About Mammals

For the One who created mammals.

—*Genesis* 1:24

Published by
PEACHTREE PUBLISHERS
1700 Chattahoochee Avenue
Atlanta, Georgia 30318-2112
www.peachtree-online.com

Text © 1997, 1999, 2014 by Cathryn P. Sill
Illustrations © 1997, 1999, 2014 by John C. Sill

Illustrations created in watercolor on archival quality 100% rag watercolor paper
Text and titles set in Novarese from Adobe Systems

Printed and manufactured in April 2014 by Imago in Singapore

10 9 8 7 6 5 4 3 2 1 (hardcover)
10 9 8 7 6 5 4 3 2 1 (trade paperback)
Revised Edition

Library of Congress Cataloging-in-Publication Data

Sill, Cathryn P.
   About mammals: a guide for children / Cathryn Sill; illustrated by John Sill.
 p. cm.
   Summary: Explains what mammals are, how they live, and what they do.
   ISBN 978-1-56145-757-1 (hardcover)
   ISBN 978-1-56145-758-8 (trade paperback)
   I. Mammals—Juvenile literature. [I. Mammals.] I. Sill, John, ill. II. Title.
   QL706.2.S547 1997
   500—dc20   96-36402

About Mammals

A Guide for Children

Revised Edition

Cathryn Sill

Illustrated by John Sill

PEACHTREE
ATLANTA

Mammals have hair.

They may have thick fur,

John Zill

sharp quills,

PLATE 3
North American Porcupine

or only a few stiff whiskers.

PLATE 4
Walrus

John Gill

Baby mammals drink milk from their mothers.

PLATE 5
American Bison

Some mammals are born helpless.

Others can move about on their own soon
after they are born.

PLATE 7
Elk

Mammals may run,

climb,

swim,

PLATE 10
Blue Whale

or fly.

PLATE 11
Big Brown Bat

Mammals eat meat,

John Sill

plants,

PLATE 13
American Pika

or both.

PLATE 14
American Black Bear

They live in cold and icy places,

hot and dry deserts,

or wet marshes.

It is important to protect mammals and the places where they live.

PLATE 18
Humans
Northern Raccoon
White-tailed Deer
Eastern Gray Squirrel

Afterword

PLATE 1
There are more than 5,000 species of mammals in the world. About 450 different kinds live in the United States and Canada. Hair is adapted to protect mammals according to the needs of each species. The coats of the Northern Raccoon grow thicker in winter to keep them warm and dry. Northern Raccoons are found in many different habitats across much of North America.

PLATE 2
Hair protects mammals in different kinds of weather. It also helps keep the animal's skin from being injured or sunburned. Many mammals have more than one kind of hair. The hair most easily seen is called "guard hair." Beneath the guard hair is a layer called "underfur." Muskoxen have a thick outer coat of long guard hairs and a dense undercoat that keep them warm in frigid temperatures. Muskoxen live in the cold Arctic region.

PLATE 3
Some mammals have thick, stiff guard hairs on parts of their bodies. North American Porcupines have sharp quills on their backs and tails. The quills are loosely attached and will come off and stick into an enemy's body. North American Porcupines live in the northern and western parts of North America.

PLATE 4

Whiskers are a special kind of hair that helps mammals learn information about their surroundings. Some marine mammals have only a few coarse whiskers. Walruses use their sensitive, bristly whiskers to find food on the ocean floor. They eat snails, clams, crabs, and shrimp. Walruses live in the Arctic Ocean and some northern parts of the Pacific and Atlantic Oceans.

PLATE 5

Mammals get their name from the special mammary glands that make milk for their young. American Bison babies drink milk from their mothers for about seven months. American Bison (also called "American Buffalo") were nearly hunted to extinction in the late 1800s. Laws now protect them and their numbers are slowly increasing. American Bison are the largest land animals in North America. They live in central and western United States and Canada.

PLATE 6

Mother mammals usually take good care of their babies. They feed, groom, and protect them until they are able to live on their own. White-footed Deermice are born blind and hairless. Their eyes open when they are about two weeks old. The babies are weaned at around three weeks. By the time they are ten or eleven weeks old, they have grown to adult size. White-footed Deermice live throughout most of the eastern United States. They also live in parts of Canada and Mexico.

PLATE 7

Grazing mammal babies must be able to travel along as their mothers search for food. The young animals must be able to run very fast soon after birth to avoid danger from predators. Elk (also called "Wapiti") babies can stand up about twenty minutes after they are born. Elk used to be common over most of North America, but hunting caused them to disappear from eastern North America. They have been successfully reestablished in several places where they used to live.

PLATE 8

Most land mammals walk or run on all four legs. Pronghorns must be able to run fast to escape from danger since they live in open areas without many hiding places. They can run over 50 miles per hour (80 kmh) for several miles. Pronghorns are the fastest mammals in North America. They live in western and central North America.

PLATE 9

Animals that climb must be able to hold on to keep from falling. Squirrels have sharp claws that help them grasp trunks and branches and allow them to make their way easily through trees. American Red Squirrels are small, noisy tree squirrels that stay safe from predators by moving quickly. They live in forests in parts of the United States and Canada.

PLATE 10

Mammals that live in the water all of the time use their flippers to steer and their tails to push themselves as they swim. Blue Whales are the largest animals that have ever lived on Earth. They swim in all the oceans of the world.

PLATE 11

While some mammals can glide from tree to tree, bats are the only ones that truly fly. Big Brown Bats are one of the fastest bats. They can fly at speeds up to 40 miles per hour (64 kmh). Big Brown Bats eat flying insects, including beetles, moths, flies, and wasps. They live in North America, Central America, the northern part of South America, and the Caribbean Islands.

PLATE 12

Animals that eat meat are called "carnivores." Some mammals, such as wild cats, eat only meat. Although Bobcats can kill animals larger than themselves, they hunt mainly rabbits, squirrels, and mice. Bobcats live throughout most of North America.

PLATE 13

Animals that eat plants are called "herbivores." Some plant eaters store food for winter. In midsummer, American Pikas begin to gather plants and pile them into stacks to dry in the sun. They often tuck the dried plants under a rock or log to protect them from the weather. When snow covers the ground, they move through tunnels they have built to find their "haystacks." American Pikas live in the mountains of western North America.

PLATE 14

Animals that eat meat and plants are called "omnivores." Most kinds of bears are omnivores. American Black Bears will eat many different things, including roots, berries, insects, and small mammals. They are able to live in forests, swamps, and tundra. American Black Bears are the most common bear in North America. They live in Canada, the United States, and northern Mexico.

PLATE 15

Many animals migrate from cold areas when winter comes. Those that stay are protected from the cold by thick layers of fat or dense fur coats. Arctic Foxes have white winter coats that change to brown in summer. This camouflage or protective coloration allows them to hide from both predators and prey. They have fur on their paws so they can walk on ice and snow. Arctic Foxes live throughout the entire Arctic Tundra.

PLATE 16

Desert mammals have special ways of surviving in their hot, dry habitat. Black-tailed Jackrabbits have large ears that carry the heat away from their bodies. Their excellent hearing helps them avoid predators. Jackrabbits are hares, not rabbits. Hares are usually larger than rabbits and have larger back legs and feet. Jackrabbits live in central and western North America.

PLATE 17

Many mammals are able to find food and shelter in marshes or other types of wetlands. Common Muskrats build domed houses in water using marsh vegetation. Their tails, which are flattened from side to side, help guide them as they swim. Common Muskrats live in most of Canada and the United States.

PLATE 18

One of the greatest dangers to mammals and other wildlife is habitat destruction. When we protect the environment, we benefit mammals as well as whole communities of different animals by providing places where they can find space, shelter, food, and water. *Can you find the animal in this picture that is not a mammal?*

GLOSSARY

Glide—to move smoothly without effort
Graze—to feed on growing grass
Groom—to clean fur or skin
Habitat—the place where animals and plants live
Marine Mammal—a mammal that spends all or part of its life in the sea
Predator—an animal that lives by hunting and eating other animals
Prey—an animal that is hunted and eaten by a predator
Species—a group of animals or plants that are alike in many ways
Wean—to help a nursing baby learn to find other food

BIBLIOGRAPHY

BOOKS

Eyewitness Books: Mammal by Steve Parker (Dorling Kindersley)
Kaufman Focus Guides: Mammal by Nora Bowers, Rick Bowers, and Kenn Kaufman (Houghton Mifflin Company)
Peterson First Guides: Mammals by Peter Alden (Houghton Mifflin Company)

WEBSITES

http://kids.sandiegozoo.org/animals/mammals
http://www.enchantedlearning.com/subjects/mammals/
http://www.arkive.org/mammals/

ABOUT... SERIES

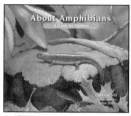

ISBN 978-1-56145-234-7 HC
ISBN 978-1-56145-312-2 PB

ISBN 978-1-56145-038-1 HC
ISBN 978-1-56145-364-1 PB

ISBN 978-1-56145-688-8 HC
ISBN 978-1-56145-699-4 PB

ISBN 978-1-56145-301-6 HC
ISBN 978-1-56145-405-1 PB

ISBN 978-1-56145-256-9 HC
ISBN 978-1-56145-335-1 PB

ISBN 978-1-56145-588-1 HC

ISBN 978-1-56145-207-1 HC
ISBN 978-1-56145-232-3 PB

ISBN 978-1-56145-757-1 HC
ISBN 978-1-56145-758-8 PB

ISBN 978-1-56145-358-0 HC
ISBN 978-1-56145-407-5 PB

ISBN 978-1-56145-331-3 HC
ISBN 978-1-56145-406-8 PB

ISBN 978-1-56145-795-3 HC

ISBN 978-1-56145-743-4 HC
ISBN 978-1-56145-741-0 PB

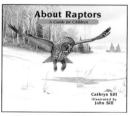

ISBN 978-1-56145-536-2 HC
ISBN 978-1-56145-811-0 PB

ISBN 978-1-56145-183-8 HC
ISBN 978-1-56145-233-0 PB

ISBN 978-1-56145-454-9 HC

ALSO AVAILABLE
IN BILINGUAL EDITION

• About Birds / Sobre los pájaros
  ISBN 978-1-56145-783-0 PB
• About Mammals / Sobre los mamíferos
  ISBN 978-1-56145-800-4 PB

Deserts

ISBN 978-1-56145-641-3 HC
ISBN 978-1-56145-636-9 PB

Forests

ISBN 978-1-56145-734-2 HC

Grasslands

ISBN 978-1-56145-559-1 HC

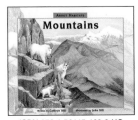

Mountains

ISBN 978-1-56145-469-3 HC
ISBN 978-1-56145-731-1 PB

Oceans

ISBN 978-1-56145-618-5 HC

Wetlands

ISBN 978-1-56145-432-7 HC
ISBN 978-1-56145-689-5 PB

THE SILLS

Cathryn Sill, a former elementary school teacher, is the author of the acclaimed ABOUT… series and the ABOUT HABITATS series. With her husband John and her brother-in-law Ben Sill, she coauthored the popular bird-guide parodies, A FIELD GUIDE TO LITTLE-KNOWN AND SELDOM-SEEN BIRDS OF NORTH AMERICA, ANOTHER FIELD GUIDE TO LITTLE-KNOWN AND SELDOM-SEEN BIRDS OF NORTH AMERICA, and BEYOND BIRDWATCHING.

John Sill is a prize-winning and widely published wildlife artist who illustrated the ABOUT… series and the ABOUT HABITATS series, and illustrated and coauthored the FIELD GUIDES and BEYOND BIRDWATCHING. A native of North Carolina, he holds a B.S. in Wildlife Biology from North Carolina State University.

The Sills live in Franklin, North Carolina.

COUNTRY THINGS

From the Pages of The Magazine, *Antiques*

Country Things

From the Pages of The Magazine, *Antiques*

EDITED, AND WITH AN INTRODUCTION,
BY ERIC DE JONGE

THE PYNE PRESS
Princeton

Distributed by Charles Scribner's Sons, New York

Contents

Introduction

ERIC DE JONGE

The Shelburne Museum

ALICE WINCHESTER

The Interiors (*Old Sturbridge Village*)

FRANK O. SPINNEY

Antiques in New Mexico

E. BOYD

Something About Stencils

A GALLERY NOTE

Some Colonial and Early American Decorative Floors

ESTHER STEVENS FRASER

The Painted Decoration (*Farmers' Museum, Cooperstown*)

NINA FLETCHER LITTLE

Country Furniture

FRANK O. SPINNEY

Sources of Some American Regional Furniture

JOHN T. KIRK

Slat-Back Chairs of New England and the
Middle Atlantic States—Part I

WILSON LYNES

Slat-Back Chairs of New England and the
   Middle Atlantic States—Part II

   WILSON LYNES

Windsor Chairs at Williams College

   KARL E. WESTON

Ebenezer Tracy, Connecticut Chairmaker

   ADA R. CHASE

An Interpretation of Shaker Furniture

   EDWARD D. & FAITH ANDREWS

Random Notes on Hitchcock and His Competitors

   ESTHER STEVENS FRASER

The Furniture (*Old Sturbridge Village*)

   MARGARET B. MUNIER

Cabinets and Chests from the Middle Atlantic States

Southern Provincial Furniture

Simple Furniture of the Old South

   MARY RALLS DOCKSTADTER

Chests from Western Long Island

   HUYLER HELD

Painted Chests from the Connecticut Valley

   J. L. CUMMINGS

Birds, Quilted, Patched and Woven

   FLORENCE PETO

Three Generations of Quilts

   FLORENCE PETO

Quilts and Coverlets from New York and Long Island

    FLORENCE PETO

Quilts and Coverlets: The Old Northwest Territory

Weavers of New York's Historical Coverlets

    JESSIE FARRALL PECK

Ohio Coverlets

    IRMA PILLING ANDERSON

The Attitude of the Eagle

    ANNE WOOD MURRAY

When Treen Ware Was "The" Ware

    EDITH MINITER

Early New England Woodenware

    MARY EARLE GOULD

The Burl and Its Uses

    MARY EARLE GOULD

American Woodenware

    JANE BOICOURT

Woodenware of German Pennsylvania

    EARL F. ROBACKER

Pennsylvania German Wood Carvings

    EARL F. ROBACKER

Early American Pottery: A Résumé

    JOHN RAMSAY

The Collections: Pottery (*Old Sturbridge Village*)

    FRANK O. SPINNEY

The Stoneware of South Ashfield, Massachusetts

    LURA WOODSIDE WATKINS

Ohio Pottery and Jugs

    RHEA MANSFIELD KNITTLE

Early Rhode Island Pottery

    CHARLES D. COOK

The Potters of Poughkeepsie

    JOHN P. REMENSNYDER

A Note on Early North Carolina Pottery

    JOE KINDIG, JR.

Early Pottery Lighting Devices

    WILLIAM J. TRUAX

American Pottery Lamps

    LURA WOODSIDE WATKINS

Decorated Tinware

    MARGARET MATTISON COFFIN

Decorated Tinware East and West: New Mexico

    E. BOYD

Decorated Tinware East and West: Pennsylvania

    EARL F. ROBACKER

The Case for Pennsylvania German Painted Tin

    EARL F. ROBACKER

Pennsylvania Cooky Cutters

    EARL F. ROBACKER

Zachariah Brackett Stevens

    ESTHER STEVENS FRASER

Old-Time Foot Stoves

LURA WOODSIDE WATKINS & EVAN W. LONG

A Note on a Victorian Foot Stool

Notes on the New England Blacksmith

MALCOLM WATKINS

Notes on Early Ohio Lighting Devices

RHEA MANSFIELD KNITTLE

Stage Coach Luggage

I. T. FRARY

Paintings on Velvet

LOUISE KARR

The Henry S. Borneman Collection of
Pennsylvania-German Fracturs

GEORGE H. ECKHARDT

Shaker Inspirational Drawings

EDWARD D. ANDREWS

Introduction

The past few years have witnessed a resurgence of interest in American country antiques. A resurgence, not a birth, for the interest is hardly new. Already in the 1920's, when American interest in the subject was great enough to support a new quality magazine called simply *Antiques,* there was at least a trickle of serious attention being paid to country materials. By the 1930's the trickle had become a flood, as can be seen from the dates of many of the most important articles in the following pages. Country objects did not, however, share prominently in the great antiques boom of the 1950's and early 1960's. The preference of most serious collectors seemed to be for Queen Anne and Chippendale and such "new" antiques as Tiffany glass and Art Nouveau silver. But now quilts, which until recently were shown mainly for their craft and quaintness at antique shows and historical society museums, are displayed as fine art at the Smithsonian Institution and New York's Museum of Modern Art. The prices of redware and stoneware have not just doubled, but tripled and quadrupled in the past five years.

The vagaries of taste are unpredictable. But the renewed popularity of country things is not really surprising. The discriminating collector, of course, has never lost sight of them. He values the objects he selects for the quality of their workmanship, for ingenuity and boldness of design, for color and for originality. To the untrained eye it may appear that there is a good deal of constancy and a certain conformity in the design and decoration of country pieces. The connoisseur has trained his eye, however, to discern the various patterns, the often very subtle shadings in the traditional forms that differentiate the work of one area, or perhaps even one individual craftsman, from another.

Yet it is not the connoisseur alone who accounts for the popularity of country antiques. The simplicity and functionalism that have captured the imagination of many as the ultimate in modern design and style often find a compatible echo in country objects. Functional simplicity is high fashion for architecture and for the objects sheltered within such architectural form. Many country objects "go well" with contemporary furnishings. They relieve the curse of newness and sterility without disturbing or contradicting the uncluttered lines characteristic of much modern design.

Country antiques may also be achieving popularity because of the reassuring qualities of the associations they convey. In recent years we have experienced various major socio-economic upheavals, often as the aftermath of wars. We should not be surprised to find that many of our young people are seeking what they consider the simple life, that they want to "get back to nature." In reaching for a utopian situation, theirs is a dream of a piece of ground, of a home of their own. Many yearn to get away from urban turmoil and big city pushes and pressures. The eternal American dream of an abode on one's *own* soil is, alas, only a dream for many. It may be partially in substitution for that dream that many are attracted to "country stuff." These objects offer tangible evidence of country or rural solidity and respectability. It is encouraging that many people instinctively feel the merits of these objects, although some are misled by the insults inflicted upon us under the guise of "Early American" reproductions.

Perhaps this sort of interest in country antiques is somewhat akin to the sartorial and tonsorial plunges of some young people. In any event, we should be able to understand both phenomena. These expressions, and many others, are the reaction of the young to the increasing pressures, disappointments and contraditions affecting our society today. Their attitudes reflect, by and large, not so much a rejection of the present Establishment, but the yearning for an Establishment of the past, the "Good Old Days." Despite much evidence to the contrary, we tend to think of the past in carefree terms, of life then being simple, and the objects of those days, ideal. What more is needed to recapture some of that simple, glorious past than a modicum of the tangible evidence which remains? And it appears that, all other means lacking, this journey back through time can be accomplished by the acquisition of "country stuff" with which to live. Perhaps visions of rural serenity, bucolic endeavor and gamboling rusticity can be transmuted into reality by possession of a sufficient number of the objects produced before the plastic age. Who is to say that this pursuit of the past, so enriching of the present, cannot be a worthwhile endeavor?

But what are country things? Are there criteria by which we can say, "yes, this belongs in the country category," and, "no, this does not"? The question is simple; the answer is not. The word "country" is in many ways a misnomer, although it has acquired, through long usage, the virtue of being generally understood. Yet many objects which collectors and dealers alike would readily categorize as "country"—Windsor chairs and redware pottery, for example— were made and used as frequently in urban areas as in rural.

There seems, however, to be no term more satisfactory. Primitive will not do. While the feed-box knocked together for a farmer may indeed be both country and primitive, many other objects in the "country" category certainly are not. One has only to look at the highly sophisticated decorative devices of the Ohio stoneware shown on pages 161 and 162 to understand that the artisans who produced them were primitive neither in skill nor design sense. Naive, as a general term, has the same deficiencies. An untutored original like Wilhelm Schimmel, one of whose elaborately carved eagles is illustrated on page 147, might be considered naive, although certainly not primitive. On the other hand, the manufacturers of early Windsor chairs, trained through an apprentice system, and consistently tempering their designs to function and to the materials with which they worked, were hardly naive.

Folk art or folk craft may come closer. For certainly there is much of folk quality in the tinware of New Mexico, the painted furniture of New England, the woodcarving and frakturs of Pennsylvania. The term *folk* implies a long tradition, specifically rooted in the lives and art of a close-knit population. These strains were transmitted to the New World from the Old and survived with particular force within those ethnic settlements where the ties of language and custom remained strong. Much of the decoration on country objects is based on folk tradition. Even when the symbols and motifs derived from the past had lost their precise meaning, they were still used not as embellishment for embellishment's sake, but because it was still dimly felt they had a meaning, some special relevance for the local area in which they were produced. This respect for the past led to a good deal of conservatism in design; ornament in country pieces does not follow the shifts of fashion with the rapidity of goods made for the less tradition-bound urban centers. In one sense, of course, all the settlers in the New World were ethnics who brought with them forms and motifs with a long history in England and the Lowlands, as well as from the more readily recognized "folk" cultures of Germany, Scandinavia or Spanish Mexico. These folk elements in the mainstream are cogently revealed in John Kirk's authoritative article, "Sources of Some American Regional Furniture." But other pieces which we rightly classify as country, Hitchcock chairs, for instance, were derived not from folk culture, but from the high-style and, indeed, academic designs disseminated through the publication of Thomas Sheraton's design books.

Functionalism and simplicity are characteristics often associated with country objects. Many of them, particularly those associated with specific tasks such as the preparation and storage of food, were, indeed, designed with respect for their appropriateness to such uses. But more than sheer utility was in the minds of the craftsmen. The wrought iron hinges and latches pictured in Malcolm Watkins' article, "Notes on the New England Blacksmith," are surely utilitarian. But in contrast to the majority of mass-produced modern counterparts, these iron pieces go far beyond mere utilitarianism. They express the craftsman's delight in the potentialities of his medium; he has enhanced his product with scrolls and arrowhead and "swordfish" motifs purely for decorative effect.

Functionalism and simplicity ought not to be confused. A high-style Philadelphia Chippendale slant-top desk shares with its country cousin the functionalism of a flat, closeable writing surface and a multitude of drawers, cubby and pigeonholes. In fact, in its greater multiplicity of storage spaces, the former may be more functional than the latter. Furthermore, one aspect of the function of the high-style piece was undoubtedly to attest to the wealth and status of its owner. William Savery, the noted Philadelphia cabinetmaker, made desks and chairs and tables for both wealthy Philadelphia patrons and for the farmers of neighboring Pennsylvania and New Jersey. Both groups of furniture served the same practical function; each expressed a view of the purchaser's social and financial status. Both have some share of the quality of beauty because of Savery's skill. Yet the country pieces, whether actually used in the metropolis or the hinterland, do differ from their high-style counterparts in their relative simplicity and freedom from added adornment, in the degree of their departure from academic design sources.

This leads, perhaps, to the most accurate definition of country things. They are the articles made by craftsmen, artisans and even factory workers operating at some remove from the academic centers of design. The distance is not necessarily geographic. The criterion is not the skill of the object's creator, but rather his degree of removal from such sophisticated design sources as Thomas Chippendale's *Director,* as well as the extent of reinterpretation and filtering down of major stylistic trends, their adaptation and modification according to local needs and tastes. The strong regional flavor created by this process is reflected in the titles of many of the articles in the following pages. The subjects are not "Sheraton Country Chairs" or "Early Nineteenth-Century Pottery," but, rather, "Painted Chests from the Connecticut Valley," "Ohio Coverlets," "The Potters of Poughkeepsie," "Pennsylvania Cooky Cutters."

In the sense of being provincial, of being at least once removed from the high-style design centers of England and the Continent, almost all American antiques made before the mid-nineteenth century might be classified as country. But the objects represented in this volume are those which are *country* in a far narrower sense—that large American sub-category of things made for purchasers whose tastes were not conditioned by what was currently fashionable overseas or in the upper circles of America's own metropolitan centers. Certain categories have been excluded. Some of these have been omitted because they have become relatively independent fields of study and because the techniques of their manufacture are uniform enough to blur the distinction between high-style and country. Silver and glass fall into this group. To a lesser extent, so does pewter. Porcelain has been excluded because, until the late nineteenth century, none was made in America as anything but a novelty or a luxury. Other categories that might well be considered—country store items, farm implements, tools— do not appear because the materials do not exist. In this, and in other respects, the selection has been controlled by what has engaged the attention of

Antiques' contributors. Finally the fine arts, painting, sculpture and architecture, have been largely excluded.

But what richness there is in what has been selected. The geographic range covers the entire eastern seaboard, much of the Midwest, and dips, thanks to two articles by E. Boyd, into the less well-known traditions of the Southwest. The time span embraces three centuries, from the joinery of the Pilgrim fathers to nineteenth-century, factory-produced chairs and tinware. Several articles, particularly those on the Shelburne Museum and Old Sturbridge Village, will be of interest to the generalist, covering, as they do, everything from painted wall decorations through furnishings and decorative objects to hardware. For the specialist there are authoritative articles on wallpaper-covered bandboxes, Shaker items, frakturs and lighting devices. The experts who produced these articles form a roster of pioneers in the scholarly approach to American antiques. Here is Mary Earle Gould on woodenware, Lura Woodside Watkins on pottery and lighting devices, Earl F. Robacker on the Pennsylvania Germans, Florence Peto on quilts, Esther Stevens Fraser on stenciling, and Edward D. and Faith Andrews on Shaker materials. More recent scholarship has, in some cases, modified their conclusions. Still, what they wrote, and the examples they first examined and illustrated, remain of tremendous importance to anyone who wishes to know and understand American country antiques.

BY ALICE WINCHESTER

The Shelburne Museum

Beyond the covered bridge (right) are the schoolhouse, stagecoach inn, stone cottage, Shaker shed, and old Vermont houses which now house specialized collections. The yellow building in the left foreground is the country store, formerly the post office of Shelburne. The great red horseshoe barn beyond the meeting house was copied in plan from one near St. Albans and constructed of enormous old timbers from all over Vermont. In it is installed the superb collection of wagons, sleighs, coaches, fire equipment, carriages, and other vehicles.

The buildings

A PANORAMIC VIEW OF THE SHELBURNE MUSEUM includes the little Vermont town of Shelburne with which it seems to merge, the Green Mountains around it, and Lake Champlain beyond. Winding dirt roads link the buildings, which represent characteristic types of Vermont architecture set in green lawns among lilacs and fruit trees, elms and maples. The great covered bridge through which one enters from Route 7 is the only one with two lanes and a footpath surviving within Vermont. Built about 1845 over the Lamoille River at Cambridge, it is 165 feet long, a splendid example of the arch truss patented by Theodore Burr in the early 1800's. Through its network of huge timbers one sees the 1840 brick meeting house, brought from Charlotte, Vermont. Most recent additions to this "architecture collection" are an 1820 house with original stenciling on its sheathed walls, and an 1850 high-gabled frame dwelling moved from Dorset to house the Joel Barber collection of duck decoys.

110

The little schoolhouse, only 38 by 22 feet in size, was built in Vergennes, a few miles south of Shelburne, in 1830. Of local pink brick, it has a projecting vestibule entered by an arched doorway and surmounted by an octagonal belfry with acorn finial. The one-room interior, still bearing the scars of generations of schoolchildren, is now refitted with old desks and blackboards, stove and books. Long disused and dilapidated, this was the first building moved to the Shelburne Museum, in 1946.

From 1783 the stagecoach inn at Charlotte, Vermont, built and operated by Captain Hezekiah Barnes, offered shelter to travelers between Montreal and New York. After his death it passed through many ownerships with attendant alterations, and in 1949 was reconstructed at Shelburne in its original state, with wide central hallway, ten fireplaces, and second-floor ballroom. It has the simplicity of the frontier which Vermont was in the late 1700's, but its ample proportions suggest comfort, and it contains some of the widest boards and longest timbers still to be seen anywhere. The folk art collection is displayed here.

The tiny slate-roofed stone cottage, such as sheltered many an early Vermont family, was built in 1840. The interior, furnished with simplest necessities, has two minute bedrooms and an attic besides the kitchen-living room. The mellowed building on the left (c. 1800), once the town barn of Shelburne and now known as the hat and fragrance unit, houses some of the most feminine collections in the Museum —appealing early hatboxes and parasols, shell dolls and miniature doll houses, quilts and rugs. The houses beyond, where ceramics, glass, pewter, dolls, and toys are shown, typify the "continuous architecture" of Vermont.

111

Specialized collections

WHILE THE ARCHITECTURAL ELEMENTS of the Shelburne Museum give it the external aspect of a typical New England village, the specialized collections displayed within the buildings give it a character quite its own. The all too few examples selected from them for illustration here only suggest their variety, scope, and quality. The folk art collection is the largest and finest group of American primitive sculpture on public view, and also includes noteworthy primitive paintings. The extent of the textile collection is only hinted at by the specimens shown here. Among the ceramics are rarities in delft, an impressive group of Toby jugs, and the pair of Chelsea swans shown in ANTIQUES for June 1954.

The mermaid weathervane, combing her flowing tresses and gazing forever into the metal mirror clasped in her hand, originally floated over a barn in Wayland, Massachusetts. She is 52 inches long, carved of one piece of pine, with separate arms. Most numerous in the collection are weathervanes of copper and iron, which include Indians, birds and animals, the American eagle and Columbia, a locomotive and a centaur.

The life-size pottery bust of George Washington, 26 inches tall, is a great rarity in American ceramics, exceptional for its size and artistry. Similar to New Jersey stoneware of the early 1800's, it was molded no doubt from an original carved in wood. It was found near Trenton, and is believed to have been made in the vicinity.

Design in decoys: a rare crane (center) and a seagull (right foreground), equally rare. The long-legged shore birds, pintail duck (left), and canvasback are from the well-known Joel Barber collection which is now part of the Shelburne Museum.

Among a number of examples of American crewelwork the finest is this early eighteenth-century bedspread, colorful, well composed, and exquisitely worked in a variety of stitches. The design is more intricate than was usual in America, though still not so compact as in much English work. This piece is remarkably well preserved. The collection includes also fine examples of blue resist, wool-on-wool coverlets, samplers, and a brilliant display of quilts including appliqué and pieced and all-white specimens.

Among the floor coverings are rare examples in needlework, including one in fine crewelwork and one in silk, and an outstanding group in the hooked technique. The latter are admirably represented by this engaging lion, worked in tawny shades against a butternut brown. The initials *J J* are faintly discernible at the left. The rug is believed to have been made in New England about 1830.

Circus figures, trade signs, toys, eagles for many a decorative purpose, as well as weathervanes and figureheads give the collection of American primitive sculpture originality, humor, vitality, and often striking design. The most recent acquisition is this carved figure of Christopher Columbus, which once rode on a circus wagon.

The smallest of these jugs (1810-1820) is nine inches high. Made by Fifield of Bristol, it is painted in colors and inscribed as a marriage jug. Of the giants shown with it, that at left, of creamware, 24¼ inches tall, was a trade sign for "J. Rolf's Wholesale Staffordshire Warehouse." Also a trade sign was the metal-covered one, 25½ inches over-all, decorated with transfers and luster. The polychrome jug at right is 14 inches tall.

Mammoth too are a pair of American blown-glass punchbowls, one of which is shown here; they measure nearly two feet in diameter. American bottles and flasks in the collection include rare historical as well as conventional designs.

Dolls of all ages and sizes: above, English (early 1700's) and French (c. 1750); below, English peddler doll (c. 1800), French knitting and nodding doll (c. 1850), French shell doll (c. 1760), and a miniature "penny wooden" of the early 1800's.

The Cavendish house

Two of the old houses at the Shelburne Museum are now completely furnished as they might have been originally. In both architecture and furnishings the Cavendish house demonstrates the time lag in styles always seen in remote regions. It was built in 1782 in Cavendish, Vermont, by Salmon Dutton who brought with him from Massachusetts memories of the early saltbox houses that had long since gone out of style in the older-settled parts of New England. His red-painted house is of typical saltbox construction, with narrow entrance hall from which the stairs rise steeply in front of the large central chimney, a room on either side, and the kitchen behind. A long ell at the rear adds space as well as architectural interest.

The furniture, like the house itself, recalls early traditions. In the parlor the butterfly table with its fine turnings, the red chest with applied black spindles and painted decoration, the racheted candlestand, the Spanish-foot chair, the ball-foot desk with its unusually handsome interior, are all characteristic of the very early 1700's. Primitive paintings of a century later hang on the walls, and a striped carpet gives life to the floor.

Stenciling discovered under layers of wallpaper was reproduced where the original could not be saved. Outstanding here is the William and Mary highboy with painted decoration, signed *RLG 1738*. A fascinating play of pattern is seen in the varied leg turnings of the highboy, the gateleg table, the unusual high chair, the cross-stretcher table, and the music stand—all dating close to 1700.

A painted pine bed with posts turned in the classic taste is hung in contemporary fringed dimity, matching the window curtains. The ball-foot chest is brightly painted in red and white on a black ground. Another furniture rarity is the Spanish-foot stretcher table.

Under the eaves of the ell is tucked a low-post bed whose urn finials show the classic influence on country furniture of the early 1800's. At its foot a painted pine cradle swings from a frame.

Great rarities in the bedroom shown below are the William and Mary lowboy, a New England piece of the early 1700's, of pine and painted black; and the seventeenth-century mirror with extraordinary stuffed beadwork surround and carved wood frame.

The northeast bedroom is stenciled, too, and has a deerskin rug on the floor. At the foot of the low-post bed stands a painted round-top chest dated *1799*. About a century older is the paneled chest opposite. The carved head is to hang a bonnet on. The seventeenth-century stumpwork pictures here are a collection in themselves.

The ground floor of the ell is furnished as a harvest room, a comfortable eating and gathering place. Windsor chairs are drawn close to the checkerboard; Bennington ware and pewter brighten the hanging shelves and cupboards. The high lift-top desk is an unusual eighteenth-century New England piece, mounted on a sawbuck trestle like that of the table in the kitchen.

The long kitchen is big enough for all the culinary activities of a busy rural home, which are suggested by the butter churn, cheese sieve, yellow slipware dishes, burl bowls, the long trestle table, and the two rare benches beside it. Equally fitting are the musket and powder horn, and the wash-stand by the door. The big open fireplace and oven are out of view at the left.

A painted pine corner cupboard in the kitchen is garnished with American pewter from one of the Museum's collections, including work of the Vermonter Richard Lee, and of the Board-mans and Danforths of Connecticut.

The Vermont house

The plan, the frame, and much of the material for this house came from a clapboarded dwelling that had stood since about 1790 in Shelburne Township but was so worn out that both interior paneling and exterior surfacing had to be replaced. The stonework was copied from a contemporary Vermont house. The interior plan is related to that of the saltbox, with central chimney, small entrance hall, a room on either side, and long kitchen in back, but the stairs rise from the kitchen instead of the hall and there is, surprisingly, a fireplace facing the front door. The lower rooms are furnished as the home of a sea captain of some means who retired to the Vermont hills in the late 1700's.

The feather-edge sheathing of the fireplace wall in the dining room is painted a soft brown, offsetting the bright blues of delftware and of the painted paper on the other walls. The ship motif recurs in the printed panel of Fulton's *Clermont* above the fireplace. Massachusetts Chippendale chairs are used with the round Queen Anne drop-leaf table. A delft posset pot stands on the lowboy, delft tobacco jars with Indian decoration on the blockfront chest. The engraving above the latter is a rare impression by Amos Doolittle of Washington's inauguration at Federal Hall.

In the hall, which is really a small room, stands a mahogany spider-leg table, believed to be unique in American furniture (see ANTIQUES, December 1934, p. 220). The early fretwork mirror is one of a pair. Throughout both this house and the Cavendish house, lighting devices and fireplace equipment are of special interest.

Surveying the parlor is Colonel Jacobus van Slyke, portrayed by the Hudson Valley painter Pieter Vanderlyn (1682-1778); the work is inscribed *Born May: 26: 1704.* New England Queen Anne chairs are drawn up to the Queen Anne gaming table. A mirror labeled by John Elliott & Sons of Philadelphia hangs above a most unusual Connecticut lowboy of cherry, with leaf and flower carving on frieze, legs, and widely overhanging top. On it stand a fine pair of brass candelabra and a Lambeth delft lobed dish.

A notable Queen Anne cherry secretary in the parlor is ascribed to the Connecticut craftsman Benjamin Burnham. Its closed bonnet top curves boldly above arched paneled doors with handsome brasses, the ornamental interior has molded drawers and vine carving of Connecticut type, and the frame stands on short cabriole legs with pad feet. The fine New England Chippendale chair contrasts with the straight seventeenth-century oak chair, which is covered in contemporary Turkeywork rich in blues and reds and extraordinarily well preserved.

A small room off the parlor is fitted up as the captain's study, with nautical mementoes and convivial paraphernalia. On the early pine desk-on-frame is an English pewter dish of the mid-1600's. The pastel portrait above it is one of a pair attributed to the eighteenth-century Salem artist Benjamin Blyth.

The fine arched and fielded paneling of the parlor came from a house near Essex, Connecticut. Painted blue-green, it provides a lovely background for rare pieces of eighteenth-century New England furniture. Outstanding among these is the chair at right, whose arms terminate in carved parrot heads, a unique feature; the stopped fluting of its sturdy legs indicates Newport origin. Also believed unique, and also of Newport make, is the octagonal tea table whose legs have the "collar" seen on a few examples ascribed to the Goddard-Townsend group and terminate in a curious paw-and-pad foot. The slipper-foot walnut chair with flaring crest is another fine example.

The kitchen has a big brick fireplace fully equipped with pots, pans, trivets, peels, spit and clock jack, oven, strainers, and all the other necessities of iron, brass, and tin. American pewter shines against the red-painted wall; interesting pieces of treenware on the octagonal hutch table include an English brose spoon of about 1750. A pine settle made of enormously wide boards separates this part of the kitchen from the end shown in the frontispiece.

The interiors

AS IN A NEW ENGLAND VILLAGE of the early nineteenth century might have been found a variety of homes, some surviving from a considerably earlier period and others more recently constructed, so at Old Sturbridge Village the houses range in date from the beginning 1700's to a century later. And just as in any house occupied over a period of years by successive generations with different ideas of convenience and comfort, and with a responsive interest in changing fashions of use and decoration, so the different residential structures of this re-created community reflect the accumulations of style, the impulse toward modernization, and the acceptance of varying tastes.

Throughout the Village homes, moreover, runs a major theme or premise that has guided their exhibit development—the typical or representative, not the unique or spectacular; the everyday home, not the "period" room; the house that was lived in, not one designed for display. The visitor to Old Sturbridge Village finds not so much a textbook of style as an anthology of homes with all the contradictions of good and bad, antiquated and modern, neatness and disarray one might expect in any house occupied by a busy family intent on its daily round of domestic activities.

It occasionally disconcerts the ardent antiquarian to discover a Connecticut sunflower chest tucked away inconspicuously in the sparsely furnished work room of a Village house rather than displayed proudly and prominently with all the reverence its rarity seems to deserve. In 1800, however, probably more often than not such an obsolete chest was relegated to the attic or shed chamber as something hopelessly old-fashioned but still usable.

Thus peering into the kitchens, bedrooms, parlors, and other corners of the Village houses shown in the interior scenes that follow, the visitor catches a glimpse of the homes his ancestors may have known—ashes on the hearth, loom in the attic, rooms filled with their furniture, their cooking utensils, all suggestive of the daily routine of thousands of obscure New England families a hundred and fifty years ago.   FRANK O. SPINNEY

Oak Carver chairs with yellow linen squabs, or cushions, are seen against the gray-blue paneling and whitewashed walls of the parlor of the architecturally plain JOHN FENNO HOUSE. Other seventeenth- and early eighteenth-century furniture includes a gate-leg table and paneled chest. To the right of the fireplace hangs an English brass lantern clock, c. 1650. A lamp, a pipe box with heart and swirl-circle motifs, and pipe tongs are convenient to the hearth. *Photograph by Samuel Chamberlain.*

Yellow linen curtains the small windows of the combination bedroom-parlor of the FENNO HOUSE, and a nut-brown quilted coverlet of glazed wool covers the low oak bed. For storage of clothing and linen in households without closets, the high chest was most useful. This one, of the William and Mary period, is of tulip poplar, or whitewood, painted to simulate the grain of walnut. The desk-on-frame, 1700-1725, is of curly maple.

In the east chamber of the FENNO HOUSE, the whitewashed walls and ceiling, the wide, untreated floor boards, and the sparseness of furniture reflect the poverty and austerity of most New England farm homes of the early 1700's. The oak bed, with its straw-filled tow ticking and homespun sheets and blankets, is covered with an indigo glazed-wool coverlet from Massachusetts. The curtains are white linen, the only floor covering a bearskin rug. The polychrome-painted pine chest, found in Connecticut but probably made in New Hampshire, is marked with the initials E B under the center decorated panel. Another view of this room is shown on the frontispiece.

The brick fireplace of the FENNO HOUSE kitchen has a beehive oven opening into the chimney. From the iron chimney-rod iron kettles hang on trammels, and equipment on the hearth includes a gridiron or broiler, toaster, and sausage baker or roaster for small birds or fish. A bake kettle with concave cover rests in the embers. On the fireplace shelves are pewter and redware vessels, with wrought-iron utensils hanging in the center, a betty lamp at the side, and drying herbs above. The pine hutch or chair table, dating from close to 1700, was found in New Hampshire.

Built-in shelves in the FENNO HOUSE kitchen hold a useful array of redware dishes and jars, woodenware, and pewter. The ladder-back high chair is red-painted pine.

In the upper-floor weaving room of the FENNO HOUSE the itinerant weaver helped the family work up the year's needs in cloth, or rag rugs like that in process here—and seen in use in the Richardson house—were made of otherwise useless scraps. The clock reel for measuring yarn has a dial and indicator hand. Beside it an early three-panel oak chest for storage has shallow tulip carving, pine top, and single drawer. A six-board pine chest opposite is nearly hidden by the large hamper of woven splint.

The soft tones of old pewter, brass, iron, red paint, and wood combine to make the west parlor of the STEPHEN FITCH HOUSE warm and inviting. The fireplace is distinguished by a granite lintel and equipped with andirons of iron with brass finials. Isaac Blaisdell of Chester, New Hampshire, made the tall clock (c. 1760) that stands against the vertical pine sheathing; his name (here spelled "Blasdel") is on the brass dial. Beside the fireplace, two country versions of the Queen Anne chair show the retention of early features in legs and stretchers.

Feather-edge pine sheathing in the FITCH HOUSE east parlor makes a pleasing background for early furnishings. Interesting pattern is provided by the turned legs and stretchers of the maple gate-leg, c. 1720, the scalloped apron of the table at the window, and the low relief carving in a stylized tulip-like design which covers the front of the Hadley chest. There is color in the blue six-boarded chest and the red and black ladder-back chairs, with touches of gilt in the armchair. The contraption on the chest is a niddy-noddy, used to wind wool into skeins.

On the fireplace wall of the FITCH HOUSE east parlor hang a colorful Delft wall plate and tin candle sconces, a red-painted pipe box with scalloped edge, and painted bellows. The tall clock was made by a country craftsman about 1790. Its imported dial has been repainted with a stylized landscape, and its weights are carefully shaped and balanced field stones. Here are two versions of the ladder-back chair, one painted red and the other black, with rockers added. *Photograph by Samuel Chamberlain.*

The red kitchen in the FITCH HOUSE has a granite fireplace with two openings below the oven; andirons, kettle, pots, and griddle are of the sort used in the eighteenth century. An early charger and teapot of English pewter stand beside the flatirons on the mantel, and at the left are a pine box for clay pipes, wrought-iron trivet, and tongs. A betty lamp is suspended from a wooden trammel, and against the red-stained horizontal wall boards hang tools of fireplace cookery—wooden peel, strainer, and long-handled ladle.

In the FITCH HOUSE bedroom, a beautifully quilted glazed-wool coverlet with patchwork center covers the curtained and canopied field bed. It was made in Northbridge, Massachusetts, about 1800. The chest is red-painted pine, as is the crude country candlestand. A doll's cradle stands at the foot of the bed.

Vertical feather-edge boarding covers the walls of
lower hall and stairwell in
the SOLOMON RICHARDSON
HOUSE, a saltbox of fine proportions dating from the
1740's. In the dining room
beyond, the corner cupboard
is garnished with colorful
English earthenware, China
Trade porcelain, and glass of
the early 1800's. *Photograph
by Samuel Chamberlain.*

Opposite page, top
The parlor of the RICHARDSON HOUSE gains an air of distinction from its paneled wall and dado, painted blue. Resist-
dyed cotton (a reproduction) covers the Sheraton easy
chair. The cherry roundabout chair (c. 1770) came from
Connecticut. An interesting feature of the Queen Anne
maple high chest (c. 1740) is the deep cove molding of its
cornice which forms a shallow drawer for papers and
documents.

Opposite page, bottom
In the RICHARDSON HOUSE west chamber, the pattern of
the red-printed cotton coverlet is a Shakespeare-David
Garrick scene; canopy and flounce are reproduction dimity.
The oval-top table with its chunky pad feet is pine, painted
red; on it a painted towel rack, pewter basin, and brass
candlestick await the guest. The tripod candlestand, also
pine, has a square molded top.

The parlor of the PLINY FREEMAN FARMHOUSE is a room of many uses. The farm's accounts are kept at the tulip-poplar desk, and relaxation is offered by the rocker, contoured for comfort. There is sewing and knitting equipment on the Queen Anne drop-leaf table with its diaper-patterned linen cover, and a painted tole candle-stand with shades. Against white-washed walls and putty-colored wood-work, red-and-yellow cotton print curtains complement the red tones of painted furniture. A courting glass hangs on the wall, between a framed paper cutout and a silhouette portrait of Stephen Badlam, Jr., nineteenth-century Boston cabinetmaker. *Photograph by Samuel Chamberlain.*

A pine folding or press bed in the FREEMAN FARMHOUSE bedroom is cov-ered with a cotton appliquéd and quilted coverlet in vivid green, yellow, and red. The child's windsor chair is pine. A wrapper, morning gown, and calash may be glimpsed in the closet. *Photograph by Samuel Chamberlain.*

The fireplace of the FREEMAN FARM-HOUSE kitchen has a granite lintel, oven at the side. Kettles hang from a swinging crane, and on the hearth are a bake kettle, toaster, iron peel, and tongs. The molded board top of the pine table is well scrubbed; the kitchen chairs are painted yellow and stenciled. The shelves of the utilitarian built-in cupboard hold early nineteenth-century Staffordshire ware. *Photograph by Samuel Chamberlain.*

In the gentlemen's game room of the Village TAVERN are windsor chairs of several patterns. The pine tavern table has unusual block-and-turned legs and stretcher, and its top has a wide overhang; the cribbage board is of ivory and ebony. There are horn cups on the hanging shelves, and on the high mantel a wooden spill or taper box, and an interesting clock made in 1786 by apprentice Levi Hutchins as a farewell gesture and demonstration of skill to his master, Simon Willard of Roxbury, Massachusetts.

A "pencil-post" bed in the TAVERN bedroom is dressed in homespun linen curtains with wool binding and a printed cotton coverlet dated 1813. Windsor chairs, oval-top table, chest of drawers, shaving stand, and candlestand are all New England maple. The record of Mary Morrison's birth in 1766, which hangs above the little oval-top table, was "wrote" by her nephew in New Hampshire.

On the bar of the Village TAVERN taproom stand deep dishes, quart-size mugs, and candlestick of English pewter, and a wooden lemon squeezer. The wall shelves are lined with old glass flasks and tankards staved and hooped in wood. Beams from a dismantled covered bridge support the ceiling.

Fig. 1 — "Nuestra Senora de la Concepcion." *Retablo* made in New Mexico. Native cottonwood (poplar) or pine was covered with gesso, made of gypsum, and painted in tempera with simple vegetable and mineral colors. They range in size from large altar pieces to fragments as small as a playing card. Similar sacred subjects painted in oil on canvas or copper are usually products of *old Mexico. From the collection of Mrs. C. H. Sawyer; drawing by Emile Cero, Index of American Design, Metropolitan Museum.*

Fig. 2 — "Sacred Heart of Mary" (1846). Lithograph by N. Currier of New York, published for sale in Spanish America, and possibly also in French Canada. Title in English, French, and Spanish. *From the collection of James MacMillan; photo by Wyatt Davis.*

Fig. 3 (*below*) — Our Lady of Guadalupe (c. 1750-1800). A *bulto* of the patron saint of Mexico, carved in cottonwood, painted with tempera on gesso. The nimbus, cherub, and crescent moon are distinguishing features of the Guadalupe *bultos.* The later work of the *santeros* became more highly stylized. Height, 30 inches. *From the Museum of New Mexico; photograph by Ernest Knee.*

ANTIQUES IN NEW MEXICO
Products of Craftsmanship in the Spanish Southwest

By E. BOYD

IN THAT PART of the United States which has been longest inhabited by Europeans, the assiduous collector can still unearth various products of the early colonists. The Spaniards who settled in New Mexico — which then included Arizona and parts of Utah, Colorado, and Texas—were relatively poor, and isolated from European influences. The battle against surrounding Indians did not end until less than a century ago, and frontier conditions persisted until after the Civil War. Few colonists were skilled craftsmen; most of their products were crude, although characterized by the charm of other "primitive" efforts.

A collector who cares only for the rare woods and subtle elegance of the styles of Queen Anne, Chippendale, Sheraton, and Phyfe will find no such delights in New Mexico. But those whose taste runs to farm interiors, whitewashed walls, and cottage furniture, the gay and handsome "Pennsylvania Dutch," and primitive art, will be well rewarded by extending their collecting activities to the Southwest.

Coronado explored the Southwest in 1540, but it was not until 1598 that Onate arrived with a caravan of settlers. By 1610 they had made Santa Fe the capital of the colony and the center of trade. The peaceful agricultural Pueblo Indians and the Spaniards were surrounded by nomadic warlike tribes which traded with them, but more often raided the settlements in the Rio Grande valley.

Eighty years of exploitation of the Pueblos as virtual slaves brought a revolt; the Spaniards were driven back to El Paso and their buildings were destroyed. With the reconquest by De Vargas in 1692 the Spanish settlements became permanent. Thus no Spanish-colonial antiques can be found which antedate 1700, but from then until the Civil War period nearly everything used in the Southwest was made there.

Included in the infrequent freight arriving by wagon from Mexico City were arms for defense, ecclesiastical furnishings such as altar services, vestments, religious paintings and images, as well as olive oil and wine in earthenware jars, seeds, clothing, boards, tools, nails, rope, canvas, tires, and coins. Otherwise the colony became almost self-sufficient. With the decline of the Spanish Empire, fewer and fewer travelers risked the hazardous journey over desert and mountain, and by the time Mexico became independent in 1821 the isolation of New Mexico was nearly complete.

One distinctive result of this self-sufficiency was the creation of an indigenous religious folk art by the *santero* school of craftsmen—the anonymous village carpenters and primitive artists who made images of the saints, called *santos*. The paintings, of earth and vegetable pigments on board panels are called *retablos* (Fig. 1 and Cover). Figures of saints carved in the round are called *bultos* (Figs. 3, 10, and 13). These paintings of sacred subjects on native pine or

cottonwood, covered with gesso and painted in tempera. There were four or five anonymous artists to whom most extant examples of the period can be ascribed, by certain mannerisms and characteristics of their work. One always brushed into the composition two red peppers; another had a unique way of coloring his faces white, cheeks red, with eyes underlined with gray. These itinerant "makers of saints" supplied every home and church for a century with these holy figures. The wooden images are a blend of peasant naïveté with remote echoes of the Spanish baroque.

The sweeping reforms introduced by Archbishop Lamy after 1851 included the suppression of the *santeros;* their images were discarded from most churches as pagan, and replaced in time by imported plaster-gilt figures. Thus most *santos,* were made in the century before 1850. All but a few were unsigned and undated.

Yankee traders arriving over the Santa Fe trail found an illiterate people living among large herds and cultivated fields with little more in the way of material goods than had the Indians. To barter for fur with the Indians and Spaniards, the Yankees brought such goods as beads, bales of cloth, combs, mirrors, ribbons, and colored chromos of the saints. Rarely, before the Civil War, a wagon-train brought a square piano

Fig. 5 — Spanish-Colonial Window Girlle and Chairs. The 6 cut-out panels of the grille are fitted without nails into slots in frames. Outer boards of grille are extended to form pivots which swing in sockets in the window frame, as did the early doors. Simple hand-forged hook fastening has rude engraved design. Such grilles were used in place of shutters, and without glass. Chair (*left*) of pine; spindle back, hand-lathed; chip carving (*1750-1800*). Chair (*center*) of pine, one of a pair; chip carving, as on chair at left, on back panels and apron. Chair (*right*) of pine; seat and one side stretcher are replacements (c. *1830*). All three chairs made without nails. *From Museum of New Mexico; photograph by Ernest Knee.*

Fig. 4 — New Mexican Altar. The upper figures represent St. Lawrence, the Holy Trinity, and Bishop Athanasius; the lower figures, the Madonna of the Rosary and St. Joseph, with the Virgin and Child, carved in the round (*bulto*), in the center niche. This structure of hand-hewn planks was taken from a church in the Santa Cruz Valley. *From the Taylor Museum of Colorado Springs; photograph by courtesy of the Museum of Modern Art, New York City.*

or sofa for some relatively wealthy ranchero or high official.

The full impact of progress as known in the eastern states came only with the building of the railroad in 1880. It brought a flood of goods as well as settlers, and expanding commerce marked the end of an era. Thus 1880 is the deadline for acceptable antiques of New Mexico. However, 1700 to 1860 is a better, if arbitrary, time limit.

The foregoing paragraphs give a sketchy notion of how remote was the province of New Mexico from the comparative opulence and splendor of contemporary Spain and Mexico. No lavish use of sheets of gold and silver in palace or church occurred in this colony. There church, palace, and hovel were all built of adobe (mud bricks) and roofed with pine beams. No sumptuous fabrics were known, only homespun and leather. Despite the presence of many metals in the rocky hills, Spanish methods of separating metal from ore were inadequate for utilizing the grades found in New Mexico. Some copper was worked in the Santa Rita mines, and a tiny amount of gold from a relatively pure deposit within sight of Santa Fe, but this was not until the early nineteenth century. Such tools and utensils as were made of metal were so few and so difficult to work without proper implements that they were mended until they are now a mass of patches. From inventories and wills of a century ago we learn that such items as "one iron hoe" were valuable enough to itemize among bequeathed property. Indeed, quotations like the following are not uncommon: "to my elder son I leave—one iron hoe, one woollen cover two *varas* long [*vara*—about one yard], one painting of a Saint on board three fingerbreadths wide."

FIG. 6 — NEW MEXICAN BENCH (*c. 1810-1820*). Unfinished wood. *From the Southwest Museum, Los Angeles.*

Due to the abundance of soft wood available — cottonwood and pine — and the scarcity of other materials, wood served every possible use to which the ingenuity of the people could shape it. This ingenuity to some extent canceled the lack of metal implements with which to work wood, as well as the limitations of the material. On the large and prosperous ranches, numerous female servants were kept everlastingly spinning and weaving more blankets, more homespun, and preparing the simple food in slow and primitive ways, while the men were busy with the stock or making more rawhide ropes and wooden implements. All of these activities varied little, except in degree, among rich and poor *rancheros.*

In most homes the family sat on the floor to do the endless routine chores, cleaning grain, beans, chili, and wool, grinding meal, making bread, doing other cooking, spinning and weaving, as well as to eat and foregather socially. Cooking was done in the tiny corner

Glass was not available, ceramics were almost non-existent. The Indian pottery was cheap and common, but settlers mainly used wooden bowls, copper and rawhide buckets, copper kettles. Rarely is a piece of Spanish majolica or one of the Mexican derivatives of it unearthed, and then in fragments. Even the use of roofing tile, so common in Mexico and Spain, was never adopted in New Mexico, except in the isolated chain of mission settlements set up in the Pimeria by Father Kino. This tile, as well as brick, the builder-priests had made on the spot for their use, but these mission settlements were short-lived, and never had any effect on the older villages on the Rio Grande.

FIG. 7 — CARVED CHEST (*c. 1800-1850*). The legs are a part of the chest. Usually the chest was separate from the base, a sort of cradle on legs. The braces strengthening the legs of this example are decorative as well as functional. The chest is dovetailed and doweled. The lid has no hinges or fastening. The coarse, severely geometric carving is characteristic of the period, when curvilinear and naturalistic forms had been forgotten. *From the Museum of New Mexico; photograph by Ernest Knee.*

FIG. 8 (*below, left*) PINE CHEESE PRESS AND COTTONWOOD SHOVEL. Tray of press is hollowed from a single plank 2 inches thick; crude legs penetrate the plank. Used in making native cheese, usually of goat's milk. When the milk is curdled by slight heating to a junket-like consistency, the curd is broken up and the whey drained off in the press. The curds are kneaded with the hands until all the whey is out, then molded into a compact flat cake, which may be eaten at once or wrapped in a cloth and allowed to hang a day or two. Cheese is still made by this simple process, but modern kitchen aids have replaced this type of press. The shovel, made from a single slab, was used for grain or beans. *From the Museum of New Mexico; photos by Ernest Knee.*

FIG. 9 — PINE CHEST WITH DRAWERS (*1700-1750*) (*two views*). Made from 1½-inch planks, handhewn and planed. Dovetailed construction. Molding, affixed with wooden dowels, was originally studded with copper bosses of which only two remain. Lid, originally one plank, has been split and reinforced with cleats. It is attached with two iron hinges. Hasp and escutcheon are plain. The low-relief carving shows Spanish influence in the traditional motifs — rosette, lion, and pomegranate. The interior is fitted with a bank of six drawers which do not rest on the bottom, thus permitting storage of long objects below. Originally the drawers were finished with simple molding and wooden knobs, some of which are now missing. Probably made for storage of vestments and other paraphernalia in a church sacristy. Length, 48 inches. *From the Museum of New Mexico.*

fireplace or in an outdoor oven, and the family sat on the floor around a communal bowl and dished out the food with neatly managed bits of tortilla. In homes of government officials and priests, there were a few chairs, as there were one or two in the churches (*Fig. 5*). Sometimes there was a bench (*Fig. 6, 14*) but most of those still surviving are church pews. Many families had stools made from a cross section of log, or a little footrest of three pieces of board. Sometimes there was one rough-hewn table in the kitchen.

The main piece of furniture was a trastero — a cupboard with doors — crude, heavy, with simple molding and carved design and a thong latch. It may be remarked that the usual style of chip carving used in native wooden ornament is remarkable chiefly for the variety of design the maker was able to produce with a single chisel. Some of the trasteros were painted. Other pieces of furniture were a large wooden box on legs to protect flour, grain, and staples from mice (*Fig. 7*), chests for storage of clothing and papers, and a hanging shelf or two with rude molding and cornice. Few homes in the pre-Civil War period had beds.

Wooden utensils in daily use included dough tray, cheese press, bowls, ladles and dippers, spinning wheel, shuttle and wool combs, shoe and stocking lasts, scales, shovels, hooks, candlestands and sconces, and homemade handles for the few metal implements there were (*Fig. 8*).

Valuables were stored in chests (*Fig. 9*). Some of these were of carved pine, others of hide. Early in the nineteenth century one or two itinerant craftsmen from old Mexico apparently came up into the colony and brought with them oil paints; the latter were not in use in New Mexico. These traveling artists painted chests, of New Mexican pine, with gay designs in the same manner as those on chests which are known to have been brought up from Chihuahua at that time. They were fitted with simple iron scutcheons, hasps, and locks. A very few are still available, although the painted surface has frequently suffered from abuse.

Smaller boxes, plaques, and candle sconces were made of soft cottonwood and blackened with a mixture of soot and pitch, then inlaid with delicate designs in wheat straw.

Musical instruments and wooden stirrups virtually exhaust the list of extant wooden items unless the collector cares for examples of old doors, shutters, corbels, grilles, and other elements of building construction.

FIG. 10 (*right*). THE HOLY FAMILY. Polychrome *bulto*. From the Taylor Museum of Colorado Springs; *photograph courtesy Museum of Modern Art.*

FIG. 11 (*below*) — NICHO (*1830-1840*). A three-dimensional frame of tin with or without glass. This example contains a water-color drawing of the *Santo Nino de Atocha* with his chair, pilgrim's basket, staff, and gourd. Glass panels of doors are neatly bound in tin strips. Ornamentation achieved with a nail on reverse side. Later designs in tinwork became more florid and sprawling; birds, leaves, flowers, and painted areas were introduced. Height, 13½ inches. *From author's collection; photograph by Ernest Knee.*

FIG. 13 (*below, right*). "CRISTO NAZARENO." Such grim and bloody representations of the suffering Savior were used in the ceremonies of the flagellant sect, the *Penitentes*, excommunicated by Archbishop Lamy. They were carried in the Easter procession to the hilltop, the jointed arms swinging weirdly, the chanting penitents following and flagellating each other with cactus whips. At the end of the ceremony an individual selected for his religious devotion was "crucified," tied to the cross until he fainted. Thus were the sins of the community vicariously atoned. This practice is still secretly carried on at night in remote New Mexican mountain villages during Holy Week. *From the Taylor Museum; photograph courtesy Museum of Modern Art.*

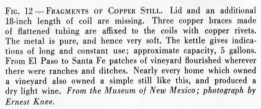

FIG. 12 — FRAGMENTS OF COPPER STILL. Lid and an additional 18-inch length of coil are missing. Three copper braces made of flattened tubing are affixed to the coils with copper rivets. The metal is pure, and hence very soft. The kettle gives indications of long and constant use; approximate capacity, 5 gallons. From El Paso to Santa Fe patches of vineyard flourished wherever there were ranches and ditches. Nearly every home which owned a vineyard also owned a simple still like this, and produced a dry light wine. *From the Museum of New Mexico; photograph by Ernest Knee.*

The use of tin began soon after the establishment of the Santa Fe Trail, early in the nineteenth century. Prior to this time tin was not available in the colony. Since it came at first in small amounts the objects made from it were carefully worked and not large. Two chandeliers, formerly in the chapel at Cañoncito, New Mexico, are alleged to have been hung in the chapel about 1820. These were both similar to mediaeval crowns, concentric circles of tin not over seventeen inches in diameter, embossed in simple punched designs and supporting a number of plain strap candelabra.

A frequent subject of tincraft was the cross. Decorative objects in this shape hang in many a church and home. The small inset glass panels were painted on the reverse in brightly colored etched designs. This was done with a comb while the paint was still wet. Slightly later the glass and tin panels framed scraps of Victorian wall paper. A contemporary group of tin crosses was made framing bits of paper painted in imitation of wall paper, a sufficient commentary on the value of real wall paper in the colony. Other forms of tin include very decorative processional staves with fanciful crown, cross, or scroll at the head.

Older examples of tinwork were sometimes joined together with pitch instead of soldier. As tin became more common its pliability, the simple tools needed to work it, and its resemblance to silver, made it a popular medium. Even today large quantities of tin mirror frames, candle sconces, and lighting fixtures are made in Santa Fe. Early New Mexican tin is readily distinguishable by its restraint and simplicity, as well as by its primitive construction. Never did New Mexican tincraft (*Fig. 11*) approach the sophistication of Mexican work.

Copper trays, basins, ewers and lamps, pewter boxes and inkstands, all severely simple in shape, were among church furnishings made in the colony. Scattered examples of brass crucifix, candlstick, or dish may be assumed to have been brought from Mexico, as were the small bronze crucifixes still found now and then.

A type of blanket known as the Rio Grande blanket was made by the Spanish colonists. The blankets were light in weight, well but not tightly woven, and of pleasing colors. Some of the older ones were in imitation of blankets from old Mexico but the limitations of cruder spinning implements and looms and the limited dyes available make them readily distinguishable from the true Mexican blanket. They are not to be confused with Indian-made blankets.

The weaving was done on a narrow loom and two strips were sewn together to form one blanket. If this was intended for use as a serape an opening for the head was left in the center. A popular design of a century ago was a series of broad and narrow bands of indigo blue, natural brown, and cream. Sometimes stepped lozenges were worked into the corners. Additional colors used in sparing amounts were yellow, bayeta red, and light green. The Brazil was a blanket in which a good part of the ground color was dipped in logwood dye which gave a pleasing café-au-lait color.

Since about 1860 or 1870 such textile weaving has been extinct. A modern revival, now a flourishing cottage industry in many small hill towns, produces the Chimayo blanket, named for one of the better-known villages. This blanket is quite different from the earlier ones in yarn (commercial), dyes (aniline), and designs (exotic).

A beguiling pursuit is collecting old steel and wood engravings illustrating a text or the Scriptures. Examples are found here and there, framed in wood or tin. These are all of Mexican or European origin, and date variously from the sixteenth to nineteenth centuries. No press existed in the colony of New Mexico before the coming of the Americans, with the exception of a small hand press brought in by an enterprising priest, on which he turned out a few issues of a newspaper and single-sheet handbills.

Even the amateur of Currier and Ives prints will find a highly specialized source of these in New Mexico. The New York firm issued a series of popular saints captioned in Spanish for the Latin American trade. These are refreshingly different from the better-known Currier and Ives depictions of the American scene (*Fig. 2*).

Mid-nineteenth-century lithographs struck in Mexico may be found occasionally. A fairly well-known series of these depicting daily life gives us an excellent picture of the dress, domestic manners, and homes of the New Mexicans about 1850, and for lack of other documentation make an interesting sidelight on the local material.

The objects fashioned by these frontiers-folk in colonial New Mexico were made for constant use in home or church, and most of them were worn out long since. There are good examples to be studied in the museums and private collections of the Southwest, but not a vast quantity remains to be picked up readily. The collector with patience and knowledge can, however, still assemble enough to make it well worth while. Examples of the work of the colonists of New Mexico deserve a place in every well-rounded collection of American "folk art." The Spanish colonists and their descendants were and are an integral and unique part of this melting-pot called America. The relics of the era before that section was united politically with the other States evoke a romantic picture of the old Southwest, and are possessed of historical associations which transcend their esthetic value.

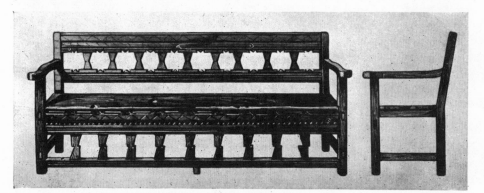

FIG. 14 — MISSION BENCH. Made of pine. *Now in the Southwest Museum, Los Angeles; water color rendering by Index of American Design.*

Something About Stencils

A GALLERY NOTE

THE restoration of old houses invariably raises questions as to the suitable decorative treatment of walls and floors. Most people incline to disregard the second part of their problem and to install a hardwood substitute for the worn and splintered pine boards that they usually find in place. However, if they chance to be purists, and their dwelling is of the late eighteenth or early nineteenth century, they turn to plain paint, marbling, or random spatterwork. Few have the hardihood to keep unfinished floors in condition by daily scrubbing — as I fear was a not infrequent custom of the good old days. As an alternative to the floor treatments enumerated, stenciling might well be tried. The subject is discussed at length and with an amplitude of illustration by Esther Stevens Fraser in ANTIQUES for April 1931. The cost for thus covering the area of an entire room might be high. If the pattern is restricted to a wide border strip, the financial hazards should not be perilous.

Fig. 1 — PANEL DECORATED WITH THE AID OF EARLY STENCILS
Such patterns should suggest manifold possibilities to the restorer of the old or the creator of the new in the field of wall decoration

Stenciling is even more readily applicable to walls than to floors, and there is ample precedent for its employment — particularly in dwellings erected between the late 1790's and about 1840, the flourishing period of stenciling in the United States — especially, perhaps, in New England. As far back as April 1922 ANTIQUES published a number of furniture stencils discovered in Montague, Massachusetts, by Esther Stevens Fraser. More recently Miss Janet Waring of Yonkers, New York, has made similar finds in Massachusetts and New Hampshire, and with them a large group of wall stencils prepared by Moses Eaton and his son, long-time inhabitants of Hancock, New Hampshire.

During the summer of 1933 selections from Miss Waring's collection of more than a thousand examples were exhibited at the Berkshire Museum, Pittsfield, Massachusetts. For this event an interpretative bulletin was prepared by Miss Laura M. Bragg, director. To Miss Bragg I am indebted for the material upon which the present hint to householders is based.

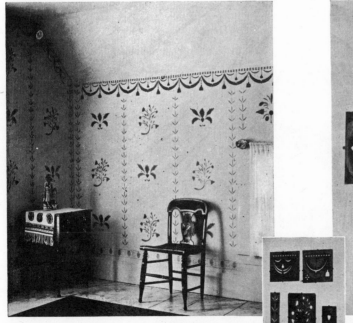

Fig. 2 — A STENCILED WALL
Bedroom stenciled by Miss Janet Waring in her summer home, a restored farmhouse in Monterey, Massachusetts. Old stencils cut by David Eaton were used. Particularly reminiscent of the eighteenth century are the swag-and-tassel frieze and the dado strip whose pattern recalls the decorative punchwork on mantels and other wood surfaces of the early 1800's

Fig. 3 — STENCILS
The pine cone, or pineapple, in dull orange with a rich mantling of green leafage, was capable of achieving quite impressive effects. Some of the actual stencils used to decorate the wall shown in Figure 2 are illustrated in the insert at the left.
Photographs by courtesy of the Berkshire Museum, Pittsfield, Massachusetts

Some Colonial and Early

By Esther Stevens Fraser

RECENT years have witnessed the expenditure of much effort in recreating proper backgrounds for our inherited or acquired antiques. Museums have sought in every way to obtain the subtle artistic illusion of true old-time homes, correct in every detail — from wall decoration to curtain tie-backs. In some instances concealed electric globes are so arranged as to simulate candlelight or the glint of a setting sun sifting through a kitchen doorway. But what do we know of floors in Colonial houses? Were they, most of them, wide pine boards pinned down with wooden pegs or hand-wrought nails, and painted "pumpkin yellow"? Were others painted in a monotone, and spattered over with many-hued dots of variegated size? Were there still other forms of floor finish in the Colonial mansions?

In seeking to find a definite answer, I have made it a practice to record all the old-time floor finishes that gave evidence of being authentic. It will doubtless surprise many that, among the numerous types of underfoot decoration that have rewarded my investigation, I have yet to see traces of a really ancient spatter floor. Several antiquaries, whose official occupation takes them into many old houses, report the same experience. It would be interesting to know whence came this now widely adopted type of floor painting. Doubtless it is based on some old custom — perhaps it is an imitation of sanding; but if spatter dates prior to 1840, it is strange that we have encountered no earlier traces of it. Personally, I strongly suspect that spatter floors originated in the Victorian era.

All in all, I am convinced that our resourceful ancestresses demanded stylish and interesting floors, in keeping with the new wall papers and fresh paints that suited their feminine hearts. Living much at home, oftentimes leading a rather drab existence, they indulged their yearning for beauty by making their homes as ornamental as resources would permit.

Some of the various floor finishes I have noticed may lend themselves to reproduction; others may have to be modified to meet present needs. Be that as it may, let us briefly review them.

First of all, of course, our dauntless pioneers erected cabins, on whose dirt floors they spread a layer of sand for greater cleanliness and comfort. Even when the luxury of board floors could be afforded, sanding was not soon abandoned. Sand proved advantageous in absorbing the tracks of many boots, and was an aid to sweeping. Today, sanded kitchen floors are far from practical, but they were quite universal in Colonial houses until well after 1750, and were in use fully a century later, not only, as my husband's grandmother told him, in Mid-Western pioneer log cabins, but in the Eastern countryside as well. It is traditionally believed that patterns were wrought in the fresh sand by dexterous manipulation of a fagot broom, and that housewives vied with each other in evolving novel designs. Widely used were herringbone treatments and swirled dots obtained by quick twists of the broom.

The association that has restored the Harlow House at Plymouth has likewise afforded us a complete picture of an old-time kitchen-living room. Here the sanded floor is in perfect keeping with the low ceiling, the great beamed fireplace, the tiny windows, and the mellow brown sheathing of vertical featheredged boards.

But I digress from my subject. Next, in point of time, came board floors, kept carefully scrubbed by the fastidious housewife. I have the temerity to champion such floors as highly practical, even today, in simple homes or in kitchens. They do not require perpetual varnishing or painting. A good scrubbing

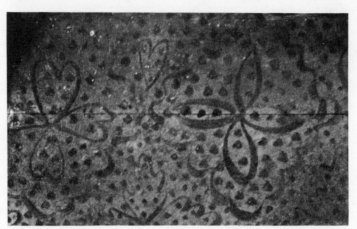

Fig. 1 — Painted Floor in Barnstable (*early eighteenth century*)
Dark gray on light gray ground. The design is in the first and only coat of paint, and gives evidence of a crude, free-hand execution.
Owned by Mrs. Joseph Iasigi

Fig. 2 — Painted Floor, Norwell, Massachusetts (*eighteenth century*)
Owned by Arthur S. Dewing

American Decorative Floors

Drawings by the Author

once a week with strong soapsuds imparts to them a silvery whiteness that shows no dust and a minimum of dirt. Contrary to present-day custom, no pride was taken by our ancestors in floors of wide boards. In fact, we generally find narrow boards in the best rooms, with the wider planks reserved for upstairs and kitchens. The very widest are likely to occur in attics. Doubtless there were excellent reasons for this distribution. Narrow boards were not subject to knot holes, or to warping and shrinking. Between wide boards, gaping cracks often developed.

Paint, as an interior finish, appears to have come into use in the Colonies about 1725. Before that date its advantages as a preservative may not have been recognized; or, again, the scarcity of pigments and oils in this country may have prevented its employment. With the removal of such disqualifications, primary colors were at first the favorites. Pumpkin yellow (mainly yellow ochre), since it came the nearest to the color of dust and dirt, was widely used on floors. Indian red also appealed to our ancestors' love of cheering tints; but it required more care in its upkeep. I have never actually seen a blue floor in original paint; though the prevalence of cart-wheel blue about old farms suggests that this color occasionally found its way to household floors. Then, of course, gray and brown were used by those practical folk who were not concerned with enlivening decorative effects.

From the first application of paint to floors, a brief step carried the householder to attempt varied patterns. I am convinced that the custom of ornamenting floors became quite general; but few are the old houses surviving today that retain even a vestige of evidence to that effect. The few instances here discussed are only samples of a technique once widely honored.

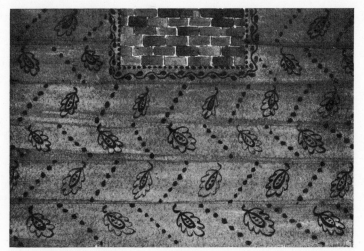

Fig. 3 — PAINTED FLOOR, BARNSTABLE *(early eighteenth century)*
Brownish-yellow ground.
Owned by Henry C. Everett

Fig. 4 — MARBLED PAINTED FLOOR, MYSTIC, CONNECTICUT *(c. 1790)*
By permission of Mrs. Davis

In the little Cape Cod town of Barnstable stands an early two-story dwelling, with hip roof and large central chimney. The "best room" displays a very early form of paneling, dating perhaps from 1720 or 1725. On its floor (*Fig. 1*), protected now by a large carpet, the first and only coat of paint is still visible. The background color, a very pale gray, is covered with an allover pattern in a dark, but transparent, gray. Along the sides of the room runs a narrow border that closely follows the hearth line. The centre of the floor is marked off into diamonds with undulating edges, sprinkled with diverse conventional designs resembling oak leaves, hearts, and flower petals. Between these major elements dots are scattered, as if the painter abhorred a plain surface. The whole was executed rather crudely with a brush that must have been nearly an inch in width. A final coat of white shellac or varnish gives the surface a slightly yellowish tone that makes the effect more pleasing. It is my belief that all decorated floors were kept carefully protected by some such finish.

Scarcely more than three doors away is another old house with beautifully paneled parlor, whose floor (*Fig. 3*) is finished with an early painted decoration. While the pattern differs widely from that described above, it has the same flavor, and is undoubtedly the same man's handiwork. The floor itself is constructed of boards of nearly equal width, painted a medium tone of yellow brown, not much darker than yellow ochre. A narrow border follows the hearth, but does not run around the entire room. Each board is decorated with wavy-edged oak leaves laid diagonally at intervals, and with dotted parallel lines midway between them. The direction of the diagonals reverses with each board, so that a zigzag effect is achieved. Fortunately, there are not

Fig. 5 — Room with Stenciled Floor in Newton, Massachusetts (*c. 1790*)
Owned by Arthur S. Dewing

One of four rooms and a hallway having floors painted with stenciled designs for centre patterns and borders, in yellow ochre, Indian red, verdigris green, white, and black. When discovered, most of the patterns were badly worn, but in one room, a protective straw matting had perfectly preserved the work. The colors are so toned down as to give the effect of parquetry in varicolored woods

Fig. 6 — Border Detail from "Valet's Chamber" in the Wayside Inn

Fig. 7 — Border Detail from South Deerfield House (*c. 1790*) *By permission of Mrs. Sheldon*

many dots in this pattern. The condition of the paint in this instance is remarkably perfect, because of the kindly protection of varnish and heavy carpeting. Here again the paneling suggests the year 1725, and leads us to conclude that the room and its neighbor in the same town were probably completed and decorated — floors and all — approximately at that time. The large scale of the floor patterns and the simplicity of their design suggest painting I have seen on certain early chests from rural Massachusetts and New Hampshire.

Once in a while, I dare say, a floor painting did double duty, and was not conceived primarily as an ornament. I remember once being shown a remarkable hooked rug, of full room size, whose proud owner informed me:

"Mother evolved the design herself, painting it on the floor of an upstairs bedroom to see if it was satisfactory. It took her two years to hook the carpet, still in grand condition, but the floor she painted is now covered with new boards." The rug with its flower wreaths was hooked about 1860. Earlier patterns may have been similarly composed.

In the old-fashioned town of Norwell, Massachusetts, stands a weather-stained shingled house, built in 1695, and successively occupied by several generations of shipbuilders. Here, in an upstairs bedroom, is a painted floor (*Fig. 2*) that was not designed purely for ornament. In the centre is a circle, some five feet in diameter, within which is drawn a many-pointed star. Outside the circle occurs an ornamentation of broad zigzag bands, in yellow ochre and chocolate brown. Each point of the star is divided by a midrib, to the left of which the member is yellow, and to the right, brown.

At first glance, I jumped to the conclusion that this was a

Fig. 8 — Detail of Floor Shown in Figure 5

compass star. Then, by slow degrees, it dawned upon me that something was wrong. The north-northeast, the east-northeast, and corresponding points were improperly painted. Such an error would never have occurred in a shipbuilder's home! For several years I remained unenlightened concerning this eight-pointed star. Then it was identified as a kind of templet for cutting the sails for ships. I do not guarantee the correctness of the identification; but I feel that such a pattern as this, or the true compass star, would be most appropriate in a restored Cape Cod house, the lives of whose erstwhile occupants were doubtless swayed by favoring winds or stormy seas.

In Colonial mansions I have found several floors laid off in squares of alternating color like six or eight-inch marble tiles. There is, for example, the yellow ochre and black floor in Tutor Flint's study at the Dorothy Q. house in Quincy, Massachusetts. When it was painted was not definitely known, but I would hazard the guess of sometime between 1760 and 1770. The mid-eighteenth-century Wentworth Gardner mansion at Portsmouth, New Hampshire, has its entrance hallway painted with eight-inch black and pale gray squares. Fortunately this original paint was in sufficiently good condition to be preserved, though other floors throughout the house have required refinishing.

With Adam influence reflecting the refinements and luxuries of ancient Rome, the advent of marbled floors in this period was quite to be expected. At Nantucket, my attention has been attracted by the number of simple 1780–1800 type homes whose parlors and best rooms rejoice in marbled floors. Usually these were painted a medium gray, with realistic feather graining in white and black, the whole kept carefully varnished. Even at

Siasconset, where rambler roses and century-old ivy clamber lovingly over low shingled roofs, I found a tiny fisherman's cottage with a marbled floor in perfect condition.

Curiously enough, in the old Newbury, Massachusetts, home of Tristram Coffin — Nantucket's first settler — there is another example of a marbled painted floor. Both entrance hall and staircase are painted pale gray with dark gray veining. On the risers of the staircase, the original marbling is still intact, with here and there a glimpse of yet older yellow ochre underneath. While part of this Tristram Coffin house dates back to 1650, the marbled floor lies in a less ancient portion, said to have been built about 1725. Adjoining the hall stands the parlor, whose superb 1800-type wall paper is quite intact. In all probability, new paper and fresh paint were demanded by some housewife just coming into residence at that date.

The surmise is substantiated by an article on the Coffin house published recently in *Old-Time New England*, the bulletin of the Society for the Preservation of New England Antiquities (July, 1929). Here we learn that, in 1785, the parlor section fell to the lot of Edmund Coffin, an unmarried son in the household, who remained a bachelor until 1792. Six years later, upon the death of his widowed mother, Edmund came into possession of the living room on the other side of the marbled hallway. At that time, doubtless, his previous living room, which has a more northerly exposure, was newly papered and turned into a "best room," and the hall was painted to harmonize with it. In 1803 the first wife died, and in 1809 a new helpmeet was installed. Apparently her advent was not hailed with fresh paint; for the year of her coming seems a trifle late for the marbled floor.

At Mystic, Connecticut, a house built about 1790 reveals a floor (*Fig. 4*) painted with a striking and intricate pattern. Tradition maintains that the original owner, who suffered from asthma, believed that he could not sleep in a room containing any vestige of carpeting. So he fooled both himself and the asthma with a painted imitation. While some decorated floors (particularly those with border and centre designs) may be old-time substitutes for expensive imported rugs, this is the first time, in my experience, that thrift has disguised itself as asthma.

Be that as it may, what a floor this is! The background color is a pinkish tone of ochre, as if a small amount of burnt sienna had been added to the yellow. Around the edge runs a broad border of scrolls stenciled in burnt sienna brown. In the centre, alternating black and white diamonds (marbled) are so placed as to resemble a two-colored ribbon turning back and forth, revealing first one side and then the other. Between these dynamic

diamonds are left square reserves, each filled with a shapely urn suggestive of Hepplewhite or Sheraton designs. These vessels are painted in a pinkish ochre one tone darker than the background, and are shadowed to roundness with burnt sienna.

In time, stenciling came to be a popular method of ornamenting painted floors. Various traveling decorators with their stencil kits journeyed through towns remote from busy wall-paper stores and carpet emporiums, and succeeded in persuading many housewives to permit the decoration of either walls or floors with methodically repeated ornament.

At Deerfield, Massachusetts, we find a floor with a stenciled border in black on a yellow ochre ground (*Fig. 7*). Here there appears to have been no centre pattern, an omission that is unusual, but not unique. One feature of this stencil design is the minuteness of its component parts. So dainty and delicate are they that we must ascribe the work to the period of extreme delicacy between 1780 and 1800. Although the stenciling has been entirely renewed, I have no doubt that it is very like the original. Such is my faith in the owners of the house; for they have been Deerfield's chief historians.

A stencil outfit consisting of four borders, two centre patterns, and five colors — yellow ochre, Indian red, verdigris green, white, and black — was used to ornament five floors in one old Newton, Massachusetts, home. As it was originally a tavern, built in 1734, its floors were doubtless unpainted for many years, until, in 1790, the place came into the hands of fresh owners. At that time, a new mantel with slender double columns was placed in the parlor, and the painting of the four main rooms and hallway was accomplished. (See *Figs. 5, 8, 10.*) When discovered recently, most of these floor patterns were badly worn or painted over; but in one room, the work is entirely original and excellently preserved, thanks to the protective grace of straw matting. Old shellac or dull varnish has so toned the colors — yellow ochre ground with centre stenciling in black and white, border in Indian red — that the effect is similar to parquetry in varicolored woods.

Across the hall, the same coloring is repeated, but the patterns are quite different. One upstairs bedroom is decorated with the centre design of the parlor and the border of the living room. The other bedroom has precisely the same centre as the living room, used with a border quite different from anything else in the house — green and white rosettes with a festooned swag between. The hallway pattern, a simple geometric design, border only, is not continued up the stairway.

Recently, an old house from Hanson, Massachusetts, was

Fig. 9 — DETAIL FROM STENCILED FLOOR IN THE WAYSIDE INN (*c. 1790*)
By permission of Henry Ford

moved, piece by piece, to North Chatham. In one downstairs room the much worn remains of a stenciled floor were still visible. While the house, with unpainted pine paneling, dates from 1720 or 1730, the stenciling cannot claim any such antiquity. The pattern of jagged leaf scrolls in dark green suggests 1825 or 1830. This V-shaped design, making, by its repetition, a zigzag line across the floor, leaves diamond spaces wherein a creamy-white rosette with dotted background is painted by means of a stencil.

Early in my study of decorated floors, someone volunteered the information that there was one such piece of workmanship at the Wayside Inn in Sudbury. Sure enough, beneath a rug in the Lafayette room, I uncovered a design (*Fig. 9*) of alternating diamonds in dull blue and black on a yellow ochre ground. Traces of the same design survive near the less worn edges of the room. In the adjoining room, known as the "valet's chamber," I likewise found fragments of a very beautiful border decoration (*Fig. 6*), reminiscent of those in the Newton home. At the time, I was not permitted to sketch the design; and as its visibility is steadily decreasing, I became alarmed for its existence. Fortunately, my request to make a direct tracing was granted before the record had been completely obliterated. I am told that Mr. Ford declines to have this floor restored for fear it will look too new. If this is really his decision, it is unfortunate that no attempt was made, long since, to preserve what traces of pattern were existing when the Inn first passed to its present owner. The care expended in perpetuating other features of the old hostelry convinces me that the rarity of this stenciled floor pattern is even yet underestimated.

I have found it difficult to date the design in the Lafayette room. At first, I supposed it to be 1825, at which time the distinguished French envoy was visiting America. Then I considered the charmingly delicate wall paper, which must be of the 1790's. The border in the tiny adjoining chamber also reflects this period of grace. The use of parallel bars of uneven length on the floor of the Lafayette room recurs in the Newton house decorations. Both might be attributed to

the same workman. Lastly, when I learned that Lafayette never stopped at the Wayside Inn, I concluded that the assumption of 1825 as the date of the floor design must be incorrect. In all probability this room was never put in order for the foreign visitor, but was papered and painted at some time in the neighborhood of 1790.

In restoring decorated floors that are quite worn, I suggest that the places in finest condition be carefully preserved with spar varnish (applied on a clear, dry day) before the missing portions are renewed. In this fashion a record is kept for matching colors and pattern. But it is necessary to be certain that the colors are matched. Dull overtones of varnish, shellac, or dirt are to be taken into consideration. One must scrape through these overtones to ascertain what colors the decorator employed. Personally, I prefer to brush a dull-toned varnish over all new work, thus reducing its rawness. But the background color must be several shades lighter than the finished product.

I sympathize with the regret of the Editor of ANTIQUES that it is impossible to reproduce here, in full color, a number of the old free-hand and stenciled floor decorations of whose hues and patterns I have a very complete record. In several instances, however, it has been possible to obtain photographs of sufficient clarity to illustrate these notes. Where camera work has been unprocurable, I have supplied sketches from my notebook. The possibilities that these various pictures will suggest to architects and decorators I can only surmise.

[The present generation usually demands at least some expanse of pile fabric underfoot, and is not likely to alter its prejudice in that respect. The painted pepper and salt, or spatter, floor, now much in vogue for small country homes and cottages, may not be historically authentic; but it is easily produced and has the further advantage of offering an excellent background for hooked rugs. Interesting effects, however, might be obtained by framing the spattered area with a stenciled border, or by using such a border with a floor of natural wood finished in shellac and wax. — *The Editor*.]

Fig. 10 — Stenciled Floor in Newton, Massachusetts (*c. 1790*)
Colors: yellow, red, green, black, white. In another room the same pattern is repeated with a different border, shown in the accompanying detail.
Owned by Arthur S. Dewing

The painted decoration

BY NINA FLETCHER LITTLE

Barroom of the Bump Tavern with overmantel painting from the Van Bergen house (built 1729), Leeds, Greene County, New York. When this house was demolished in 1862 the board was removed to a new house erected on the same site, where it remained until acquired by the New York State Historical Association in 1954. Here it is installed in such a way that it can be removed for exhibition. *Except as noted, photographs by LeBel Studio.*

DURING THE LAST DECADE there has been increasing interest in early decorative painting, and the collection of the New York State Historical Association now contains documented examples in all the major categories. This material has been installed in the Farmers' Museum buildings with the intention of showing it in its original context.

Ten years ago the public was unaware of the number of landscape panels and stenciled walls still in existence in New York State. But as interest increased through information made available during the Seminars in American Culture, reports began to come in concerning decorated walls, floors, woodwork, and furniture in many parts of the state. Correspondents were urged to photograph and describe their finds and to deposit the data at the Association's headquarters where they are kept on file for the use of all interested scholars.

Decorative landscapes painted on sections of room paneling became popular in the seaboard states during the mid-1700's. They began to go out of fashion by 1800 because post-Revolutionary architectural styles did not emphasize the overmantel. Of the few eighteenth-century examples found in New York State, a particularly fine one is in the Bump Tavern barroom. This originally formed part of the woodwork in the home of Martin van Bergen, a stone farmhouse built in 1729 in the present town of Leeds.

A second architectural painting executed on a wood panel was found, framed by short pilasters, below the

Center section of the Leeds overmantel (mid-eighteenth century), showing Van Bergen's stone farmhouse and its outbuildings with the Catskill Mountains in the background. The owner and his wife stand before the house, watching a loaded wagon pass, while other members of the family, Negro servants, and farm animals enliven the scene. In the foreground an Indian with gun is meekly followed by his squaw with papoose. Apart from its liveliness and charm, this painting is the finest pictorial record yet discovered of early eighteenth-century farm life in the Hudson River Valley. Length of entire panel, 7½ feet.

Architectural painting from Potter Hollow Tavern, Greene County, mid-1800's; signed *W. W. Cornwell Pin . . .* The artist emphasizes the coming of steam to the Hudson Valley with sidewheelers plying the placid river and a wood-burning locomotive drawing a train of small passenger cars. *Fenimore House.*

bar in the old Potter Hollow Tavern in Cornwallville, a well-known landmark destroyed by fire in March 1957. This scene, painted about a hundred years later than the Van Bergen panel, illustrates with naive charm the coming of steamboat and railroad to the Hudson River area. An unusual feature is the signature of the otherwise unidentified artist, *W. W. Cornwell pin. . . .*

A comparison of the various stenciled plaster walls which are gradually emerging in central and upper New York indicates that itinerant decorators traveled westward in the wake of the pioneers during the first half of the nineteenth century. New England houses of this period exhibit many patterns similar (and some identical) to those now being discovered west of the Hudson River.

In the Bump Tavern, which originally stood in Ashland, Greene County, several rooms of stenciling were found under later wallpaper. The motifs are attributed on stylistic evidence to the itinerant artist "Stimp," a shadowy personality whose distinctive designs are identified with a group of houses in western Connecticut. Similar patterns in the Perry house in Dover Plains suggest that he may have crossed the New York border near that point, and, proceeding northwesterly, eventually arrived in Ashland. There he was probably lodged by the landlord in return for decorating the upper hall, chamber, and ballroom of the Bump Tavern.

The floor stenciling of the Lippitt parlor is typical of farmhouse floors in central New York between 1790 and

Stenciled walls in upper hall of the Bump Tavern (c. 1830), painted in dark green, red, and black on a white background. Discovered after the building was moved from Ashland to Cooperstown, the original stenciling had to be, for the most part, removed when the room was replastered; but the center section, customarily concealed behind a removable panel of wallboard, may be seen here as found. Border, frieze, and several wall patterns closely resemble designs attributed to an itinerant called "Stimp" in Janet Waring's *Early American Stencils on Walls and Furniture. Rollins photograph.*

Stenciled floor in the parlor of the Lippitt Farmhouse. Black motifs painted on a gray ground, copied from a design in a house in West Edmeston, twenty miles west of Cooperstown. Such decoration was typical of many floors of the first quarter of the 1800's. The chest is grain-painted in black on a yellow-tan background. The larger box is of pine embellished with a wreath of red, black, yellow, and white flowers on a dark blue-green background. Bride's boxes were repositories for feminine treasures and were frequently decorated by their owners. This example is cream-white, with panels outlined in green and red enclosing colorful birds, butterflies, and grapes, with the initials *M.A.B. Rollins photograph.*

1820. This small repeat pattern was taken from one in West Edmeston. That in the gentlemen's reading room of the Bump Tavern was copied from a floor in nearby Willowbrook, a house built in 1816 and now known as the Cooper Inn. This design (shown on the cover as well as in the illustration) is more formal than most painted examples and appears to simulate a woven ingrain carpet of the 1830-1840 period.

A group of decorated walls painted freehand, also in the collection, will soon be installed in the lower hall of the Bump Tavern. They were originally in the Carroll house, an early nineteenth-century turnpike tavern in East Springfield, about twelve miles north of Cooperstown, and the decoration was found under layers of later

Section of plaster wall from the Carroll house, East Springfield, New York. Painted freehand with a bold technique in strong dark colors; a type of decoration popular from 1825 to 1840. Two walls from the house are signed *William Price 1831*.

Romantic Scene with Lion. Fireboard, oil on canvas mounted on a wood frame. An interesting combination of the techniques of the ornamental painter in which a stenciled border frames a freehand landscape. So-called Oriental scenery was of great popular interest during the 1830's. *Fenimore House.*

Bear and Beeves. Fireboard painted on wood; height 33 inches. The humorous title derives from a note in Hedrick's *History of Agriculture in the State of New York* mentioning Timothy Bigelow's trip to Niagara Falls in 1805, during the course of which he heard that the settlers hung fresh meat in the trees to keep in hot weather. If the large red objects hanging from the branches are intended to represent meat, the bear is apparently climbing the wrong tree. Paintings believed to be by the same unknown artist have been found in houses in Grafton and Lisbon, New Hampshire. *Fenimore House.*

A country washstand found in Waterloo, New York. Painted gray and decorated freehand in silver. The striping is effectively painted in shades of gray and black. *Bump Tavern.*

Three painted side chairs. *Left,* a Hudson Valley chair painted black with swan splat and decoration of gold leaf with burnt umber and red detail. *Center,* a Rhode Island arrow-back chair with unusual top rail decorated with a tiger in a landscape, painted black with yellow and red striping. *Right,* a Pennsylvania chair painted gray with striping in green and brown. *Fenimore House.*

paper. The plaster of almost every interior wall was painted with scenery and semitropical landscapes which included naval battles, military figures, a parade of ladies and gentlemen, and Indians lurking behind trees. The signature of the artist, *William Price 1831,* appears twice, in the east upper chamber and in a closet. These walls have been divided between the Winterthur Museum and the New York State Historical Association.

Painting fireboards was also an important part of the repertoire of the traveling artist. Made of either wood or canvas, they were used to close fireplaces when these were not in use. Several interesting examples are in the collection, representing the romantic taste and the primitive techniques of the first half of the nineteenth century.

Decorated window shades, painted on thin cambric to render them "transparent," added gaiety and color to the nineteenth-century home. A pair exhibiting picturesque scenes is installed in the reading room of the Bump Tavern. Some such shades were manufactured and sold commercially, while others were made at home after directions in contemporary art-instruction books.

The Tavern and the Lippitt Farmhouse contain some interesting decorated furniture illustrating the types used in country homes during the first half of the nineteenth century. Pine chests were skillfully grained by local artisans to simulate more costly woods. Others enriched their surroundings with colorful, informal patterns applied by brush, cork, or feather. Many pieces were ladies' work, stenciled with patterns laid on bright backgrounds, or painted freehand with graceful vines and flowers. Sets of chairs, factory-decorated during the second quarter of the century, were an important item in the home. Several regional examples in Fenimore House exhibit stenciled and freehand decoration typical of their locality and period.

Photographs on this page by Rollins.

A corner of the gentlemen's reading room, Bump Tavern. The fireboard is from Jefferson, New York. Slots allow the andirons to rest outside on the hearth. The stenciled floor has a yellow ochre ground with red and green designs (a sample of the original from which it was copied is kept in the room for comparison). The painted window shade was used in the Knapp house, Morris, New York. Such shades were manufactured from 1830 to 1860.

Country furniture

BY FRANK O. SPINNEY

Note: This article presents in condensed form the main thesis offered in a talk on *Country Furniture of New England,* given at the Antiques Forum held at Williamsburg in January 1953.

IN THE VARIOUS ARTS at different periods of history one can trace two parallel streams of culture and taste. On the one hand there is the sophisticated taste of the social, economic, and governing leaders and the fashionable artists, musicians, jewelers, cabinetmakers, and other craftsmen who worked for them. Their activities are usually carried on in the centers of population, wealth, and power. These craftsmen set the pace and create the main stream of style. They are thoroughly immersed in it, understand it, contribute to it, and design and create within its spirit and principles.

A little below this apex of the social, economic, and fashion pyramid are other workers. They are aware of the main stream, but their grasp of its meaning is not so complete nor their skills so highly developed. Their customers are less critical and demanding and are unable to afford the most magnificent examples of the prevailing taste. And so on down the pyramid to the simplest, palest, least well-understood reflections.

Simultaneously there exists a second main stream, often just as vigorous but fundamentally different and independent of the sophisticated one. In music there are the folk songs, the ballads, the popular tunes. In art there is a popular culture quite separate from the concepts of the sophisticated artists. In dress one can trace the co-existence of a high-style current of fashion and a folk type of costume. In furniture too, perhaps, one may distinguish two divisions, the sophisticated and the popular or country type.

To think of country furniture as the cabinetmakers' equivalent of what has been called folk, popular, provincial, or primitive in the field of art may be a useful concept. The struggle often made to see the simple chairs, tables, chests, and other pieces turned out by the country craftsman as an effort on his part to ape the modes of Chippendale, Sheraton, or Hepplewhite may cause one to overlook the possibility that these pieces represent a very different set of ideas. Granted the existence of two parallel streams in the crafts of cabinetmaking as in music and art, certain confusions are thereby avoided and certain similarities do not have to be imagined. The work of the country craftsman can then be judged on its own merits, and not admired or rejected on the basis of how well or how poorly the artisan adapted or imitated a current style.

Throughout the rural parts of New England, the simple and the elegant in architecture and in furniture are found side by side. A good instance is the village of Charlton, in south central Massachusetts, where for fifty years, starting in 1799, Chapman Lee carried on a part-time craft of cabinetmaking. Like most other country craftsmen, he worked his fields in the spring, cut his hay in the summer, harvested his corn in the fall, traded off work with neighbors, patched roofs, replaced rotted sills, got out the frame for new barns, and did all kinds of farm and handy work when not occupied in his shop. In this period Lee recorded in the account book the making of several hundred pieces of furniture—chests, tables, beds, cradles, chairs, desks, stands, cupboards, and ultimately coffins—for over eighty families in Charlton.

In 1803, Lee made a settle for Daniel Bacon. He worked in his shop the better part of a day and by nightfall had finished the job. In his account under Bacon's

Simple pine chests with lift lids were made by all rural cabinetmakers, and were necessary equipment in country homes. Painted decoration, popular in the nineteenth century, added gayety and color to unpretentious pieces.

name he noted, "one settle 6/0 = $1.00." During the same year Lee supplied other Charlton families with various pieces they required in their households. Benjamin Stow bought a chest for $1.67 and a "chest and draw" at $3.00. Edward Cleaveland ordered a coffin for his child and paid 64 cents, while a bedstead cost him $1.75. Lieutenant Richard Blood was charged $1.50 for a "Candle Stan" and Aaron Woodbury purchased a writing desk for $1.83. Altogether during this year Chapman Lee pursued his furniture making and repairing trade to a total of $25.95, about 26 working days at the rate of $1.00 per day, his usual rate.

Contemporary with Lee in the village of Charlton was Major General Salem Town, a man of considerable wealth and position. The General built, as befitted his prestige, a rather elegant home incorporating as much of the fashionable architectural detail of the period as his purse and his builders' skills could provide. When it came to the matter of furnishing the house, and later when his son, General Salem Town, Jr., and his family became a part of the household and additional pieces were required, Chapman Lee was not approached. No account for the two generals appears in his book. Family tradition says that the furnishings were purchased in Boston and carted the fifty miles to the new mansion. Surviving pieces tend to corroborate this tradition.

It is difficult to estimate how many times this pattern of action was repeated, but one suspects it to have been a frequent one. A great gulf separated the Goddards, Saverys, Phyfes, and Frothinghams from the Chapman Lees.

If one takes the point of view that the rural craftsman was largely the country cousin of the skilled worker catering to sophisticated urban tastes, lacking knowledge

Pine chest with two "draws." The lid is hinged and the upper drawers are false. This chest is an eighteenth-century piece, but the red and black painted decoration was probably added many years after the chest was made.

of styles and rusty in technique but still striving to produce for his customers the nearest possible approach to the fashionable modes of the day, it is hard to see where the settle built by Chapman Lee for Daniel Bacon fits into the picture. Was this 1803 settle a country version of a sophisticated piece designed by Chippendale, or did it reflect the Sheraton influence, or possibly a Hepplewhite trend? What style term will adequately describe the common six-board chest, the slat-back chair, the simple table, the low bed, and other pieces that the country craftsman made in tremendous quantities, without a thought of following any London design? How vigorously can it be maintained that the reds, blues, and greens or the frankly non-realistic decorative painting adorning so much country furniture represent the rural craftsman's interpretation of the furnishings of the court or the "stately homes" of England?

There are suggestions, of course, in country furniture of the prevailing winds of fashion, just as primitive paintings and popular music show borrowings from the sophisticated stream of taste. This is natural. No fixed, immutable boundary exists between the two. Cross-pollenization takes place in either direction. Great composers have used themes from folk music and fashion designers have been inspired by country costumes. Like all divisions, there is a blurring at the edges, but from a distant view it is possible to see that Chapman Lee is not simply a poor copyist of Thomas Chippendale, but with his fellow craftsmen was creating a popularly accepted type of country furniture that deserves to be examined, collected, and admired on its own merits, as an expression of what may be considered an independent stream of taste and culture.

A form of the popular pine chest of the nineteenth century incorporating four small "draws" below the lift-lid compartment. Red paint, a favorite cheap country finish for chests, tables, beds, and other pieces, has been used here.

115

Chairs were made by most rural cabinetmakers in all periods and of many types. The slat-back, with or without arms and rockers, was one of the most common.

Settles were easy to make, useful, and persisted as a country style until stoves became common. The chair settle is not seen as often as the wider type.

Simple backless benches have for the most part been discarded, but undoubtedly were once widely made and used.

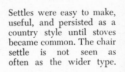

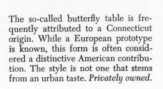

The so-called butterfly table is frequently attributed to a Connecticut origin. While a European prototype is known, this form is often considered a distinctive American contribution. The style is not one that stems from an urban taste. *Privately owned.*

Cupboards often appear in country cabinetmakers' accounts. Many were simple shelves with doors above and below. The open-shelved type, frequently called a Welsh dresser, was popular in rural homes. *Mission House, Stockbridge, Massachusetts.*

The comfortable interior of a rural inn contained sturdy country furniture that defies a period style classification. *Wayside Inn, Sudbury, Massachusetts.*

Sources of some
American regional furniture

BY JOHN T. KIRK, *Assistant curator, Garvan and Related Collections of American Art, Yale University Art Gallery*

IT IS WELL KNOWN among students of American furniture that American styles depended on European designs for their basic forms and decoration. How much originality is to be attributed to American makers is less clearly established. Some have felt that it was limited to a few motifs or forms of construction, while others have seen our early cabinetmakers as creators of many original designs. The matter of what areas of Europe were most influential on American work also remains in question. While attention has been paid in recent years to Ireland's influence upon the furniture designs of Philadelphia (ANTIQUES, March 1961, p. 276), a systematic search for just what parts of Europe influenced what parts of America, and a thoroughgoing attempt to determine just exactly what came to this country, are yet to be made.

In 1963-1964 it was possible for me to spend nine months in Europe studying this problem. It was obvious that only a preliminary study could be made. The first five and a half months were spent in London, working at the Victoria and Albert Museum and visiting local manor houses, antiques dealers, and other museums. Then two weeks were spent in the Low Countries and Denmark. The remaining three months were spent crisscrossing England visiting National Trust houses, private collections, museums, and antiques shops in all but two of the counties.

This is the first of two articles dealing with some of the discoveries that resulted. The present one is concerned chiefly with country furniture: certain types made in Connecticut and Pennsylvania, and also New York, and their design relationships to each other and to English prototypes. The second article, to appear in ANTIQUES for April, will deal mostly with high-style or city furniture.

CONNECTICUT VALLEY CARVED CHESTS

It has long been known that Connecticut and the Connecticut Valley produced several types of chest decorated either with two-plane, low-relief carving or with painted designs. The basic carved groups are the sunflower (or aster) chests, now believed to be by Peter Blin of Wethersfield, and the Hadley chests. The latter were divided into three subgroups by Clair F. Luther in his book, *The Hadley Chest* (1935): the Hadley type, the Hatfield type, and the Hartford type.

Figure 1 represents the sunflower type from Wethersfield. Note the central panel with the so-called sunflower flanked by tulips, some asymmetrical with long curved central petals, others with dogtooth central petals, all attached to a single central stem growing from a mound, or earth motif. The tulips are repeated with variations on the outer panels. Figure 2 represents the Hatfield type of Hadley chest. It has in the central panel a sunflower-type carving flanked by tulips, leaves, and scrolls. The outer panels have tulips both symmetrical and asymmetrical with dogtooth centers, all springing from an earth motif. The framing around the panels and drawers is carved with a continuous undulating vine with asymmetrical and dogtooth tulips. Figure 3 represents the Hadley type of Hadley chest, with the so-called basic Hadley pattern of scroll, tulip, and two forms of leaf: one with a smooth outline in the center panel, one with a notched edge in the outer panels, and both on the drawer, one above the other. All these forms, which appear in low relief, are incised with lines and curls. The same undulating vinelike motif is found on the Hatfield chest (Fig. 2) and on Figure 4, a related Connecticut chest, where the undulating carving is clearly defined as a tulip motif. Here the inner panel is also related to that of Figure 2, while the outer panels resemble those on chests of the sunflower type. This chest, then, forms a link between Wethersfield and Hatfield. A Connecticut Valley Bible box (Fig. 5) is carved with asymmetrical and dogtooth tulips and is in this way related to the group formed by Figures 1 to 4.

These distinctively Connecticut designs have puzzled students of American furniture. Are they purely local creations or are they adapted from a European, particularly an English, source?

Figure 6 is a small English cupboard which has in its central panel the basic motifs of the Hadley chest—the scroll, the tulip, and two forms of leaf with incised line carving, all springing from the same point. The panel is bordered on the frame by undulating vine carving, which combines features of grape and tulip carving popular in England, and is related to the vine carving on Figures 2 and 4. Figure 7 is another English piece with carving related to Figures 2, 4, and 6; note particularly the band of undulating tulip carving above the doors of the bottom section. Thus we begin to see a relationship between Hatfield-Wethersfield and England.

The carved central panel of the English wainscot chair in Figure 8 shows smooth-outline leaves and elongated tulips growing from an earth motif, and elongated tulips appear in the crest rail as well; also carved in the central panel is a conventionalized Tudor rose. These carvings

Fig. 1. Connecticut chest; 1670-1710. Oak, pine, and maple. Possibly made by Peter Blin (active c. 1675-1725) of Wethersfield, Connecticut: for attribution see article by Houghton Bulkeley, Connecticut Historical Society *Bulletin*, January 1958. Height 39⅝ inches. *Yale University Art Gallery; Mabel Brady Garvan Collection.*

Fig. 2. Connecticut Valley chest, probably Hatfield, Massachusetts; 1670-1710. Maple and pine (oak and sycamore secondary), initialed *M. D.* Height 45½ inches. No. 24 in *The Hadley Chest* by C. F. Luther. *Yale University Art Gallery; Garvan Collection.*

Fig. 3. Connecticut Valley chest, probably Hadley, Massachusetts; 1670-1710. Oak and pine. Height 34¾ inches. Luther, No. 65. *Yale University Art Gallery; gift of C. Sanford Bull.*

Fig. 4. Connecticut Valley chest; 1670-1710.
Oak and pine. Height 39½ inches.
Connecticut Historical Society.

Fig. 5. Connecticut Valley box; 1670-1710.
Oak and pine, initialed *S. L.*
Width 28⅝ inches.
Yale University Art Gallery;
Garvan Collection.

Fig. 6. English cupboard;
1640-1700. Oak.
Height 13 inches.
Victoria and Albert Museum.

are related both in design and in execution to the Connecticut carvings on Figures 1 to 4. Another English wainscot chair (Fig. 9) has asymmetrical and dogtooth tulips flanking the central conventionalized rose, again related to the American carving on Figures 1, 2, 4, and 5.

The "sunflower," then, is actually a Tudor rose, and this and the other motifs are basically of English origin. Moreover, these four English pieces are not isolated instances but are typical of a particular school of English provincial cabinetmakers and carvers. We must therefore recognize that the Wethersfield sunflower chests, the Hatfield-type chests, and the other related chests and boxes all draw directly upon a particular English background. The Hadley-type chests seem to form an offshoot from them, dependent upon but not so closely related to English models. Probably, then, the decorative designs were transmitted to America by men who had worked in England and who, when they came to the Connecticut Valley, selected and recombined motifs that they had used before.

It seems possible to identify the region of England from which the designer-craftsmen came to the Connecticut Valley by studying the origins of these English pieces. Figure 7 is from Turton Tower, Turton, Lancashire. Two related cupboards were found nearby in

Fig. 7. English cupboard; 1640-1700. Oak and pine. Top finials and upper edge scalloping new; upper case a separate unit from the lower. Height (without shortened feet), 62½ inches. *Turton Tower, Turton, Lancashire.*

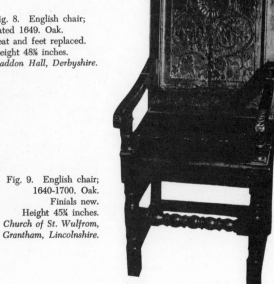

Fig. 8. English chair; dated 1649. Oak. Seat and feet replaced. Height 48⅞ inches. *Haddon Hall, Derbyshire.*

Fig. 9. English chair; 1640-1700. Oak. Finials new. Height 45¼ inches. *Church of St. Wulfrom, Grantham, Lincolnshire.*

Fig. 10. Connecticut chest; 1680-1710. Upper part of a chest over drawers.
Pine, oak, and poplar. Width 44⅝ inches.
Yale University Art Gallery; Garvan Collection.

Fig. 11. Connecticut chest of drawers; 1680-1710.
Oak, pine, and poplar. Height 43 inches. *Wadsworth Atheneum.*

Rufford Old Hall. Rufford Old Hall, with much of its furniture, was given to the nation by Lord Hesketh, in whose family it had descended. Some of the furniture bears the initials of his ancestors and the family emblem of a wheat sheaf; some of it also carries dates in the second half of the seventeenth century. The Tudor rose, looking like our sunflower, was also found on pieces which, according to tradition, have always been in Rufford Old Hall. Another related press cupboard was found in Astley Hall, near Chorley, only a few miles away. Figure 8 is from Haddon Hall, near Bakewell, Derbyshire, and has a history of having been among the early furnishings. Related carving appears in the frieze above the paneling in the long gallery of that house and shows the Tudor rose above thistles, symbolizing the union of England and Scotland under James I. The thistle reappears on the outer panels of the Connecticut chest of Figure 4. Figure 9 is from the church of St. Wulfrom, Grantham, Lincolnshire, and there are related chairs in Gainsborough Old Hall just to the north, and in Belvoir Castle just a few miles to the west. The concentration, then, seems to be in southern Lancashire, Derbyshire, and to a lesser extent Lincolnshire. It is probable that the originators of the Connecticut Valley style of carving came from that area.

But again we must ask whether the motifs originated there, or whether, as in Connecticut, the carvers of that region of England drew upon traditional designs common to other areas and only varied them because of local tastes. Much work will have to be done before we are certain. However, we know some sources which they could have used; for example, designs similar to the carved designs were sold as embroidery patterns and appeared also on Dutch tiles and on cut velvets imported from Italy.

CONNECTICUT PAINTED CHESTS

Having dealt with the source of the designs of the Connecticut Valley carved chests, can we trace the other famous type of Connecticut chest—that with painted decoration—to the same English source? Traditionally this painted type has been considered a product of Guilford, Connecticut. Some students now think that these chests were painted in Saybrook, but the facts are as yet not clear. It is, however, possible to discuss the European origin of the design even if we do not know the exact town in Connecticut in which it reappeared.

The distinctive features of these chests are seen in Figure 10, which shows the top part of what was once a chest over drawers, or blanket chest: typical are the central accent of flowers and, flanking it, freely undulating vines. In the center of the horizontal panel is a two-handled vase holding roses and vines flowing right and left from the center, terminating in leaves, tulips, and carnations. The corners of the panels are marked with fleurs-de-lis. Figure 11 shows another Connecticut piece, a chest of drawers with related decoration. The topmost long drawer has floral scrolls flowing right and left on either side of a central carnation, all springing from an earth motif. The second long drawer has a two-handled cup or vase holding a central carnation and flanking floral vines supporting birds. The bottom drawer has a central fleur-de-lis supporting a crown and birds, flanked by floral vines terminating in thistles supporting crowns.

One might have expected that if a European source

Fig. 12. English chair; 1600-1670 (related pieces were made into the eighteenth century). Oak, inlaid with holly, "bog oak," cherry, and stained woods. Height 48 inches. *Victoria and Albert Museum.*

for this decoration were found, it would also be in a painted form; this, however, is not the case. An English wainscot chair (Fig. 12) has floral inlay of colored woods of a type which is apparently the source. The lower panel shows, rising from an earth motif, a carnation in the center and floral vines at right and left supporting birds and filling the panel, which in this case is square. Similar inlay in the upper panel flows more horizontally because of the shape of the panel, which is like those in Figures 10 and 11. This type of English inlay is also found with the flowers rising from a vase instead of from an earth motif. The fleur-de-lis occurs in closely related but more elaborately inlaid pieces intended for the court.

Here, then, we find designs in inlaid colored woods transferred to Connecticut and there executed in paint so as to achieve a decorative pattern with less time and effort. There is evidence that this type of decoration reappeared in an inlaid form in Pennsylvania; one example is found on a dressing table top in the Philadelphia Museum of Art. It suggests a connection between Con-

Fig. 13. English chair; 1745-1760. Walnut and walnut veneer; front and side seat rails (under veneer) oak, rear seat rail beech, slip seat new, back feet restored according to related examples. Knee blocks are thin in depth with added blocking behind, not common in America. Height 37 inches. *Victoria and Albert Museum.*

Fig. 14. English chair from East Anglia (purchased in London); 1700-1750. Cherry. Back feet restored. For related American chairs see Wallace Nutting, *Furniture Treasury*, Nos. 1892, 1893, 1894, 1897, 1898, 1903, 1904, 1907. Height 46⅝ inches. *Yale University Art Gallery.*

Fig. 15. English chair; 1680-1710. Ash. Seat formerly rush. The front stretcher, feet, lower side, and rear stretchers are restored, as are the arms, but they are replaced according to evidence on the chair and local tradition, and are not the parts that affect our study. Height 43¼ inches. *Strangers' Hall, Norwich.*

necticut and Pennsylvania which we shall investigate further in a moment.

This form of English inlaid decoration is found in Norfolk, Suffolk, Derby, Lancashire, and the southern part of Yorkshire; the finest and most diversified group of examples is possibly that in the West Yorkshire Folk Museum in Halifax. It seems to have been popular from East Anglia through the southern part of the north country, over a slightly larger area than the source of the carved chests we have already considered. The rural English inlayers probably took their inspiration mainly from textile designs. Various textiles in the Victoria and Albert Museum have similar scrolling vines, on either side of central carnations, springing from earth motifs and supporting birds.

RELATED CHAIRS OF
PENNSYLVANIA, CONNECTICUT, AND NEW JERSEY

Ever since American furniture began to be collected it has been observed that Connecticut and Philadelphia furniture have characteristics in common. Research has revealed that various Connecticut cabinetmakers went to Philadelphia to be apprenticed or to receive additional training and later returned to Connecticut to practice.

Benjamin Burnham and Eliphalet Chapin are two famous Connecticut cabinetmakers of whom we have definite proof that this is true. Therefore it has been assumed that Connecticut's style of furniture was heavily conditioned by Philadelphia taste. This, however, turns out to be only partially true. For instance, the two chairs shown in Figures 13 and 14 were made in England, and each reveals both Connecticut and Philadelphia characteristics.

The Philadelphia features of Figure 13 are these: the pad feet rather than simple club feet—that is, there is a disk or ring around the edge of the foot; the flaring of the back feet as on many Philadelphia Queen Anne chairs; the veneering of the seat frame, back posts above the seat, splat, and crest rail; also the scrolling of the ears and of the front ends of the arms. The movement of the strapwork of the splat is characteristic of New England work in general and of Connecticut chairs made by Eliphalet Chapin in particular. The corner blocks, quarter round in section, vertical grain, made in two pieces fitting around the top of the leg, are found in both Philadelphia and Connecticut work. The flowing movement of the front legs is also common to both areas. This chair is stamped S:SHARP NORWICH. The will of

Fig. 16. English chair; 1680-1710.
Ash. A lady's or three-quarters chair.
Compare Nutting, Nos. 1799-1802.
Victoria and Albert Museum.

Fig. 17. English chair; 1700-1750.
Ash. Legs probably cut down.
No securing pins were used in the construction.
Finish original; no traces of paint.
Height 43¼ inches. *Haddon Hall.*

Samuel Sharp, filed April 27, 1760, and now in the Norwich public library, records his work as a chairmaker in that region.

The ladder-back chair (Fig. 14) is from the same part of England, perhaps a little farther north in the fen country. It is related to Philadelphia and vicinity in the shaping of the top edge of the back slats, though the dip in the bottom edge is not American. Also Pennsylvania-like are the turnings of the front stretcher and of the posts under the arms, and particularly characteristic of that area are the back posts, left plain without ring turnings or other decoration. Typical of Connecticut are again the turnings under the arms, and the front legs and feet. Close to Connecticut work are the finials, the arms, and the front stretcher. This chair is made of cherry. Cherry was popular in both Pennsylvania and Connecticut, so much so that Connecticut imported it from upper New York State. Related English chairs are found with the rear legs raking sharply backwards below the bottom stretcher, a practice found on Connecticut Queen Anne and Chippendale chairs. Thus we see again overlapping in Pennsylvania and Connecticut work.

Also from the Norwich area of England comes a chair (Fig. 15) which is a direct parallel to American late seventeenth-century work. The shape of the back slats, the flat arms, the turned secondary arms (again typical of Connecticut), the knob handholds, the turnings of the posts and the finials obviously are related to and represent the source of one of the great American ladder-back chairs, pictured in Wallace Nutting's *Furniture Treasury*, Number 1822, and now at the Winterthur Museum.

Figure 16, related to Figure 15, is a heavy seventeenth-century English chair resembling American work, here with spindles like those we find in American chairs, particularly in the famous Brewster chair. Figure 17 is interesting because it is an English banister-back chair. Elaborately turned and carved English banister-back chairs are published, but this simpler chair relates closely to ours, combining some Connecticut and some Pennsylvania features. The split balusters of the back are inserted with the rounded side forward. This practice is found on some Connecticut chairs but is unusual elsewhere. The large central ball in the front stretcher is found in some early Pennsylvania ladder-backs and on a Connecticut banister-back side chair.

It is therefore possible to assume that some of what Connecticut and Philadelphia have in common is that

Fig. 18. New York or New Jersey chair;
1680-1720. Walnut. Height 35¾ inches.
Yale University Art Gallery;
Garvan Collection.

Fig. 19. Chair from the Low Countries;
mid-seventeenth century.
"Nutwood." Height 40¼ inches.
Rijksmuseum, Amsterdam.

Fig. 20. Chair from the Low Countries;
mid-seventeenth century.
Rijksmuseum.

designer-craftsmen came from the same locality of England to these two regions of America. The differences
that arose between the American regions seem to be
due in part to the fact that Philadelphia was a large
style center with a sophisticated production that con-
tinually looked to Europe for modes and manners of
design, while Connecticut and the Connecticut Valley
were made up of small individual style centers developing an originality of interpretation which is known in all
countries in the rural, country, or peasant furniture.

To turn to another factor in the situation, Figure 18
shows an American chair that has been thought to be
of New Jersey origin since several examples have been
discovered in that area. They have in common more
elaborate ball turnings than are found on New England
examples, sausage-turned stretchers, and vase-and-ball-
turned finials. A related chair (Fig. 19) is in the Rijksmuseum in Amsterdam. Note its similarities to Figure
18, particularly the ball turning, the sausage turning, and
the small button top of the front legs. In the Plantin-
Moretus Museum in Antwerp a set of similar chairs was
found in which the top rail was similar to that of the
American chair. The finials of Figure 20 complete the
picture. This chair too is from the Rijksmuseum in Amsterdam and its finials are similar to those of Figure 18.
It also has spiral-turned stretchers. New York was one
of the few places where spiral turning appeared in America, and it may well be that the type exemplified by

Figure 18 was made in New York rather than New Jersey, though Dutch influence is also often seen in New
Jersey work. Chairs similar to Figures 19 and 20 appear
in Dutch seventeenth-century interior paintings.

Now, what is the relationship among the Low Countries, England, and America? Note in Figures 20 and
15 the use of ring-and-reel, or baluster, turnings on the
back posts rather than the simple ring turning common
in America. The influence of the Low Countries was
strong in East Anglia and the fen country because of a
long-existing interdependence resulting from the wool
trade. Then, as we have seen, that area of England influenced Connecticut and Pennsylvania. In other words,
the Low Countries influenced America indirectly, by way
of England, as well as directly, by way of New York,
and it is thus not surprising to find similarities in the
work of Connecticut, Philadelphia, New York, and related regions.

In the light of this study it is apparent that the American craftsmen did not attempt to depart entirely from
their traditions, nor did they cling to them slavishly.
What they did was to reinterpret them, simplifying and
reassorting as they responded to their new environment
and to new influences from other local and European
sources. Their genius lies in the way they used these
traditions. While they did not create something wholly
new, they drew upon their heritage to create something
distinctive, and to that extent original.

Slat-Back Chairs of New England and the Middle-Atlantic States

A Consideration of Their Derivation and Development

Part I

By Wilson Lynes

Note. In so far as ANTIQUES is aware, the following article represents the first attempt to present a careful analysis of a type of early chair so frequently encountered and including specimens of such wide diversity in design and in quality as seemingly to defy classification either chronological or geographical. Both author and editor view Mr. Lynes' contribution as exploratory rather than definitive. But now that the field has thus been courageously invaded, other students, it is hoped, will be inspired to volunteer their aid in bringing it to a state of complete cultivation. — *The Editor.*

SLAT-BACK chairs were made in Europe as early as the fifteenth century, or earlier. Judging from the fragmentary evidence available, the common primitive form was distinguished by heavy, hewn, rectangular posts, and flat, rived slats. With increasing employment of the turning lathe, hewn-post slat backs were gradually superseded by those with turned posts; but the former were not entirely obsolete until as late as the nineteenth century. Indeed they still occur in European peasant work.

Seventeenth-Century Slat Backs of New England

Slat backs handed down from the pioneer days of New England exhibit features common to both hewn and turned European prototypes. Doctor Irving P. Lyon has called attention to the existence of seventeenth-century New England slat backs of the hewn-post class (*Fig. 1*). The chairs discovered by Doctor Lyon seem to indicate that the type is characterized by heavy, hewn, rectangular posts and two or three flat, rived slats (ANTIQUES, October 1931, pp. 210–216).

Surviving slat backs, with turned posts of the same period, familiarly known as "Pilgrim slat backs," are distinguished by heavy posts and two or three rived and slightly bent slats, straight-edged at top and bottom except for a concave quarter circle in each upper corner. The stylistic kinship between the Pilgrim slat backs and the contemporary spindled chairs (so-called Brewster and Carver types) is apparent. For example, the only essential difference between the Pilgrim slat back of Figure 2 and the Carver

Fig. 1 — NEW ENGLAND (*seventeenth century*). Rectangular-post type.
From the collection of Dr. Irving P. Lyon

Fig. 3 — NEW ENGLAND (*seventeenth century*)
Carver type. Contemporary with the Pilgrim slat back of Figure 2. Similar turnings of the posts.
From the Wadsworth Atheneum

Fig. 2 — NEW ENGLAND (*seventeenth century*). Pilgrim slat-back type.
From the Metropolitan Museum of Art

were less massive than their predecessors, and were taller. This change in proportion was, perhaps, in deference to the slender, high-backed Carolean chairs that became popular in England and America after the restoration of Charles II to the English throne. The ratio of turned to hewn-post slat backs was doubtless greater in the eighteenth than in the seventeenth century. With the colonies better established and more

chair of Figure 3 lies in the treatment of the back, which in the former is slatted, and in the latter, spindled.

One may surmise, from a general knowledge of economic and social conditions in the early New England colonies and from inventories of the period, that well-turned chairs, such as those of Figures 2 and 3, were scarce and were greatly outnumbered by more readily contrived articles such as stools and hewn chairs. I have seen no authenticated examples of seventeenth-century American slat backs, other than those of New England origin. Doubtless such chairs were made south of this section before 1700. A type so well known in Europe must almost inevitably have been reproduced by immigrants to the Middle-Atlantic and Southern colonies, as well as by their neighbors to the northward.

"Northern" Slat Backs of the Eighteenth Century

Both the hewn and turned-post chairs continued to be made during the eighteenth century; but, in general, they

Fig. 4 — PROBABLY CANADIAN (*eighteenth century*)
Rectangular-post type. The rockers appear to be later additions. The arms, almost seventeenth-century French in feeling, are unexpectedly fine in contour, considering the roughness of the piece. Slats essentially Gallic. All horizontal members completely pierce verticals.
From the collection of D. P. Powers

Fig. 5 (left) — "NORTHERN" (*eighteenth century*)
Characteristic of the more elaborate slat backs of the period.
From the Wadsworth Atheneum

Fig. 6 (right) — "NORTHERN" (*eighteenth century*)
A simplification of the contemporary type of Figure 5.
From the collection of J. H. Dilts

Fig. 7 (left) — "NORTHERN" (*eighteenth century*)
Shows localized elaboration, probably northern New Jersey.
Courtesy of American Art Association Anderson Galleries, Kauffman collection

Fig. 8 (right) — "NORTHERN" (*eighteenth or nineteenth century*)
A rudimentary type. Much used.
From the collection of S. Hansen

prosperous, there was decreased necessity for using rough furniture. A hewn, rectangular-post arm chair, apparently of the eighteenth century, is shown in Figure 5 of Doctor Lyon's previously cited article. Another is pictured in Figure 4 of the present group of illustrations.

The normal eighteenth-century turned slat back differed from seventeenth-century prototypes not only in its proportions but in the design of its turnings, and in the shape and number of its slats. Figure 5 exhibits the usual characteristics of the more elaborate examples. These are: four or five thin, bent slats, with straight lower edge, but cut in a sweeping curve at the top; posts deeply ring-turned, with bold spherical or spheroidal finials; and an abrupt and well-defined separation between post and finial, and front leg and foot. Similar chairs were made in New York and northern New Jersey. In view of this extra-territorial occurrence of the so-called New England type in the eighteenth century, I shall henceforth refer to such chairs as "Northern."

Comparison between the eighteenth-century chair of Figure 5 and a turned chair of analogous quality and elaboration representative of the preceding century (*Fig. 2*) immediately reveals radical differences. Besides the differences already specifically cited, the finial and post turnings of the earlier chair are more complex in design than those exemplifying the later era. Its front posts are unturned below seat level. Its front stretchers are virtually devoid of decorative importance. This stylistic break between turned slat backs of the seventeenth and eighteenth centuries was not accomplished without some transitional confusion. Many slat backs made about 1700 betray mingled influences, some features of their design following the early style of Figure 2, others imitating, or approximating, eighteenth-century practice. Turned eighteenth-century slat backs often lack the elaboration of that of Figure 5. A comparatively simple example is shown in Figure 6. In the latter, simplification consists in the omission of turnings on the rear posts between slats, on front posts below the seat, and on stretchers. The well-turned chair of Figure 7 shows localized elaboration on the foremembers, the rear posts being comparatively simple.

The utmost in simplification is achieved in the skeletal chair of Figure 8. This rudimentary specimen is reminiscent of the rectangular-post type in its economy of design. It fulfilled, as did the

other, the need for a cheap, sturdy, and easily constructed article.

This almost elementary form, and similar forms adorned only with simple finials, were used in large quantities during the eighteenth and nineteenth centuries. Their province was the homes of the poorer classes; kitchens and servant's quarters, and porches of the more affluent. Comparison with the splendidly designed and sophisticated chair of Figure 27 (to be illustrated in Part II), for example, emphasizes the fact that slat-back chairs, as such, were used by poor and prosperous alike, and may not be universally classified as a strictly "cottage type" of furniture.

Turned Northern slat backs of the eighteenth century show numerous individualities in design. Finial and stretcher turnings are almost endless in variety. Posts are usually ring-turned as in Figure 5, or plain. Slats are commonly straight on the lower edge, and cut in a dynamic curve along the top, as shown in the diagram of Figure 9. Other types are likewise shown in the same diagram.

The salamander slat was popular with French provincial chairmakers, but appears to have been rarely, if ever, used by the English, Dutch, Germans, or Swedes. It seems fair to assume, therefore, that chairs with salamander slats found in this country were made by persons of French extraction, or, more probably, are importations. For example, the salamander-back chair with square posts of Figure 4 was found some twenty years ago in a district strong in French influence on a farm just this side of the Canadian border.

The elaborate type of salamander-back chair of Figure 10, although often credited with New England or Canadian manufacture, is so distinctively French in design that it seems more logical to believe its origin to be French rather than North American. Besides the shape of the slats, this type of chair has additional French flavor in its redundancy of turning and its recessed arms. Recessed arms were much used on French slat-back armchairs. A French provincial armchair with arms almost identical to those of Figure 10 is shown in ANTIQUES for October 1930 (*Fig. 9, p. 315*).

"Central" Slat Backs of the Eighteenth Century

The eighteenth-century slat backs of Pennsylvania, southern New Jersey, Maryland, and Delaware are distinct in design from the contemporary Northern product, and are known as the

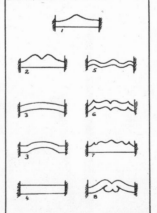

Fig. 9 — SOME EIGHTEENTH-CENTURY TYPES OF "NORTHERN" SLATS
1, Curved; *2*, notched; *3*, arched; *4*, horizontal; *5*, serpentine; *6*, cusped; *7*, crested; *8*, salamander (French)

"Pennsylvania" type. There seems to be no valid reason for this appellation, as the chairs are not exclusively indigenous to the Quaker State. I shall refer to them as the "Central" type.

The more elaborate members of the tribe of Central slat backs (*Fig. 11*) are signalized by the following features: Rear posts are without turnings other than small, simple finials. Slats, four to six in number, are ogival at top and bottom. Front posts are vase-turned between stretcher and seat. Feet and front stretcher are boldly turned, the former in a vase, ball, or ring design, and the latter in ball and ring or vase and ring. Simplifications of the above consist in partial or complete omission of post and stretcher turnings.

The Central group of slat backs appears to show less diversity in the design of turnings than does the Northern. Central slat backs occur — rarely, to be sure — with slats cusped in various patterns. An example is shown in Figure 12. Sometimes the slats of the Central chairs are straight along the lower edge, as are the slats of the chair illustrated in Figure 24 (see Part II).

As previously indicated, the sphere of influence of the Northern slat backs extended well into northern New Jersey, and that of the Central into southern New Jersey. Chairs made in the intermediate territory of central New Jersey, and an adjoining section of eastern Pennsylvania,

Fig. 10 (left) — ORIGIN UNCERTAIN
French style of *c.* 1700. *From the collection of R. H. Maynard*

Fig. 11 (right) — "CENTRAL" (*eighteenth century*)
Exemplifying the more elaborate "Central" slat backs of the period. *Courtesy of American Art Association Anderson Galleries, Kauffman collection*

may betray the influence of both the Northern and Central types. The chair of Figure 13, which is said to be of central New Jersey origin, has the ogival slats and turned front stretcher of the Central chairs, associated with the ring-turned posts and form of foot more characteristically Northern.

There is good reason to believe that the slat back of Figure 14 represents a style local to central New Jersey. It lacks the mingling of influences apparent in the former example, and is not unlike certain slat backs found in New England.

The interesting chair of Figure 15 was obtained recently at Sellersville, Pennsylvania (eastern Pennsylvania, just west of central New Jersey). Whether or not it was made in or near Sellersville is beyond telling. Nevertheless, the piece shows the mingling of styles logically to be expected in the section where it was found. The plain rear posts, with small, simple, finials, the vase-shaped foot turnings, and the six slats are in the manner of the Central slat backs; whereas the ring-turned front posts and the shape of slats are in accord with Northern design.

(The second, and concluding, part of Mr. Lynes' article, which comprises a discussion of slat-back chairs of the Southern colonies and states, nineteenth-century types, variants, European prototypes, materials, and methods of construction, will appear in an early issue.—*Ed.*)

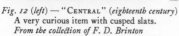

Fig. 12 (left) — "CENTRAL" (*eighteenth century*)
A very curious item with cusped slats.
From the collection of F. D. Brinton

Fig. 13 (right) — SAID TO BE CENTRAL NEW JERSEY
(*early nineteenth century*)
Shows influence of both "Northern" and "Central" types.
From the collection of J. S. Stokes

Fig. 14 (left) — PROBABLY CENTRAL NEW JERSEY (*eighteenth century*)
A well-designed local type, suggesting certain New England chairs.
From the collection of J. H. Dilts

Fig. 15 (right) — PROBABLY CENTRAL NEW JERSEY OR EASTERN PENNSYLVANIA (*eighteenth century*)
A mingling of "Northern" and "Central" elements.
From the collection of F. D. Brinton

Slat-Back Chairs of New England and the Middle-Atlantic States

A Consideration of Their Derivation and Development

Part II

By WILSON LYNES

IT SEEMS doubtful that hewn-post slat backs were made in this country during the nineteenth century, except in isolated communities. In both the New England and Middle-Atlantic states, turned slat backs generally followed the designs of the preceding century. According to the Editor of ANTIQUES, a few minor stylistic differences, usually of a decadent nature, distinguish the majority of nineteenth-century slat backs from their eighteenth-century prototypes. In most eighteenth-century chairs, the turnings are bolder than in those of the nineteenth. The separations between post and finial and post and foot are more abrupt and deeper, and are often marked by a crisp collar. The curves of the slats show a finer sweep. A deeply turned eighteenth-century post is shown at the left of Figure 16. At the right, for comparison, is a post of the mid-nineteenth century, with shallow turnings and indefinite separation of elements. A form of shallow turning sometimes found on nineteenth-century slat backs consists of a series of parallel grooves (*Figs. 17 and 23*).

The shallow, lifeless turnings on the fore-members of the Central slat back of Figure 18 suggest nineteenth-century origin. Somewhat similar chairs, known to be of Victorian vintage, are illustrated in *The Ware Chairs of South Jersey* by Mabel C. Powers (ANTIQUES for May 1926). These late, superficial turnings permitted economy in time and material, and were, perhaps, foreshadowings of the dawning machine age, with its sacrifice of quality to speed and low cost.

Shallow, nineteenth-century turning is again well illustrated in the late northeastern New Jersey chairs of Figures 19 and 20, a type that I have had opportunity to study. In addition to the decadent quality of the turning on these chairs, the notched slats are soggy in curvature. This may be readily appreciated upon comparison with the deeply notched slats of an earlier type of chair found in the same locality (*Fig. 21*).

I have located thirty-four chairs identical with that of Figure 19 within a radius of ten miles of Ridgewood, New Jersey, and none elsewhere. Thirteen are die-stamped CAD on the top of the front posts. Five of these thirteen were, until recently, in the possession of Miss C. E. Hopper. Miss Hopper says that her father, Garret J. Hopper, of Ridgewood, had eight of these chairs, and a child's chair for her (*Fig. 20*), made to his order in 1867.

Three chairs similar to that of Figure 19, and die-stamped HZ, have been located (*Fig. 22a*). They differ essentially from the other only in the

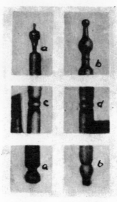

Fig. 16 — COMPARISON OF EIGHTEENTH- AND NINETEENTH-CENTURY POST TURNINGS
a, from an eighteenth-century chair; *b*, from a nineteenth-century chair. Note the following: *a*, abrupt and deep; *b*, gradual and shallow; *c*, deep; *d*, shallow

Fig. 17 (left) — NORTHEASTERN NEW JERSEY (*probably c. 1835*)
According to seemingly reliable information from a descendant, originally belonged to John C. Van Riper (*1834–1910?*), of Lodi, New Jersey. The shallow, grooved turnings on the back posts, and the fairly gradual and shallow post-finial transitions are suggestive of nineteenth-century design.
From the collection of John Eitzenboffer
Fig. 18 (right) — "CENTRAL" (*probably nineteenth century*)
The shallow turnings suggest nineteenth-century manufacture.
Courtesy of American Art Association Anderson Galleries, Kauffman collection

shape of the central components of the finials, which in the latter are urn-shaped, and in the former, spheroidal. The owner of two of them, Mrs. A. T. Zabriskie, states that her husband's grandfather, Henry Zabriskie, of Hawthorne, New Jersey, made the chairs in 1852, as a wedding present for his daughter.

Attempts to determine the identity of CAD have been unsuccessful. The search has resulted, however, in the discovery of an interesting account of two local chairmakers of the period. This appears in the *Genealogical and Memorial History of the State of New Jersey*, by F. B. Lee. In part, it is as follows: Abraham John Demarest (*1812–1897*) was first a carpenter's apprentice. After marriage, he entered the employ of his father-in-law, Cornelius Cooper, engaged in the manufacture of chairs at Kenternernick, New Jersey, later New Milford. After two or three years he purchased a farm at River Edge, then known as Old Bridge. "Here he erected a small factory for the manufacture of chairs, employing four to six workmen, and much of his stock he let out to be made up by workmen in their homes. He manufactured the old straight back chair with rush bottoms [slat backs], then in great demand. He found a ready market in New York for his product, driving there twice each week, selling to the different furniture firms. Much of his stock was shipped to southern markets. He followed chair-making up to within a few years of his death."

The foregoing remarks on the superficiality of nineteenth-century turnings should not be interpreted as suggesting that the tendency toward shallow turning became immediately prevalent in the year 1800. The classification of slat backs into those of the eighteenth and nineteenth centuries is admittedly arbitrary. Slat backs of true eighteenth century design were probably made long after nineteenth-century influences had begun to make themselves felt. There is some evidence to indicate that the first few decades of the period witnessed a considerable output of slat backs stylistically indistinguishable from those of the preceding century. In the illustrations of this article, therefore, it is assumed that chairs listed as eighteenth may have been made in the early part of the following century.

Essentially a rural product, the slat back seems to have largely escaped the extreme decadence of Victorian commercialism. That the evasion was not complete is demonstrated by the meretricious factory product of Figure 23. Nail and glue construction is used in this chair. The slats are thick, machine-scrolled, and flat. Proportion

Fig. 19 — NORTHEAST-
ERN NEW JERSEY
(1867)
A good chair, con-
sidering its late
date. Departure
from usual eight-
eenth-century de-
sign may be ob-
served in the gradual
transitions from
post to finial and
post to foot, shal-
low ring turnings,
and shallow notch-
ing of slats. Early
methods of con-
struction have been
retained.
*From the author's
collection*

and turnings are
likewise decadent.

Fig. 20 — NORTHEASTERN NEW
JERSEY *(1867)* Child's chair from same set as
Figure 19. *From the collection of
Raymond Hopper*

Fig. 21 — PROBABLY
NORTHEASTERN
NEW JERSEY
(eighteenth century)
From an old Bergen
County family. The
finely contoured
slats, sharp post-
finial and post-foot
transitions, and
deep ring turnings
are in the eight-
eenth-century man-
ner. Compare with
Figure 19, which is
a later chair found
in the same locality.
The differences are
easily seen.
*From the collection
of Mrs. F. A. Storm*

New Jersey chairs of
Figures 19 and 20.

Slat Backs of the Southern Colonies and States

Reference has been avoided to the slat backs made in the South, as
my knowledge of the subject is slight. The many varieties, distinct
from the northern slat backs, offer an interesting and neglected study.
It is hoped that this article will stimulate a survey of the field. It is also
hoped that some of the deficiencies in my discussion of the New England and Middle-Atlantic types will be supplied by those possessing the
information, and that, in this way, many hitherto overlooked facts will
be brought to the attention of collectors.

Persistence of Type in Slat Backs

Attempts closely to date slat-back chairs on the basis of design are
liable to error. Makers of rural types of furniture, such as the slat back,
were, for the most part, removed from the stimulus of close contact with
changing European fashions, and came, in addi-
tion, largely from the racially conservative
stocks of England, Germany, and Holland. It
would not surprise me, therefore, to learn that
some of the "Pilgrim" slat backs were made
during the early part of the 1700's. There is no
question that types probably popular in the first
half of the eighteenth century were
being made essentially unchanged
at its close.

For example, Maskell Ware
(1776-1855) of Roadstown, New
Jersey, made slat backs almost
identical to the finely turned and
proportioned chair of Figure 11
(see ANTIQUES for December 1933).
The type of turning employed by
Ware was in use on Central slat
backs probably before the middle of
the eighteenth century; yet, being
born in the first year of the Revolution, he could not have begun his
chairmaking activities much before
the year 1800. For a description of
the work of Maskell Ware and his
descendants, see *The Ware Chairs of
South Jersey (loc. cit.).* The chair of
Figure 24, which is said to have been
made between 1780 and 1800, also
illustrates perseverance of type.

The persistence of early eighteenth-century design in slightly
altered form into the mid-nineteenth-
century has already been discussed
in connection with the northeastern

Fig. 22 — NINETEENTH-CENTURY SLAT BACKS
Die-stamped on top of front posts with initials of makers. *A,* Northeastern New Jersey; *1852.* HZ — Henry Zabriskie. *B,* Probably northeastern New Jersey. Maker unknown. Note use of seventeenth-century
form of slat. *"A" owned by Mrs. A. T. Zabriskie; "B," by J. Eitzenboffer*

Material and Construction

The standard material for eighteenth- and nineteenth-century slat
backs is maple for posts, and hickory for slats and stretchers. In the
seventeenth century, this practice had not become established, ash and
oak often being used as well. Seventeenth-century chairs are usually of
ash, oak, maple, or hickory, or combinations of these woods.

The usual practice in assembling a slat-back chair was to use posts of
green wood, with well-seasoned stretchers and slats. Subsequent shrink-
age of the unseasoned vertical members held the horizontal ones firmly
in place. In the nineteenth century, this method of differential seasoning
was frequently abandoned for the glue pot, to the detriment of quality.

The top slat, receiving as it did the major thrust of the occupant's
back, was almost always secured by dowels or brads. Sometimes the two
upper slats were thus reënforced; rarely, all the slats were. In the
nineteenth century, brads were used more than
hitherto in place of dowels. These brads were
usually machine-made rather than handmade.
Machine-made brads in the rear post-slat or
front post-arm junctions are reliable indications
of nineteenth-century workmanship.

Slat-back armchairs show several variations
in arm construction. In the seventeenth century, arm rails were likely
to be tenoned into the front posts
(Fig. 1), rather than front posts
tenoned into arm rails *(Fig. 6).* In
the eighteenth and nineteenth centuries, the reverse was probably
true. An occasional practice was to
recess the arm rails and join them to
the upper side stretchers by means
of vertical or diagonal spindles, as in
Figure 10. This device may have
been a concession to the ample skirts
of prevailing fashion. The use of an
intermediate spindle between arm
and seat rails, as in Figure 25, was
an occasional device in the eighteenth and nineteenth centuries.

Seats were formed by weaving
twisted rush or strips of inner bark
(splints) over the seat rails. Rarely
was a slip seat used, as in Figure 26.
The seats of many early European
slat backs were made of wooden
boards, and it is entirely possible
that some of the early colonial
examples were thus equipped.

The underbody of a slat back is

always braced by stretchers, the number used for this purpose varying considerably. On the Northern chairs it was common practice to use one stretcher in the rear and two in each of the other sides, as in Figure 5. I know of one maker cautious to the extent of using three on each side — twelve in all. At the other extreme, the chair of Figure 28 carries only one stretcher to a side. The usual distribution in the Central chairs is one stretcher in both front and rear, and two on each of the sides, as in Figure 11. F. D. Brinton tells me that an exception to this rule is found in western Maryland, where two stretchers are ordinarily used in front, the upper being turned and the lower plain. Ornamental turning is usually confined to the front stretchers. The chairs of Figures 10 and 25, showing decorative stretchers on all sides, are exceptions. (Figure 10 is probably of French workmanship.)

Fig. 23 — "Northern" (nineteenth century)
A late, degenerate type.
From the collection of John Eitzenhoffer

Fig. 24 — "Central" (said to be c. 1780–1800)
According to a direct descendant, this chair originally belonged to Mrs. J. Thatcher of Lambertville, New Jersey. She is said to have acquired it between 1780 and 1800. The early type of turnings on a seemingly late eighteenth-century chair is a warning to daters.
From the collection of J. H. Dilts

Fig. 25 — "Northern" (eighteenth century)
Intermediate spindle at arm. Stretchers all turned.
Courtesy of American Art Association Anderson Galleries, Kauffman collection

items made about the year 1700. Its employment on the posts of a slat-back chair, however, is rare. This chair is also exceptional in its combination of slats. The upper two are of seventeenth-century form; the lower two, of eighteenth.

A slat-back variant in cherrywood, which partakes of the forms common to the so-called Chippendale ladderback chair, is illustrated in Figure 32. It is taller and narrower than the Chippendale variety, its proportions being more nearly those of the contemporary slat-back type. The slats lack the piercing of the Chippendale design, and the slip seat is rushed rather than upholstered. The chair is similar to the Chippendale ladder-back in the shape of the posts, the top, and the seat rails, and in the outline of the slats. It is essentially rural and perhaps the supreme effort of a maker of slat backs.

Quality

Among the indications of good quality are: sturdy construction, pleasing proportions, bold and well-designed turnings, dynamically curved slats, and crisp post-finial and post-foot separations.

Variants

Slat backs show interesting variants. In Figure 27, for example, Queen Anne influence is obvious. The combination of a Queen Anne underbody with slatted back is rare in this country, but common in eighteenth-century English examples. Unusual features of Figure 28 are: abruptly slanting arm rails, individualistic post turnings, and the use of only four stretchers.

The chair of Figure 30 shows influence of the spindled chairs. I have seen four other slat backs with vertical spindling within the past few months. In two of them, this decoration is placed between arm rails and seat; in the third, between arm rails and seat, and between slats; and in the fourth, the distribution is the same as in Figure 30. Evidently, spindled slat backs are not excessively rare. It would, perhaps, be more correct, therefore, to treat them as representations of a distinct type rather than as variants.

The combination of turning and blocking shown on the posts of the footless chair of Figure 31 was much used on tables, chairs, and other

European Prototypes

Seventeenth- and eighteenth-century New England was overwhelmingly English in descent. It seems fairly safe to assume, therefore, that slat backs made there were copied or adapted from English models.

The assumption of English derivation for similar types made in New York and northern New Jersey is not so readily justified. The Hudson River region of New York and the Hackensack River section of northern New Jersey were largely settled by Dutch colonists. Slat backs made in these sections may either have derived from similar chairs made in the Netherlands, or have been copied from New England examples.

The resemblance of certain slat backs made in the Netherlands to the usual Northern type of the eighteenth century is well illustrated in *The Turner* (Fig. 33), an etching by Jan Joris Van Vliet (1610–1635?). This print is one of a series of twenty-two, depicting the arts and crafts. Three are dated 1635; the others, including the one illustrated, are undated, but were doubtless produced in or about the same year. Here is testimony to the early development of this type of slat back on the Continent.

The region of manufacture of the Central type of slat back contained a more heterogeneous population than New England. In Pennsylvania, the important racial elements were German, English, Scotch, and Irish; in southern New Jersey, English, Dutch, and Swedish; in Maryland, English.

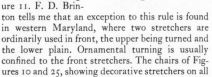

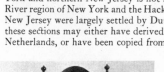

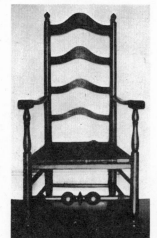

Fig. 26 — "Central" (eighteenth century)
Unusual in having slip seat.
From the collection of George Batten

Fig. 27 — "Central" (eighteenth century)
Shows Queen Anne influence in the underbody.
From the collection of J. S. Stokes

Fig. 28 — "Northern" (*eighteenth century*)
Unusual in type of post turning, abruptly slanting arm rails, and use of only one stretcher on a side.
From the collection of J. S. Stokes

Fig. 29 (left) — Northeastern New Jersey (*probably nineteenth century*)
Descended in the Demarest family of Bergen County. Said to have been originally owned by Mrs. Lena C. Demarest (*1763–1853*). An interesting slat-back variant. The low back, raked rear posts, and unusual slats possibly reflect the influence of the early fancy chairs. The post turnings were perhaps inspired by the bamboo Windsors. The front stretcher and foot turnings are of nineteenth-century design.
From the collection of Dr. L. M. Demarest

Fig. 31 — "Northern" (*eighteenth century*)
Shows rare use of blocking on posts.
From the Metropolitan Museum of Art

Fig. 30 (right) — "Northern" (*late seventeenth or early eighteenth century*)
Elaborated by means of vertical spindles.
From the Wadsworth Atheneum

A careful search of the limited pictorial and written sources at my command and correspondence with foreign museums and collectors have resulted in the location of but a few European specimens at all resembling the American Central chairs. These examples are from England. One, shown in Figure 34, has been drawn from a photo-engraving (Plate XLIV) in *Old English Furniture*, by F. Fenn and B. Wylie (G. Newnes, Ltd., London). The author's description is as follows: "Beechwood — probably Stuart Period. This form seems to have been usual for many years, only varying in the legs, which gradually became plainer and plainer. The club feet and turned front rail gradually disappearing." The points of similarity between this chair and the Central type of Figure 11 are: plain rear posts, ogival slats,

vase-turned front posts, and boldly turned front stretcher.

On page 60 of *Old West Surrey*, by G. Jekyll (Longmans, Green & Co., London), a simple slat-back armchair is illustrated, which, again, has ogival slats and plain rear posts. The front posts and arm rails are similar to those of Figure 6. Beside it is shown another armchair, closely resembling that of Figure 6, except for omission of the finials. G. Jekyll says of this pair of chairs: "Two of the most usual patterns of arm-chairs in use [West Surrey] within the last two hundred years are shown side by side."

As stated in Part I of this article, the present study is exploratory rather than definitive. It is hoped that other students will offer material that may serve to clarify the subject.

Fig. 33 (above) — "The Turner." Dutch School
Etching by Jan Joris Van Vliet (*1610–1635?*).
From "L'Œuvre des Élèves de Rembrandt," Vol. II, Rovinski, St. Petersburg

Fig. 32 (left) — "Northern" (*eighteenth century*)
Imitative of Chippendale ladder-back design.
From the collection of Henry W. Erving

Fig. 34 (right) — English Slat Back
Shows some similarity to "Central" chair of Figure 11 (see Antiques for December 1933)

WINDSOR CHAIRS AT WILLIAMS COLLEGE

By KARL E. WESTON

IN THE COLLECTION of early American furniture bequeathed to the Lawrence Art Museum by Charles Milton Davenport there are fifty-one windsor chairs and settees. These comprise nearly one third of the entire collection of which every piece is of exceptional interest and merit, while some are rare specimens of their kind. A few outstanding pieces were shown in ANTIQUES for February 1944 (p. 73). The superior quality of the collection itself and the many discriminating descriptions of the individual pieces in his letters and, in some cases, in attached labels, give evidence of Mr. Davenport's knowledge and connoisseurship. His interest in furniture with historic associations is seen in several pieces, among them the Wirt writing chair *(Fig. 11)*. The windsor chairs include almost every variety of the low-back, fan-back, and bow-back types of arm and side chair, with and without combs and back braces, and with five, six, seven, eight, or nine spindles. There are also two remarkably fine double seats and three settees with arrow-shaped, bamboo, or whittled spindles.

Many of the chairs are shaped to conform to the body and are extremely comfortable, which seems to refute the recent assertion of Mr. Robsjohn-Gibbings, in his joyous obituary of Mr. Chippendale, that "chairs are now being designed to fit the body, *an idea really never attempted before*" (italics mine). Moreover, most of the old windsor chairs seen today have had the paint removed and exhibit the beautiful tone and grain of the natural hickory, maple, ash, and pine, "the color and grain of which are left in their natural state," as that writer recommends for his brave new furniture, and "keep their clear colors indefinitely." Again as in modern furniture, "the surfaces [are] plain with none of the elaborately carved leaves, masks, and rocaille gathering the dust into every crevice, and requiring constant waxing and polishing to take away some of the dead ponderousness that keeps settling over it."

Yes, indeed, we are "glad to be living in the twentieth century — rather proud, in fact, to be a part of it," and, sitting comfortably in a windsor armchair, to watch with open mind and lively interest the modernistic parade.

FIG. 1 *(above)*—BRACED LOW-BACK SIDE CHAIR *(1725-1750)*. The eight whittled spindles with slight swellings, the continuing curve of the bow as it joins the seat, as well as the entire underbody, are characteristic of the very early windsor type of which this is an outstanding example. The saddle seat is chamfered to a marked degree at each side.

FIG. 2 *(right)*—BOW-BACK ARMCHAIR WITH KNUCKLE ARMS *(c. 1760)*. The bow back is particularly high and the saddle seat is of striking conformation. It has the almost unique feature of coil springs applied to the front legs, suggesting a precursor of the rocking chair. Painted a rich red, with gilt trimmings. From the Sheedy collection, New Oxford, Pennsylvania.

FIG. 3 *(right, below)*—KNUCKLE AND LOW-BACK SETTEE *(Connecticut, c. 1760)*. This piece with a right-angle turn at one end and unequally spaced legs—features which no one has ever seen in another settee—was an enigma until careful examination indicated that it was ingeniously refashioned at an early date as the result of a fire, traces of which can be seen on the under side of the wide, hollowed-out seat. Evidently it was originally a straight settee nearly seven feet long (now 4 feet, 10 inches), with both ends like the present left end. When part of it near the center was damaged by fire, someone with Yankee cleverness cut out the burned section and mitered the two uninjured parts together at a right angle, possibly intending the projecting part for a fireside cradle, at all events making a comfortable lounge with an arm rest. From an inn at Stafford Springs, Connecticut.

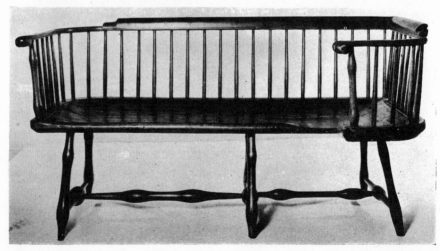

Fig. 4 (left)—Loop-Back Writing Chair. Hickory and pine. It has nine slender spindles and a circular writing arm of uncommon design and attachment, containing a drawer with rounded front. Legs are flaring with bamboo turnings. Such turnings are usually, though not always, taken as indicating a date after 1800, but Mr. Davenport, who gave many discriminating descriptions of individual pieces in letters and attached labels and was usually very accurate, credited the piece to *circa* 1770. Concerning the types and dating of windsors, see the article *The American Windsor Chair*, by J. Stogdell Stokes, Antiques, April 1926.

Fig. 5 (right)—Triple-Back Armchair with Comb. The comb rising above the double back is always an interesting feature. The arms have exceptionally delicate three-finger ends and side scrolls matching those of the rail-crest ears.

Fig. 6 (left)—Armchair with Braced One-Piece Back and Arms (*New England, c. 1760*). This rare chair, in its original condition except the refinish, combines in one piece all the finest qualities of the windsor type. It has knuckle arms, which are extremely rare in this type of chair, braced back, continuous arm, nine graceful spindles with a slight swelling, and quite perfect arm supports, leg turnings, and underneath stretchers. The bow back has a delicate beading. Nine spindles in chairs with braced backs are much less frequent than in chairs without the back brace since the two bracing spindles take up considerable space. In the Davenport collection there are three bow-back chairs with continuous arms but without back braces which have nine spindles; two similar chairs without back braces have seven spindles; two bow-back side chairs with braces and seven spindles; and one with eight spindles.

Fig. 8 (below)—High Comb-Back Rocker. The high comb is attached by five slender spindles to the horizontal back rail of a well-proportioned rocking chair which has four arrow-shaped spindles of graceful design. The rail of the comb conforms in pattern to that of the chair. Arm posts, spindles, legs, and stretchers have bamboo turnings. Compare with comb-back chair shown in Figure 5. The seven spindles carried through the two backs support an especially graceful and wide crest rail which balances the spread of the arms in a harmonious manner. The two outside spindles are bent in sharply to gather with equal spacing all seven spindles on the saddle seat.

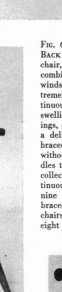

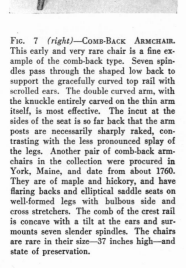

Fig. 7 (right)—Comb-Back Armchair. This early and very rare chair is a fine example of the comb-back type. Seven spindles pass through the shaped low back to support the gracefully curved top rail with scrolled ears. The double curved arm, with the knuckle entirely carved on the thin arm itself, is most effective. The incut at the sides of the seat is so far back that the arm posts are necessarily sharply raked, contrasting with the less pronounced splay of the legs. Another pair of comb-back armchairs in the collection were procured in York, Maine, and date from about 1760. They are of maple and hickory, and have flaring backs and elliptical saddle seats on well-formed legs with bulbous side and cross stretchers. The comb of the crest rail is concave with a tilt at the ears and surmounts seven slender spindles. The chairs are rare in their size—37 inches high—and state of preservation.

FIG. 10 (below)—ONE OF A PAIR OF SHERATON WINDSOR SIDE CHAIRS (c. 1800). Maple and pine. Distinctively flattened T-shape stretcher extends from center front of the seat to the cross stretcher. The raked back has double cross rails. The seven spindles are alternatingly round and flattened. This is the only pair of just this type of chair with the unique T-stretcher known to exist today.

FIG. 9 (above)—BRACED FAN-BACK SIDE CHAIR (New England, c. 1770). Maple and hickory. Posts, legs, and stretchers are attractively turned in vase and bulb pattern. The crest rail with upturned ears forms a deep crescent which with the deep and narrow saddle seat gives vaguely a wing-chair effect. The slight bulb of the spindles indicates whittling by hand. Rare in this small size and shape.

FIG. 12 (below)—COMB-BACK ARMCHAIR (c. 1740-1750). The unusually high and wide flaring top rail of the comb with its scrolled ears, and plain well-shaped arms, and the admirable turnings of the arm posts, legs, and stretchers make this chair a striking example of the New England windsor type.

FIG. 11 (above)—WRITING ARMCHAIR (late eighteenth century). Nine spindles support a plain, horizontal top rail. The squared writing arm measures 19 by 28½ inches and has a drawer and a small tab for a candle rest. Severe in all its details, this chair is extremely solid and practical. It belonged to William Wirt (1772-1834), who was Attorney General of the United States from 1817 to 1829 under Presidents Madison, Monroe, and John Quincy Adams. Previously he had been appointed by Thomas Jefferson to assist in prosecuting Aaron Burr for treason. Wirt began his *Letters of a British Spy* on the writing arm of this chair in August 1803, as he himself states, "to while away six anxious weeks which preceded the birth of my daughter." The name Wirt is marked in black on under surface of seat. This chair, acquired from a direct descendant of the original owner, attests Mr. Davenport's interest in furniture with historical associations.

FIG. 14 (below)—LOW HORSESHOE-BACK ARMCHAIR. Fourteen spindles of excellent turnings support the arms. The most distinctive feature is a saltire or four-pointed stretcher, reminiscent of those found in earlier roundabout chairs but apparently unique in windsors. Compare the cruder, but also rare, asymmetrical X-stretcher of the windsor in Figure 7, page 27, ANTIQUES, July 1944. Although the bulbous feet have been cut off and casters inserted, the saltire stretcher puts this chair in a class of its own.

FIG. 13 (above)—FAN-BACK SIDE CHAIR (c. 1760). The striking feature of this chair is the boldly curved crest rail with upturned ears, supported by six walnut inside spindles and two choice side posts. Concerning the relative merits of American windsor chairs of this and other basic types, see the article *Windsors: Suggested Criteria*, by Henry B. Stoddard, in ANTIQUES for January 1938 (p. 21). The ABC's of American windsors were given in a *Hornbook* in ANTIQUES for April 1942 (p. 253).

Ebenezer Tracy, Connecticut Chairmaker

By ADA R. CHASE

ALTHOUGH it is well known that in the 1700's able clock-makers were working in Norwich, Connecticut, little has transpired regarding the town's early cabinetmakers. Since the Norwich folk were notably industrious, and inclined less to agriculture than to manufacture and commerce, we may reasonably assume that among them were furnituremakers capable of equipping the substantial homes of their ambitious and wealthy fellow citizens.

The name of one such craftsman has recently come to light. And though he appears to have devoted himself chiefly to the production of wind-sor chairs, his work is of such outstanding quality as to entitle the man himself to a place in the arti-san gallery of New Eng-land immortals. Perhaps a prophetic feeling that such skill and integrity as his must be honored by future generations led this maker to emblazon his name upon many, if not all, of his creations. At any rate, this he literally did, using a red-hot iron to implant his name, EB: TRACY, beneath every shapely chestnut seat that he fashioned.

Ebenezer Tracy was born in that part of Nor-wich which is now the town of Lisbon, April 20, 1744. Lisbon was originally known as Newent, or the Third Ecclesiastical So-ciety. With what is now Hanover, it was segregated from Norwich as an incorpo-rated town in 1786. It borders on Preston, where such mechanical geniuses as John Avery and Thomas Jackson were making clocks, while Thomas Harland was simi-larly engaged in Norwich. Situated on the post road from Norwich to Boston, as well as in the crotch between the Shetucket and Quinebaug Rivers, Lisbon enjoyed means of transportation unexcelled in those days, and well calculated to encour-age commerce.

Ebenezer Tracy was the son of Deacon Andrew and Ruth (Smith) Tracy. The Deacon, though a farmer, living on the west bank of the Quinebaug, about one mile south of Jewett City on the Norwich road, had artisan blood in his veins. His great-great-grandfather, Lieutenant Thomas Tracy, one of the founders of Norwich in 1659, was a ship carpenter. So inheritance as well as opportunity directed Ebenezer to the vocation in which he achieved preëminence.

Fig. 1 — COLONEL EBENEZER TRACY'S DWELLING AND INN, LISBON, CONNECTICUT
The workshop stood at the rear. The original paneled double doors of the eighteenth century are still in place. The estate has never passed out of the family's possession, and the present owner, Paul Geist, is connected by marriage with the Tracy descend-ants in the female line

Where or how Ebenezer learned his trade we do not know.

We find record of his purchasing twenty-five acres of land in Newent, November 9, 1769, when he was but twenty-five years old, and but recently a benedict. He was thrice married. His first wife, Mary Freeman of Preston, succumbed after bearing seven children, one of whom, Ebenezer Junior, became a car-penter and dwelt in Norwich until his demise in 1823. The senior Ebenezer's second matrimonial venture joined him in wedlock to Thankful Ayres, who presented one addition to the family brood before passing on to make way for a successor. It is not surprising that, with a considerable assortment of children on his hands, Ebenezer should hasten to acquire a third helpmeet. Within a year Anne Very (Kirtland), or Annevera, as he names her in his will, had valorously ac-cepted the position. Ebe-nezer was now fifty-six and old for his years. He died in March 1803.

In his will, evidently prepared in expectation of the end, for it is dated February 7, 1803, he de-scribes himself as "being advanced in years, and having a bodily infirm-ity." His bequests were to his "loving wife Annevera Tracy," one third of his per-sonal estate, to be hers forever, and also the use and improvement of one third of his real estate, the rest to be divided equally among his eight children, except £35, to be shared by Mary and Rebecca "in consideration of their services."

His inventory, which amounted to the goodly sum of $8,228.13, reveals an amaz-ing array of belongings. After enumerated articles of a generous wardrobe, with silver buttons, knee and shoe buckles, a silver-hilted sword and bridle, two pairs of over-alls, there appear: a sideboard, £23; desk and bookcase, £15; best table; maple table; circular ends for ditto; pembroke table; maple tea table (with complete set of china); "Ketching table"; low bureau with 4 drawers; low bureau; 4 old ditto, with legs; "Writing chair and cushing, £4"; "8 Cushinged botomed Chairs, £12"; 6 yellow ditto; 22 green ditto; 1 large fiddle-back ditto; 6 fiddle-back chairs, £3; rocking chair; brass-wheeled clock, £30; 6,400 chair rounds and legs, 277 chair bottoms; clockcase; large table; high-post bed, and under bed; another

Fig. 2 — Two Windsors by Ebenezer Tracy

Stripped of their paint, these examples clearly reveal the chestnut wood of the seats. An oak stretcher is discernible in the side chair. The thickness of the seats, modified by careful "saddling" of the surface and by undercutting the edges, should also be noted. Chairs with back and arms in one piece were difficult to make and were inclined to fragility. Observe the careful thinning of the back strip in the armchair. In the side chair, shown below, the inward curve of the hoop back where it meets the seat is an eighteenth-century feature. In later chairs the hoop splays outward just above the seat line. The Tracy label branded beneath the seat is pictured below.
From the collection of Orton Loring Clark

pembroke table and a candlestand. In addition, we find these significant items: a sideboard *unfinished;* a great deal of lumber (mahogany, 148 feet, cherry boards, birch and beech, 111 mangrove boards, pine, whitewood, maple, chestnut, oak joists); 52 molding tools; 37 joiner's planes; 76 chisels & gouges; 24 paintbrushes, with varnish, lampblack, stone yellow; and, as our country auction announcements read, other articles too numerous to mention, among them a washing machine!

The list of household furniture and of stock in trade in hand is worth pondering. Evidently Ebenezer was prosperous, and, despite the necessity for supporting a large family, lived well, and, on suitable occasions, clothed himself in brave attire. The plenitude of his furniture may be in part explained by the fact that he maintained his commodious home as an inn for wayfarers along the Boston turnpike. Its quality, however, bespeaks the man of means and good taste. Since we know Ebenezer primarily as a maker of windsor chairs, generally recognized by historians as a craft distinct and separate from that of cabinetmaking, we should normally assume that his highly appraised family sideboard, desk, and "cushinged botomed" chairs were purchased from other artisans. Probably they were. The fiddleback chairs may well have been direct Tracy heirlooms or souvenirs of successive marriages.

It is really the recital of stock in trade

that gives us pause. The 6,400 rounds and legs, enough to sustain more than 900 windsor chairs, of course need occasion no surprise, though they are indicative of a large business. But what of the stores of mahogany, cherry, birch, and beech, the molding tools, joiner's planes, chisels, and gouges? Their evidence unmistakably implies that Ebenezer Tracy supplemented the manufacture of windsor chairs with the execution of fine cabinetwork. This striking revelation should set the old families of Norwich and its vicinage busily at work searching their furniture for labels and their trunks of documents for bills that will confirm their townsman's versatility.

Tracy's house was well stocked with linen, with "London Brown bed quilt, green ditto, pied ditto," with rose blankets, "new check'd blankets." Quite modern they sound.

When Annevera, third wife of Ebenezer Tracy, died November 11, 1807, she too left a will, and for a relict, a tidy sum of money, $743.14. She specially remembered those two mainstays of the family, Mary and Rebecca: to Mary, "all my estate which I dye posesed of except what I hereafter & herein give away," and to Rebecca "one bed and bedstead with suitable beding for the same, also my black and red lutestring gown." She also provided for her brothers, Jabez and Joshua Kirtland, her sister Hannah Bushnell, Nemira Bushnell, and her granddaughter Very Ann. It is interesting to find in the inventory,

Fig. 4 — TRACY BOW-BACK WINDSOR
Eight spindles instead of the nine occurring in the brace-back chair of Figure 2. Since the back in the present example is not braced, we may assume that the piece was not designed for heavy duty. Hence its seeming lightness.
From the author's collection

Fig. 3 — TRACY WINDSOR
Compare with the example in Figure 2. Here the arch of the back seems to be slightly lower, and the legs show no signs of abbreviation. It is reasonable to believe that the long, tapered section of windsor legs was devised to permit shortening to accommodate the customer's stature. *From the collection of Raymond Case*

Fig. 5 — TRACY BOW-BACK WINDSOR
The usual handsome turnings of legs and posts, ample stretchers, and delicate tapered spindles characteristic of Tracy's work are here in evidence. No spindles more pleasing than those fashioned by Tracy are to be found in chairs by other makers.
From the collection of Doctor Ier J. Manwaring

besides numerous bed quilts, her "mourning appairel, and every day wearing aparel," and some pieces of furniture easily identified in her husband's inventory: a sideboard, pembroke table, stand table, candlestand, maple tea table, low bureau with drawers, £4, "writing chair & cushing £4," brass-wheel clock, £30, and other pieces.

Ebenezer Tracy enlisted August 3, 1778, in Captain Wheeler's company, and was discharged September 12 of the same year. In October 1778 he was made ensign of the 4th Company or trainband, in the 20th Regiment. In the

Fig. 6 — TWO TRACY FAN-BACK WINDSORS
That at the left has eight spindles in the back; its neighbor but seven. Hence the slightly pinched aspect of the latter chair.
Left, from the collection of Miss Mary E. Richards; right, from the collection of Julian L. Williams

papers relative to his estate and on his gravestone he appears as *Colonel Ebenezer Tracy*, and we can picture him with his silver-hilted sword. Fortunately, his branding iron burned deep and lasting impressions, so that we have authentic illustrations to show the sturdy turnings, fine spindles, and comfortable seats that he provided in his chairs for the delectation of his customers and of their children and children's children unto the third and fourth generation and unnumbered generations to come.

Colonel Ebenezer Tracy, his father and mother, his three wives, and an infant daughter, "A tender flower, Scarce seen to rise, Before it droops its head and dies," sleep in a row in an old burying ground in Lisbon.

Critical Note. If the back were

removed from any one of the chairs pictured with the preceding discussion, the remaining seat and four intact legs would still constitute a stool capable of affording rest to the weary. The same statement applies to all chairs in the windsor category. Hence any chair whose back consists of members rising directly from the seat and in no wise connected with the rear legs qualifies as a windsor. The best of such chairs are both handsome and comfortable. The worst are trash. American windsors are supposed to have been first made about 1725. Their manufacture has not yet ceased.

The most desirable of the old windsors exhibit thick, handsomely shaped seats whose apparent weight is modified by undercutting of the edges. Legs are boldly turned and generously spread. Arm posts are likewise well turned, as are the back posts of the fan-back type. Spindles are light and gracefully tapered. Stretchers are bulbous in form and of ample proportions. All these characteristics are observable in Ebenezer Tracy's windsor chairs.

About the year 1810 windsor design underwent a change for the worse. So-called bamboo turnings, or equally ugly club turnings, largely supplanted the previous vase shapes; stretchers became meagre, seats lean, and other members coarse. The rhythmic composition of parts that gives a noble windsor its special dis-

Fig. 7 — Tracy Writing-Arm Windsor
A monumental chair with huge tablet equipped with a drawer and supported on massively turned posts. The drawer beneath the seat has disappeared.
From the collection of Doctor Ier J. Manwaring

tinction was thereafter quite lost.

The materials of windsors vary. Tracy made his seats of chestnut, bows of oak, legs of maple, stretchers of oak, spindles of hickory. The usual practice of other makers was to employ pine for seats, maple for legs and stretchers. Hickory, white oak, and ash, according to Nutting's *American Windsors*, were used for curved backs and for spindles. Whatever their material, seats were in one piece, and not of several sections glued together.

Traces of paint cling to most ancient windsors. Probably nearly all such chairs were originally painted. Indian red, dark green, and black were the usual colors. Tracy's inventory suggests that he used yellow as well — although, to be sure, the stone yellow may have been used for mixing green.

It will he helpful to bear in mind the period of Ebenezer Tracy's life span. Born in 1744, he must have been making windsor chairs for at least a decade before the outbreak of the Revolutionary War. In so far as may be judged from available chairs carrying his brand, he attempted no significant alterations in the style of his product from the time when he became an independent master until his death. In short, whether an individual "Eb: Tracy" chair was actually made in 1770 or in 1800, it belongs in the pre-Revolutionary class.
— *The Editor*

Fig. 8 (left) — Tracy Writing-Arm Windsor
Less masculine in outline than the chair of Figure 7, but exhibiting a tall comb back. A rare example of Tracy's proficiency.
From the collection of Mrs. Frederick J. Kerr Alexander

Fig. 9 (right) — Tracy But Not Ebenezer (c. 1800)
This spindle bow-backed chair marked E. TRACY is not the work of Ebenezer. The son, Ebenezer Junior, may be responsible. Apparently an Elisha Tracy (*1744–1809*), perhaps a chairmaker, lived in Scotland, Connecticut. He may be the person whose birth and death dates are confused with those of Ebenezer Tracy by a correspondent quoted in ANTIQUES for February 1926, *p. 97.* Evidences of decadence in design are observable in this chair. Nevertheless, its merit is what Mr. Nutting would probably call "high for the period."
From the author's collection

An Interpretation of
Shaker Furniture

By Edward D. and Faith Andrews

Illustrations, except as noted, from the authors' collection

"To me more dear, congenial to my heart
One native charm, than all the gloss of art."
— Oliver Goldsmith, *The Deserted Village*

Fig. 1 — Swivel Sewing Chair
A Shaker derivative of the Windsor type. Chiefly of maple

IN THE program of the early Shakers, little place was left for the intentional cultivation of beauty. Not only did the practical aspects of making a livelihood lead to neglect of the decorative arts, but the tenets of the Believers were so interpreted that the beautiful was considered unnecessary to the highest life, and therefore wrong. Thus Elder Frederick Evans, one of Shakerdom's chief spokesmen, is quoted as stating, "The beautiful . . . has no business with us. The divine man has no right to waste money upon what you people would call beauty, in his house or his daily life, while there are people living in misery." (*The Communistic Societies of the United States*, Charles Nordhoff, *1875*.) If he were to build his dwellings and shops again, he would aim, not to make them more beautiful, but to assure more light, a better distribution of heat, and a more inclusive regard for protection and comfort, because such concerns promote health and long life — a basally functional point of view. The members of the sect have always been known as "strict utilitarians." In a book entitled *Two Years' Experience among the Shakers (1848)* a certain David Lamson writes: "In all they do, the first inquiry is, will it be useful? Everything therefore about their buildings, fences, etc. is plain."

In this attitude the Shakers differed little from other communal societies in this country. Only the Harmonists, who were taught by Father Rapp to love

music and flowers, and the Oneida Perfectionists, who fostered musical and theatrical entertainments and landscape gardening, appear to have encouraged the æsthetic side of existence.

The utilitarian conception voiced by Elder Evans strongly influenced the furniture craft among the Shakers. The necessary relationship between utility and sound workmanship was obvious. Shaker furniture was always fashioned in the spirit of Mother Ann's injunction: "Do your work as if you had a thousand years to live and as if you were to die tomorrow." The same care that was expended on chests, tables, chairs, and beds was lavished on workbenches, broom vises, shoe benches and racks, sanding machine frames, and the trays for carrying berry baskets from the field. Moreover, everything had to be plain in aspect, not only because all ornament or embellishment was believed to be wrong, but because, as ardent disciples of cleanliness, the Shakers knew that the simpler a piece was, the more easily could it be kept unsoiled.

The character of Shaker furniture was in no small measure determined by the fact that each item was utilized in the immediate community where it was made. Thus the general household requirement was often modified by the particular need of the individual. The purpose that a given piece was to serve, and even the place where it would stand, were known to the maker, and tended to emphasize the functionality of the finished work.

Fig. 2 — Shaker Chair
Ironing chair with seat twenty inches above the floor

Fig. 3 — Shaker Chairs
a. Child's chair. *Height: 11 inches to seat, 24 inches to topmost slat. b.* Adult's rocker. The bar across the top is to permit application of an upholstered back. *Height: 43 inches to cushion rail*

This accounts in part for the large number of unduplicated pieces that has come to light. Committed though they were to independence from worldly sources of supply, the Shakers could not prevent the element of variability from entering into the production of their shops. They had to turn out not only such essential pieces of furniture as tables, chairs, chests of drawers, and beds, but countless accessory forms, such as clocks, bookcases, washstands, soap boxes, sinks, knife boxes, brushes, brooms, trunks, benches, mirror frames, stools, foot warmers, wood boxes, measuring sticks, sewing boxes, dust boxes, mixing bowls, bean boxes, squash squeezers, foot measures, letter boxes, trays, pincushion holders, coffins, counters, tailoring benches, and so on. The Shaker cabinet-maker, obviously, was forced to be unusually versatile.

Unless, however, one grants to the craftsman some very clear appreciation of the beautiful for its own sake, it is difficult to explain how Shaker craftsmanship so long maintained its excellence. Its inherent æsthetic quality must have won a degree of recognition that helped to maintain the tradition of good workmanship and supplied inspiration for some of the fine pieces constructed during the midyears of the last century. Though even as late as the 'seventies and 'eighties

Fig. 4 — HIGH WORK BENCH
Made especially to support three mixing bowls for preparing white, graham, and unleavened bread. Omission of braces in front permits worker to sit at his task

Fig. 5 — SHAKER STOOLS
The two-step stools were equally useful as foot rests and as portable steps. They are exclusively Shaker. The legs of the tripod stool are characteristic

Elder Evans and other leaders officially repudiated "beauty," evidences of a more liberal conception of the place of the arts in a desirable community life are not lacking.

A reaction had set in against the constraints that accompanied the revivalistic ardors of the founders. The natural desire of newcomers, especially young people, to enjoy some gratification of the senses also had its slow effect. Flowers, for instance, came to be appreciated for their color and fragrance as well as for their value in the making of extracts and medicines. By the early 'seventies a Shaker Elder, Giles B. Avery, proclaimed that "Creative Providence made flowers beautiful, and made the eye with capacity to drink in their beauty, to contribute to the happiness of His creatures." Music and poetry also advanced beyond their strictly religious function to play a part in a gradually increasing, though always limited, recreational life. During the last half of the nineteenth century several volumes of poetry were published, while *The Shaker* — the official monthly publication of the sect — as well as its successor, *The Manifesto*, printed words and scores of many hymns and songs.

The Shaker author of the book *The Aletheia* went so far as to predict that "the arts as well as the sciences would some day

Fig. 6 — SMALL SEWING "DESK" OR CABINET
Of maple and cherry, painted Shaker red. Unusual because of size

Fig. 7 — BUREAU DESK
A Shaker version of a type of desk that was much in vogue at the beginning of the nineteenth century

flourish under the patronage of those living the highest life, the Shaker life"; and Hinds, in his *American Communities (1902)*, noted that "there is a growing party of progressives, who, while firmly adhering to all the essentials of Shakerism, demand that non-essentials shall not stand in the way of genuine progress and culture."

But the best of Shaker furniture had been made before this conscious broadening of culture. All the more reason for praising the early cabinet-

Fig. 8 (right) — SMALL CHEST OF DRAWERS Of butternut. The brasses are a recent substitution for original Shaker knobs. *Size: 25 ¾ inches high by 24 ½ inches wide. From the collection of Mrs. Carl de Gersdorff*

Fig. 10 (below) — PINE CASE WITH DRAWERS AND CUPBOARDS Fine paneling distinguishes early Shaker work such as this. Best examples are found on doors and window casings of meetinghouses. In the piece illustrated, the doors spring open when pressure is applied to protruding wrought-iron pins

Fig. 9 (above, right) — PINE CHEST OF DRAWERS
Marked *Lucy Bishop's Case. Made by A. B. April 3, 1817.* The initials stand for Amos Bishop, an early cabinetmaker of the Mount Lebanon community. In general, the piece follows late eighteenth-century precedent

Fig. 11 (below, right) — PINE CUPBOARD. Unique and apparently quite early

makers who anticipated the subsequent attitude and, in an atmosphere of apparent indifference to any consideration but that of utility, created and maintained a school of design which later won honor. The conventions that kept their work simple in character could not bind their imaginations, but, on the contrary, gave purity and direction to their skill.

In the early days of the Shaker communities no pieces of furniture were more widely in use than benches. Constructed in heavy native pine, sometimes with basswood tops, they were a frequent substitute for chairs. Deal benches ten feet long, or longer, were placed in the dining and meeting rooms. Shorter forms, sometimes equipped with a drawer, were used as spinning stools, for holding flowerpots, keeping sundry containers above basement floors, supporting coffins, and so on. One of these benches is shown in Figure 4. It has a medial brace tightly keyed on the outside of the leg, somewhat in the manner of Swedish refectory tables. The braces are dovetailed, and the vertical members are mortised, Windsor fashion, into the top. The two-step stools (*Fig. 5*), designed as foot rests, and the "three-steppers," used to reach tall chests of drawers and sometimes equipped with a

— small chests, cupboards, table desks, wall racks, and so on, which show that the producers recognized the convenience of appurtenances. It is true that members of the sect were amply provided with efficiently designed furniture and tools that lightened the daily tasks — even though the emphasis was always on usefulness and durability, and no concessions were made to what the Shakers believed was the human weakness for vulgar display. In the items that have been selected to illustrate this study, we perceive constant evidence that æsthetic satisfaction accompanied the creative effort. And

Fig. 12 (above) — WORK TABLE
Interesting and convenient disposition of drawers

Fig. 13 (right) — RARE STRETCHER TABLE
An exceptionally dignified piece. Originally an ironing table, later used for canning. Top strengthened by addition of strips under the edges. On the table are a small hanging cupboard and a dovetailed chest

supporting rod or rods for the hand, belong in the same category. Strength is their outstanding characteristic; but they are a delight to behold, especially when covered with the soft-hued mat work from the sewing rooms of the Sisters.

The passion for utility among Shaker cabinet-makers is nowhere better illustrated than in the high pine chests (*Fig. 10*) which were used for nearly every room in dwelling house or shop. Often they were built into the wall structure; sometimes, as in this case, they stood out from the walls and were equipped with cupboard space. Though of generous dimensions, rising on occasion almost to the ceiling, they never seem ungainly or ill-proportioned. The paneling of the cupboard doors is finely achieved, the knobs are delicately turned, and the total effect is one of chaste perfection. In contrast to this chest is the small butternut stand pictured in Figure 8, a diminutive bureau of most charming quality. Many such pieces have come to light

we are glad that strict limitations defined the character of the work, for, in the instinctive and perhaps unconscious evasion of the prescriptive letter, the free spirit of the craftsman has become unfailingly manifest.

Fig. 16 (above) — PAN CUPBOARD
On the wall above is a hanging rack

Figs. 14 and 15 (left) — TWO UNUSUAL STANDS (*early*)
For convenience the former stand has a tilted top and the height is adjustable

Random Notes on Hitchcock and His Competitors

By Esther Stevens Fraser

Fig. 1a — ADVERTISEMENT OF SEYMOUR WATROUS (*1824*)

FOR the reader's convenience, these notes may as well begin with a brief résumé of the already familiar events in the life of Lambert Hitchcock, chairmaker. Hitchcock was born in Cheshire, Connecticut, June 28, 1795. He died, apparently at Unionville in the same state, in 1852. In 1818 he settled in the village of Barkhamsted, where he established a chair factory. In 1821 the community was rechristened Hitchcocksville; in 1866 it assumed the name of Riverton, evidently a satisfactory appellation, since it has not since been altered.

Hitchcock is said to have engaged first in the making of chair parts which were shipped to Charleston, South Carolina, and other southern coastal cities. This does not mean that he turned out fragments of chairs, but the unassembled elements — backs, seats, slats, stretchers, and so on, which were easily and inexpensively packed and shipped and could be put together by the ultimate purchaser. This method is said to have been widely adopted by manufacturers of cheap furniture, who in the heyday of the traveling peddler and of the country store used such agencies for the distribution of their product.

After a few years, Hitchcock seems to have abandoned the selling of knocked-down furniture. At any rate he embarked on the more ambitious project of manufacturing completely constructed and more or less elaborately painted chairs for middle-class homes. Such articles were known to the trade as "fancy chairs." Fancy chairs had enjoyed a considerable measure of popularity since the 1790's, though with the passing of time the delicate early forms were supplanted by sturdier designs, and quickly applied stenciling superseded the more delicate and costly process of hand painting.

In 1826 Hitchcock had reached his peak of prosperity, which he celebrated by erecting a new factory employing upward of a hundred hands, including women and children. In 1829 financial reverses compelled a reorganization of the business. Arba Alford, who was previously general manager of the concern, was admitted as a partner, and manufacturing continued under the name of Hitchcock, Alford & Company. The arrangement thus made continued until 1843, when Hitchcock withdrew to establish a business of his own in Unionville. The old establishment was, however, carried on by Arba Alford and one Josiah Sage under the name of Alford & Company until 1853, when a new and different industry supplanted

chairmaking in the old shop. Meanwhile, Hitchcock's venture in Unionville had proved unsuccessful and was gradually abandoned.

AS WE pass from personal biography to a study of furniture, it is necessary to emphasize the fact that the term "Hitchcock chair," as usually employed, is generic rather than specific. In other words, most persons use it to designate a wide diversity of chairs whose only common characteristic is a painted surface adorned with stenciled designs in gold or colors. Such chairs were turned out by many shops, in many places, over a long term of years. Among these shops, the one owned and operated by Lambert Hitchcock was apparently the most consistent in labeling its products. Despite the wear and tear of time, many fancy chairs of the 1820–1840 period still retain the inscription clearly lettered on the back strip of the seat: *L. Hitchcock, Hitchcocksville, Conn. Warranted.* So by virtue of his enterprise in advertising himself, while most other manufacturers were content with anonymity, Lambert Hitchcock has been popularly accepted as the originator of the general style exemplified in the painted chairs of his day, and as the genius from whose creations his contemporaries derived their inspiration.

One hesitates to hurl down the statues of the gods, and thus incur punishment for sacrilege. If now I seem to be embarking on such a perilous adventure, let me defend myself in advance by saying that, while Lambert Hitchcock was evidently a good citizen, an honest man, and a conscientious chairmaker, he is not to be reckoned among the deities who have ruled the tastes of humankind. All the essen-

Fig. 1b — ADVERTISEMENT OF SEYMOUR WATROUS (*1824*)

Fig. 2 — CHAIR APPARENTLY BY WATROUS (*c. 1824*)
Compare with illustration in the Watrous advertisement. Back shows better proportions, better turnings, and greater delicacy of detail than we find in Hitchcock chairs. Leg turnings less fussy. Shaping of lower part of front legs more carefully treated.
From the collection of Mrs. Madeline Wiles

tial motives discoverable in his earlier chairs — notably the turned top rail with a rectangular bar in its midst — will be found in Sheraton's design book of 1803. (Strange, *p. 345, No. 27.*) The leg turnings of Hitchcock's chairs are decadent versions of those to be found in Sheraton's drawings. Other makers of fancy chairs in America apparently had a hand in developing the type prior to Hitchcock's advent. Two newspaper advertisements dated March 2, 1824, by Seymour Watrous of Hartford testify to this probability. One portrays a round-seated chair of a type that we incline to associate with the modes of 1815, the other a chair with rectangular seat — much cheaper to construct than the round type, and in its major features very like the early Hitchcock product.

Again we find that one William Moore, Jr., a man old enough to be Hitchcock's father, was a resident of Barkhamsted at least twenty years before Hitchcock set up business. Moore was a manufacturer of chairs and so continued, more or less in competition with his new neighbor, until forced out of business in 1829. An inventory of assets filed at the time of Moore's insolvency affords an interesting view of the business ramifications of a country manufacturer more than a century ago. The inventory in question lists 100 chairs on their way to Philadelphia; 46 in the hands of G. & I. Wills, Northampton; 30 with Lewis Baily in New York; and many others in less distant communities. The wholesale valuation of these pieces was 62 cents each. It is appalling to think that anyone should have to conduct business at the meagre margin of profit implied by such a figure.

Thus far I have found only two chairs by William Moore, Jr., both in

Fig. 3 — Two Chairs by William Moore, Jr. (*c. 1824*), and One by Hitchcock (*c. 1826*), All Labeled
Centre item by Hitchcock; others by Moore. Seat of the chair at the left apparently changed from cane to rush type before painted finish was applied. This chair is almost identical in style and decoration with the Hitchcock example. The reduced splay of the latter's front legs constitutes a point of difference.
Moore chairs from the collection of Mrs. Gilbert Jones. The other from the collection of Mrs. Arthur Oldham

possession of one whose family lived in Westfield near Springfield, Massachusetts, when the chairs were purchased. The decoration of both is adequate, and the striping exceptionally fine. An edging of braided cane around the seat of the caned example is a touch of elegance seldom encountered (*Fig. 3*). The second of these Moore chairs is signally important because of its resemblance to the labeled Hitchcock example of Figure 3. The stencil units of the two are so nearly identical as to suggest that they are the work of the same painter working for two manufacturers. If this is not the case, we must assume that one shop was actually tracing the designs of its rival. One leaf in the two patterns precisely matches a leaf in the other — a circumstance not to be explained on the ground of pure accident. It may be that Moore joined forces with Hitchcock. Mrs. Mabel Roberts Moore, author of a pamphlet on Hitchcock, thinks she remembers seeing the name of William Moore, Jr., in a list of Hitchcock employes.

In this connection it is worth observing that, though Lambert Hitchcock is said to have established himself in Barkhamsted in 1818, I find his first recorded purchase of local property to have been in 1820. Mrs. Moore, his recent biographer, states that he built his large factory about 1826 and thereafter changed from manufacturing chair parts for foreign shipment to producing complete chairs. Fully decorated Hitchcock chairs would therefore date from 1826 or somewhat later, if they carry the label *L. Hitchcock, Hitchcocksville, Conn. Warranted.* Such early chairs, in my opinion, exhibit a finer sense of line and proportion and a

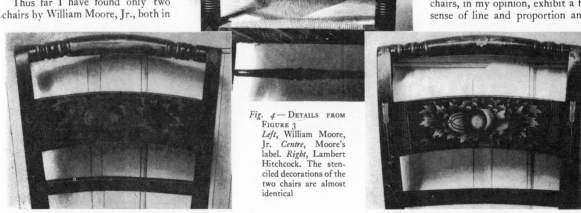

Fig. 4 — Details from Figure 3
Left, William Moore, Jr. *Centre*, Moore's label. *Right*, Lambert Hitchcock. The stenciled decorations of the two chairs are almost identical

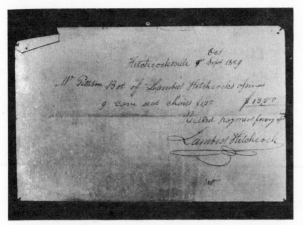

Fig. 5 — BILL RECEIPTED BY LAMBERT HITCHCOCK (*1829*)
 The chairs, of which five still survive, are precisely like that shown in
 Figure 3.
 By courtesy of H. S. Bailey

Fig. 6 — THE STENCIL KIT OF Z. WILLARD BROOKS
 From Hancock, New Hampshire. Velvet dauber at extreme right. The
 stencils, cut from copybook paper, are late.
 From the collection of Maro S. Brooks

keener appreciation of good turnings than contemporaneous chairs by William Moore, Jr. Their bronze stenciling is unsurpassed — well designed and superb in its brilliance. Such excellence is not apparent in Hitchcock's later products. We cannot say when Moore began making chairs of the style exemplified in Figure 3. But we know that Hitchcock was turning out virtually the same article in 1829. Evidence supporting this statement is afforded by the receipted bill for nine chairs here reproduced (*Fig. 5*). Five of the original set recorded in this bill still survive. Since they are identical with the example pictured in Figure 3, it is not necessary to repeat the portrait. At the time of this sale, October 1829, Lambert Hitchcock was suffering financial reverses. The retail price of his chairs was $1.50 each. William Moore's wholesale figure, we recall, was 62 cents each.

A finer labeled Hitchcock than that pictured in Figure 7 would be hard to find. The stenciling is in almost mint condition, lustrous as if burnished. Around the frame of the caned seat runs a braided-cane border like that to which attention has already been called in a chair by William Moore, Jr. Even before

Hitchcock's business was reorganized the lustre of his stenciling began to fade. Evidence of a timid use of bronze is found in the chair of Figure 8. The design on the slat is compressed and relatively uninteresting, while the urn and scroll motive in the midst of the upper rail is wholly inadequate to the space occupied. The previously mentioned braid about the seat is missing.

In her biography of Lambert Hitchcock, Mrs. Moore tells us that the application of stencil patterns was accomplished by women. In this process, she says, the workers first dipped their fingers in oil, then in dry bronze powder, which they forthwith rubbed through the stencil apertures on the still slightly damp painted surface of the chair. As a result of this constant rubbing, the women's fingers in time became hard as boards. Though I have had much practical experience in stenciling, my attempts to emulate the practice described have been so unsuccessful that I fear Mrs. Moore may have been misinformed by someone anxious to withhold the jealously guarded secret of stenciling. A book whose fifth edition was published in 1826, and available to Hitchcock, directs the manipulation of stenciling powder with a pad of soft glove leather stuffed with cotton wool.

Fig. 7 (*left*) — A SUPERIOR EARLY HITCHCOCK CHAIR (*c. 1829*)
 Early label on seat. The handsome stenciled design still retains its original brilliance. This form of chair may have been less expensively produced than the form already illustrated and represents a departure from the first style adopted by Hitchcock. We may not assume that the first style was abandoned as soon as the second was adopted.
 From the author's collection

Fig. 8 (*right*) — A LESS SATISFACTORY EXAMPLE (*c. 1829*)
 Compare the pinched and timid stenciling with the rich design shown in the preceding illustration. Because of the shape of its solid slat and the associated protuberances, such a chair is popularly termed a "turtle back." The resemblance to a turtle is more pronounced in some other examples.
 From the author's collection

Fig. 9 — MARKED HITCHCOCK, ALFORD &
COMPANY CHAIR (c. 1829)
With basket of fruit and flowers.
From the collection of Mrs. Marean

Fig. 10 — HITCHCOCK, ALFORD & COMPANY ROCKER
Compare scroll design applied to top rail with that
of the chair of Figure 7. The deterioration is evident.
From the author's collection

Fig. 11 — CHAIR LABELED BY J. K. HATCH
Perhaps a New Hampshire item. Heavy
seat and nondescript legs.
From Higgins Antique Shop

The ninety-three-year-old craftsman who taught me the art and mystery of stenciling used a similar dauber covered with velvet instead of leather. Likewise a stencil kit recently found at Hancock, New Hampshire, is equipped with a velvet pad (*Fig. 6*). With such an apparatus the texture and shading of the old-time bronzing may be perfectly reproduced. The horny handedness of Hitchcock's female employes may have been due to a process known as "handing," which calls for rubbing a foundation coat of paint with pumice and water under the bare palms of the worker.

AFTER the reorganization of the Hitchcock enterprise under the name of Hitchcock, Alford & Company (*1829*), the factory continued chairmaking very much in the old manner. However, we now find pieces in which a fine, irregular graining is superimposed upon a black ground. Formerly, the two-tone effect had been achieved on a red undercoat — a circumstance responsible for the erroneous assumption that *all* Hitchcocks were given a preliminary brushing of red. During the period beginning about 1829, a basket of fruit and flowers was added to the firm's repertoire of stencil pat-

terns. We find it alike on chairs bearing the label of L. Hitchcock and of Hitchcock, Alford & Company (*Fig. 9*).

A Hitchcock and Alford rocker in my collection displays a flower and leaf pattern and scrolled ears that hark back to earlier designs, though evidently a later and, in the scrolls at least, less careful cutting. On the legs, front stretcher, and back posts occurs a conventional vine pattern in freehand stroke whose cost at today's wage scale would be more than the Hitchcocksville concern received for the chair complete (*Fig. 10*).

WHILE Lambert Hitchcock had many competitors and some imitators, few of them marked their products. Figure 11 pictures a stenciled chair with heavy wood seat and nondescript legs, which exhibits the branded label *J. K. Hatch, Warranted*. I believe it to have been made in New Hampshire. Again, the three-chair-back rush-seat settee of exceptional excellence and fairly early date pictured in Figure 12 is emblazoned with the words *C. Johnson's Patent*. This piece recently found its way to a Salem antique shop, but of its original source I have no knowledge. To the advertisements of the Hartford chairmaker, Seymour Watrous, I have

Fig. 12 — STENCILED SETTEE, "C. JOHNSON'S PATENT" (*c. 1820–1825*)
From the collection of J. S. Metcalfe

already referred. The pictured example of what may well be his work is from a set which, strangely enough, was purchased by the present owner in Seville, Spain (*Fig. 2*). Of their American origin I have never entertained the slightest doubt. Hartford was one of those New England ports whence ventures were shipped on sundry vessels to unforeseen and often strange destinations.

In conclusion I wish to pay brief tribute to one of the last old-time stencilers, Z. Willard Brooks, who was born in 1812, and, from 1840 until his death in 1906, was a resident of Hancock, New Hampshire. Not long since his decorating equipment was found tucked away under the eaves of his farmhouse dwelling. Brooks was not a chairmaker. He purchased furniture, unfinished, from a local manufacturer in Peterboro or Jaffrey and adorned it according to his own fancy. This he did in 1835 in behalf of his new bride, Eliza Gordon. At the advanced age of eighty he was the only gilder in the locality who had the nerve to climb the spire of the village church to restore its shining glory. Some of the stencils that he cut with his own hands survive with his kit of tools; but the pattern according to which men of his kind were fashioned seems to have been irrevocably lost.

Returning for a

Fig. 13 — STENCIL DECORATION BY Z. WILLARD BROOKS (*1835–1840*)
Left, chair stenciled in 1835 for the artist's bride. Rush seat replaced by splints. *Right*, a late Windsor type of chair made in New Hampshire.
From the collection of Maro S. Brooks

moment to Lambert Hitchcock, I trust that my notes may assist in reaching a fair appraisal of the man and his work. Though he may have been surpassed by some, he was equaled by few. He made chairs that were pleasing to the eye, comfortable, honestly and enduringly constructed, and extremely reasonable in price. He gave employment to a small multitude of country folk. To that extent he was a public benefactor. And though he seems ever to have been hovering on the verge of bankruptcy, he never lost his valiant spirit. He worked hard, traveled widely in search of markets for his wares, and yet found time to serve his state as a member of its legislature. If only for reasons of pure sentiment we set special store upon examples of his work, we need not be ashamed of our weakness.

References

Hitchcock Chairs, by Mabel Roberts Moore, published 1933 for the Connecticut Tercentenary Commission. A careful account, though illustrations lack adequate and authentic annotations. Besides the preceding article, ANTIQUES has published the following significant contributions to the general subject: *Hitchcock of Hitchcocksville*, by Mrs. Guion Thompson, August 1923. *Robertsville and Its Chair Makers*, by C. H. Nickerson, September 1925. See also three articles, *Painted Furniture in America*, by Esther Stevens Fraser, June 1924, September 1924, January 1925; and chair labeled *Holmes and Roberts, Colebrook, Conn. Warranted*, November 1924 (*p. 244*).

Fig. 14 (left) — TURTLE-BACK CHAIR (*c. 1829*)
Here the turtle form of the slat is clearly in evidence. The turning of top rail and form of "pillow" distinctly different from those employed by Hitchcock. Probably by another maker, unknown.
From the collection of Mrs. Roland Thaxter

Fig. 15 (right) — PROBABLY A RHODE ISLAND CHAIR (*c. 1825*)
Top rail resembles that of Hitchcock chairs. Slat, leg turnings, and seat frontal different. Note slight splay of front legs, reminiscent of earlier technique.
From the author's collection

The earliest dated piece of furniture in the Old Sturbridge Village collection is a six-board, notch-sided chest marked 1678. The initials I W, two hearts, two diamonds, intersecting lunettes, and crossed lines are impressed into the soft pine with a tool such as a leather stamp.

The furniture

BY MARGARET B. MUNIER

THE VILLAGE FURNITURE COLLECTION, covering the period from the late 1600's to the 1830's, is extensive, varied, and, because of its frequent deviation from formalized styles, of special interest to the collector who delights in creative and individual expression. Some of the pieces were produced by the finest cabinetmakers; others should be considered in terms of their original use and the needs of the first owner. Many early households had "best," "middling," and "common" furniture, and the Village collection reflects these distinctions. A common bench may have been as soundly constructed as the best table in the parlor, but more care was given to the selection of wood, the proportion of the parts, the execution, and the finish, of the parlor piece.

Country furniture was the work of the local cabinetmaker or joiner, the turner, or even the farmer supplying his own needs. That is why so much of it has individuality

Cupboards for storing kitchen and eating utensils were a form of furniture needed in any household. This seventeenth-century one is made of chestnut. Most of the pewter here was made by the Danforth-Boardman group.

Butterfly table, Connecticut, c. 1700, of cherry. Block-and-turned legs, bold curves of the leaf supports, the subtle cant of the base are characteristic of this New England form.

The form and the fan motif of this high chest indicate a date of about 1800. The painted graining, which may have been done then or later, is so well executed that many people have thought the chest really made of mahogany.

Cyma arches and scalloping of the skirt, cabriole legs, and pad feet are all Queen Anne features of a red-painted chest-on-frame made in Massachusetts about 1730-1750. The torus molding of the cornice forms a wide, shallow drawer.

Red-painted pine table (c. 1800) in the Freeman farmhouse (see Interiors). The plainness of this square-topped table is relieved by the grooving or fluting of the tapered legs, the semicircular notchings of the drawer, and the serpentine curves of the apron.

Like the simple chest, the stretcher table persisted in country furniture throughout the eighteenth century and even later, with simplification of the turnings. This octagonal top is an unusual variation: square, round, or oval tops are more common. Originally painted red, the base is maple and the top pine.

and an unconventional character. Fashion played only a small part in its basic design and decorative techniques, and the styles set down in the design books of professional cabinetmakers were modified or but dimly reflected in the form of a chair, the shape of a foot, the carving of an ornament. These were likely to be determined instead by tradition or personal preference. Even when the country craftsman attempted to emulate his more sophisticated contemporaries, his limitations gave his work a flavor of its own.

The woods used had a great deal to do with the design of country furniture. Basic form was influenced by the innate qualities of the material, and many pieces retain the feeling of the boards from which they were cut even when their abrupt angles are refined by beveling, notching, a molded rim, or incised lines. The variety of trees

This well-proportioned tulip-poplar desk (1710-1730), originally painted red, stands in the Freeman farmhouse (see Interiors). It is distinguished by its molded separators, deep well, small slide supports, and sturdy turned feet. The teardrop pulls are replacements.

Red-painted pine chest-on-frame (1725-1740) in the Freeman farmhouse (see Interiors). The four drawers are set into a low, stocky frame which has the unusual feature of a shallow drawer. The teardrop pulls are replacements.

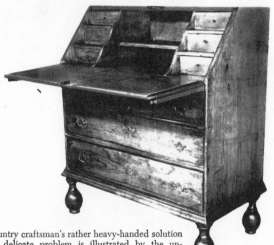

Black paint on a white base applied with a feather or dry brush in knots and cyma swirls imparts an air of bold exuberance to the simple chest form. This decoration may be considerably later than the piece itself, which exemplifies an eighteenth-century type.

A country craftsman's rather heavy-handed solution of a delicate problem is illustrated by the unusual interior of this desk (early 1700's). It is pine, with molded base and high turned feet.

found throughout the eastern part of the United States was a challenge to the craftsman, and each one was used in such a way as to take advantage of its peculiar qualities. Hickory was selected for the graceful bow of a windsor chair because of its toughness and resiliency. The hardness and flexibility of maple recommended it for the turned legs of a chair, and, as with walnut and cherry, the choicer boards were used for flat surfaces.

Geometric patterns, scratched or carved, embellished much country furniture, with variations of the circle appearing frequently. The heart and other traditional designs were also used, sometimes symbolically but more often just as ornaments. When classical motifs and natural forms became a part of the decorative vocabulary during the second half of the eighteenth century, country furniture responded to fashion by adopting the acanthus

leaf, honeysuckle, and bellflower, the cornucopia overflowing with fruit, and the pineapple; but these motifs were more likely to be painted, stenciled, or applied on the surface than carved or built into the form.

In contrast to more formal pieces, country furniture was often painted, especially when the material was a soft wood with little textural graining. Blue, red, brown, dark green, and black were typical colors throughout the period represented at the Village. Occasionally an item constructed of soft wood was painted to simulate the grain of a hard wood such as walnut. A piece of furniture handed down from one generation to another may have been repainted by successive owners; it is often impossible to say just when a coat was applied.

All these types and many others are represented in the furniture collection at Old Sturbridge Village.

Of all American furniture forms the windsor chair is perhaps the most individual and varied. From 1760 on, it was widely used in homes and public institutions. Its makers advertised comb-back, round-top, high-back, low-back, and sack-back chairs useful as garden, parlor, and dining furniture for children and adults, and low chairs for the very young. Left to right: a child's sack- or hoop-back chair, a continuous-arm-and-back windsor made by E. B. Tracy of Connecticut, and a similar child's low chair.

No makeshift but a piece worthy of the "best" room is this walnut Queen Anne side chair, 1740-1750, competently fashioned in the New England tradition. The seat is covered with a reproduced embroidered flame stitch in shades of rose, blue, green, brown, and yellow.

Transitional pieces, combining elements of an old style with a new, are frequent in country furniture. This black-painted pine chair (c. 1750) has the turned legs and stretcher and the Spanish foot of the early 1700's with the pierced splat and back of mid-century mode.

A country cabinetmaker's expression of the shield-back Hepplewhite style. Made of maple, its plainness is relieved by black walnut and fruitwood inlay at the base of the shield. The legs and stretchers are a sturdy continuation of the Chippendale straight-leg style and the seat is rush. Its history indicates a New Hampshire provenance.

Following the windsor chair in popularity, the fancy chair, derived from Sheraton design, came into full flower by 1825. This one in the Freeman farmhouse (see Interiors) is gilded, and decoratively stenciled on the cross splat with a patriotic eagle atop the world.

WALNUT STANDING CUPBOARD (c. 1750). Found in Richmond, Virginia. Such cupboards are a rare persistence of sixteenth- and seventeenth-century styles and were seldom made in this country. This piece has a trim smartness of line and proportion, and escapes heaviness thanks to its delicately scrolled feet. The crisp raised panels of the doors are nicely edged with moldings.

PINE BLANKET CHEST ON FRAME (c. 1720). Half-round moldings surround the real drawers and the two simulated drawers above them, and a base molding overhangs the supporting frame. Such chests mounted on frames are seldom seen. An uncommon feature of this piece is that the front legs are trimmed down into long spikes which extend through the turned feet.

CORNER HANGING OR "RAIL" CUPBOARD (c. 1760). Found near Winchester, Virginia. It is of curly Virginia walnut and the hardware is original. The cornice molding has been restored. The raised and molded center portion of the drawer is unusual in its elaboration.

CABINETS
AND CHESTS

From the Middle Atlantic States

IN THE DAYS BEFORE BUILT-IN CLOSETS were considered a prime requisite in a home, cabinets and chests of various sizes and shapes served the same purpose. Surviving examples range all the way from convenient little wall cabinets a couple of feet wide to the huge and handsome cupboards usually known by their Dutch name, *kasten*, common in early New Netherlands and in Pennsylvania. The pieces which are illustrated here were selected not so much to represent types as to emphasize the individual differences to be observed in this one category. All were found in the Middle Atlantic region — Pennsylvania, Maryland, and Virginia — and all seem to have a homespun quality, native to the rural parts of that section. In strong contrast with the richness of Philadelphia furniture of the Chippendale period, or the elegance of Baltimore furniture in the Federal era, they have a robust simplicity that appeals to those who enjoy the essential quality of our American craftsmanship.

PINE HANGING CUPBOARD (*c. 1725–50*). Found near Wilkes-Barre, Pennsylvania. This cupboard appears to be entirely original. It had no cornice molding and was never intended to have doors, as is evident from the fact that the side and top members are molded along their inner edges and this molding is continued along the top and bottom edge of the center shelf. This cupboard and the walnut hanging cupboard below are scrolled at the bottom in a manner typical of the best ones of their period.

WALNUT HANGING CUPBOARD (*c. 1725*). Found in Maryland near the Pennsylvania line. It has rat-tail hinges, iron escutcheon, and beautifully scrolled open lock. The inside is fitted with one shelf below which is hung a row of three small drawers.

WALNUT KAS OR PRESS (*c. 1725*). From eastern Pennsylvania. The open scrolled lock, iron escutcheon, and rat-tailed hinges are almost identical in design with those on the walnut hanging cupboard above and could well have been made by the same craftsman. The top section as in many similar pieces is a separate cabinet unit. Cut-out openings in the bottom of this top section provide access to its "cubbyhole" where hats were stored. The straight bracket feet on this piece, less usual than ogee bracket feet on Pennsylvania items of this kind, are set on the outside limit of an extremely wide molding. The feet were strengthened in the making by long blocks, the same depth as the feet and secured to them, and hewn thinner as they extend diagonally across the bottom of the piece, to which they are also secured.

All illustrations except the blanket chest, from the collection of George H. Kernodle

Southern Provincial Furniture

SINCE elsewhere in this issue ANTIQUES is publishing a somewhat lengthy, though admittedly tentative, discussion of the old furniture of Charleston, South Carolina, the moment seems propitious for the portrayal of several furniture items from other parts of the South. Unfortunately, it is virtually impossible to subject the style of these pieces to any comprehensive analysis, since material for comparison is either quite lacking or is scattered beyond immediate hope of its reassembling for intensive study. It must suffice to let the illustrations speak for themselves, assisted by promptings from the Editor's chair.

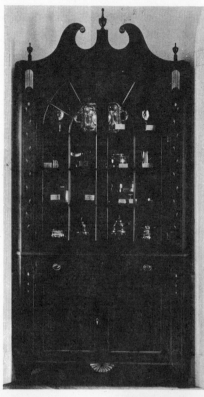

Fig. 1 (left) — CORNER CUPBOARD PROBABLY FROM VIRGINIA (*1790–1800*)
Of cherry. The general proportions, the delicate vine inlay, and the broken-arched top without crowning molding and with excessively small terminal scrolls, point to the Shenandoah Valley as the source of this quite impressive piece of cabinetwork.
From the collection of Mrs. J. Amory Haskell, lent to the Monmouth County Historical Society, Freehold, New Jersey

Fig. 2 (below) — VIRGINIA SECRETARY AND CORNER CUPBOARD (*1790–1800*)
Of mahogany. Made for Tusculum, the home built in the late 1700's by William Sidney Crawford near New Glasgow, Amherst County, Virginia. While tradition maintains that the furniture for Tusculum was imported from England, the style of the two pieces illustrated affords clear evidence of their local Virginia origin. Both are evidently the work of the same cabinetmaker. Seemingly characteristic of Virginia is the exceedingly delicate, almost attenuated form of the pediment scrolls. Like many other provincial pieces, the two illustrated combine mid-eighteenth-century features with others of considerably later implication.
From Tusculum, now owned by John Williams, a collateral descendant of William Crawford. Photographs by courtesy of Mary S. Yancey

Fig. 3 (*above, left*) — NORTH CAROLINA PINE HUNTBOARD (*c. 1800*)
While North Carolina cabinetmakers were partial to walnut, they also used pine extensively, not only for dressers, but for more sophisticated pieces such as this sideboard, which, because of its exceptional height, qualifies as a huntboard (see ANTIQUES for September 1932, *p. 105*). The severe lines of this piece suggest a date not far from 1800, though the legs, whose plainness is relieved by passages of fluting, apparently derive from Chippendale. A crude item, yet in design and execution showing evidence of the maker's intelligence and care.
From the collection of J. E. Catlin

Fig. 4 (*above, right*) — SOUTHERN PINE SERVING TABLE (*c. 1800*)
Found in Georgia, but not improbably made in the Carolinas. Thoroughly provincial in design but in its details betraying the hand of a careful workman.
From the collection of Mrs. F. A. Thayer

Fig. 6 (*below*) — NORTH CAROLINA WALNUT HIGH-POST BED (*eighteenth century*)
From Bath on the Pamlico River, one of the oldest communities in North Carolina, though now reduced to a few houses at a crossroads. Somewhat similar beds from the same locality have had tapered legs instead of the cabriole form. Note the chamfering of the inner line of the legs and the embryonic hoof feet. The scrolled board at one end may be a later addition. Rails are bored for ropework to support the mattress. Such provincial items, though lacking the refinement and elegance of form and craftsmanship that characterize the work of the notable cabinetmakers of New England, New York, and Pennsylvania, have a distinctive and agreeable flavor of their own. They do not mix well with more daintily constructed pieces, nor are they quite at home in highly stylized architectural surroundings; but in rooms such as the North Carolina installation in the Brooklyn Museum they are appropriate and effective.
From the collection of J. K. Beard

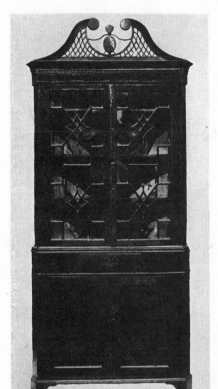

Fig. 5 — NORTH CAROLINA WALNUT CUPBOARD (*c. 1790–1800*)
From Hertford, on Albemarle Sound. Eighteenth-century houses and furniture from this part of North Carolina often exhibit highly individual traits. Something of Pennsylvania influence seems to be apparent in the pediment scrolls of this cupboard. The elaborate design of the door muntins finds almost exact counterpart in Chippendale's *Director* of 1754, Plate LXIII.
From the collection of J. K. Beard

Simple Furniture of the Old South

By MARY RALLS DOCKSTADER

Illustrations from the collection of Thomas R. Keesey

LITERALLY anyone equipped with technical knowledge and plenty of time and money can make a distinguished collection, whether it be of furniture, first editions, postage stamps, or bookplates. But it takes more than ordinary knowledge, backed by a compelling interest, to make a representative collection of such a commodity as rural Southern furniture without expending any great amount of either time or money. That it can be done, however, has been proved by Thomas Keesey, an Indiana man whose business has taken him frequently during the past several years through the states of North and South Carolina, Georgia, Alabama, and Tennessee. Since his intention has been to transplant his acquisitions to a lodge in an Indiana forest, he has been on the watch for simple domestic things, without specific concern as to their precise place of origin. Some of his finds are no doubt emigrants from other states than those in which Mr. Keesey has done his hunting. But, whatever their source, with the exception of a few items from Indiana, they are all Southern, at least by adoption.

A number of years will probably elapse before Mr. Keesey's dream is realized. In the meantime the collection has furnished his apartment in Atlanta with suitability and comfort, proving that good old furniture, like a real lady, is charming in any surroundings. Likewise it offers food for reflection. For example, it is pleasant to realize that simple though characteristic antiques are still comparatively plentiful and readily come by: Mr. Keesey's were picked up here and there, mostly from country dealers, without, as has been said, any undue outlay of time or effort. Perhaps this statement should be qualified by adding that antiques are fairly easy to find in the hands of dealers — not elsewhere.

And to the impersonal student, if one is ever impersonal concerning antiques, there is the evidence that more old-time middle-class furniture exists in the South than has formerly been supposed. From the time of settlement until well into the nineteenth century there were in this part of the country, especially along the seaboard, two main classes of inhabitants — the wealthy planters and the slaves; but there was also a sufficiently large less wealthy class, still far removed from the "poor whites," to leave behind a considerable legacy of attractive native furniture. The persons composing this class were farmers, with few or no slaves, as differentiated from the planters and from the tradesmen and others of moderate means belonging to the towns and cities.

The well-placed and traveled planters, we know, imported a large part of their household furnishings from Europe, and likewise patronized the fashionable cabinetmakers in New York, Philadelphia, Baltimore, and New Orleans. But all the furnishings of the early South did not come from outside her borders. The relentless hunt for the possessions of our forefathers is developing fresh evidence, both verbal and concrete, to show that, even in this preëminently agricultural region, there was many a little shop turning out maple candlestands, and pine cupboards, and walnut or cherry sideboards, for the local trade.

It even appears that, contrary to popular opinion, there were clockmakers in the South. While it is, of course, true that the factories of Terry, Thomas, Willard, and some others in New England made by far the greater percentage of the first American timepieces, in Georgia alone a number of clockmakers seem to have been at work. At Augusta, the firm of Dyer, Wadsworth & Company was well known, and clocks bearing the label *A. Sage & Company, Wholesale and Retail, Savannah, Geo.* are still found. In the Savannah *Georgian* for March 17, 1829, one Balthazar François announces that he has lately arrived from France and set up an establishment on Bull Street, where he is prepared to make clocks and firearms for the community. Darwin & Seymour of Macon, and Davis & Barber of

Fig. 1 — HUNT BOARD FROM COWPENS (*c. 1800*)
Built of walnut and pine. Comfortably tall, after the fashion of such pieces. The crockery is English ware; candlesticks probably Sandwich dolphins. Wall lights are coach lanterns

Fig. 2 — Pine Bookcase Secretary
   A curious piece evidently of rural Southern design and construction. The chair is an early nineteenth-century Southern Windsor

Greensboro, were other Georgian firms selling clocks. Whether they made both works and cases, or merely the latter, buying the works from the indefatigable New Englanders who peddled their clockworks on horseback about the country, it seems impossible now to determine. Since all of the examples bearing these names are of the tall, shelf variety, they must have been made sometime between the years 1815 and 1850.

In Alfred Coxe Prime's volume, *The Arts and Crafts in Philadelphia, Maryland, and South Carolina, 1721–1785*, published by the Walpole Society, 1929, a number of clockmakers are quoted as advertising their trade in Charleston during the eighteenth century — notably Joshua Lockwood and William Lee. A handsome long-case clock, made by William Lee, who was working in Charleston in 1717, is cited by Hudson Moore as still in that city, and in working order.

But to return to the subject of general furniture. Now that the South has been practically cleaned of its finer pieces, except those to be found in private collections or in the hands of important

dealers, the plainer things such as those Mr. Keesey has sought have begun to emerge in increasing numbers. It is surprising that so many should have survived the wear and tear of usage, the hazards of war, and the demands of the class ever on the alert for gifts of second-hand furniture — which gifts, once bestowed, usually suffered a swift dissolution.

A number of pieces in the Keesey collection can be traced to their origin in the communities in which they were bought. There is an especially good six-leg, cherry table with wood of a bright, rich color, which was found in Tennessee. Recently I have seen two others of the same type from the same state, clear indication that all were from the shop of some local Tennessee cabinetmaker. So much good cherry furniture — beds, tables, chests, and cupboards — has been located in Tennessee, and so abundant are the wild cherry trees in the Cumberland Mountains, that there can be no doubt that the furnituremakers of the state simply made use of the materials that they found ready to hand.

Fig. 3 — Walnut Dresser (*early eighteenth century*)
   An imposing specimen, found near Greensboro, North Carolina. Foreign and American pewter dominated by the fine covered pitcher at the top. The chair is a slat back from Georgia

The *pièce de résistance* of this collection is a huge old walnut dresser from North Carolina (*Fig. 3*). It was found near Greensboro, and is entirely original, even to the handwrought H and L hinges. Previous to its acquisition by Mr. Keesey, it had stood in a cellar for fifty years, a repository for preserves. Mr. Keesey has its family history; it is unquestionably of North Carolina origin and is contemporary with the walnut stretcher table (*Fig. 8*) that was purchased with it.

Both pieces have taken on new life under the sympathetic hands of the refinisher. Instead of preserves, the dresser now harbors pewter, which is quite as it should be. Old inventories show that pewter, some of it imported, some native, was a familiar household accessory in the South. Mr. Keesey has fine examples of English, Dutch, and American make, most of it found in North Carolina. Even more interesting, historically, are the pewter molds picked up in isolated sections, indicating that the traveling pewterer was a familiar figure in the earlier-settled states.

Alluring because of its age and materials is a small tavern table from Spartanburg, South Carolina, with walnut top, and legs and stretchers of chinaberry wood (*Fig. 6*). The chinaberry tree, or "pride of India," as it was once romantically called, is a tender, soft-wooded tree incapable of withstanding the cold Northern winters, which is proof enough that this little table origi-

Fig. 6 — WALNUT AND CHINA-BERRY TABLE (*c. 1750*) From Spartanburg, South Carolina

nated somewhere in the South. It is only rarely that one finds chinaberry wood used for furniture. The table would hardly date later than the middle of the eighteenth century and might be earlier, since, with Charleston to set the pace by both importing and manufacturing quantities of furniture, South Carolina was extremely well supplied with the newest and best in household equipment. One old dealer who has

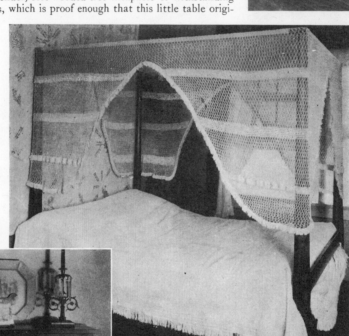

Fig. 5 — FOUR-POST BED IN YELLOW PINE (*eighteenth century*) A piece deserving of less uncompromising draperies

spent a long life in traveling up and down through the region mentioned vouches for the truth of the statement that there was one cabinetmaker in Charleston who employed sixty slaves in his workshop. However this may be, there were certainly furnituremakers in the lovely old city by the sea, and their advertisements are quoted in Mr. Prime's book.

A notice from Savannah of a quite different order catches my eye. Among the death records for the year 1803 occur those of "A Cabinet Maker" and of "A Windsor Chair Maker." At the date mentioned, Windsor chairs had already passed the meridian of their popularity, so that we may safely assume that the deceased was not the first maker of Windsors in the state of Georgia.

Mr. Keesey's Windsors are of various types, ranging from very early, low-backed examples with vase-turned legs, to the later fan backs, whose legs display the less desirable bamboo turnings. He has also slat backs, both splint and rush bottomed. One of a matched pair of the latter, from Georgia, is shown in Figure 3 standing at the side of the big Carolina dresser. The slats and stretchers are hickory and the legs, maple.

Among the larger pieces are a six-foot maple bench, worn satin-smooth, and two specimens of yellow pine — a tester bed with slender posts and fishnet canopy (*Fig. 5*), and a curious bookcase secretary (*Fig. 2*). A sturdy

Fig. 4 — SMALL HUNT BOARD (*c. 1800*) A delicate and well-constructed piece, of walnut

examples were acquired chiefly from country dealers in a sparsely settled section, where household goods were seldom wont to travel far from the neighborhoods that knew them first.

This collection, then, while interesting in itself, seems likewise to point a moral, or at least to adorn a surmise, to the effect that among the original Colonies there were fewer divergencies of style than has often been believed; that, as someone has put it, William Byrd of Westover and John Hancock of Boston warmed themselves before much the same kind of mantels and ate their food from much the same sort of tables, the difference being that one preferred Virginia "spots," and the other, cod.

Note. — My thanks are due all those persons who so kindly assisted me in ascertaining the facts preserved in this article. I am especially indebted to Mrs. Craig Barrow, Savannah, Georgia; to the staff of the Charleston Museum, Charleston, South Carolina; to that of the Carnegie Library, Atlanta, Georgia; and to Wallace Nutting, Framingham, Massachusetts.   — M. R. D.

Fig. 7— WALNUT SUGAR CHEST
An unusually good example. The pottery pitcher above it is of more than passing interest

Fig. 9 (below) — WALL SHELVES Showing an interesting collection of iron and pottery lamps

sugar chest of walnut (*Fig. 7*), from Tennessee, with businesslike lock and key to preserve the precious white sugar from the depredations of servants, is characteristically Southern. Equally Southern in type and origin is a walnut-

Fig. 8 — LONG TABLE OF WALNUT
From near Greensboro, North Carolina. The chairs are typical Southern slat backs. The contents of the corner cupboard range from Staffordshire to Sandwich

and-pine bow-front hunt board (*Fig. 1*) — considerably smaller than the usual run of these boards — from the historic village of Cowpens. It stands under a good copy of that rollicking picture, *The Melton Breakfast.* Such hunt boards became popular early in the life of the Colonies, especially from Virginia southward, where there were vast territories over which to pursue the elusive fox. They must have been a great boon to gentlemen who, having spent arduous hours in the saddle, riding neck and crop across field and ditch, returned at length to stand at ease about these little long-legged boards, partaking freely of the baked hams and the game and the rum punches generously provided. It was all very British and very delightful.

Of the array of old china, glass, bottles, and other small objects that find themselves so much at home on the shelves of the pine cupboards probably the only items of native manufacture are those of wrought iron and pottery. The Betty lamps (*Fig. 9*) are quite unusual in their delicacy, and at least one of the crude pottery fat lamps was still in use when found in the Tennessee mountains. But Staffordshire, Stiegel, Bennington, Sandwich are here in unmistakable array to demonstrate their wide distribution from early times. These

CHESTS FROM WESTERN LONG ISLAND

By HUYLER HELD

FEW types of furniture made prior to 1710 and specifically characteristic of the New York area have thus far been identified and classified. Perhaps not more than a dozen types would suffice to cover the known field. To this number, insignificant in comparison with the many known forms of New England seventeenth-century furniture, may well be added the Long Island ball-footed chest.

Two examples of this type were shown at Mineola, Long Island, in 1936 as part of Nassau County's celebration of the Long Island Tercentenary (*Figs. 1 and 2*). The interest they aroused was based primarily on the fact that here was an obviously early item of New York origin which had not been generally known, presented in a museum, or discussed in writings on American antiques.

Despite a search covering eight or nine years, I have seen but four examples of this type of chest. Three are here pictured (*Figs. 1, 2, and 3*). The fourth appeared at an auction sale on Long Island several years ago, with newly constructed bracket feet replacing the original ball feet, and the original form of the chest concealed by other extensive alterations. I have learned of the existence of a fifth example, but have not had opportunity to inspect it. All of the four chests I have seen were found in one locality, namely, within a section ten miles square in Nassau County, Long Island. Thus, the chest of Figure 1 for several generations was owned by the Allen family of Mill Neck. That of Figure 2 was found in Roslyn, Long Island; while the chest of Figure 3 came from Oyster Bay, and is now on exhibit there at Old Raynham, headquarters of the local chapter of the Daughters of the American Revolution.

In my opinion, the date of these chests would probably not be later than 1715; it might be as early as 1690. In arriving at this estimate I have considered the scarcity of examples, the early form of keyplate, and above all, certain points of construction rarely found in pieces made later than 1715. The body of the chest itself is of stile and rail construction, and to that extent reminiscent of paneled chests of New England origin. However, unlike the earlier Connecticut Valley oak chests, the rails at top and bottom run completely across the front of the chest, and the stiles connect them instead of serving as corner posts. Each of the square panels is rabbeted into the stiles, in accordance with New England practice, and is outlined with molding affixed to the panel itself. A later period would probably have produced a drawer with lip or bead molding.

My conviction as to the approximate age of this type of chest was recently shaken by the discovery of a somewhat similar example, illustrated in Figure 4. This chest bears brasses, affixed with bolts, of a type that was probably not used in this country before 1730, or manufactured in England before 1720. Further variations between this chest and the other three occur. The wooden pins used on the face of the earlier chests show a certain symmetrical arrangement, which differs from that of the pins in the later chest. Moldings around the panels of Figure 4 are sunk below the surface of the piece instead of projecting. Dimensions of all four chests — depth and width of carcass, depth of drawers, and height — are approximately the same. Variations are negligible, ranging from a fraction of an inch to about two inches.

Figure 1 is hinged with butterfly hinges; the lid of the till box of Figure 2 is attached with the same type of hardware. Such hinges were probably not employed on Long Island furniture after 1710, although they continued in use in New England perhaps as late as 1730. Figure 4 carries the cockscomb hinge, unquestionably later than either butterfly hinges or the staple hinges on the lid of Figure 3. The cockscomb hinge is found in the New York two-paneled chest with early bracket feet, which usually dates between 1720 and 1740. So far as I know, such chests never exhibit the butterfly form of hinge.

During the fourth quarter of the seventeenth century and the early part of the eighteenth, chests were a common article of furniture on Long Island, as in New England. Presumably chests identical in type were used in both localities. This would be true

FIG. 1 — LONG ISLAND TWO-PANELED CHEST (*c. 1700–1710*)
Mentioned in a will of 1749. For several generations owned in Mill Neck, Oyster Bay. *From the collection of George Allen*

FIG. 2 — LONG ISLAND TWO-PANELED CHEST (*c. 1700–1710*)
A section of the base molding is missing from the right end of the chest. *From the author's collection*

FIG. 3 — LONG ISLAND TWO-PANELED CHEST (*c. 1700–1710*)
On exhibit at Old Raynham, Oyster Bay The base molding on the front is probably an early replacement. The drawer handles on this piece, like those of Figures 1 and 2, were attached not with bolts, but with cotter pins

FIG. 4 — LONG ISLAND TWO-PANELED CHEST (*c. 1700–1710*)
Brown varnish or stain has been applied over the original finish, which was probably "Dutch blue" paint.
From the collection of Mrs. Frederick W. Seaman

particularly of the eastern end of Long Island, where there was little, if any, Dutch influence. The ball-footed chests of our present concern, however, clearly show blending of Dutch and English characteristics.

Dutch influence is revealed chiefly in the so-called ball feet, which are virtually identical with the feet found on certain local *kas*. The turned ball in front is connected with the bootjack foot in the rear by a plain board, nailed on. As in the case of the local *kas*, this support is never attached to the bottom of the chest itself (*Fig. 5*). When we compare the separate feet shown in Figure 5 with the feet of New England chests, we find that in the latter the ball, turnip, or similar type of foot was doweled into or, on rare occasions, nailed to the frame.

In the body of the chest itself we find further unusual structural features. In both Long Island and New England chests a cleat is usually found under the projecting side edges of the lid. On the Long Island chest there is also a strip of wood or molding under the front projection of the lid. In New England the side cleat was usually nailed from the bottom and was not flush with the edge of the overlap. In Long Island practice the cleats or moldings on sides and front were fastened with nails driven through the lid from the top and were made flush with the edges of the lid. The nail heads were driven deep and covered with wooden plugs.

While New England chests may have one, two, or three drawers, I have not discovered any of these Long Island paneled chests with more than one drawer, nor have I found an example without a drawer, although unpaneled chests of the same period without drawers but with identical lid construction and ball feet have come to my attention. It should be noted that, while all the chests

under discussion have two panels, in New England the use of three panels was the general, though not the absolute, rule.

In these Long Island chests the material used for lid, front, sides, and drawer fronts is pine. I do not recall ever having seen local *kas* feet made of wood other than oak stained or painted black, perhaps to imitate ebony. Yet the feet on the chests of Figures 1, 2, and 3, otherwise analogous to *kas* feet, are of pine. In concealed portions, such as drawer slides and horizontal supports of the feet, almost any kind of wood may be found. In these chests several varieties of hard wood occur.

So far as I can judge, the chests were always painted. Figures 1 and 2 are still covered with the blue paint so popular among the Dutch in New York and its environs, which, with the passing of time, has changed almost to gray. The paint on Figure 2 is original; that on Figure 1 was presumably applied within a few years after the chest's construction, since under it vestiges of red remain on all surfaces and a trace of black remains on all moldings and feet.

Certain minor differences occur among the three chests. The feet of Figure 1 are more nearly spherical than those of the other chests, though all belong to the ball category. The base molding of the same chest is somewhat less elaborate than that of Figure 3, which I believe to be a replacement. (That of Figure 2 is so worn as to be indistinct.) Upright moldings at either end of the drawer vary slightly in each case. Nevertheless, it seems reasonable to conclude that all three chests are the work of one craftsman. Chest 4 I do not believe to have been made by the same person, unless at a considerably later date. It might possibly have been made by an apprentice or son of the original joiner. In these conclusions I am supported by J. L. Cummings of Hempstead, Long Island.

FIG. 5 — "KAS" AND CHEST FEET
a, *b*, and *c* are typical *kas* feet; *d* and *e* are, respectively, from the chests of Figures 2 and 1; *f* may have come from a small, unpaneled chest; *g* is the front post of a Long Island chair showing a foot similar in outline to some *kas* feet and apparently peculiar to the locality

PAINTED CHESTS
FROM THE CONNECTICUT VALLEY

By J. L. CUMMINGS

DURING the summer of 1933, I chanced to be calling in a historic town in central Massachusetts. Here I was shown a very interesting painted or japanned chest of drawers. It was black, decorated with crude figures in many respects like those found on the japanned furniture of the early eighteenth century. This was not particularly startling; but I was surprised to discover high on the right side of the chest and toward the rear the painted date *1735* with a line above it. The measurements of this piece of furniture I found to be: depth, 21 inches; width, 34 ½ inches; height, 37 inches. Its fittings consisted of two small drawers in the top and three large ones below, with their early cotter-pin brasses still in place. Apparently original and untouched, the piece was still in possession of the family that first owned it.

Three years later I found in a small country antique shop a first cousin to the chest just described. This example differed from the first chiefly in

FIG. 1a — DATE ON CHEST OF FIGURE 1

showing three, instead of two, drawers at the top (*Fig. 1*). Its construction and decoration were to all intents the same as those noted in the previously described item. However, this second example carries the date *1738*. Said to have been found in the vicinity of Amherst, Massachusetts, it is in reasonably good condition, and retains almost its entire quota of cotter-pin brasses.

In the fall of 1936, I met with a third member of this curious group of chests (*Fig. 2*). It is identical with the second except for its date, *1737*, and for the fact that it stands on turnip-shaped feet, whereas its relatives are supported on crude brackets. The finish of this last example is rather the worse for wear, and the brasses are missing; but its decorations and its inscribed date are visible. The dimensions of these three pieces do not vary by more than a fraction of an inch.

About this time, I observed a small two-drawer chest, then owned by Charles O. Cornelius, on exhibition in the Metropolitan Museum of Art.

FIG. 1 — "JAPANNED" CHEST OF DRAWERS (*dated 1738*)
Of pine; with maple drawer fronts. Decorated with curious designs applied with heavy yellowish paint, perhaps ochre. This piece and its fellow (*Fig. 2*), while in technique of decoration painted rather than japanned, qualify in the general category of japanned furniture. The date, more distinct than it appears in the illustration, is shown above

FIG. 2 — "JAPANNED" CHEST OF DRAWERS (*dated 1737*)
Evidently by the artisan who produced the chest of Figure 1. The term *lacquer work*, strictly speaking, is applicable only to oriental decoration accomplished with a natural varnish, derived from the sap of certain trees. "Japanned work" is a western imitation of the oriental product. It really consists of coats of paint protected by sundry varnishes

FIG. 3 — NEW ENGLAND PAINTED HIGHBOY (1730–1740)

Apparently undated. But in the form of its upper case and in general decoration clearly associated with the dated chests of drawers here illustrated. The fact that the tops of the latter show dovetailing, and in general design accord with the upper case of this highboy, suggests that they may once have been similarly supported on a base. They were found north of the Connecticut boundary. This highboy, on the contrary, is reputed to have come from Windsor, Connecticut. Whatever their particular source, highboy and chests of drawers are evidently the product of the same shop.

From the collection of Mrs. J. Insley Blair. Photograph by courtesy of the Metropolitan Museum of Art, New York

It was of the same workmanship and finish as the three described. On this chest, the place where the date may once have been painted is discernible. The construction and decoration are very like those of the other articles mentioned.

We have, then, four chests exhibiting characteristics that seem to proclaim their common origin, and their fabrication and decoration during the second quarter of the eighteenth century. All seemingly are of rural Massachusetts provenance. The case of these pieces is invariably of pitch pine; the drawer fronts of maple, which in some instances is figured. No drawer runs are in evidence, separation and support for the drawers deriving from fairly wide lengthwise boards. The drawer bottoms are secured to the sides by nailing from below, and are faced with thin strips to facilitate their sliding to and fro. The chest tops are secured with board dovetailing and are finished, though not decorated. The molding between drawers and along edges is of the double-arch variety. All the features enumerated pertain to years at least as early as the dates painted on the furniture.

The paint, or japan, which constitutes the ground for the decoration differs somewhat from usual paint in that it may be softened with pure alcohol and removed with dilute ammonia. The ornamental figures are perceptibly in relief and are heavily laid on with some thick, light-colored, highly resistant pigment. Except for a slight darkening, they have successfully defied the effects of time and wear. They are even immune to the action of many of the chemicals used for the removal of paint.

The decorative motives consist of figures of men and women; lions, camels, deer, foxes, dogs, and even squirrels; birds, especially peacocks; trees, foliage, and flowers. The figures, singly and collectively, suggest Chinese inspiration, but have been metamorphosed into the American vernacular, with a distinctly provincial flavor. Their naïve whimsicality is unusually attractive.

I record these chests without any insistence upon their value or importance. I wish only to call to the attention of antiquaries certain pieces showing almost identical features of structure and decoration, and without doubt hailing from the same shop in the Connecticut Valley. Perhaps, then, I have uncovered part of a considerable furniture group whose precise source and authorship may be determined by further investigation. In such an undertaking the unusual occurrence of inscribed dates on the pieces observed should prove helpful. The locality where enquiry and investigation might be productive is the Connecticut Valley, probably south of Hadley, Massachusetts, and north of the Connecticut boundary. Yet in these limitations we must not place unquestioning confidence. Early in 1933, the Metropolitan Museum of Art staged an exhibition of American japanned furniture. Among the more significant articles shown was a highboy whose decorative embellishment in all respects conforms to that of the chests here considered. This highboy, in the collection of Mrs. J. Insley Blair of Tuxedo Park, New York, is reputed to have come originally from Windsor, Connecticut. The arrangement of the drawers of its upper section is almost precisely what we encounter in the chests found in Massachusetts. This circumstance raises question as to whether or not these chests were at the outset the tops of highboys, which, to facilitate transportation, were subsequently deprived of their lower members. Some such process of dismemberment and belated substitution of new underpinnings should be viewed as at least a possibility. Mrs. Blair's highboy is illustrated on page 47 of the Metropolitan Museum *Bulletin* for March 1933, in conjunction with a brief but illuminating discussion by Joseph Downs, and with Mrs. Blair's permission is again portrayed in conjunction with the present note (*Fig. 3*).

BIRDS—QUILTED, PATCHED, AND WOVEN

By FLORENCE PETO

peacock was the proud bird of Juno. In early Christian art the peacock was the symbol of immortality and, therefore, of the Resurrection, of Christ risen from the dead; the bird was frequently depicted with a nimbus. In Europe and in America a live peacock added the final touch of grandeur to the country

FIG. 1 — PATCHWORK QUILT (*dated 1858*)
The stylized design of the patches and more particularly of the quilting suggests peacock feathers. *From the collection of Mrs. Paul Sturtevant*

FIG. 2 — APPLIQUÉ QUILT (*prior to 1800*)
Chintz pheasants appliquéd to homespun cotton. The quilting of the ground is so fine as to be imperceptible in the reproduction. *From the collection of Mrs. Philemon K. Wright*

WHENEVER birds appear in the ornamentation of American-made patchwork quilts and coverlets, their grace and color contribute to richness of plan and pattern. At the same time, it seems that the quiltmakers must have had an appreciation of symbolism, and often employed different feathered species for the sake of allusion and sentiment.

Artists, craftsmen, and many needlewomen succumbed to the fascination of the peacock's decorative form and brilliant plumage. In some localities the cock's feathers were considered unlucky; in spite of the superstition, his plumes collected dust in many old-time parlors. My own New York Dutch grandmother had a vase of showy tail feathers on her marble-topped table; at every hint of misadventure to any member of the family she blamed the feathers and threatened to throw them out — but never did. In mythology the

226

estate; on a golden platter, roasted, he satisfied the epicurean taste of royalty; on the farm he was not only a weather prophet but a reliable "watchbird," giving his shrill cry at the approach of strangers. Pennsylvania-German artists portrayed the peacock's iridescent splendor on bridal chests, bandboxes, furniture, and crockery, on birth and baptismal certificates and house blessings done in *fractur*. In old books of German Pennsylvania he is placed on representations of the Ark; the artists show him sitting on the ridgepole side by side with the dove and the pelican. Aware of this strong predilection, English manufacturers designed printed chintz and other cotton goods especially for the Pennsylvania market, lavishly sprinkling them with peacocks.

The quilt of Figure 1 bears, in ink, the signature and address of the maker, *Thomas W. Nable of Claysville, Pa.*, and the date, *October 26, 1858.* Its colors are green (once patterned but now faded and indefinite), brilliant red, and tawny orange, on a white muslin background. This appliqué

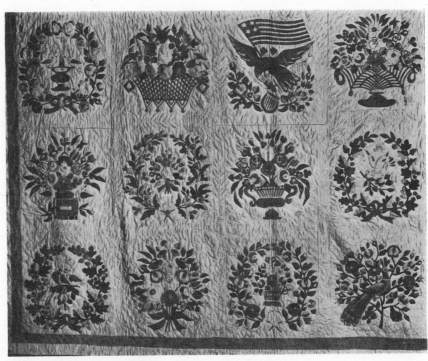

FIG. 3 — DETAIL OF BALTIMORE BRIDE'S QUILT (*dated 1851*)
Showing American eagle, peacock, and — appropriately — love birds in profusion.
Formerly in the collection of Mrs. Lawrence Ullman

FIG. 4 — DOUBLE-WOVEN COVERLET (*c. 1830*)
In three colors — blue, red, and natural — resplendent with peacocks and turkeys. A striking and unusual design.
From the collection of Mrs. E. H. Mays

piece, unusual in having been made by a man, is interesting too for its highly stylized design. In the applied patches, though they are floral in general appearance, the peacock is suggested: slender spines for leaves and "eyes" of tail feathers for blossoms; the technique of reverse appliqué, in which the flowers are made, adds to the illusion. In the quilting stitchery the implication is stronger, for long, feathery plumes ending in clusters of "eyes" have been disposed skillfully to preserve the integrity of their natural form and still to cover the background surface. Lest this interpretation of the design seem far-fetched, one single, rather lonely-looking peacock, perched on a flower spray, left and below center, supplies the decorative motive.

After the middle of the eighteenth century, when the new process of machine-printing by means of copper rollers had revolutionized the cotton-printing industry, upholstery furnishings and draperies of all sorts made of the new material soon appeared in well-to-do households in the colonies. The new prints were monochromes — blue on white, brown on white, and pink or red on white. They displayed classical or pastoral scenes and historical allegories, and not a few featured in their compositions magnificent bird groups. The peacock dominates a repeat pattern a yard square which is reproduced as the Cover design of this issue of ANTIQUES.

Peacocks are not the only birds used in old coverlet patterns. In the spread of Figure 2, pheasants cut from a handsome English chintz are appliquéd to a background of fine homespun cotton cloth which has become, with the magic of passing years, a deep cream in tone. Flowers and branches are softly pastel in shades of brown and rose, but the birds still sparkle with iridescent shadings. The intermediate area has been closely covered with quilting stitches, so minutely spaced as to give a crêpelike effect suggestive of stippling. A hand-knotted fringe finished the edges. Such bedcovers, thinly interlined, were intended for use as counterpanes — for beauty, not warmth. This quilt descended to a cousin of General Richard Thomas. The General, who was born at Piney Neck, Queen Anne County, Maryland, in 1815, claimed that it had been made by his aunt (name unrecorded) at some time prior to 1800. At Kenmore, home of Betty Lewis, George Washington's sister. there is on exhibition a piece of quilt with almost identical arrangement and similar print, which, it is claimed, was made just before the Revolution.

A coverlet of the double-woven variety (*Fig. 4*) displays an impressive repeat pattern of peacocks and turkeys. The piece was made on the Harris farm, near Belmont, Ohio, about 1830. It is rich in three colors — dark-blue and coppery-red filling of wool on a warp of natural flax. According to Mary Meigs Atwater, double weaving was within the capacity of the domestic weaver who possessed a suitable loom; yet such an intricate design as is shown here involved a complicated technique, and it is more than likely that *Peacocks and Turkeys* was the product of a professional weaver — possibly one of the traveling craftsmen who set up his own loom somewhere on the farm property and wove a coverlet from yarn already prepared, spun, and dyed by the housewife. Support is lent to this theory by the striking resemblance between this coverlet and one reproduced on the cover of ANTIQUES for December 1936. Though the two differ in border and in minor details, they are so similar in form and disposition of the fowl, of the leafy branches, of the stars and rosettes, and even of the grapevine — or is it a fountain? — between the confronted turkeys, as to leave little doubt that both were made by the same weaver. The example previously illustrated, which is now in the Thayer Museum of Art of the University of Kansas, was made, according to an inscription in one corner, in Cadiz, Ohio. As the crow flies, Cadiz is less than twenty miles from Belmont, so it is entirely likely that the two towns lay in the itinerary of one weaver. As for their inspiration, turkeys were portrayed often enough on early textiles. Doctor Franklin, it will be recalled, regretted that the wild turkey was not chosen as the bird to ornament the Great Seal of the United States, for he considered the turkey a "true native of America and a respectable bird, moreover." To Americans, the turkey is the symbol of abundance, everlastingly associated with Thanksgiving.

Even a confirmed misogamist can do no less than admit the romantic appeal and significance of love birds, and smile at those adorning the Baltimore bride's quilt of which a detail is shown in Figure 3. On the entire quilt, composed of twenty-five autographed and dated (*1851*) blocks, love birds appear fourteen times — always in pairs and facing each other in attitudes of mutual adoration. A magnificent American eagle assumes protective posture in the center of the quilt. With less spirit but with great pride a peacock poses on a rosebush; a wavy-figured, plum-colored print ingeniously suggests plumage, while round patches of turquoise blue make "eyes" in his tail feathers. This example of needlework shows appliqué technique at its peak of elegant finesse and exquisite workmanship. Small details on the opulent flowers, fruits, leaves, and birds have been penned with India ink, not embroidered. Signatures show fanciful flourishes and scrolls. Theoretically, each square in this type of quilt was made by a different friend of the bride — truly an album piece, for remembrance — but it is my feeling that autographed quilts were not always made by those whose names appear on the separate blocks. Sewing, like penmanship, reveals personal characteristics; twenty-five women, however expert with the needle, were not likely to

have produced uniformity of style and accomplishment. There might have been professional needlewomen in Baltimore and possibly in other localities who specialized in making fine quilts and spreads for bridal trousseaux, though thus far I have come across no evidence to support the idea except the character of the work itself.

The dove, which appears on the Baltimore bride's quilt directly above the peacock, was significant of various concepts. On a bride's quilt it was a prophetic symbol of conjugal felicity; hovering over a cradle (as on one of my Pennsylvania-German quilts) it was an emblem of innocence; olive branch in beak, it was the harbinger of peace. Figure 6 shows a detail of a friendship quilt; each of the blocks was made by a different young female acquaintance or relative of William Henry Vernon of Baltimore, on the occasion of his coming of age in 1840. Such quilts were often known as freedom quilts. At that period a young man was entirely under the jurisdiction of his father until he reached his majority; even wages earned by him were payable to his male parent. A freedom quilt, signalizing his attainment of personal independence, usually abounded in symbols and figures intended to strengthen his patriotic loyalties and develop manly virtues; the eagle, the flag, anchors, ships, guns, horses, and dogs, were plentiful, and invariably included were many insignia and devices of the various fraternal orders in which the young man, now adult, was eligible for membership. The first lodge of Odd Fellows in this country was founded in Baltimore the year of William Henry Vernon's birth, and he later became a member. The quilt was not assembled until the year of William's marriage to Henrietta Le Compté Lusby in November 1846 — which happened to be the year that had seen the death, in May, of Major Samuel Ringgold. This Maryland soldier, born in 1800, fought with valor against the Florida Indians, and eventually died from wounds received in the battle of Palo Alto, the first engagement of the Mexican War. For inclusion in her young husband's freedom quilt, Henrietta Vernon made a block to commemorate the soldier-hero's death. Below and to the right of the eagle is Ringgold's monument in brown calico, with crossed flags, stacked guns, floral tributes, and, on the tombstone, a plaque showing the eagle, bursting shells, and the name *Ringgold*. Above the peak of the monument hovers a dove; its upward flight suggests the warrior's spirit on its quest for eternal peace. One recalls depictions of the dove in religious art, issuing from between the lips of dying saints.

The bald-headed eagle as a symbol of American independence is almost commonplace. Artists and craftsmen have wrought his figure in both precious and humble materials; the quiltmakers depicted his protective spread of wing on innumerable patchwork quilts. Sometimes the likeness of the noble bird was executed with rare skill; often the results were ornithic enigmas, but the intention to do honor to the symbol was obvious.

The uncommon technique of Italian quilting was used by Mary Ann Mount on a white spread (*Fig. 5*). A coverlet of this type was not designed for warmth — its purpose was solely decorative. By sewing double rows of quilting stitchery through two layers of cloth a narrow channel was made through which cord or roving was introduced from the back; the lower layer of material had to be something coarsely woven, to allow the introduction of the cord and also to facilitate additional padding with wool or cotton for completing details of the design. In this quilt thirteen stars, crossed flags, the protective American eagle. and a scroll inscribed *Mary Ann Mount/September 1. 1864*, hold central interest. Two houses represent the Mount homestead before and after an extension had been added to accommodate a growing family; the dwelling still stands, at Navesink, New Jersey (formerly called Riceville), on a branch of the Shrewsbury River. The quiltmaker made three matching quilts — the large one illustrated. one of crib size, and a cradle cover — for her sister, Cornelia Mount Peto; the initials *M.A.M. to C.M.P.* appear on each piece. The Mounts were a family of closely-knit affections and intense fondness for their home. These sentiments are reflected in Mary Ann's needlework designs. Beautiful shade and fruit trees surrounded the little house and — special pride of Mary's father — water fowl, domestic and wild, paddled happily in the secluded stream. Swans, a turkey, a peacock, and unidentified water birds apparently of the genus duck, vie with patriotic motives.

Wrapped in the folds of the age-mellowed quilts was found a *Scriptural Album with Floral Decorations;* it had belonged to Cornelia, and in it the whole Mount family and its friends had expressed their sentiments in verse, with the tinge of Victorian gloom which conformed to the era's standards of gentility and fashion. While these have no bearing upon birds or quilts, I cannot resist quoting a few, by Cornelia, her brother, and her sisters.

FIG. 5 — DETAIL OF ITALIAN-QUILTED BEDSPREAD (*dated 1864*)
From the collection of Mrs. Cornelia Bird Spahn

FIG. 6 — DETAIL OF FREEDOM QUILT (*1840–1846*)
From the collection of Miss Grace Vernon Smith

MISS CORNELIA MOUNT'S ALBUM
My Album is a chosen spot
Where all my friends may sow
Where thorns and thistles flourish not
But flowers alone may grow.

I never from my father heard
Through all my happy life
A single false deceitful word
Or one of angry strife;
For power or place he has not sought

But for his country's weal
His heart has always had a thought
Of patriotic zeal.

Life's end is hastening and time wings his rapid flight
And earth with all its loveliness must soon fade from thy sight.

Cornelia! my love for thee
Is like the cornel tree
Once taken root, though slow, its growth is sure;
It is no passion flower
Lasting one summer hour;
While my heart lives — that feeling will endure.

TO MY SISTER CORNELIA LATELY MARRIED
Let not my sister, though a wife
Bid all her fears adieu,
Comforts there are in married life
But there are crosses too.

I do not wish to mar your mirth
With an ungrateful sound;
But yet remember bliss on earth
No mortal ever found.

Though you have left a parent's wing
No longer ask its care
It is but seldom husbands bring
A lighter yoke to wear.

They have their humors and their faults
So mutable is man;
Excuse his failings in your thoughts
And hide them if you can!

In spite of this frank family pessimism, Cornelia Mount Peto lived to be eighty-two years old, adored by her husband and beloved by eight children. The spreads are now owned by a great-grandchild, Mrs. Cornelia Bird Spahn.

THREE GENERATIONS OF QUILTS

By FLORENCE PETO

EXAMINATION OF PATCHWORK quilts made through successive generations will reveal interesting cycles of taste in composition and design. From the earliest days of patchwork, through the years when needlework was practiced by every female member of the household, to the time when the sewing machine appeared, the influence of expediency is increasingly apparent. Convenience in handling and availability of manufactured cloth were factors in this evolution. Thus designs on quilts show a relationship to the eras in which they were made. The three quilts here reproduced may serve to illustrate the point.

The Ann Heck spread (*Fig. 1*) is a fine example of late-eighteenth-century patchwork. From a central medallion the pattern is built out in a series of five borders of varying widths; these alternate piecework with appliqué. Though simplicity and restraint prevail the finished work has an air of elegance. Except for the vases and flower bouquets cut from highly glazed English chintz, the material is homespun, home-dyed linen, ivory white for the background with a peculiar yellow-gold flecked with black predominating in the inner borders. The outer border displays rose tones, as do the flowers of the Chinese-patterned chintz. Pleasing blue is seen in the vases. The excellent quilting, in homespun thread, treats each border as a unit; *princess feather* in graceful curves surrounds the central vase, while *lover's knot, clam shell, loop,* and close horizontal lines enrich the succeeding borders. The dimensions are very large, the width greater than the length; the binding is hand-loomed braid.

Paul and Barbara Heck came to New York from Ireland on the ship *Perry* in 1760. Barbara (*1734-1804*) helped Philip Embury to organize the first Methodist Society in this country; for her zeal she was called the mother of Methodism in America. When the Revolution came, the Hecks, who were Loyalists, went to Canada, where they were again founders of Methodism, in the province of Ontario. In spite of tireless devotion to a cause, Barbara found time to instruct her daughter Ann in the domestic arts. This quilt, product of Ann's handiwork, was owned by the Brookfields, an old New Jersey family, who lived in Newark for over a hundred years. It is now the bequest of Mrs. August Baker Brookfield to the Newark Museum in memory of her husband.

Soon after this quilt was made, the favorite way of constructing a patch quilt came to be in unit blocks, a method more convenient for handling, as most of the work may be done before the final joining together. Moreover, great variety may be achieved, for the blocks may be set together with latticework, strips, or alternate white blocks, or square to square for an all-over, kaleidoscopic effect. Many an otherwise undistinguished pattern achieved interest by originality of "set," while many another, pleasant enough in its own right, lost significance with a cluttered setting. The *ship's wheel (Fig. 2)* was and still is a popular pieced pattern. The red, green, and white diamond-shaped patches of the eight-pointed star, set together point to point, have a clean-cut, cool look. To this quilt the *sawtooth* patch borders add smartness and simple, sparkling beauty. Did the name of the pattern have special meaning to the quiltmaker? Here is the story:

Joseph Fleming and Francis Scott Key were first cousins; their families were intimate and occupied adjoining plantations in Maryland. Joseph had two daughters, Harriot and Charlotte. It is not clear which of them made the quilt — probably both worked on it. It was made shortly after their father's cousin Francis had his exciting experience as a prisoner aboard a British ship on the night of September 13-14, 1814. Francis became a hero to his young cousins and it is not difficult to believe that a ship's wheel meant something more to them, as their needles flew, than a quilt pattern. Charlotte presently married James Stover who became Sergeant at Arms in the Ohio Senate, 1866–1867. In 1884 Harriot Fleming gave the *ship's wheel* to her niece, Alice Stover, who in turn gave it to her niece, Edna Stover Seybolt, in 1908. It is now owned and shown by courtesy of Mrs. Edna M. Seybolt, great-granddaughter of Joseph Fleming.

Figure 3, though made in blocks, is diverse in pattern, informal and gay. It resembles the album quilts of the 1840's though it bears no signatures. Made during the Civil War in the family of Barbara Hundloser of Maryland, it is a

FIG. 1 — APPLIQUED QUILT (*late eighteeenth century*). Made by Ann Heck of homespun linen decorated with English chintz. Large enough to cover a pair of twin beds. *From the Newark Museum.*

quilt typical of later work, reflecting the imagination and individuality of the maker and a perhaps unconscious humor. It must have been fun to make. Colors are red, dark green, orange, blue, yellow, and rose tones; borders are of red and white strips. Birds of red-dotted yellow calico placed at intersections of the unit blocks vary the "set" of this quilt. The square above the prancing red horse shows a green tree bearing many red apples while a brown serpent twines about the base. In the block below the horse is a sheaf of wheat neatly tied with a bow. And do not miss the birds encircling a nest with three eggs defying gravity above it. This merry quilt was sold once during the war to raise money for Confederate soldiers. It now bears a blue-ribbon award taken at the Maryland State Fair and Agricultural Society in Timonium, September 1939.

FIG. 2 (*above*) — QUILT IN "SHIP'S WHEEL" PATTERN. In red, green, and white, with *sawtooth* patch border. Made by Harriot and Charlotte Fleming, nieces of Francis Scott Key, shortly after September 1814. *From the collection of Mrs. Edna M. Seybolt.*

FIG. 3 (*right*) — PATCHWORK QUILT MADE IN BLOCKS. Made during the Civil War in the family of Barbara Hundloser of Maryland. *From the author's collection.*

QUILTS AND COVERLETS

From New York and Long Island

By FLORENCE PETO

ALL of the quilts and coverlets here pictured in company with brief notes were made in or near New York City. Their range of dates is from the 1780's to 1853. In so far as may be judged from a study of these examples, and others more or less similar, the domestic art of quiltmaking in the New York zone developed no marked individualities of design or technique during the period in review. Thus, for instance, the district has yielded nothing, either in originality or in richness of effect, comparable to the splendid eighteenth-century hooked wool bedspreads of the Connecticut Valley (see ANTIQUES for November

FIG. 1 (*right*) — FRENCH KNOTS ON HOMESPUN LINEN: WHITE (*dated 1800*)

The foundation material, woven on a narrow loom, sewed in three strips and embroidered by hand. The cornucopia filled with flowers or fruits, symbolizing abundance, was a favorite decorative motive in the early 1800's. Happily Marcy Huntting of East Hampton, Long Island, who made this coverlet, inscribed her own name and that of her place of residence on her handiwork and added the date *December 1800*. Marcy was born in 1781. Hence she was nineteen years old when she completed her bedcover.
Owned by a descendant, Mrs. Etta Hedges Pennypacker

FIG. 2 (*below, left*) — WOVEN COVERLET (*late eighteenth century*)

Made in two strips on a simple four-harness loom; flax warp with wool filling. In design, if not always in fact, wool coverlets exhibiting such geometrical patterns antedate by many years the more elaborate double-

faced coverlets whose decorative motives include involved scrolls and attempts at pictorial representation. The present piece is the work of Ida Stillwell of Gravesend, Long Island, and was probably made about 1786, when the young woman was twenty years old. She was twice married, the second time to Jacobus Voorhees. *Owned by a great-grandnephew, James Voorhies*

FIG. 3 (*below, right*) — "STAR OF BETHLEHEM": PATCHWORK AND APPLIQUÉ

Delicate border design, chain edging, and graceful vases recall eighteenth-century design. Sunflower strip and diamond patchwork are distinctively of the 1800's. Ascribed to Mary Totten of Staten Island, who was born in 1781. It seems reasonable to place the date of this piece in the neighborhood of 1810. The appliquéd pattern shows an interesting mixture of printed flowers cut from English chintz and silhouette leaves of formally figured calico. *Owned by a collateral descendant, Miss Ella Butler*

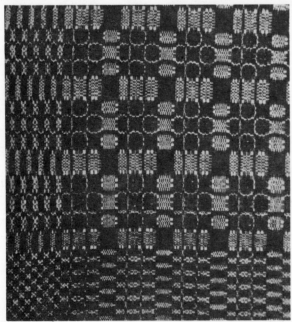

FIG. 4 (*upper, left*) — "SNOWBALL AND STAR" DOUBLE-WOVEN COVERLET

Made for Maria Kouwenhoven of Flatlands, Long Island, who was born in 1805. Maria's name and the date, *December 10, 1817*, are woven into the border. The coverlet is made of two strips seamed together. For an American coverlet of this type this date is very early.

Owned by a great-granddaughter, Mrs. Bernard Bennett

FIG. 5 (*upper, right*) — "COMPASS" OR "CHIPS AND WHETSTONES" QUILT

An involved patchwork pattern in calicoes on a homespun ground. Like most quilts made by the practical Dutch women, heavily padded for warmth and hence lacking fine stitchery in the quilting. Said to have been made by Cornelia Van Sicklen of Flatlands prior to her marriage in 1828 to Jacobus J. Voorhies.

Owned by a great-granddaughter, Mrs. Phoebe Voorhies Lott

FIG. 6 (*lower, left*) — "WILD GOOSE CHASE" QUILT

A seemingly unimaginative pattern until the long strips of triangles are seen to represent flocks of wild geese winging their way above the Long Island marshes. Johanna Bergen of Bergen's Island, Flatlands Bay, records in her diary (*1825–1829*) "grate flight of geese. I have seen 17 flocks." Johanna made the quilt here pictured.

Owned by a great-granddaughter, Mrs. Jane Voorhies Lyman

FIG. 7 (*lower, right*) — "TRIPLE STAR" LINEN AND CALICO QUILT

A curious item credited to a man, Obadiah Smith of Smithtown, Long Island, who was a successful farmer, a musician, and, because of a crippled wife, a handy man about the house. The most remarkable feature of his quilt is its star and swastika border. Probably made late in Obadiah's life, perhaps in the 1830's or 1840's.

Owned by a great-granddaughter, Mrs. Edith S. R. Scott

FIG. 8 — "GRAPEVINE AND OAK-LEAF" QUILT

Made by Elizabeth Glover of Brush Neck Manor, near Sag Harbor, Long Island. Born in 1824, Elizabeth began working her quilt when she was eleven years old. She worked her daily stint on this opus during a period of some years. It was finished in time to be placed in her dower chest. But the patient seamstress did not live to use it. Shortly before the date set for her marriage, she died of bronchial trouble, when she had barely passed her twenty-first year.

On loan, Whaling and Historic Museum, Sag Harbor. Owned by a grandniece, Mrs. Miriam Foster Gates

FIG. 9 — A WHIMSEY IN APPLIQUÉ

Made in 1853 by Irene B. Forman, who was properly brought up in a brownstone house on the corner of Lexington Avenue and 23 Street, New York City. The piece is made up of 56 appliquéd blocks of highly ingenious designs executed in bright-colored calicoes. Background of designs and intersecting strips are white muslin. Irene, who ultimately became Mrs. Purdy, was a resourceful person. When financial difficulties overtook the family, she turned the brownstone mansion into a boarding house, which she operated successfully for some years.

Owned by a descendant, George Read

FIG. 10 — PRESENTATION QUILT

Presented in 1843 to Joshua K. Ingalls, a lay preacher in Southold, Long Island, by appreciative womenfolk of his congregation. Each appliquéd block, a wreath or floral design on a white cambric background, was a separate donation. When all were finished, they were sewed together, padded, and quilted. The half squares along all four edges of the quilt are filled by blue-purple clusters of grapes and green leaves. Some one person of taste must have directed the undertaking, for the individual offerings are, on the whole, well related in scale and pattern. One or two of the sisters, however, appear to have had ideas of their own. Each block is signed inconspicuously in indelible ink with the name of the woman who made it. Less elaborate "Friendship" quilts are sometimes made today.

Owned by Mrs. Charles Ingalls

1934, *p. 169*). The latter items, however, are in a class by themselves. Something of their influence seems to have been carried over from New England into rural communities in central New York State, but apparently avoided metropolitan neighborhoods. Even though the pieces here illustrated betray no conscious or unconscious adherence to a particular local tradition in design and workmanship, they may each boast a reliable pedigree, and may be dated with reasonable accuracy. As a group they illustrate certain trends in design

and workmanship that were manifested decade by decade almost simultaneously in almost every locality in the United States. The telepathic process by which new ideas in household handicrafts were transmitted long before the days of women's magazines and women's pages in the daily and Sunday newspapers is yet to be explained. But apparently it worked rapidly and efficiently.

(Figures 3, 9, and 10, courtesy of the Art Service Project, W.P.A.; Figure 5, courtesy of the Photographic Division, Federal Art Project, W.P.A.)

Quilts and coverlets

THE FRONTIER HOUSEWIFE's homespuns and hand weavings were supplemented from the 1830's on by the work of professional weavers with jacquard looms, many of whom were itinerant, and soon also by the products of spinning and weaving mills. Such utilitarian textiles as woven coverlets were often highly decorative, and so were the samplers, quilts, and other creations of the housewife's busy needle.

Friendship quilt. Inscribed in fine stitchery *Presented by your scholars at Sunnyside, Ohio. 1814*, with many signatures and a verse:

Accept our valued friendship,
And roll it up in cotton,
And think it not illusion,
Because so easily gotten.

Cotton; red, yellow, blue, orange, and green. Length 7 feet, 3 inches. *Keene.*

Quilt, appliquéd and stuffed, c. 1850. Marked *Ohio*. Cotton; red, pink, green, and yellow. Length 8 feet. *Brunner.*

Jacquard coverlet.
Found in Carrolton, Ohio, 1835-1845.
Wool, cotton;
red, blue, and white.
Length 7 feet, 4 inches. *Fowler*.

Jacquard coverlet. Woven in corners *1840 Ohio*.
Wool and cotton; indigo and white. Length 8 feet. *OHS*.

Jacquard coverlet.
Signed *Zoar 1845 G. Kappel & Co.*
Wool and cotton;
scarlet, blue, and white.
Length 7 feet. *OHS*.

Jacquard coverlet.
Signed *A. W. Van-Doren.*
Weaver Avon 1849.
and *Oakland. Co.*
Michigan. Wool and cotton;
rose and white.
Length 8 feet, ½ inch. *Crumb.*

Jacquard coverlet, c. 1850. *J. Huber. Jakson. Township.*
Dearborn. Co. Indiana. Wool and cotton; brown, green, and white.
Length 7 feet, 8 inches. *HFM.*

Jacquard coverlet. *Made By D. Cosley, Xenia Greene Co, Ohio.*
1850. Wool and cotton; red, blue, green, and white.
Length 7 feet, 8 inches. *Brunner.*

Fig. 1. — HORSE AND EAGLE (*detail*)
    The centre medallions are clever combinations of Scotch thistle and English rose. Woven in the corners, *Mary Van Dorn* (name of owner), *Liberty &
Independance, Ithaca, 1837, A. Davidson, Fancy Weaver.* Color, indigo blue and white.
This and other coverlets illustrated are from the author's collection.

Weavers of New York's Historical Coverlets

By JESSIE FARRALL PECK

While American woven coverlets of the second quarter of the nineteenth century have received considerable attention, little has hitherto
been done in the way of tracing their authorship or of estimating the relative quality of their designs. This phase of the subject is of primary
interest to Mrs. Peck, whose investigations, now in progress, will form the basis for a book. The present article offers new material on certain of the New York State weavers. The coverlets of Harry Tyler were discussed in ANTIQUES for March, 1928. — *The Editor.*

SEVENTY-FIVE or a hundred years turn most of human-
ity into mere names. That's what is happening to the old
Jacquard loom weavers of America. If you are treasuring
a blue and white coverlet with the name of its first owner and the
date of its making tucked into a corner, aren't you curious sometimes about the artist who fashioned it; or interested in the
thread of history woven into its fabric?

Archibald Davidson's shop offers a splendid illustration of the
place of the professional weaver during that phase of our industrial history — the period of transition between home-craft and
factory. He called his shop a "carpet factory," but it still had the
home way of doing things. Picture the Ithaca Carpet Factory on
a certain cold day in December of some such year as 1838:

On the site of the old Cornell farm east of Ithaca, snuggled
close to the bridge over Cascadilla Creek, extends a long, shedlike
structure, with cheerful wisps of smoke puffing from its chimney.
Twenty-year-old Cordelia Wilsey canters up on horseback,
blankets her horse, and bustles in — a trifle late, but three miles
on a morning like this, with the wind blistering one's face! Red
hands are limbered beside the comforting chunk stove. In a few
moments, the idle spinning wheel is buzzing: Cordelia is the
champion spinner of the countryside.

Three clanking looms, two wheels, and a steaming dye pot —
these, with their six attendants, make up the Ithaca Carpet
Factory. Archibald Davidson is the master weaver. He is the one
who, in the borders of his coverlets, skilfully perpetuates his

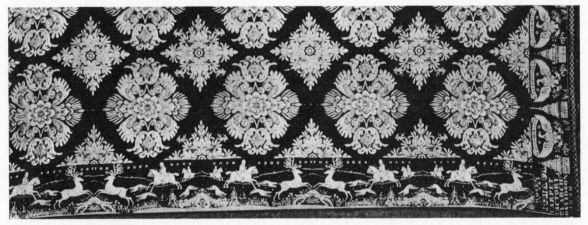

Fig. 2 — THE DEER HUNT (*detail*)
    Notice the delicate bit of weaving showing the tiny flowers and grass; the outlines of the hills; the perspective of the distant horsemen; the action depicted
in the lithe bodies of the pursuing hounds. Woven inscription, *Woven at the Ithaca Carpet Factory by Arch^d Davidson, 1838.* Color, indigo blue and white.

memories of the horse and hound in old Scotland, and thoughts of the deer so plentiful in this newer country. John Davidson helps, sometimes, with the carpets. There is one on the loom now, with tiny meeting-houses scattered over it. The third weaver takes care of the clothmaking.

Cordelia's spinning wheel is slowing up. Twenty knots, two skeins — the "run" is finished. Now for the little dance that helps take the chill out of a winter's day. All join in with heartiness, and here is the song that guides their steps:

Hey, jin along, jin along Jessie,
Hey, jin along, jin along Joe.
The black-bird said, said he to the crow,
"If you ain't black then I don't know."
Hey, jin along, jin along Jessie,
Hey, jin along, jin along Joe.

Hey, etc.
First to the courthouse, then to the jail:
Hang your hat on a rusty nail.
Hey, etc.

The dance is similar to the Scotch sword dance, two sticks being used. There is much action, including patting of knees and stamping of feet. Ten minutes, and all are back at their tasks — till the spinners have finished one more "run" of twenty knots, two skeins.

ARCHIBALD DAVIDSON, FANCY WEAVER.

AT his Shop about 50 rods south of Otis Eddy's Cotton Factory, and a quarter of a mile east of the village of Ithaca, respectfully informs the publick that he has purchased a patent right for the town of Ithaca, superiour to any patent heretofore in the United States, for weaving Carpets and Carpet Coverlets of any pattern or figure that can be wove in the United States; and the work not inferiour to any in Europe or America.

He will weave the owners' name, date of the month and year, if required. If the yarn is good, and not cut, he flatters himself that he will show and give better work than has ever been by any patent loom heretofore invented. From his long experience and practice in the weaving line in Scotland and in the United States, and the great expense he has been at in procuring a patent so valuable, he hopes to merit the publick patronage.

Also, at his shop he weaves Broad Cloath, Sheeting, two and one half yards wide, in kersey or plain; Diaper of all kinds, and country work of every description done with punctuality and dispatch.

Yarn spun fo coverlets ought to be spun 3 runs to the pound, doubled and twisted, and cotton, No. 7, doubled and twisted. Carpet yarn spun two runs to the pound, doubled and twisted, or one run to the pound, single. And he likewise, for their accommodation, will, if required, get their yarn coloured to suit the pattern Ladies are requested to call and examine the work before they engage their weaving.

Nov. 9, 1831.   43tf

Fig. 3 — ADVERTISEMENT OF THE ITHACA CARPET FACTORY
From the files of the *Ithaca Journal*, at Cornell University.

The location of the first Jacquard loom in America is open to question. The earliest I have been able to trace was in the Northrup Woolen Mill, at Roanoke, Genesee County, New York, which was built, in 1820, on a portion of the forty-eight acres purchased by the Northrups from the Holland Land Company. Its chief output was cloth and carpets; coverlets were made when ordered. In 1822, Isabella Norris of Morganville wanted the "latest thing in woven spreads" for her hope chest. It turned out to be quite an historic affair (*Fig. 4*). It shows, first, that Elijah Northrup was one of the pioneer Jacquard loom weavers in America; and, second, that he was the originator of the New York Masonic coverlet, with pillars, square, and compass in its border.

Northrup was a Mason, but the near-by trouble with Morgan and the consequent rise of the Anti-Masonic party cooled his ardor. Besides, after the stirring times of 1825, these emblems were unpopular. In a coverlet woven for Hulda Hudson, Pavilion, in 1829, we find thin pine trees taking the place of pillar, square, and compass. The Masonic border crops up again, however, in the Independence coverlet, done by J. A. Getty,

Fig. 4 — MASONIC COVERLET
One of the earliest of the double-woven type. The Masonic emblems and patriotic symbols harmonize, because patriotism is a cardinal principle of Masonry. Color, indigo blue and white.

Fig. 5 — INDEPENDENCE COVERLET
Most of the Independence Halls in coverlet borders lack the Liberty Bell. This pattern shows the influence of the earlier Masonic coverlet by Northrup. Color, indigo blue and white.

near Auburn, in 1839, and here illustrated in Figure 5.

In 1824, John Getty belonged to the same Masonic Lodge as Northrup — the Olive Branch Lodge at Bethany — and, once in a while, weavers passed along a few patterns. Both coverlets picture Independence Hall, but the later piece adds the Liberty Bell to the tower. Let me remind you of a bit of history; one needs it to appreciate this Independence pattern.

In 1752, Philadelphia ordered a two-thousand-pound bell from England. On its shining surface, the following words were engraved, like a prophecy: "Proclaim liberty throughout all the land, unto all the inhabitants thereof." On July 4, 1776, hundreds were gathered around Independence Hall. Within, something was whispered to a small boy. Breathlessly he rushed up the steps to the tower, shouting to the bellman, "They've signed it! Ring! Ring! Ring!" And the bell sent out its solemn message, while, from the steps below, the Declaration of Independence was read to the waiting crowds. When the British occupied Philadelphia, the Liberty Bell was hidden. But it completed the story of liberty, ringing out the signal that peace was declared. Ninety years ago, people were fairly close to our vital history; and they enjoyed having the things which they revered woven into an enduring fabric. Surely this memorial to American Independence ought to bring some credit to its author, John A. Getty.

Ira Hadsell was one of the later craftsmen. As a little twelve-year-old boy, in 1825, he came adventuring into Palmyra, and went to work on a farm. At fourteen, we find him traveling weary miles over the old Erie Canal towpath, urging along the "power" for a brand-new packet boat. Nine years more, and he is running his own boat, the *Eclipse*, loaded with wheat for Rochester. Having reached the height of his canal ambitions, he seemingly lost interest in waterways: it was time he was seeing more of the world. Soon he is making his way through Michigan, Ohio, Indiana — on foot. Finally, his wanderlust satisfied, he returns to Palmyra, and takes up weaving on Vienna Street with his friend Van Ness. In 1848, the old-fashioned loom is remodeled to weave seamless coverlets; and three years later it belongs to Hadsell.

There are no lovelier designs for coverlets than those given New

York State by Ira Hadsell. He was the naturalist among the weavers — spent hours tramping through the woods, learning the shape of leaf and flower and vine, and their ways of winding and clustering. His diaries still treasure some of his pressed models. The two examples of his work pictured here show his fondness for natural forms. One is a fascinating study in all kinds of leaves. The other has additional interest: first, in the fine drawing of the four heads of Liberty; and, second, in its historical meaning. The inspiration for the design as a whole came with the first signs of dissension between North and South: the two joined flags representing the union of the two sections; the eagle as the national emblem for both; the horn of plenty as a prophecy; and *E Pluribus Unum* as a motto. Truly a powerful plea against civil war! (*See Cover.*)

One old resident of Palmyra relates an incident in the life of the Hadsells that still amuses her greatly. "It was circus day," she says, "and almost the whole town turned out. The circus folk had begun unloading, when up over the hill poked Uncle Ira's old white horse, trailing the family market wagon. That horse didn't approve of a thing he saw, or heard, or smelled. Wheeling, he sent a double kick toward the whole business — a kick that upset the market wagon and sent the two passengers skyrocketing. Poor, proper Aunt Lydia. Her bonnet flew off; her switch, being pinned to it, followed. Both sailed over the fence and lit on a bramble bush, where they dangled disgracefully. No one was hurt, unless you count feelings."

Fig. 6 — WOOD AND GARDEN
Hadsell is usually known by his E Pluribus Unum coverlet. This example shows simply his deep-rooted love of nature. It takes a magician so to control the threads of a loom that they weave themselves into a picture like this. Color, indigo blue and white.

Another aged settler told of living alone on the hill with a widowed mother. They bought milk and butter from the Hadsells — the richest milk and the sweetest butter in all the country. On butter day, "Uncle Ira" always pulled an "extra" out of the wagon. Sometimes it was a bag of mixed vegetables, sometimes a bushel of apples; but always something to make living easier.

In seeking information concerning weaver James Cunningham, I was almost discouraged. I had browsed around cemeteries, been through countless dusty newspaper files, written twenty or thirty letters to old inhabitants and to wardens of vital statistics. Then I found Miss Allie Davison of New Hartford, and she remembered. I am giving the account as nearly as possible in her words:

"James Cunningham lived on Oxford Road — 'twas South Street then — the second house from the church. William Winship built that house more'n one hundred and forty years ago. Was one of the first frame houses west of Albany they say. Built when New Hartford was bigger'n Utica. Cellar kitchen, fireplaces all over, comfortable. And I remember *him*, a small old man with long white chin whiskers. He had four boys and two girls: Arthur was my age, born in 1847. George and William went to war and William was killed. Broke his father all up. Mr. Cunningham liked reading, mostly history things. Used to loan 'em around to the neighbors. My father would borrow his war books. We lived near by, just down the road a piece."

This weaver's coverlets are, as one would expect, historical. Washington on Horseback was first woven about 1835, when Cunningham was working his last year with his partner Butterfield. The early specimens of this pattern had four large circular medallions in the centre, and were nearly square. Later on, two elongated figures were added at the top, making the "bolster covering" for the pillows (*Fig. 7*).

Cunningham's New York State Emblem coverlet was designed about 1840. It is much rarer than the Washington on Horseback — the knightly figure of the latter seemed better to suit the hope chest fancies of young lady customers. The Emblem design, however, is historically more interesting. The arms of New York were adopted March 16, 1778. They have been called the happiest choice made by any state of the Union. The surmounting eagle belonged first to New York — the United States chose its eagle in 1782. Liberty and Justice as supporters of the shield could hardly be bettered; and the device on the shield, picturing the passage of the Hudson River through the mountains to the ocean, suggests the very foundations of the State's history. The whole rests on the motto *Excelsior* (*Fig. 8*).

Fig. 8 — The New York State Emblem

A fine piece of weaving. The floral design of the border is worked out with the tulip as a basis, a tribute, perhaps, to the Dutch founders of the State. Color, copper red and white.

By 1798, the old seal needed repairing, and a new one was made. "Without authority some details were changed — such as removing the bandage and the scales from Justice; and, from this time on, many artists took all sorts of liberties." To Cunningham, with his English background, this loose conception of the State's coat of arms must have seemed a desecration.

Finally the Legislature was roused to action. The State had preserved no records of the original arms; but, luckily, an old military commission signed by Governor Clinton, June 25, 1778, was unearthed and the device upon it served as corrective material. Governor Cornell spoke the general feeling when he said, "The citizens of the State who are proud of her position and history should also delight in her insignia. The device of Arms of this State is so perfect in its conception that our aim is mainly how we can best restore the original." How Cunningham would have delighted in this awakening of the State's conscience! The correct design was restored in 1882.

During the Civil War, there was almost no coverlet weaving: the soldiers needed the wool. After the war, there was no call for it. The era of machinery was in full swing. In 1866, there crept into Ithaca a new railroad called the Shoefly. It was a queer little road, whose trains would stop for anyone, anywhere; but its chief business was to haul lumber from Cortland to the fast growing city. The workmen on this road discovered one day a dilapidated old building near Judd Bridge, on the bank of the Cascadilla. It would make a handy place for tools, and a fair shelter from the weather; so it was used that way. The old Ithaca Carpet Factory was rendering a last service to the commercial age which had rung its death knell. Yet changing fashion may have had something to do with the passing of elaborate coverlets. Commercialism is not to be blamed for everything.

Fig. 7 — Washington on Horseback

Artists have always considered the depiction of the horse a difficult feat. Cunningham, with his shuttle and loom, seems to have succeeded unusually well. Color, rose red (cochineal dye, softened by age) and white.

OHIO COVERLETS

By IRMA PILLING ANDERSON

AT THE TIME of the founding of the first permanent settlement in Ohio, at Marietta in 1788, the spinning of yarn and the weaving of cloth were foremost essentials of pioneer domestic economy. Necessarily at first, weaving equipment and also flax seed and sheep as sources of tow and wool were brought from the east and from New England. The fact that the textile arts developed early and rapidly in the Ohio country is evidenced by the census report of 1810 which listed a total of 10,586 looms at the time.

Since decorative bed coverings have always appealed to the homemaker, it is probable that coverlets were made in early times as well as household linens and cloth for garments. From advertisements in old newspapers, from legends woven into the coverlets, from county histories, and from information secured from descendants of pioneer weavers, the story of coverlets in Ohio is becoming increasingly clear. The quality of the work, as exemplified by coverlets still in existence, is high. All of the principal types of weaving used in coverlets have been found in this state.

The processes for preparing materials such as wool, flax, and cotton, are familiar to those interested in the subject and therefore need not be discussed here. Time, patience, and skill were required for this work and since the finished piece is dependent on the quality of the spinning, there is considerable evidence that many accomplished spinners resided in Ohio in the early 1800's. However, machines for the "making of cotton and wool rolls for the benefit of the home spinner" were operating in 1806, and two years later an advertisement of a spinning machine appeared in the Cincinnati *Liberty Hall* which guaranteed that the "yarn spun will be more even and in every way better than can be spun on a common wheel." How grateful the pioneer housewife must have been for this! Careful examination of the yarn in the coverlets will show whether it was hand-spun or produced by machine. The twist of the former is tight with some unevenness, while the latter is both regular and even. In hand-woven coverlets the materials employed were colored wool yarns with either linen or cotton in natural color.

Within a few years the work of the home weaver was further lightened by that of the professional weaver and by the establishment of numerous mills for the processing of materials and the weaving of fabrics. The professional weaver might reside in one community over a period of years or he might be an itinerant weaver, moving from place to place according to the demand for his services. The majority of the coverlets of the first decade of the nineteenth century in Ohio were, however, unquestionably produced in the home.

The home weaver also became a dyer, and with the exception of blue, much experimentation must have taken place before satisfactory colors were obtained. Indigo was easily secured, produced a beautiful blue, and combined harmoniously with other colors; hence, blue predominates in many of the early coverlets. This is particularly true of the double-cloth weaves of Ohio. In the overshot weave soft reds, bordering on rose, light blue, and light green are frequently seen, and brown, lavender, and orange occasionally appear. "The pioneer housewife commonly manufactured her own dyes from butternut, hickory, oak-galls, sumac and other materials which were near at hand, using alum as a mordant" (William T. Utter, *The Frontier State, 1803-1825*, Carl Wittke, ed., *History of the State of Ohio*, Columbus, 1924, II, 252).

As early as 1814, however, dyestuffs were an important item in Ohio's imports. Logwood, indigo, madder, arinetta, camwood, and redwood were offered to the public in general stores and the home dyer as well as the professional made use of them. Many advertisements by men appear in early newspapers but at least one enterprising woman, Ann Yaman of Cincinnati, conducted a dyeing establishment in 1809 and returned "her most grateful thanks to her friends for their custom."

Instructions for using dyes were available to early Ohioans. A handbook on dyeing published in London in 1800 is known to have been used in Ohio during the first quarter of the century. It is a compilation by James Haigh of Leeds and extracts from it were copied into an account book (*1814-1834*) which also contained drafts for weaving as well as diagrams of looms. Both the book on dyeing and the account book were owned by the MacFarland family of weavers who lived at Center Belpre, now Porterfield, Washington County. (They are now the property of Norris F. Schneider, great-grandson of Johann Schneider, a coverlet weaver of Lowell, Washington County.)

The types of weaves used in Ohio coverlets may easily be recognized, and to the owner of a handwoven piece this information is important. The four principal types in the chronological order of their appearance

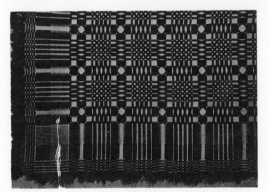

FIG. 1 (*right*)—OVER-SHOT WEAVE. Woven at the Zoar Separatist community, (*c. 1840*). Wool and cotton. Blue, green, a soft red and white. *At Zoar Museum, Division of State Memorials.*

FIG. 2 (*below*)—DOUBLE-CLOTH WEAVE (*c. 1840*). Wool and cotton. Blue and white. Geometric design. Woven by Sarah Whinery Coleman, Columbus. The design is single snowball with pinetree border.

FIG. 3 (above)—DOUBLE-CLOTH WEAVE. Blue and white. Wool and cotton. Floral design. *Coverlets are property of Ohio State Archaeological and Historical Society, gifts of residents of the state.*

are overshot, double-cloth, summer and winter, and Jacquard.

The overshot weave is characterized by a plain tabby weave with the design in colored wools. Instead of the wool being closely interwoven with the linen or cotton background, it is floated or skipped over the background and so creates the design, which is always geometric (*Fig. 1*).

Double-cloth is the most easily recognized of all coverlet weaves but is more difficult in technique than the overshot. Briefly, it is two webs interwoven at the point of design. These webs can be separated easily, determining the double-cloth feature. Both geometric and floral types of designs are found in the double-cloth weave (*Figs. 2, 3*).

Summer and winter weave is the rarest of the weaves found in Ohio coverlets. It has been stated by Mary Meigs Atwater in her authoritative book that "it appears to be wholly of American invention" (*The Shuttle-craft Book of American Hand-weaving*, New York, 1928). The weave is difficult to describe and should be seen to be definitely recognized. The fabric is closely interwoven at every point. The distinguishing feature is the fine honeycomb-like appearance which is most easily seen on the light side of the coverlet (*Fig. 4*). All coverlets show the design in colors on a light background on the face or obverse side and in light on a colored background on the reverse side. I have seen only two coverlets and one fragment in this weave in the more than three hundred which I have examined in Ohio.

The Jacquard coverlet was made on a loom invented by a Frenchman of that name. The first loom of this type in America was set up in Philadelphia in 1826. The earliest weavers on this loom were professionals, for both the designs and the loom were complicated. Most Jacquard coverlets have the name of the weaver, the date, and other information in one or more corners (*Fig. 5*). The designs are never geometric in type and vary from floral to realistic representations of many subjects. Jacquards are hand-woven if they have a seam in the middle, which is true of other types of coverlets as well. In Ohio, there seem to be more Jacquards than any other kind, with the double-cloth weave second in number.

Very important to the early housewife were the drafts or designs for her

coverlets. Many of the designs here are common to other parts of the country though variations were worked out by skillful weavers. The drafts were written on paper and no doubt passed from weaver to weaver just as a treasured recipe was, but they seem to be rare in Ohio. They are fascinating documents with small crosses or tiny, black squares carefully arranged on parallel lines. The designs are generally placed in two classes: geometric and floral. The earliest were geometric and are to be seen in the overshot, double-cloth, and summer and winter weave. The floral designs are found in the double-cloth and Jacquard weaves.

The geometrics have a charm not surpassed although a few of the later Ohio geometrics are somewhat monotonous. In the hands of an artistic weaver, the floral patterns produced were lovely and they must have pleased the pioneer woman very much since we find so many examples. As the coverlet designs became more ornate and additional colors were employed, the results were less artistic and satisfying. When railroad trains, buildings, flags, scales of justice, lodge emblems, and the like appeared, skill in handweaving had reached the peak of excellence but design was at the lowest point. There are, at times, evidences of real artistic feeling in the composition of some of the earlier designs. The border, which usually severed the design of the body of the coverlet in an abrupt way, occasionally was planned to complement the overall design (*Fig. 4*).

The names of one hundred and seventy-four Ohio weavers of coverlets have been recorded at the Ohio State Archaeological and Historical Society's Museum, with the coöperation of Mrs. Rhea Mansfield Knittle, Mrs. J. V. Cochran, and the Anne Simpson Davis Chapter, D. A. R. Additional names are constantly being found. Jacob and Michael Ardner, J. Heilbronn, L. Hesse, Benjamin Lichty, and G. Stich, prominent Ohio weavers of the double-cloth and Jacquard type, are names found most often on coverlets I have seen.

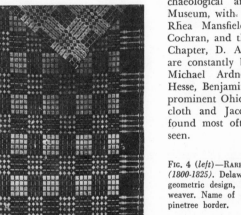

FIG. 4 (left)—RARE SUMMER AND WINTER WEAVE (1800-1825). Delaware County. Blue and white, geometric design, linen and wool. By a home weaver. Name of design is sixteen states with pinetree border.

FIG. 5 (below)—JACQUARD WEAVE. Wool and cotton. Red, white, and blue. The design is four roses and sixteen-pointed star.

THE ATTITUDE OF THE EAGLE

As Portrayed on an Outstanding Group of "Liberty" Quilts

By ANNE WOOD MURRAY

E VER SINCE THAT MOMENTOUS DAY toward the end of the eighteenth century when Freedom "called her eagle bearer down, and gave into his mighty hand the symbol of her chosen land," the American eagle has appeared as a patriotic design in numerous arts and crafts of our country, as well as on goods prepared for American markets by foreign countries. But nowhere has he been portrayed with a more earnest patriotism than on the patchwork quilt, for the early quiltmaker was sharply aware of what her freedom had cost in toil and tears.

Many devices were considered by various committees before the Great Seal with the American bald eagle was agreed upon and adopted by Congress in 1782. It is said that Benjamin Franklin complained that the eagle selected looked more like a wild turkey than an eagle and he regretted that it was not, since "the turkey is a true native of America."

Doctor Franklin would be pleased with the eagle which decorates the hempen quilt made in 1793 at Canterbury, Connecticut (*Fig. 3*). The domestic attitude of this "fowl of freedom" reminds me of a Thanksgiving turkey. The quilt, combining pieced and appliquéd work in nine-patch blocks and a large center square showing the eagle with stars motif, came from the Brown-Francis family homestead at Canterbury. The hemp for the quilt was made from a small patch of marijuana grown in the yard on the family homestead, which was occupied by the Francis family about 1743. Norman L. Kilpatrick, the present owner of this quilt, received it from his grandmother in Canterbury, who had inherited it.

Could it be possible that the maker of this quilt copied her eagle from one on a piece of Oriental export porcelain? The eagle

FIG. 1 (*above*) — EAGLE QUILT made in Saratoga County, New York (*1846*). *Photograph courtesy United States National Museum.*

FIG. 2 — EAGLE DESIGN on Oriental export porcelain coffeepot (*late eighteenth century*). *From the Rhode Island School of Design.*

on the Great Seal of 1782 has his wings uplifted and outspread; he holds an olive branch in the claw on the left of the design and arrows in the claw on the right; the stars above his head are completely encircled. Now the eagle on the quilt has drooping wings, and the stars appear in a sunburst which is joined to his wings, as in the porcelain eagle (*Fig. 2*). The tail feathers correspond in number and arrangement to those of the bird on the porcelain. The shield is not set on as the device appears in the Great Seal, but is made by cutting slits in the applied material and allowing the cloth beneath to show through, approximating the shield of the United States in somewhat the manner of the Chinese craftsman in his china decoration. The quilt eagle has his beak parted slightly, as has the porcelain eagle, while the eagle of the Great Seal closes his beak firmly to hold the *E Pluribus Unum* ribbon. And finally, and rather significantly I think, the calico from which the quilt eagle was fashioned is a dull brownish-red color which is not too far removed in tone from the reddish-brown of the porcelain eagle against a sunburst background. The two designs below the eagle and the flowers around him are the same brownish-red color as his body and the sunburst, and the fifteen stars are sky-blue.

R. T. H. Halsey, in *The Homes of Our Ancestors*, suggests that United States coins carried to the Orient by American sailors may have served as examples from which the Chinese porcelain decorators derived their conception of the American eagle. Homer Eaton Keyes, in his article in ANTIQUES for June 1930, seemed to agree with Mr. Halsey, and also called attention to the fact that the spade shield used by the Chinese decorators fronts the eagle on some American currency of the period; an eagle with drooping wings appeared on Massachusetts copper cent and half-cent pieces of 1787–1788, and these Massachusetts pieces appear to be the only American coins on which the laurel appears on the left and the arrows on the right of the design. However, the droop-winged eagle of the Massachusetts coins lacks the

FIG. 3 — EAGLE QUILT made at Canterbury, Connecticut (*1793*). Eagle with sunburst surrounded by nine-patch blocks. *Collection of Norman L. Kilpatrick. Photograph courtesy of United States National Museum.*

sunburst, which first appears on two and one-half dollar gold pieces of 1796.

The Massachusetts coins would probably have been available to the quiltmaker, and also an imprint of the Great Seal. But it is quite possible, too, that she owned an Oriental export porcelain teaset, in American eagle design, since the ware was imported in rather large quantities before and at that time. Women usually take their designs from something near at hand and what could have been simpler than setting a plate on the table before her while she cut out her pattern for the quilt?

Whether the Canterbury quiltmaker used one of her plates when she cut out her eagle, or whether he was a combination of the design on the plate and her impression of the Great Seal, is interesting but not too important. What does matter is that she created a unique and sturdy design. Her eagle is the most naïve and delightful eagle I have ever encountered on a quilt. There he stands with his beak parted breathlessly, holding his lone arrow-head and trefoil sprig of laurel, surrounded by stars and flowers that have bloomed for over one hundred and fifty years. And though they are of faint color which does not show up well in the photograph, if you look carefully you can see on each of the curled leaf designs below the eagle a pair of tiny fowl that look as though they may have been intended for eaglets.

The bald eagle framed by four curved sprays of flowering laurel, and holding a flowering twig in his beak, is a resplendent bird (*Fig. 5*). The quilt which he adorns was made shortly after 1790 by Hannah Thomson of Connecticut, who later migrated to Ohio and settled there. After the death of Mr. Thomson, Hannah married again, a Doctor Wood, and had several children by him. This quilt has come down to Mrs. Willauer, the present owner, from a cousin who was the daughter of Hannah Thomson's son and only child by her first husband. The eagle is blue with stripes of rose-red and white, which gives a feathered effect, and the thirteen stars above his head are pink. The flower baskets in the

FIG. 4 — "DELECTABLE MOUNTAINS" pattern, with eagles around border. Made in Westchester County, New York (1810). *From National Gallery of Art, Index of American Design.*

center are blue filled with rose-colored flowers, and the baskets which border the quilt are a soft brown. Brown and rose pheasants perch on the rosy fruit which fills each basket. The sprays of laurel leaves are blue with pink buds and flowers, and the large roses in each corner are dull rose and brown. The quilt has been done in what is known as reverse appliqué or "inlay," which is related to patchwork but not as commonly used, and is much more difficult than ordinary appliqué. Marie Webster says that in the making of this style of decoration one material is not laid upon another, but into it. "For convenience all the pieces are placed upon a foundation of sufficient firmness which does not appear when the work is finished. Ornamental stitches conceal the seams where the edges meet, and it is especially adapted for making heraldic devices." Half-inch diamond quilting and a narrow blue sawtooth border further enhance the quilt, which is a very large one. Two narrow strips of blue separated by a strip of white complete the quilt. This double border is very decorative, with an unusual design of leaves and pink wheat ears.

The militant eagle surrounded by stars on a quilted ground is later than the other two, but I have chosen him because of his realistic appearance, produced by the material, and the manner in which it has been used (*Fig. 1*). The eagle is appliquéd in a brown, blue, and white floral print which gives a feathered effect, and the 28 five-pointed stars are of yellow, blue, and red print. The quilt is finished with a band seven and a half inches wide, made up of two rows of red, white, and blue; the red matches the stars,

and the blue is a pin-stripe pattern on white. It is lined and bound with bleached muslin and quilted in a combination of shell, star, diamond, and sawtooth patterns.

This quilt was made in Saratoga County, New York, in 1846, by Mary C. Nelson who was then twenty-two years of age. She later married Platt S. Pine of Sandy Plains, Greene County, New York, and went there to live.

The eagle quilt in the patchwork pattern known as *Delectable Mountains* (*Fig. 4*), with star in center, was made in Westchester County, New York, in 1810. It is of turkey-red, oil-boiled calico on white patched center with eagles in appliqué, and was designed and made by Amanda Jane Hatfield as a birthday gift for her grandfather, Captain Hatfield, who fought in the French and Indian wars as well as the American Revolution. Note the double row of quilting in laurel-leaf design bordering the quilt above and below the fat little eagles which look something like swallows.

Ruth Finley, in *Old Patchwork Quilts*, says: "That American women should have chosen from all of Bunyan's many vivid characterizations 'The Delectable Mountains' for a quilt name is confirmation of their appreciative love of country. 'The Delectable Mountains' meant peace and plenty to John Bunyan's pilgrims. In search of peace and plenty the Pilgrims of Plymouth first landed on these shores; millions of other pilgrims followed them . . . America came to mean gardens and fountains of water to the oppressed of all the world. It was a remarkably apt choice of name, 'The Delectable Mountains,' for an American quilt pattern."

FIG. 5 — LIBERTY QUILT, made by Hannah Thomson of Connecticut (*c. 1790*). American eagle framed by four laurel sprays. *Collection of Mrs. Whiting Willauer. Photograph courtesy United States National Museum.*

Fig. 1 — WOODENWARE OF VARIOUS DESCRIPTIONS
In the centre a collapsible cap stand. The other items, except for the cover of the Havana tobacco box, call for no special identification

When Treen Ware Was "The" Ware

By EDITH MINITER

Concerning early American woodenware the most that is known is its universality. In the main it is very simple stuff, not in the least comparable to the fine old treen of England, with its carefully wrought forms and frequent mountings of precious metal. Yet despite its plainness and the barriers that it offers to accurate dating and classification, the mature product possesses no little interest for the collector, as Mrs. Miniter demonstrates in a highly readable discussion. The illustrations are from many different sources. — *The Editor.*

POST FACTUM efforts have been made to supply the good ship *Mayflower* with a full complement of china, glass, and furniture at the time of her initial voyage to America. Yet about all of which we are reasonably sure is that the vessel bore such primary necessaries as a jug now in the collection of the American Antiquarian Society at Worcester, the chair of Myles Standish, and a cradle in which to rock Peregrine White. The Elder Brewster teapot, that pretty little affair decorated with gilt and red posies, may loudly declare itself *Mayflower* property, but its claims were fairly well dissipated when it was extensively reproduced in 1874. Mr. Townsend of the South Kensington Museum said it was old delft, and thus might, at some time, have been brought from Holland — except that tea was scarcely known either in Holland or in England in 1620, while teapots were not invented until considerably after tea had come into use.

These acknowledgments having been made, however reluctantly, we may enquire what our first immigrants did bring with them. One hundred and one people could not dress their food

entirely without dishes, even three centuries back. The answer, of course, is treen ware. They probably possessed plenty of it, and were also adding to their store throughout the tedious voyage. For the fact that ardent religionists — as they all were then — were busily arguing various methods of harmonizing the Gospels would by no means interfere with nimble knife play and the conversion of blocks of wood into trenchers.

Even the largest collections of things early American are rather shy on treen ware — for two reasons. One is that the stuff is not pretty, and furthermore nothing about it to settle its dating; the other is its scarcity, due to its handiness for kindling. The Pilgrim father who uncovered the coals and discovered naught but a forestick and a flicker could gain no immediate assistance from a pewter porringer or an earthenware cup, but he probably had no scruples about feeding the blaze with a wooden bowl. It was the work only of a short evening to supply the housewife with another.

Woodenware was commonly used in England in the sixteenth century. In the seventeenth it was just beginning to be superseded by pewter, but poor folk headed for a long voyage naturally took what was easily transferable and inexpensively augmented. On acquaintance with the natives of their new home, they found the Indians unconsciously in fashion, with what Governor Bradford refers to as their "wooden bowls, trays, and dishes." It was from these natives that the travelers learned the art of sticking a clamshell into a split stick and calling it a spoon.

The woodenware of which we have knowledge today includes plates in various sizes, some shallow as trays, others deepening till one cannot quite decide whether to call them deep plates or shallow bowls. There are also "noggins" — low bowls with handles. Then there are trenchers, either square or oblong. Understanding that a trencher and a plate are not the same thing, though used for the same purpose, explains that puzzling performance of the lady in Mother Goose, who "tripped upon trenchers and danced upon dishes"; and remembering the shape of the oblong trencher, one sees how a man and his wife (or even the wife of some other) might simultaneously partake of food from such a utensil. Affection and unity were thereby demonstrated,

Fig. 2 — TURNED MAPLE SUGAR BOX AND SALT BOX
Both from Lorain County, Ohio, and probably of Ohio manufacture. Similar types were made in New England, Pennsylvania, and Maryland.
From the collection of Rhea Mansfield Knittle

as well as economy in table furniture. Furthermore, if one may believe tradition, it indicated a proper spirit of democracy. A Connecticut farmer who failed to compel his children to eat two-from-a-trencher was refused election as a church deacon on the ground of undue pride!

Poplar wood was eminently suitable for treen ware, and maple knots were taken advantage of for burl bowls. These bowls, or mortars, have survived better than any other of the wooden-ware because they were employed up to very recent times, besides being substantial, and also handsome in their fine graining.

Even for a hundred years after china had come into common use, and when pewter had enjoyed its day and had largely disappeared from circulation except in bullets, treen ware continued to serve for children and old folk. My grandfather, born in 1815, ate from a wooden plate until he was old enough to earn his living, at the age of fifteen. He liked to tell a story of a harsh economist who fed a palsied father from treen because of possible breakages. One day the stern disciplinarian came upon his own little son whittling, and the following conversation took place:

"What are you making, my son?"

"A wooden plate, sir."

"And for what use?"

"To feed you on when you are old."

Shocked to find his son dreaming of sometime treating him as he was treating his own parent, the conscience-stricken man is assumed thereafter to have supplied grandpapa with the best of the family Staffordshire.

Treen ware was wrought with the ever handy jackknife, and also by turning. Some of the walnut or maple affairs were first turned by machinery and then finished by hand. Most people made their own treen; once in a while someone of meditative profession supplemented scanty pay by manufacturing wooden plates and bowls. At least one New England parson is known to have done so, claiming that the process of carving a bowl was

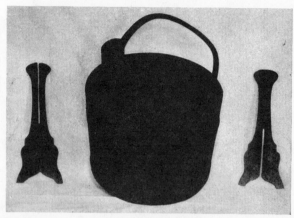

Fig. 3. — WOODEN BUCKET AND THE MEMBERS OF A COLLAPSIBLE CAP STAND

closely akin to that of building a sermon. For instance, both were first blocked out; a period of digging came after, then polishing, and finally a finishing off in which one went carefully over the whole production, removing all rough edges.

It is difficult to think of anything that could not be developed in wood. During the age of treen a saltcellar was not a metal or glass vessel, it was of curiously cut wood. One stirred one's toddy, not with a spoon, but with a carefully fashioned toddy stick. (Toddy, by the way, differed from grog in that it contained less spirits and more sugar. Flip differed from either by the absence of water, beer or cider being used instead. Flip was stirred with a hot iron called a loggerhead.)

Perhaps the most peculiar application of wood was in the making of lather boxes. But lather boxes were quite the thing,

Fig. 4 — OBVERSE AND REVERSE OF A WOODEN BUTTER MOLD · (*probably eighteenth century*) Brought to Ohio from Massachusetts. The initials w. T. are carved on each side of both molds.
From the collection of Rhea Mansfield Knittle

Fig. 5 — OBVERSE AND REVERSE OF WOOD MOLD FROM MASSACHUSETTS Perhaps carved by the maker of the mold of Figure 4. The nature of the designs — crown, rose, and thistle — suggests Scotch or English work.
From the collection of Rhea Mansfield Knittle

Fig. 6 — Germanic Butter Molds of Maple
Left, one part of mold with pine handle, from an Amish settlement in Holmes County, Ohio. Right, mold brought from Pennsylvania to Ohio, a century ago.
From the collection of Rhea Mansfield Knittle

Fig. 7 — Pie Board of Pine
Brought into Ohio from Pennsylvania in 1818. When not in use for pastry mixing, the board served to close the flour barrel; or it could be hung up by the pierced handle.
From the collection of Rhea Mansfield Knittle

Fig. 8 — Two Ohio Butter Molds (*c. 1830–1840*)
Similar molds are made today.
From the collection of Rhea Mansfield Knittle

Fig. 9 — Pennsylvania Cooky Box of Maple
The top screws on. The box is partly covered with reddish brown paint. Top and sides are decorated with a gilt stencil. Found in a Mennonite settlement in Ohio, but probably brought from Pennsylvania.
From the collection of Rhea Mansfield Knittle

and continued in use until after the Civil War. The majority of such boxes were petted by their owners and adorned with pictures. The very young man looked at Jenny Lind or Fanny Kemble while he was shaving. Later, when married, he wisely pasted the American eagle over the alluring female face.

Wood made pretty gifts from lover to beloved. If a gentleman was handy with his knife he made his sweetheart a tiny seal box, or a graceful quassia cup from which to partake of her spring corrective. If actually betrothed, he ventured on a wooden busk for the lady's corsets, the left one appropriately carved with hearts and darts. For a wedding gift a cap stand was welcome. Madame could take the two flat pieces in her capacious pocket when she went tea-visiting, assemble the stand on the bureau and put her under-bonnet cap where it would escape wrinkling while she displayed herself in its dressy substitute. As for the girls, they persuaded complaisant brothers to make bullet pushers and sand boxes to present on birthdays and at New Year's. Alice Morse Earle says that there were even wooden bottles. And P. T. Barnum in his *Life* (1854) mentions a wooden bottle that held a gallon.

The quassia cups were made from a Central American or Jamaican wood. Water left standing in the cup became tinctured with bitters. The longer it stood the worse it tasted, and the more beneficial it was supposed to be. Nowadays the same result is secured with quassia chips or bark procurable from druggists.

An extensive literature has grown up around trenchers. Myles Standish used them and left a dozen to his heirs. They were frequently mentioned in wills. For years, Harvard students ate from them; they were purchased for college use by the gross. As to their worth — in 1689 two of them, put in a lot with a couple of spoons, were appraised as worth six shillings. Of course, in this reckoning, the spoons are represented by x, but one rather fancies that they too were of treen, the fine-grained laurel best known as spoonwood. The largest of the pictured plates (*Fig. 1*) once belonged to John Calkins of Wilbraham, Massachusetts, a philanthropist without money who, from an income of less than $300 a year, gave at least $99 to charity — as he put it in his diary, "to ade the poore." He was a philosopher, without education, yet he associated with Adin Ballou, Garrison, and all the antislavery leaders in the two decades before the war.

Some of the treen ware terms are almost forgotten. Who now knows that a piggin differs from an ordinary wooden pail in having one long stave for a handle? Or that a noggin approximates a gill? Or that a rundlet stands for eighteen gallons? A tankard was a barrel in miniature; an Indian bowl was a mortar or dish made Indian fashion by burning out a false growth in a maple root. A fine example is the one that came from King Philip's wigwam and is now in the rooms of the Massachusetts Historical Society in Boston. And who would know what was asked for if someone said, "Please pass the losset"? Though if you happened to grab a flat dish you would get credit for being quick in the uptake!

Particular tenderness was felt for the trencher mate. Susceptible young gentlemen often wrote "varses" the morning after they had been seated beside some fair "marmalet madam" with a mess of succotash or hasty pudding and milk on a trencher built for two. In many ranks of society a couple announced their betrothal by choosing to eat together from one trencher. Legend also says that more than one old married couple of wealth and aristocratic presence emulated the British duke and duchess who publicly partook of food together from a trencher once a year, in order to set an example of thrift and frugality, and to present an object lesson in amicability. Indeed it is more than possible that the long-sought cause of modern divorce is to be found in the abolition of the trencher. Why should not separate plates mark the beginning of all sorts of separations?

In the heyday of treen, very little metal was employed in country districts, and people managed comfortably enough without it. Ploughs and harrows, cart wheels, piggins, noggins, keelers, firkins, churns, dye tubs, powdering tubs — all were quite naturally made of wood; all the children's toys, including dolls, were of wood; doors had wooden hinges and latches, and were locked with wooden buttons. Everybody whittled. Whittling was the one great sin in the life of that poor priggish Nathaniel Mather who died "an aged person that had seen but nineteen winters in the world," as his gravestone at Salem confesses. He did his whittling on Sundays, and, the better to hide his wickedness from the Lord, behind the door! He says so himself and dilates at some length on the temptation to whittle.

The American fondness for whittling aroused some misunderstanding. Goodrich, in *The People of New England; Their Character, Manners and Customs, Amusements, Education, &c.*, says:

> It is peculiar to these people that they are seldom found without a pocket knife, which they use with dexterity; boys at school are frequently seen *whittling*, or cutting wood into some shape, for a windmill or other toy. It is a common trait, and it is said that a gentleman in Havana, who invited a large company to dine, gave each man from New England a shingle to cut, that they might not carve his furniture.

If this incident is not apocryphal, then the New England gentlemen were doubtless able to consume the latter half of their repast with utensils of their own construction. But Goodrich is wrong in his suppositions. The New Englander had no wish to destroy, his only wish was eternally to construct.

Is it any wonder, then, that for over two hundred years almost

Fig. 10 — WOODEN MUGS FROM NEW ENGLAND
From right to left: pewter-bound mug with metal handle; copper-bound mug or measure; so-called "Indian" tankard bound with wooden withes.
From the collection of Frederic Fairchild Sherman

every resident of the United States was always on the lookout for carvable wood? Suitable chips of hickory, a maple plank, sections of poplar were to the men folk wielding the knife, not pieces of wood, but potential boxes, trenchers, plates, waiting to be whittled.

Fig. 11 — (*right*) WALNUT MOLD
Built in sections and bound with metal. The butter was pounded into the container and a removable carved disk at the bottom made the decorative imprint. From the Amish settlement in Holmes County, Ohio, though perhaps made in Pennsylvania.
From the collection of Rhea Mansfield Knittle

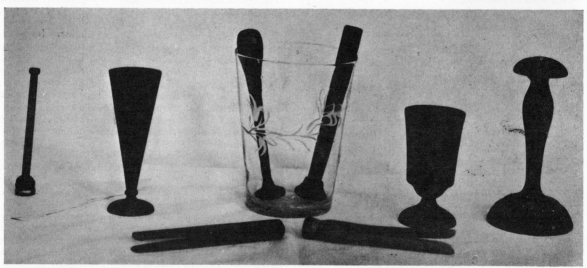

Fig. 12 — THREE TODDY STICKS, A CAP STAND, CUPS, AND CLOTHESPINS

Fig. 1 — Shaker Boxes
Exquisitely made containers, characterized by tapered laps secured by copper nails. Diameters range from about 3 to 18 inches. Copper nails also secure tops and bottoms to their frames. Made in sets and used for meal, sugar, spices, herbs, and the like

Fig. 2 — Various Pantry Boxes, Round and Oval
Methods of lapping vary. Less neatly constructed than their Shaker analogues. The employment of handmade nails to secure laps usually indicates an early date of production. Wooden pegs hold tops and bottoms in place. Diameters of oval boxes, from 2 to 17; of round, from 1 ½ to 24 inches

Early New England Woodenware

By Mary Earle Gould

Illustrations, except as noted, from the author's collection, photographed by the author and her brother, Doctor Rufus H. Gould

THE wooden utensils of olden days — boxes, bowls, buckets, sieves, tools, countless in variety — were as vital to the home as were the contemporary iron, pewter, and brass, of which we read so much. Hence it is strange that so few persons have troubled to study these alluring though humble devices, and to record them in text and photograph. Wood deteriorates through hard usage and exposure to the elements, and for that reason utensils in this material are scarce. It is seldom that their precise age may be estimated. They are to be appraised on the basis of their individual revelation of handcraftsmanship directing simple tools.

Pantry Boxes

In pantry boxes I find two distinct types of workmanship. One appears in the Shaker group; the other in what I call colony pieces. Shaker handicraft is characterized by perfection and uniformity. Each box exhibits a lapped joining of several points and a lapped cover with one point. A three-inch box has two points, and the number increases with the size of the box, until we reach the eighteen-inch size, with eight points. Copper nails are used to secure the lap points and to fasten bottom and top, respectively, to their circumscribing sides. Shaker boxes are oval in shape, and were made in sets of nine and, later, twelve, for storing meal, sugar, spices, and herbs, and for sundry other purposes.

What I term colony boxes are far from uniform. Each one betrays the personal skill or lack of skill of its maker. Hand-forged nails usually indicate a period prior to the factory era; but even at that, we may be misled in judging dates. The maker of a box may have thriftily used such old hand-forged nails as were easily available, despite the fact that machinemade nails were obtainable in the local store. Nevertheless, in general, nails and workmanship are fairly reliable indices of period.

Patterns of colony boxes are as numerous as were the makers. Points of all lengths, lapped in any position — near the end of the box or in the middle — fastened with no definite number of nails, testify to a rugged and unregulated individualism. I recall one box stitched together with shoe thread, another sewn with wire, another fastened with a splint. A fourth has points tucked into holes without reinforcing nails. In all such

boxes, the bottom is fastened to the sides and the cover to its rim with shoemaker's wooden pegs. Copper nails for fastening laps came later, but wooden pegs continued in use even in the factory-made boxes. The oval boxes vary in length from two to seventeen inches; the round items from one and one half inches to twenty-four.

I have divided boxes into three classes: (1) round boxes of large diameter for butter and cheese; (2) round and oval boxes for meal, sugar, and spices, varying from three inches to seventeen inches in diameter; (3) pill boxes, round and oval, less than three inches in diameter. Shaker and colony boxes are illustrated on this page.

Butter Boxes

The butter boxes vary in diameter — from twelve to twenty-four inches — but are of a depth to hold a pound roll of butter standing on end. They are lapped with a straight lap, or are made of staves and hoops. The period of a butter box is revealed by the method of lapping the hoops. The earliest hoops have notched ends that tuck under. In the next period more elaborate lapping appears: one end, tapered and notched to prevent slipping, is inserted through an elliptical hole in the other end. A peg further secures the fastening. The ends of later hoops are lapped and nailed, first with handmade nails or brads, and later with machinemade nails. The butter boxes with lapped sides were made of oak or ash — a strong, heavy wood. Bottoms were of pine. Covers were of pine with an oak or ash rim. A quartered-oak box with copper nails marking the lap, with a handsomely grained pine cover framed in a quartered-oak rim, is as fine an example of woodenware as any collector could desire.

Butter boxes with staves and hoops occur in oak, ash, and pine. The staves are of pine, doweled together, with a bevel at one end, fitted around a white-pine bottom. Odorless white pine did not impair the flavor of the butter. The hoops are of oak or ash, and so, too, is the cover rim.

Cheese Boxes

Cheese boxes are shallow, and their diameter is such as to accommodate the usual cylinder of cheese. Relatively few examples have survived; my collection boasts only three. One is of maple with large handmade nails securing the laps; a second, twice as heavy as the first, is of extremely thick oak

Fig. 3 — Pill Boxes
Dainty fabrications, one or two of which retain their labels with directions for effecting a sure cure

Fig. 4 — Water Buckets
Built of staves bound with hoops, variously secured. The middle item has an iron bail and iron loops

Fig. 5 — Water Buckets
Among the most appealing of old-time domestic woodenware and likewise perhaps the rarest

Fig. 6 — Milk Piggins
The elongated stave handle of the piggin at the left is expanded at the top to avert slipping

with handmade nails; and the third, possibly a factory product, is of oak with small machinemade nails, showing later workmanship.

Oval Forms

Oval meal, sugar, and spice boxes are very interesting. The Shakers, as previously observed, made their boxes in sets, regulating size and depth in exact proportion. Doubtless such boxes stood on pantry shelf or in pine cupboard in perfect order, meal or sugar in the large bottom box and spices in successive steps above. The colony housekeeper's pantry exhibited an odd array made by the handyman of the house, or by a neighboring cooper. The oval colony boxes, ranging from five to ten inches in length, are mostly of maple, with pine top and bottom. Occasionally, however, oak occurs. The laps of the smaller boxes are short, stopping in the middle of the box, or running to the end. The cover is always lapped in the opposite direction — I have but one exception. A few boxes have a straight, unpointed lap. The nails are copper or iron. In the larger boxes, oak or ash occurs, and the designs of lapping are highly varied. With few exceptions, the nails are handforged, with large heads. Depth and diameter follow no fixed rule. At a later time came the nests of round boxes, all of pine and showing machinemade nails. Often a factory name appears on a cover. In judging boxes the sense of touch plays an important rôle. New boxes have not the "feel" of the old.

Boxes were frequently painted. The color helps in determining age. We find gray, gray green, dark green, blue, and red. In some localities, the blue was called "wagon blue," since blue was a favorite color for farm wagons. The red was called by the Indians "turkey red," and by the colonists "coffin red," because coffins were once painted with that color. It was obtained by mixing red clay with scalded milk, buttermilk, whey, or the whites of eggs, together with an animal-hoof dryer.

Pill Boxes

Pill boxes seemingly made their appearance subsequent to the larger boxes. They are either round or oval, made of pine. The wood was reduced on a grindstone to a shell-like thinness. In some cases the laps are glued, as the wood is too fragile for nailing. The cover is held in its rim by friction; so is the bottom. I have a round pill box only one and one half inches in diameter, and an oval example slightly over two inches long. Other round boxes, as much as three inches in diameter, have one machinemade nail holding the lap on the box, and another single nail securing the cover lap. Wooden pegs keep top and bottom in place. The pill boxes were never painted.

Buckets

Buckets are pleasing members of the wooden family. They were made by a "white cooper" (the cooper produced barrels, while the smaller staved pieces were the white cooper's specialty). The buckets now most familiar are sugar buckets. But we also find water buckets, well buckets, milk piggins, and sap buckets. In the same category come tubs and kegs. All of these containers are built of staves and hoops. Examples originally used for liquids are now scarce, since they quickly rotted and were destroyed. The few survivors are highly prized. Staves of all such articles are of pine, bottoms of pine, and handles of oak or ash — a wood

Fig. 7 (left) — Butter Tub, Paddle, and Small Field Butter Tub

Fig. 8 (right) — Washtub and Three Old Clothes- pins

Fig. 9 — WATER KEG, POWDER KEG, AND RUM KEG
Note various methods of securing hoop ends. Kegs are similar to buckets in construction

Fig. 10 — SIEVES
The three in front, with horsehair sifters. That in the rear, a splint winnowing sieve. The smallest, oval with two covers

Fig. 11 — MAPLE BURL, AND BOWLS
The most-prized bowls are those made from the burl growth

Fig. 12 — THREE SALT BOWLS AND THREE DEEP DISHES
The standing item shows a burled grain

that bends easily. Sometimes the hoops are hickory like those of barrels. The staves are slightly curved and tapered at the bottom, some more than others. As in the butter boxes, the laps show three distinct methods of fastening. The early buckets have hoops with locked laps. Hoops of later date are lapped over and nailed.

Water buckets have two lengthened staves into which is pegged a bail handle. The two long staves also raised the bucket from the ground when it was turned over to dry. My collection includes seven unusual examples. The rarest is but six inches high — pine staves and bottom, hickory hoops lapped and tucked under, and an oak bail handle. An obviously authentic inscription on the bottom reads, "made by E. Proctor when he was 10 years old in 1770." Well buckets are made of oak staves with iron hoops — two features that make for strength and indifference to moisture.

The sap bucket is a common bucket with two extended staves. One type is equipped with a bail handle; for another type an ash or hickory stick run through the stave holes and secured with leather ties serves as a handle. These buckets were hung on spouts, called "spiles," driven into a tree when the maple sap was running. They were carried to the sheds on shoulder yokes. The milk piggin has only one stave handle. Size of bucket and length of stave handle vary: there are small piggins and large piggins; short, stubby handles and long, shaped handles.

Sugar buckets are made and used today, but examples of the prefactory era are not easily found. My collection reveals three types of hoops — two with locked joinings, another with lapped-over ends fastened with handmade nails. The largest of my sugar buckets stands twenty-four inches high and the smallest about eight inches high. A child's sugar bucket only four inches high is as perfect in workmanship as the large examples. Sugar buckets originally had covers, pine like the staves. Sugar boxes are shallow like the butter boxes, but smaller. They are lapped boxes of oak or ash with a bail handle of the same wood. The

covers are of pine with a rim of oak or ash. Such boxes were often used for conveying certain things to market, such as butter and eggs.

Tubs

Tubs are so hard to find as to be viewed as prize items. Some are round, some oval. Extra-long staves serve as handles. The family tub, the hand tub, and the laundry tub all occur. Sometimes the staves were reinforced with wooden hoops, but iron hoops were favored.

The butter tub is another member of the tub family. Tapered in form, it stands two feet high. The wooden hoop ends are tucked under, indicative of an early period. The cover is similar to that of the butter box. Such tubs were used for storing butter, which was packed with the aid of a long paddle and kept in the milk room or in the cellar.

Maple-sugar tubs are in the class of tubs with covers. Not so large as the butter tubs, they are made in the same way, of staves, hoops, and covers, and are tapered.

Kegs

Water kegs, rum kegs, molasses kegs, water canteens, and powder kegs were made by the white cooper. They are similar in construction to the buckets, but exhibit two heads like a drum. With the exception of the canteen, they have lock-joined hoops and a bunghole. Early examples were closed with a wooden plug driven in with a mallet. Later on the threaded plug made its appearance. The canteen dates well back into early colonial days. It is a lapped container with two heads and a plug hole — much like a mousetrap in appearance. Attached straps through which a longer strap could be slipped and thrown over the shoulder facilitated carrying. The lap of the oldest canteen in my collection is sewn with shoe thread.

Sieves

Horsehair sieves in a frame of maple or pine were made in sets, graduated in diameter from two to twelve inches. They were used to sift herbs and spices. A set of five was used in a doctor's office, and powder still clings to the mesh. Larger sieves were for sifting flour in bread-making. All have copper nails in the hoop fastenings, and the workmanship is of unfailing perfection. Sometimes bolting cloth was used instead of hair, and, at a later period, a very fine wire. Occasionally a large round sieve has a lid above and below. Oval pantry sieves with two covers are the most uncommon. Also to be mentioned are the winnowing sieves. Many of these are known to be about one hundred and fifty years old. They have oak rims, twenty to twenty-four inches in diameter, with a sieve of black-ash splints, often curiously fastened to the rim. One of my splint sieves is of Shaker origin, and the other is a colony item. Charcoal sieves are made of splints, with an ash rim around the top, and with holes larger than those of winnowing sieves.

Bowls

We cannot omit bowls from a consideration of woodenware, for bowls and deep dishes of wood served many purposes. Chopping bowls are found in a diversity of shapes and sizes. The earliest are hand-hollowed, and the resultant marks indicate the qualifications of the maker. Some were turned on the spring-pole lathe, which, we must bear in mind, came into existence as early as the thirteenth century. The most delightful as well as valuable chopping bowls are those made from the burl growth that sometimes occurs on trees. The Indians called this growth a "knot," and the "Down East" natives used the term "knurl." A burl bowl will not easily crack or warp. The most commonly used knot was of maple. The salt bowl, a little-known item, is five or six inches in diameter, and was intended to stand on the table as a receptacle for the family salt. It is round, made on a lathe.

Bread troughs are boxlike, with bottom, four sides dovetailed or nailed, and a cover. They are found in all sizes. More often than not, bread troughs were used as chopping bowls. In the present delicatessen days we may find it hard to realize how constantly our ancestors depended upon chopping bowls. Much food was prepared in the fall to

supply the family through the winter. Meats, poultry, fruits, vegetables passed under the chopping knife before being packed away in jars and crocks for use during the hungry days to come.

Mortars

Next to the chopping bowls in domestic usefulness came the mortar and pestle. What was not minced in the bowl was pounded or crushed in the mortar. Mortars vary quite surprisingly in form and material: small birch mortars for spices; heavy mortars of chestnut, oak, ash, or lignum-vitæ for crushing salt, sugar, herbs, or cornmeal. Still a third type — shallow, with a stubby pestle — was used for snuff. Pestles were often merely roots of appropriate form shaped for use.

Cheese Drainers and Baskets

Cheese baskets played an important rôle in every home. The making of cheese occurred two or three times a week. The crudest drainers have simply a perforated board for a bottom. Another early type was constructed of rounded sticks set in a wooden frame (*Fig. 13*). Round ash hoops, joined and bottomed with rounded slats, form another variety of cheese basket that may be termed the "windsor" type (*Fig. 14*). Of later date are the cheese baskets made from oak or ash splints, woven in hexagonal form with wide hexagonal spaces. These baskets come in various sizes, from twelve to twenty-four inches, and often in odd shapes. They served to hold the curds while these were being drained through cheesecloth. The baskets were set on racks over tubs, which caught the dripping whey — later passed on to the pigs. The curds, tied in the retaining cloth, awaited the finishing processes. Of construction similar to that of the splint cheese baskets are a funnel, an ox muzzle, a clam basket, and an odd Shaker basket (*see Figs. 15 and 16*).

Pantry Tools

Old pantry tools of many kinds tell a tale of laborious hours. Many of them were made at home with the aid of ingenuity, elbow grease, and a jackknife. Some of the scoops are works of art. There are wet scoops

Fig. 13 — EARLY CHEESE DRAINER
Originally painted red. In default of a basketmaker in the vicinity, this piece of carpentry and spindlework would suffice

Fig. 14 — CHEESE BASKET OF "WINDSOR" CONSTRUCTION, PALETTE PADDLES, PADDLE WITH BUTTER PRINT, TWO COMMON PADDLES
The paddles were used in working butter

Fig. 15 — CHEESE BASKETS AND AN EGG BASKET
Made of splints. Used in draining cheese curds. The example at the right is a Shaker basket for carrying eggs

Fig. 16 — OX MUZZLE, CLAM BASKET, AND FUNNEL
Various ingenious methods of attaching the openwork to the supporting rim were employed in making these splint items

Fig. 17 — Scoops and a Ladle

Fig. 18 — Bread Board, Graters,
Sausage Gun, Wooden Funnel,
Herb Skimmer

This sausage gun was used to force
the chopped meat into the sausage
cases. Such instruments, particularly in Pennsylvania, were sometimes of quite majestic size

Fig. 19 — Trough, Wooden Plate, Bowl, and Indian Eating Scoop

and dry scoops, for barn and pantry. One very large Shaker scoop in my collection has a double-barred handle. Of one piece and measuring fully eighteen inches, it was used for stirring apple butter. Other scoops have even more elaborate handles, but the majority are plain, for hard and frequent usage.

Butter paddles are similar to scoops in construction, but flatter, as the term implies. The woods used are birch, maple, or pine. One beechwood butter paddle has a butter print cut in the end of the handle. Two unusual paddles resemble an artist's palette and are perhaps more useful. Rolling-pins of several types occur. For the one that serves us today, over half a dozen were needed yesterday. The earliest rolling-pins had no handles. A ribbed example was used for rolling out cookies.

Spoons, forks, spatulas, toddy spoons, toddy stirrers, lemon sticks, pie crimpers, apple parers, dippers, and mashers afford an array of shapes and sizes that beggar description. Chopping knives show much individuality in shape and size. Here the blacksmith was called upon to supply the blade. Butter molds are often quite elaborate. They are made from a single piece of wood — a stamp within a boxlike case that holds a pound of butter, or a single stamp with a handle. A grater for horse-radish and carrots is a crudely shaped, broad spatula about twelve inches long. A sheet of tin, punched in a so-called pattern, and curved, is fastened over the lower part with handmade nails. The back is inscribed with initials and the date *1794*. Two others showing machine-

made nails are not so old. There are likewise the long-handled stick for stirring Indian pudding, the long stick for use in the dye pot, and another used in soap-making. There are the chubby stick for beating clothes, the broad spatula for turning over apples drying on racks, and the fancifully shaped ones for stirring food cooking in pots before the fire. Pantry tools are mute evidence of the vast amount of labor accomplished in old-time households. To a collector of such woodenware, nothing seems so interesting in the study of our early days as the life which is represented by these homely, crude, worn utensils. Each acquisition — and, as this article with its illustrations testifies, the variety of objects is infinite — reveals another bit of the home life of the past.

The way of the woodenware collector is long but alluring. It should be pursued casually lest hard work impair exhilaration. Some choice pieces cannot be purchased at any price, some are transferred with great reluctance, while others are tossed away at auctions. The possession and study of such pieces gives to history a wealth of human connotations not otherwise to be discovered or appreciated. In the realm of woodenware connoisseurship may walk hand in hand with sentiment. That is why I find it the most fascinating realm in all collectordom.

Fig. 20 (*left*) — One-Piece
Wooden Jug and a
Sugar Scoop
The scoop, with its pe-
culiar hand grip, is an
unusually fine exam-
ple. From Ohio

Fig. 21 (*right*) — Stamps
and Crimping Wheels
First three of wood,
though the second has
a pewter wheel; fourth
and fifth of brass. Pre-
sumably to speed the
glorifying of piecrust.
From Ohio.
*Figures 20 and 21
from the collection of
Mrs. Rhea Mansfield
Knittle*

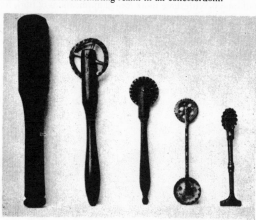

THE BURL AND ITS USES

By MARY EARLE GOULD

Except as noted, illustrations from the author's collection

oval in shape, and holes were cut for handles. These two features distinguish early Indian bowls from those made later by the colonists on the lathe or by hand.

The colonists learned valuable lessons from the Indians, but improved on the methods of the aborigines. Rather than hewing burl bowls by hand, the white men constructed a lathe that fashioned them more easily, producing round bowls with rolled edges and ornamental grooves on the outside. First charring the wood with fire, they used the axe-shape adze and the drawknife before turning the burl. The earliest lathe, called a spring-pole lathe, consisted of an arm built on a stand to hold the work, a treadle, and a pole suspended overhead. A rope or cord attached to the overhead pole went around the working arm and down to the treadle, so that in operation the pole was pulled down by the treadle and on the release flew back again, the arm working in see-saw motion. Picture the romantic scene when such a lathe was built in the dooryard and the overhead pole was an apple-tree limb that waved gracefully as the lathe worked! A later lathe, more scientifically constructed, made full revolutions. Even at that, work produced on it was never perfectly round because of the unsteadiness of the arm on the lathe.

On nearly every bowl is to be found the mark where the burl joined the tree. The annual rings of the tree show in a decided grain against the dotted wood of the burl. This grain helps to tell from what tree the burl was cut; otherwise it would be almost impossible to distinguish the burl of one tree from that of another. Though a growth may form on any tree after it has been bruised, the best burls for turning are found on the maple, ash, and walnut, since they are very hard and solid. Burls are often seen on chestnuts, elms, and birches, but their wood seems to be too light in weight and too porous to work.

Curly or bird's-eye maple and certain other woods have an ornamental grain, but it is the grain of the tree itself, not of an excrescence. Such woods should not be confused with burl and should not be called "burly." Wood taken from the crotch of a tree, from a knotty section where a limb has been cut off, from the gnarled roots, or from the base of the tree reveals to a trained expert just where it was cut. The possibility of determining from what part of the tree the cutting for a given bowl or other utensil was made adds zest to the study of wooden articles. Those who

BURL is the scar tissue that nature supplies to cover a wound on a tree. When a tree has been bruised, the rings of the trunk or branch are checked in their regularity and extend in a gnarled, twisted excrescence resembling a wart. Sometimes this growth or burl is called a tumor; the Indians called it a knot; the early colonists spoke of it as a knurl. On certain trees the burl is extremely hard and solid, and the Indians, recognizing its possibilities, made bowls of it. The American colonists, in their need for adaptation of the materials at hand to a variety of everyday purposes, followed the Indians' example, and found further use for burl in making mortars and numerous small articles. In this country and more particularly in England, burl — or burr, as it is called there — was early utilized for decorative furniture veneers and inlays. With these more formal applications of burl, however, we are not here concerned.

The natural shape of the burl suggests a bowl. After cutting the growth from the tree and allowing it to become properly seasoned, the Indians used their tools of flint, stone, or shell to produce the bowls now to be seen in museums and collections. First a fire was kindled on the flat side of the burl to char the wood and soften it for cutting. Hollowing and shaping was a laborious process, for their crude tools cut no more than sawdust chips. The bowls were

FIG. 1 — INDIAN BOWLS

a, Typical Indian shape, oval with hole handles, but not of burl. Made in the 1830's by an Indian named Huge Pie. *b*, Indian burl bowl of large size, 4 feet by 2 feet, 10 inches deep.
From the Wells Historical Museum

FIG. 2 — THREE BURL EATING BOWLS

Example at left is all of burl, as the mottled texture shows. The other two indicate that they were made from the intersection of burl and tree trunk

1a 1b 2

FIG. 3 — LARGE ASH BURL BOWL

With decorative bandings below the rim. The grain where burl and trunk joined may be detected

FIG. 4 — BURL BOWLS

a, milk bowl. *b*, grease bowl, stained very dark

FIG. 5 — CHEESE STRAINER OF BURL

Interior bleached to whiteness; cheesecloth attached to pegs below rim. *From the collection of Charles L. Hopkins*

FIG. 6 — MORTARS AND PESTLES

a, a beautifully grained example of walnut burl. *b, left*, an ash burl mortar, nearly worn through by the friction of the iron-headed pestle; *right*, also of ash burl, rather elaborately turned

wish to acquire only pieces made from burl would do well to bear these points in mind. Nothing is burl except what is cut from the burl itself, and the term "burly wood" is a misnomer.

The largest Indian bowls were about four feet in length, and the smallest bowl known is the individual salt of three inches. The colonists' bowlmaking included the broad-base bowl and that with a small base, the shallow bowl and the deep bowl, the bowl with a hole in the bottom used as a cheese strainer, the shallow washbasins, the large bowl for the family serving, and the small one for individual members of the family. By studying shapes and stains one can quite accurately identify a bowl's function. The bowl in which bread was mixed was large and deep, showing a bleached whiteness. Grease left a stain: the shallow, wide-bottomed bowl that held fat for soapmaking turned dark from the penetrating grease. Quite the opposite was the bowl in which milk was set for the cream to rise; it was bleached to whiteness. The shape of the milk bowl, which was called a tray as often as a bowl, followed the lines of early earthenware bowls — flat and shallow. The butter bowl, more commonly spoken of as a tray, shows the line left by grease. A bowl used for straining the cooked milk in making a batch of cheese has a hole in the bottom. Over it a piece of cheesecloth was fastened by means of a drawstring slipped over a protruding rim at the bottom of the bowl or by loops at the corners of the cloth which caught on wooden pegs at the upper rim of the bowl. The cloth could thus be taken off and washed after use. The bowl is very much bleached where the curds rested.

Bowls for use as chopping trays were made of a sizable diameter and show the marks of the chopping knife. Eating bowls were made of all sizes and are generally without marks — fingers and wooden spoons left no imprint. But in spite of all the purposes for which the bowls were originally designed, most old bowls appear to have felt the chopping knife sooner or later. One frequently finds bowls that have been stained a color delightful to look upon, with any identifying marks that might help the collector carefully hidden. Beware the too-finished look that might disguise a new bowl or

plate. Here, again, the collector needs a thorough knowledge of old wood as well as of old workmanship.

The burl was used for mortars, as well as for bowls, and for covered receptacles, urns, butter workers, scoops, and salts, all turned on the lathe. The mortars are frequently beautiful specimens of wood. For small kitchen mortars, the pestles were of maple; often a gnarly root of a tree was found shaped, ready for use. Occasionally the wooden pestle was mounted with a metal head, as shown in Figure 6b.

Woodenware was primarily a utilitarian expression, but its construction was not always dictated by bare necessity. Fancy receptacles and urns, sometimes of quite unusual shapes, were made for ornamental purposes. Some of the latter may have come from England, where a greater sophistication was usually apparent even in the humble objects.

An extremely large burl still attached to the trunk on which it grew stands in Wiggins' Tavern in Northampton, Massachusetts. It must measure at least five feet in diameter. One can well see why such a growth was called a wart because of its repulsive surface. From such great burls as that, and from such as appear on the two-hundred-year-old elm shown on the opposite page, the Indian made his big bowls.

A knowledge of wood can hardly be acquired from books. Part of it must be gained from the living trees, part from things made of wood. The burl seems a small part of the tree, but I have found my own study of the burl and its uses well rewarded by my increased appreciation of the burl bowls and mortars in my collection.

FIG. 8 — BUTTER WORKERS

Of burl and of curly maple. The small scoop (*right*) is for skimming cream

FIG. 9 — SHOVEL

Head of burl, handle of wood from the tree trunk. *Length*, 3 feet. *From the Wells Historical Museum*

FIG. 7 — BURL WASH-BOWL, BUTTER WORK-ER, AND CHUNK OF MAPLE BURL

American Woodenware

WOODEN TRENCHER

BUTTER MOLDS. *Right*, a typical Pennsylvania pattern. *Above*, a New England design. *Index of American Design.*

UNTIL THE SIXTEENTH CENTURY, and later, table manners were far from elegant. People ate from square wooden blocks, hollowed out in the middle, called trenchers. These went through various developments in England, generally becoming flatter. The colonists brought some of them to America, but most of the wooden dishes made here were round. One would think that trenchers might have been plentiful enough so that everybody could have his own, but as a matter of fact it was considered gross extravagance to supply more than one trencher for every two eaters. Even after woodenware, or treen, as it was called, began to be superseded by pewter in the sixteenth century, the poorer people went on using it. In the American Colonies, especially in the remoter regions, a good many people

were still eating from wooden trenchers and bowls up to the time of the Revolution.

From the Indians the colonists picked up the art of making things out of burl, a bulgy growth of scar tissue found on certain trees. The Indians cut off the burl, let it season, and then hollowed it out by charring and chipping to make oval bowls. The twisted growth of the burl not only provided an attractive grain, but made things that were not apt to warp and crack. The bowls the colonists made out of burl were round, and were usually turned on a lathe instead of being chipped out by hand. Burls from maple and ash trees were most commonly used; in fact, maple generally was the favorite wood for dishes, with ash, beech, and birch running next.

The hand lathe was used for making plates and bowls,

CARVED ROOSTER, in Pennsylvania German style, colored red, cream, and green. *Collection of Earl F. Robacker.*

MILK PIGGIN, with one stave elongated as a handle. *Collection of Mary Earle Gould.*

and also the wooden drinking vessels called noggins, which looked rather like pitchers and were produced in one-cup, two-cup, and three-cup sizes.

Buckets and tubs, on the other hand, were made of upright staves bound together with hoops, and the interesting point to note here is the variety of methods which were used to fasten the hoops—lapped under and interlocked, or secured with nails.

Almost nothing in the way of American woodenware survives from before 1700. In the early eighteenth century, commercial production got started. By 1732 we find a "Wood Turner from London" advertising in the *Pennsylvania Gazette* "all sorts of turning in Hard Wood —Coffee Mills, Pepper boxes, Punch bowls, mortars, sugar boxes."

In the early nineteenth century woodenware makers were numerous, especially in New England. There must have been many small establishments like the one operating in 1817 in Henniker, New Hampshire. Father and son worked together, one turning the lathe while the other held the tools. When they had finished a supply of bowls, plates, and other items, they went around peddling them. Barrels and buckets were the specialty of Hingham, Massachusetts, and these were distributed all over New England.

The variety of wooden utensils is almost endless— "peels" for putting bread in the oven, "Scotch hands" for rolling butter into balls, mortars and pestles, sieves, and ingenious tools like apple parers, to mention only a few. Assorted oval boxes range in size from the diminutive pill boxes to large ones, some 24 inches in diameter. The nests of boxes made by the Shakers are especially in

demand, because of the fine craftsmanship which is the hallmark of all their products.

Collecting wooden utensils can be a lot of fun, but there is one difficulty: it is almost impossible to tell how old a thing is. People speak of the "feel" of old wood, but a wooden utensil that's seen hard use gets to feeling old before its time! Another thing you hear is that you can tell an old box or bucket from the hand-made nails, but this is not very helpful either, since machine-made nails were in use from about 1825. At least, however, you can be sure that nobody would have bothered to make a wooden bucket, for instance, once metal pails had become cheap and plentiful.

Most American woodenware is characterized by a plain, down-to-earth utility, but collectors with an eye for the decorative can also find plenty to enjoy, particularly in the work of the Pennsylvania Germans. Wood carving was a traditional skill with them, and they turned it to good account in the decoration of all sorts of objects.

Butter stamps and molds, made not only in Pennsylvania but in New England and elsewhere, are especially attractive. Those from Pennsylvania feature the ever-popular tulip, heart, and star, together with sheaves of wheat, crescents, and acorns; the design is generally quite stylized. The same sort of decoration was applied to the springerle boards used for making fancy cakes. New England patterns, derived from England rather than the Continent, tend to be more naturalistic and asymmetrical, with freely flowing curves.

A later type of Pennsylvania woodenware, now being sought by collectors, is Lehnware, which was made by

WOODEN NOGGIN. *Essex Institute.*

CIGAR STORE INDIANS. *Collection of Dudley E. Waters.*

BRACKET SHELF, Pennsylvania German, with carved birds and heart. *Collection of Earl F. Robacker.*

Joseph Lehn almost up to 1900. Cups and goblets are the most typical form, turned and painted with a grayish-pink background and frequently a strawberry design.

The fondness of the Pennsylvania Germans for wood carving led them to create all sorts of fanciful animals, birds, and figure groups, which have recently been elevated to new dignity by being classified as folk art. The best-known carver was Schimmel, but there were others.

Pennsylvania wood carving, for the most part, is so closely linked with Continental European work as to be scarcely American at all, but there is one type of carved wood figure that we can claim as our own—the bird decoy, another idea we took over from the Indians. Though not intended to be "art," many of these bird figures resemble modern sculpture in their clean, dynamic lines. Some of the old wooden weathervanes, too, appeal to modern taste with their crude but vigorous designs.

One important category of objects that can scarcely be overlooked, though hardly a "collectible" for most people, is the wooden Indian. When cigar-store figures started life in England, they were not Indians but "black boys," wearing a headdress and skirt of tobacco leaves. Over here, however, cigar-store Indians were established as part of the American scene by the middle of the nineteenth century. Their gaudily painted decoration had to be renewed so frequently that some itinerant artists made a living doing nothing else. Hand-carved figures gradually gave place to cast metal ones, and the wooden cigar-store Indian faded away. According to Jean Lipman's *American Folk Art*, there were once some 75,000 of them scattered over the country. Now they are extremely scarce —in case you were planning to get one for that odd corner of the breakfast room.   —JANE BOICOURT

WATER BUCKETS, showing various methods of fastening the hoops. *Collection of Mary Earle Gould.*

SHAKER BOXES, with typical "zigzag" overlap, fastened with copper nails. *Collection of Mary Earle Gould.*

Wooden Boxes
of German Pennsylvania

BY EARL F. ROBACKER

Fig. 1—Pine candle boxes (*eighteenth century*). *Top*, constructed with wooden pegs, painted dull orange and blue with closed tulip typical of the period. *Below*, with wide dovetailing, painted dark blue with white panels inscribed *Eva Anno 1776*, said to have belonged to Eva, wife of Conrad Weiser; the top is a replacement. *Except as noted, all illustrations are from the author's collection.*

LESS WELL KNOWN than the dower chests, iron stove plates, and illuminated certificates of the Pennsylvania Germans are their boxes, but these minor articles also tell their story of ingenuity and decorative skill. Gay with the painted flowers and other devices typical of the region, they follow the same evolutionary development as the major arts of German Pennsylvania. The earliest are in general the most desirable, succeeded by those less detailed and skilled, and eventually followed by machine-made products of little interest. Their period extends from at least as early as 1750 through the Civil War, and perhaps later.

Pennsylvania boxes, made to serve all sorts of useful purposes, are remarkably varied in shape, size, construction, and decoration. Most of them are of pine or walnut, but maple was also used. Earlier ones are usually dovetailed and pegged, later ones often nailed. While many have separate or hinged lids, examples of the sliding-lid type are numerous. On most of these the thumb-catch on the lid is a single, wide, shallow gouge, but sometimes it is composed of three or more deeper, parallel gouges, for extra elaboration.

Perhaps first in importance among Pennsylvania boxes are those for candles, which often received the best efforts of the decorator. Only a limited number have survived, and probably all *bona fide* examples in existence today were made in the eighteenth century, for as the nineteenth century progressed the candle box became less necessary as a household appurtenance.

Each of the two specimens illustrated here is representative of the work of the last quarter of the eighteenth century *(Fig. 1)*.

"Bride's boxes," now conceded to be of Swiss and German provenance, range in size from the largest, about nineteen inches in length, down to miniatures of seven inches and perhaps even less. The covers of larger specimens are often painted with crude representations of bride and groom in eighteenth-century costume; when they are dated, the dates are most frequently in the 1790's. Some carry romantic inscriptions, the lettering following the oval plane of the cover. The inscription on the large box of Figure 2 reads *Ich liebe dich mit Luff*—not com-

Fig. 2—"Bride's boxes." Of European origin, these are the most colorful in the entire box fraternity. *Left*, inscribed *Ich liebe dich mit Luff*. *Right*, unusual painted decoration of angel with two swords, perhaps to guard the precious articles of the bride's trousseau kept in the box.

Fig. 3—Spice boxes. *Left*, hanging type, walnut, with X-inlays on drawer fronts, brass pulls, and heart-shaped cutout in back (*early 1800's*). *Center*, later hanging type, pine, stenciled (*1820's*). *Right*, sliding-lid type, pine, heavily dovetailed, with thick wooden pegs to secure top molding: inscribed *1750 A G D* .

Fig. 5—Bureau or trinket box. Of quarter-sawed maple, unusual in construction, with floral painted panels.

Fig. 4 — Knife boxes. *Above*, sliding-lid type, of pine, dovetailed and pegged. Painted in bold color; black, green, and red, with yellow background. *Right*, hinged-lid type, of walnut, inlaid with maple, mahogany, ebony, and oak. The brass hinges are not original.

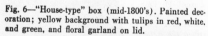

Fig. 6—"House-type" box (mid-1800's). Painted decoration; yellow background with tulips in red, white, and green, and floral garland on lid.

Fig. 7—Hinged-lid pine bureau box. Painted decoration in red, white, blue, yellow, and green, with spattered brown background. Undoubtedly garish when new, now mellowed into a pleasing blend of colors.

pletely German, and certainly not English, but perhaps a forerunner of that melding of languages and dialects called "Pennsylvania Dutch." The smaller boxes, identical in construction with the larger ones, even to the fine wooden pins or pegs and laced side fastenings, are less detailed in ornamentation. Their principal motif is the tulip—the same tulip that graces the larger oval boxes, and also one of the candle boxes of Figure 1.

Berks County in Pennsylvania has contributed notably to the total of interesting or unusual painted boxes in work often attributed to one Henry or Henrich Bucher (*Fig. 8*). The Reading (Pennsylvania) Public Museum and Art Gallery has outstanding specimens of this work, one box carrying the name *Görg Kutz*. Some of the boxes are oval, some rectangular; all have a black background on which the peculiarly individual tulips are painted in red and yellow. On any given specimen, the tulips are usually shown in variety: closed or in bud, partly open, and full blown. On the covers the foliage (green now faded to brown, with bandings of cream) fills in the space about the flowers in pleasing fashion.

Bucher-type oval boxes are like the imported bride's boxes in shape and construction, with one important difference: European boxes are fastened together with thongs or withes; the broad sheets of wood used in the Berks County boxes have been shaved to paper thinness at the point of overlapping, and glued. Neither Bucher nor any other decorator seems to have designed the flowers on the side of the cover so that they would match those on the side of the box itself when the box is closed.

Spice cabinets are among the earliest of home-made boxes—generous ones which would accommodate from four to eight or more of the highly desired condiments. The earliest I know of is an essentially crude box of pine dated *1750* (*Fig. 3*). It has a sliding lid and the interior is divided by whittled partitions into six compartments of equal size. Another type is the hanging wall cabinet, usually heavy in construction, generally of walnut, but sometimes of pine, painted and decorated. A well-known salt box of similar construction in a private collection is dated *1797* and bears the original owner's name. The one pictured in Figure 3 is perhaps a little later. Still other—and later—hanging cabinets have the drawers placed under one another in a single tier, the whole article being painted and stenciled.

Wooden boxes for lead and slate pencils are rather like the spice box with sliding lid, but narrower. Some have interior compartments, long ones for slate pencils, smaller ones for sponges or other gear. They occur in both pine and walnut. Decoration is usually painted, occasionally inlaid.

Another type of box with sliding lid, used probably for trinkets, is similar in form but deeper in proportion and smaller, about five or six inches in length. In this type, all sides are decorated similarly with tulip or other flowers but the front or top is reserved for the painter's best efforts.

Various other small boxes are known as bureau or trinket boxes. Some are plain, some decorated; in form they may be round, oval or rectangular, and the range in size is considerable, though none is very large. Unusual in construction is the rectangular box with floral-painted panels (*Fig. 5*). The cover is attached by a wooden pivot at each end of the box itself, and instead of being pegged or dovetailed, the pieces are secured by glazer's points. In design, wood, and decoration, it appears to be Pennsylvanian, but in construction and detail it is not characteristic. A later design used on Pennsylvania German boxes is the morning-glory pattern, also found on chairs comparatively late in the so-called "painted period."

A painted decoration sometimes found on Pennsylvania boxes has an all-over spattered or sponged effect, similar to that on the Staffordshire china called spatterware. The box of Figure 7 also has a six-petaled open tulip painted in red, white, and blue, like that seen on spatterware. Since spatterware is seldom, if ever, dated, the *Emma Billig 1810* on the under side of the cover is of interest. The dark brown background was rhythmically spattered with a small circular sponge.

Knife boxes are familiar objects in Penn's country, as elsewhere. Two distinctive ones, representing two different methods of construction, are shown in Figure 4.

Fig. 8—Bucher-type Berks County box. *Courtesy of the Reading Public Museum and Art Gallery, Reading, Pennsylvania.*

One has two hinged, sloping lids, attached to a lengthwise partition, with a mahogany knife inlaid on one and a fork on the other. The design of these implements may give the best clue to the age of the piece: they suggest the bone-handled tableware of the mid-nineteenth century. A variant type of knife box has hinged covers fastened to a partition *across* the middle, rather than lengthwise. Other knife boxes have separate sliding lids for knife and fork compartments.

Perhaps most familiar of all Pennsylvania boxes is the four-inch kind often called the "house" type, though the curved lid and attached thin metal hasp suggest an old-fashioned trunk more than a house (*Fig. 6*). Although the genuinely old ones are hand-pegged and bear authentic, though simple, designs, the pieces are often carelessly put together, the thin wire fastenings and the loop for the hasp not well secured, and the measurements generally irregular. There is a wide range of background color, and the purchaser should be advised that the paint usually has a water, not an oil base. These boxes, made originally about 1840-1850, are now being reproduced.

FIG. 1—REPRESENTATIVE CARVED NOAH'S ARK ANIMALS. The specimens from three different sets are shown here, the smallest figures "belonging" to the Ark in the illustration.

Except as noted, the illustrations are from the collection of the author; the photographs are by Herman Kartluke.

PENNSYLVANIA GERMAN WOOD CARVINGS

By EARL F. ROBACKER

AMONG THE LESSER COLLECTIBLES in the field of Pennsylvania German arts and crafts, various types of small, handmade wooden objects are worthy of scrutiny. Since many of the earliest settlers in Pennsylvania stemmed from woodcarving areas in Europe, especially Switzerland, it is not surprising that carved wooden toys in some variety have been found here. They are not numerous, however, perhaps because of their perishability at the hands of children, or because the demands of the new world left little time, even to the artistically gifted, for making such comparative luxuries as toys. In addition to these playtime mementos there are many objects, utilitarian or decorative.

These wooden pieces fall loosely into several categories, according to their treatment: carved, whittled, scratch-carved, and turned, either alone or in combination. Best known among actual carvings are the birds and beasts of Wilhelm Schimmel, who worked in and about Carlisle, Pennsylvania, after the Civil War (see ANTIQUES, October 1943, p. 164). But Schimmel, though his work is unique in character, is not alone among the Pennsylvania German carvers; in fact, strictly speaking, he may not have been a Pennsylvania German at all, since Germans in Pennsylvania are not considered honest-to-goodness Pennsylvania Germans unless their residence had been established prior to 1848. Occasionally one comes upon birds, domestic animals, and human figures which in execution and in applied color bear the marks of old-time Pennsylvania handwork. Noah's ark figures, now nearly non-existent save in factory-made sets; deer with branch-

ing antlers; and tiny sheep with woolly pelts like those which Schimmel used come to light in "Dutchland" areas. Sometimes their makers are known; oftener there is no information available beyond their reputed span of ownership in a given family.

The Christmas *putz* miniatures of George Huguenin, descendant of a toy-carving family of Travere, Switzerland, are of this type. The first Huguenin lived north of Stroudsburg, in Newfoundland (then Hopedale), Pennsylvania, on the upper fringe of the so-called Dutch country. Huguenin was not a professional toy carver, but now and then carved objects which were packed away and kept for display, either with the Christmas tree or in lieu of one, during the Christmas season. Incidentally, a wealth of folk material has been lost as later generations in Pennsylvania German villages have allowed the tradition of elaborate representations of the Nativity to die.

Huguenin (locally known as "Higiny") was particularly fond of sheep, and there is a family tradition that his Swiss barns, sheepfolds, stockades, and diminutive houses and churches were made largely to serve as a fitting background for his multitudinous flocks. These animals were small, not more than two inches high, smoothly executed with a careful eye for the anatomical details and then, like those of Schimmel, painted and covered with genuine sheepskin pelt. The barns were simply boxlike constructions except for the fronts, which suggested the conventional Swiss peasant form; they served as repositories, not for the flocks alone, but for all the smaller toys in the collection. Houses and churches were of single blocks of wood, usually not much larger than those used in making the sheep. They were

FIG. 2 — TOY BUILDINGS carved by George Huguenin of Newfoundland, Pennsylvania, about the middle of the nineteenth century. *Courtesy of Mr. and Mrs. Newell Felton.*

painted white, with windows and doors outlined in black (*Fig. 2*). Earlier members of the Huguenin family probably also had a hand in these carvings, for some appear considerably older than others. George Huguenin, who also made simple furniture for his own household, and such items as doll houses and cradles, died in 1882.

American in origin though they were, the Huguenin toys were probably patterned after remembered European originals. Sets made for export to America contained strikingly similar buildings, and Swiss stockinette-covered lambs may well have served as inspiration for the larger, woolly Huguenin sheep. Box labels in German and French on surviving imported sets seem to indicate a Swiss origin.

More elaborate in every way, and demonstrating a command of technique vastly superior to that of either Schimmel or Huguenin, is the finely carved rooster shown in Figure 3 (*right*). Several of these specimens have been found, so closely resembling one another that they seem to be the work of a single artist. The maker is unknown, but general opinion

them remained there permanently. It is possible that what would seem to be a Pennsylvania German rooster may actually be a New York German one.

Wood carving for utilitarian purposes is represented in such homely objects as sugar mortars, dippers, and the bowls and paddles used in processing butter as it came from the churn (*Fig 4*). These objects were carved of a single piece of wood, chosen, when possible, from a large knot or burl in the tree, to minimize the danger of splitting in actual use. Round bowls were sometimes lathe-turned, but the less common oval ones were as a rule patiently gouged out and finished to satin smoothness by hand. The butter molds used both in and out of Pennsylvania represented a combination of wood turning and carving. Especially prized by collectors is the Pennsylvania butter mold bearing the design of a cow, since for some reason cattle are less common in decorative representation than almost any other motif. The tulip, the eagle, and the acorn are also popular Pennsylvania motifs.

Akin in feeling to the designs on butter molds are those of the *springerle* boards which Pennsylvania German housewives used in baking Easter cakes, *lebkuchen,* and others. By one method the intaglio-carved board was used to form a design in bas-relief in the soft dough; by another a carved rolling pin was used (*Fig. 5*). The decorated surface of springerle rolling pins varied in width from three inches to ten or more. While some of the flat boards were so small that they would decorate only a single cake or two, others were large enough to pattern a dozen at once. Designs on the larger boards were frequently duplicated in some of the component squares, which usually measured two inches. The cakes were cut apart before they were baked. Some of the best *springerle* molds probably came from Germany and Switzerland, where they have been used for centuries, but others, often the smaller or simpler ones, are of known Pennsylvania origin.

Wooden printing blocks used for patterning fabrics in color are not dissimilar in workmanship, although they are heavier and coarser in detail. They have sometimes been confused with baking implements. A full set of these blocks, complete even to the name of the designer, was discovered in Pennsylvania within the past year. Isolated specimens are more commonly found.

Early Pennsylvania German wall spoon racks, of which a fine specimen is in the Pennsylvania German rooms in the American Wing of the Metropolitan Mu-

FIG. 4 — HANDMADE BUTTER BOWL from German Valley, Pennsylvania, with paddle and butter molds. *Courtesy of Mrs. Frank Robacker; paddle from the collection of Mrs. Lawrence J. Ullman.*

is that the work was Pennsylvania German. This claim rests partly on its comparability with the body of Pennsylvania carvings, particularly in its characteristic use of applied color.

The example illustrated was carved from a single block of pine about eight inches square. The coloring is in tones of red, cream, and green, and, as is true of Schimmel roosters, the wings are not separate members but are outlined in black paint against the body. (It will be recalled that the wings of Schimmel *eagles* were carved separately and pegged to the body.) One of these birds was found in eastern New York, a circumstance which gives rise to an interesting speculation. Many of the Palatinates who set out for Pennsylvania broke their journey by spending considerable time in New York, notably in and about Saugerties, and some of

FIG. 5 — SPRINGERLE BOARDS, rolling pin from Berks County, Pennsylvania.

seum, New York, show the same type of homespun execution. The gouge-carving of baking and block-printing molds is occasionally supplemented in spoon racks by scratch carving, and sometimes by simple reeding as well. There is a considerable range in the amount of actual carving; in some cases it is confined to the cut-out top or the slots which hold the spoons. Often the use of applied design and color enhances what would otherwise be a painfully primitive piece (*Fig. 6*).

Some of what passes for carving might more reasonably be termed whittling, since its significant decorative detail is essentially two-dimensional. An outstanding specimen of this type is the shapely little bracket shelf shown in Figure 6. Interesting as a study in the curved line, it gains added distinction through the use of the yellow and "Dutch red" which lend character to the well-cut facing birds. The background is dark brown; the simple medallions are yellow. The whittling is remarkably clean-cut throughout. The heart is of the low, broad-lobed design so often found on dower chests, *fraktur* patterns, and in such lowlier items as tin cooky cutters and the cut-out handles of bake boards, kraut cutters, and knife boxes.

Of this type of work also is an occasional comb case. The one shown in Figure 6 is crudely executed, but interesting because of its date and because of the symbolic scratch carvings. There are nine of these geometric figures in all, one of them on an inside end of the trough. Two sets of initials appear: *A.H.C.* on the bottom, and *H.A.* on the back. Some of the tiny wooden pegs which were originally used have fallen out and have been replaced with small square nails. A comb case similar in form but without the scratch-carved symbols was among the household articles made by Huguenin, but is no longer in existence. No comb cases with painted decorations have been reported.

One of the most curious of hand-carved objects is in the form of what purports to be a small scratch-carved and painted wooden book, but which in reality is the lair of a steel-tongued serpent. The snake, a fearsome curved and spotted creature, makes its appearance when the novice, discovering that the "book" is a fake, endeavors to open it by means of a slight projection in the binding. The string mechanism within is so contrived that the snake buries its single fang at the base of the nail of the experimenter's exploring finger. The box itself is hollowed out of a single block of wood. The scratch-carved tulips, which are the most significant part of the imposed decoration, are much like those of attested Pennsylvania pieces. If it is

Pennsylvanian and not European, as its nature would strongly suggest, it is the first of its type to be listed as the product of a native woodcarver's art.

Small, more or less utilitarian objects were occasionally inlaid. A characteristic specimen is the flat box of Figure 7. The box itself is of walnut, neatly dovetailed. The flat heart, the wavy line below it, and the edges of the grooved lid are of a lighter, contrasting wood. The interior is divided by partitions into two long and two short compartments. Far more elaborate is the knife and fork case also pictured. Here all the exterior surfaces are inlaid with designs in cherry, mahogany, ebony, walnut, oak, maple, and holly. These designs include the knife and fork for the appropriate covers, and a variety of leaves, animal, human, and geometrical figures.

No cataloguing of the wooden wares of the Pennsylvania Germans would be complete without a mention of the work of Joseph Lehn. Lehnware, as it is called, is actually too late properly to be considered antique, but is highly collectible nevertheless. The small pieces were lathe-turned, sanded, and painted. The characteristic body color is a grayed-pink, and the favorite decoration includes the strawberry and a strawberry-like blossom. Small cups and saucers, saffron boxes, egg cups, goblets (*Fig. 8*), and similar stemmed pieces, with or without covers, are popular among collectors. Other Lehn pieces, coopered instead of turned, include small pails, small sugar "barrels," and an occasional ice cream freezer. Lehn's work was produced almost up to 1900

FIG. 6 (*above*) — WHITTLE-CARVED SPOON RACK, bracket shelf, and comb case from Lancaster County, Pennsylvania.

FIG. 7 — INLAID WALNUT BOX from Berks County; knife and fork case from Silverdale, Pennsylvania.

but, like the pottery of Jacob Medinger, it is considered both representative and desirable.

An interesting footnote to the carving skill of the Pennsylvania Germans is found in the gourd baskets which are infrequently found. Gourd dippers were commonplace, but now and then an oversize fruit was treated in the manner shown in Figure 8. Extremely fragile, these are not often found in good condition

Even Easter eggs were carved! After the dye had been applied, a sharp instrument was used to scratch through the colored surface to the white shell beneath (*Fig. 8*). Favorite Dutchland floral and geometric patterns were thus applied to one of the most unconventional of antiques.

FIG. 8 — SCRATCH-CARVED EASTER EGG, Berks County; painted gourd basket, Lehigh County; turned spatter-decorated sugar bowl and Lehn goblet.

Early American Pottery: A Résumé

By John Ramsay

THERE are many roads by which to approach the consideration of early American pottery. That most usually followed is the highway of history. It is the logical route, and the inevitable one for whosoever would arrive at complete understanding. Nevertheless, it presents some dreary stretches, which few would be inclined to traverse were they not first tempted by being taken to a high place and given at least a glimpse of the irresistible allurements at the journey's end. Then, and then only, would the desire for a closer acquaintance with things seen from afar overcome reluctance to endure some hardships in reaching them.

The following notes are intended to provide some such bird's-eye view, taken from an altitude great enough to obscure all but major features of the scene, yet not so lofty as to prevent perception of essential details. They are not addressed to the advanced collector or the connoisseur, but to the beginner who, perhaps aware that early American pottery is desirable, has yet but the dimmest of notions as to what he should look for and how recognize it when found.

Fig. 1 — Early Massachusetts Red Ware
Crudely potted; shiny black glaze running to within about six inches of base.
From the collection of Charles D. Cook

What Is Pottery?

Strictly speaking, pottery includes all articles made from clay, but, for the sake of clear identification, the term is here restricted to more or less common household articles made from easily available clays by simple processes of manufacture. Within these limits, however, lies a field rich in examples of artistic expression, ranging from the primitive and appealingly uncouth to the finely formed and impressively handsome.

Classification

The simplest classification of the native American product is according to the clays from which it is made and the type of surface finish applied to it for purposes of protection and decoration. First we have those clays, of which common red-burning clay is typical, that are fired at a relatively low temperature and, partly because of their inherent texture, partly because they have not been fully fused by heat, provide articles whose body is somewhat soft, easily chipped or broken, and quite porous. Secondly, we have the grayish clays that, with a proper admixture of sand, may be fired at an extremely high temperature without disintegrating or warping, and that permit the production of utensils of an extremely hard, durable body, impervious to liquids. Our classification of pottery will, therefore, be that of soft-bodied types — sometimes called red ware — and hard-bodied types known as stoneware.

Glazing

The porosity of soft-bodied pottery is a drawback. Unless the pores of articles of this material are sealed in some way, they will

Fig. 2 — New England Red Ware
All except the "luck pitcher" on the extreme right, which is a New Hampshire piece, are from Massachusetts. Colors are, from left to right, dark red with black spots; russet-brown with dark-green splashes; ox-blood with moss-green splashes; yellow with dark-brown splashes; dark yellow splashed with brown and green. The luck pitcher is glazed in black and is initialed J.B., perhaps for Jeremiah Burpee of Boscawen.
From the collection of Charles D. Cook

Fig. 3 — Slip-Decorated Red Ware
Left to right: Connecticut ware splashed with yellow and green, probably made at Hartford; black glaze with yellow decoration; yellow glazes streaked with purple brown. All probably from Connecticut.
From the collection of Charles D. Cook

absorb grease and exude liquids. This sealing is accomplished by the application of a so-called glaze, which sometimes coats both the interior and exterior of the clay utensils, sometimes only the surface that comes into contact with food or liquids. Early American glazes on soft-bodied wares are what is known as slip glaze — that is, they are composed of *slip*, a compound of finely ground clay diluted with water to the consistency of cream and carrying an admixture of powdered red lead, together with various easily procured mineral substances calculated to produce a desirable color effect when fired.

Glazes of this kind were applied to the sun-dried ware, by means of dipping, brushing, or dabbing with a rag. After another brief period of drying, the ware thus glazed was fired. The outcome of the process was never quite certain. Chemical impurities in the clay body of the object occasionally exercised an unexpected influence on the chemicals in the glaze, and produced curious blotchy effects, or surprising passages of color. Overfiring at times caused simple glazes to bloom into areas of vitreous brilliancy. Happy accidents of this kind are always likely to occur in pottery glazing.

Stoneware required no such method of sealing. It was surfaced while still in the kiln, and red hot, by the simple process of shoveling common salt on the fires. The salt promptly vaporized and settled like a fog upon the ware, to mingle with the constituent elements of the clay itself and to cool in the form of an infinitude of hard, crystallized drops that presented a surface impervious even to the action of strong acids. The method outlined is known as salt glazing.

Slip glazes in whose making lead was employed were capable of emanating a subtle and deleterious poison. Vessels thus clothed could not be safely employed for storing vinegar, wines, or other liquids capable of attacking the glaze. They were unsuitable for putting down meats, pickles, or preserves, against the winter. They were, however, available as temporary containers of milk, water, and

food as dispensed on the table. Easily and cheaply made by the country potter with a limited equipment, inexpensive, attractive in color, slip-glazed articles are usually those that were more or less constantly within sight, and that, accordingly, played a part somewhat ornamental as well as useful. Stoneware, on the contrary, since it was particularly suitable for storing foods and liquids, was primarily utilitarian. And, again, since it was quite as likely to be harbored in the cellar as anywhere else, it offered little stimulus to the decorative ingenuity of the potter.

Both these generalizations as to the use of slip-covered wares and stonewares must, however, be taken with wide reservations. In certain sections of the country a great variety of pitchers, mugs, and deep dishes for kitchen and table use was made in stoneware. Red clay was employed for articles destined to inconspicuousness. But the fact remains that, for one piece of early stoneware capable of warming the heart of the collector, dozens of enticing slip-glazed items are to be found.

Local Peculiarities

Local tradition and prejudice, born of diverse national inheritances, influenced pottery styles in various sections of this country just as they influenced modes in furniture — perhaps even more emphatically. Thus stoneware was far more frequently given a significant decorative treatment in the New York, New Jersey, and Pennsylvania potteries, where the native Dutch and German fondness for this material manifested itself, than in New England, which shared the old-time English liking for the

Fig. 4 — Connecticut Red Ware
Left to right: Dark red with black splashes; dark red with black splashes; light brown with black splashes; light brown with black splashes.
From the collection of Charles D. Cook

Figs. 5, 6, and 7 — PENNSYLVANIA SLIP WARE
From the Pennsylvania Museum

Fig. 8 — PENNSYLVANIA RED WARE
From the Pennsylvania Museum

softer, more richly colored wares, even though it admitted the superiority of stone vessels for certain purposes and manufactured large quantities of them. At the same time, Teutonic fantasy in matters of form, and Teutonic delight in strong con-

trasts of bright hues led the New Jersey and Pennsylvania makers of slip-glazed wares to elaborations in the shapes and glazes of their products such as their New England contemporaries seldom thought of and still more seldom attempted.

The potteries that sprang up along the Ohio River, while in early days producers of slip wares

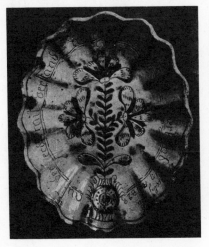

and later of so-called Rockingham, made their most significant and original contribution to the potter's art in the way of decorative stoneware. To the south, in Virginia, we encounter frequent evidences of Pennsylvania influence; while still farther down the

Atlantic coast, the habit of putting down meat in stoneware jars led to the making of some nobly proportioned pieces, whose glazes — whatever the process of their application — appear to be highly individual.

Decorative Methods

In the case of early pottery, as in that of early glass, while the everyday commercial

Figs. 9 and 10 — PENNSYLVANIA RED WARE
From the Pennsylvania Museum

articles turned out for general sale are of interest to the collector and student, it is the pieces that were specially made and that, in consequence, bear evidence of special care on the workman's part that are most highly prized. Dish pans, mixing bowls, pudding molds, and soft-soap urns exercise a less potent appeal than inscribed pie plates, milk jugs for table use, and the great crocks that occupied commanding positions upon open shelves.

New England soft-bodied slip-glazed wares, at their best, are usually reserved and dignified in both

Figs. 11 and 12 (above and left) — PENNSYLVANIA RED WARE
From the author's collection

form and color. Shapes are sturdy, well rounded, comfortable, though the quality of potting varies widely in any considerable group of specimens. Decoration is usually limited to a few incised lines — straight or curved — on neck and shoulder, and to the use of glaze either of a single color, or of a major tone splashed or mottled with another shade of a similar hue, or occasionally with a contrasting hue.

A very simple form of what is known as slip decoration also occurs in New England. This was achieved by pouring a dribble of light slip from a spouted vessel over the surface of the ware so as to form a pattern of scrolls, or an inscription such as the name of a person or the words *Mince Pie, Lemon Pie,* and so on. It is generally stated that slip decoration was applied on the raw ware, and that the piece thus decorated was then

dusted with sulphide of lead, which, in firing, spread as a glaze over background and ornament. This may be the case. It seems probable, however, that slip design was occasionally laid on a slip background of a contrasting shade.

In Pennsylvania, slip decoration was carried out far more elaborately than in New England. Bird and flower patterns were traced in slips of different colors on plates and deep vessels. Even complicated pictorial designs, including figures of men and animals, were attempted. Inscriptions were often long and involved. Effects of contrast were produced by deeply incised

Figs. 13 and 14 (above and left) — VIRGINIA POTTERY
FROM THE SHENANDOAH VALLEY
From the author's collection

outlines, and by a method of scratching through one layer of slip to expose a pattern in darker slip beneath. Ware thus treated is known as *sgraffito,* or scratched ware. Pennsylvania potters showed an inclination to crimp the edges of deep dishes and to apply ropes and festoons of twisted clay by way of added decoration. The vividness of their use of color in comparison with New England custom has already been mentioned.

Only in rare instances is New England stoneware decoratively interesting, though its quality is often excellent from the

Fig. 15 — Pennsylvania Stone-
ware Churn
Gray, salt glaze, blue decora-
tion. Stamped on two sides:
Boughner Greensboro Pa.
*From the collection of Rhea
Mansfield Knittle*

Fig. 16 — Ohio Stoneware Wa-
ter Cooler
A fine example with eagle in
relief; decoration in blue.
Height: 20 inches
*From the collection of Rhea
Mansfield Knittle*

standpoints of material and
workmanship alike. Such
decoration as it displays is
seldom more than a blue
flourish, a bird, or an animal form hastily daubed
on neck or shoulder before
the firing. Exceptions are a
few specimens upon which
the wielder of the cobalt
brush has taken advantage
of the opportunity to ex-
press his political sentiments, or to draw a more
or less elaborate picture.
Some New Hampshire
stoneware — notably that produced by Burpee at Boscawen — is
very neatly potted and tidily decorated with incised lines or impressed toolings. But perhaps the most obvious departures from
the unimaginative plainness of New England stoneware are
Norton's greyhound inkwell made at Bennington in the 1840's,
and a mid-nineteenth-
century water cooler by
Hastings and Belding of
South Ashfield, Massa-
chusetts. The former is
illustrated in ANTIQUES
for January 1924; both
are pictured in Spargo's
*Early American Pottery
and China.*

New York, New Jer-
sey, and Pennsylvania
stoneware, while seldom
as compelling as the slip-
glazed products of these
districts, indulges in a
far greater degree of decorative playfulness than does
the similar New
England product.

Ascribing
Early Pottery

Little is to be
gained by at-
tempting to learn
precisely where,
when, and by
whom unmarked
items of rural
American pottery
were made. The
rough outline pro-
vided in these
notes, supple-
mented by the
illustrations, will

help in determining the
general locality from which
certain pieces have come.
Reference to books and
current articles in AN-
TIQUES will be of still further assistance. Pictures,
however, except when
shown in color, are poor
guides to the identification
of glass and pottery. So
far, no American museum
has acquired a compre-
hensive and accurately
ascribed collection in this
field of American industrial
art. The Pennsylvania Museum, however, has an exceptionally
fine lot of Pennsylvania wares, and, thanks to the interest of
the late Doctor Barber, some specimens from other sources.
Local museums and historical societies throughout the country
house collections of local wares. Unless one has ample time and
opportunity to travel and to compare, he
will find the identification of pottery a
somewhat blind enterprise. But that circumstance need not impair the joy of his
collecting. Lacking concern as to sources,
he may apply himself more unreservedly
to observing quality of potting, variety
and relative attractiveness of form and
color, and such accidental effects as make
for special charm or significance.

Determining Dates

Dates are almost as difficult to determine as sources. Rural potters in particular passed on the secrets of their trade
from father to son through many generations. Catering almost exclusively to a
neighborhood trade, they were under no
competitive com-
pulsion to produce
novelties. An arti-
cle made in 1840
may differ little in
appearance from
one dating nearly
a century earlier.
In the main, how-
ever, the glory of
rural pottery be-
gins to fade soon
after 1840.

Within the suc-
ceeding decade,
improved means
of transportation
encouraged the
centralization of
pottery making

Fig. 17 — Ohio River Valley Stoneware
Fine examples. The water cooler in the middle of the lower row is exceptionally noteworthy. The circle
applied to the jar at the lower right appears to have been pressed in a butter mold.
From the collection of Rhea Mansfield Knittle

Fig. 18 — BENNINGTON ROCKINGHAM
Authenticated examples, whose richness of glaze is evident even in the illustration.
From the collection of Charles D. Cook

and the development of factories capable of producing wares whose appearance of sophistication the country potter could neither equal nor successfully imitate. Gradually the rural kilns were forced into idleness, or were reduced to the firing of flower-pots and the simplest of kitchen bowls, pans, and pitchers. In some country districts old potters continued to ply their trade until the close of the last century; but very few of them had the courage or the interest to produce the forms or the handsomely colored glazes of old.

The early factory era, however, achieved some interesting glazed pottery of a type known as Rockingham. Rockingham pottery — as distinguished from Rockingham porcelain, which is quite a different thing — is the term used for any brown glazed ware, either mottled in presumable imitation of tortoise shell, or virtually plain. It was the glaze *par excellence* of the early factory period of the 1840's, and still continues to be manufactured in the form of teapots, jugs, and the like. Rockingham ware was made under Fenton at Bennington, Vermont; at Baltimore; at Jersey City and Trenton; at East Liverpool and Zanesville, Ohio; and at other places besides. On the whole, the richly mottled, Rockingham glaze achieved at Bennington was the handsomest of its kind. An improvement upon it was Fenton's patent flint enamel, in which several colors are blended with an effect approximating that of the old Whieldon glazes.

As pottery glazes Fenton's Rockingham and flint enamel are admirable. They would be far more highly esteemed had they not been indiscriminately applied to certain well-modeled figures, book flasks, and other decorative or semidecorative pieces, as well as to the commonest and most vulgar of household utensils. In many minds the Bennington glazes are so closely associated with kitchen soap dishes, with cuspidors and slop basins, as to render quite impossible any appreciation of the artistic qualities of the glazes themselves. Most of the polite pieces upon which these glazes occur are, further, of decadent Victorian form. Nevertheless, the Bennington glazed dogs, lions, deer, and reclining cows are entitled to high rank in any collection of pottery. The Bible and coachman flasks, Toby tobacco boxes, and hound-handled pitchers from the same factory likewise deserve recognition, not only for their glaze but for their modeling.

Other contemporary factories imitated the Bennington forms and the Bennington glazes, and, when Fenton's ambitious projects failed in 1858, his workmen were scattered throughout the East, South, and Middle West, bearing with them the lessons they had learned in a little Vermont town. The student of American ceramic history will be interested to follow their peregrinations and to acquire specimens of their work. But the lustiness of form, the vigor of modeling, the richness of color that make pottery worth having for itself passed completely with the demise of Fenton's enterprise. They were the common attributes of the country products of an earlier day. Only in a few instances were such fine qualities achieved at the Bennington factory.

Fig. 19 — NEW JERSEY ROCKINGHAM
Though somewhat similar to the Bennington glaze, that of New Jersey is paler in tint, is less brilliantly mottled, and has less depth.
From the collection of Charles D. Cook

The collections: pottery

BY FRANK O. SPINNEY

The Village potter uses native clay in his demonstration of the craft. *Photograph by Dick Hanley.*

The shaving mug, top center, has a smaller cup attached to the inside wall. It is attributed to Gonic, New Hampshire. The other pieces (all are redware) show a variety of shapes whose functions are self-evident, so simply is the ware designed. Makers are unknown.

Top: The two pieces at right, with yellow and brown glazed decoration, are probably eighteenth-century imports from England. The redware cup, left, has a light brown glaze and is slip-lined. Its origin is unknown. *Bottom:* Slip-decorated redware pans with brown glaze of New England origin and of eighteenth-century form, turned on the wheel rather than shaped over a mold. Such wares brighten the shelves of the Village kitchens (see Interiors).

IN NEW ENGLAND THE MAKING of pottery—stoneware and redware—stayed close to the craft's earliest traditions of utility. Any collection of the simple wares of the eighteenth and early nineteenth centuries makes this clear, and it is emphasized when one sees the pieces in their natural places, on the cupboard shelves, in the buttery, near the oven, or in any of the other spots in house or shed where their use is obvious. Only the simplest of embellishments were added: an abstract design quickly incised while the piece still whirled on the wheel, a flourish of slip decoration on plates or platters, a dabbling of simple glaze combinations with colorful results.

The self-sufficient nature of rural or village life kept the New England potter hunched over his wheel turning out milk pans, bean pots, storage jars, footwarmers, jugs, crocks, bowls, and mugs. Another factor that influenced his product was New England's glacial clay, serviceable for bricks and plain earthenware, but not for the making of more delicate and ornamental things; what New

Slip decoration was frequently and attractively used by many New England potters. These forms with reddish brown glaze were shaped over a mold, not turned on the wheel.

Englanders acquired along these lines was imported. All this, of course, is not to say that New England pottery is unique or remarkable in its simplicity and utility. These traits are common to most folkware of any country or any period in this, perhaps the oldest of the crafts.

As one looks at the pottery in its living context, one sees that all the pieces are working articles, for butter-making, cooking, storage, eating, warming, drinking, or other mundane purposes. In the more formal exhibit at the pottery shop, where rarer marked specimens are shown, one feels the same insistence on utility.

Here, too, a potter shows the craft in operation. Using the Village collections as his guide, and working with clay dug from the shores of a nearby pond, once a source for earlier potters of the locality, he re-creates the early forms on the wheel, glazes, and fires them. The almost magical process by which a shapeless lump of clay is raised into a pleasing utensil never fails to excite interest and to provide a better appreciation of the craft.

Stoneware pot with brown glaze, marked BOSTON/1804. Maker unknown.

Redware pot and cover both marked JOHN SAFFORD and STEW POT NO. 3. Olive glaze flecked with red. Safford was working in Monmouth, Maine, in 1855.

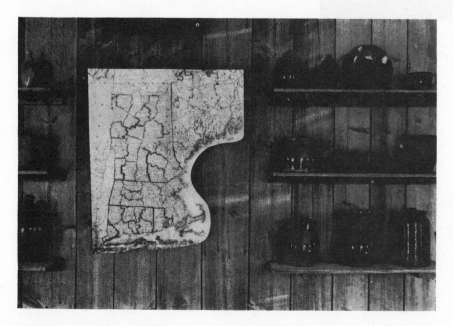

Part of the exhibit at the Village pottery. The map of New England is marked with the locations of the several hundred potters known to have worked in the region in the eighteenth and nineteenth centuries. *Photograph by Samuel Chamberlain.*

251

The Stoneware of South Ashfield, Massachusetts

By Lura Woodside Watkins

IN ORDER to understand the significance of the South Ashfield venture — a small pottery, indeed, and short-lived — it is necessary to know something of the conditions that inspired it. Why should so remote a village have attracted men acquainted with the potter's craft? Where did these men get their training? And what were the reasons for the abandonment of the business after it had survived for more than eight years? A study of local history reveals the answer to these questions.

In the decade between 1840 and 1850 Ashfield was a town of about fifteen hundred inhabitants. Situated in the Berkshires, halfway between Shelburne Falls and South Deerfield, it embraced several separate communities. Its central village, then known as Ashfield Plains, stood on high land near the mill pond. Another settlement of nearly equal importance — South Ashfield, locally called "Tin-Pot" —

Fig. 1 — Remains of the Ashfield Pottery Works
The upper part of the shed at the left is all that remains of the original building

was situated a mile and a half to the south of Ashfield Plains.

The appellation *Tin-Pot* was suggestively chosen, for South Ashfield was a centre of small industries and a starting point for peddler's activities of the kind that flourished throughout the New England states in the middle of the last century. Here were a tinware factory and a pottery. Ashfield Plains boasted a turning mill for wooden wares; and the whole township was noted for its production of essences distilled from native plants. Its manufacture of peppermint oil alone, carried on in seven places, at one time yielded no less than forty thousand dollars a year. Combs for peddlers' outfits were also locally manufactured, in a small way and in his own house, by one Richard Cook; while the making of palm-leaf hats and shirt bosoms provided pin money for many a housewife.

Every season hundreds of young men took to the road, driving peddlers' carts or traveling by stage and afoot with tin trunks filled with Ashfield products. Nathaniel Hawthorne in his *American Notes* describes such a peddler, whom he saw when he was journeying by stage through the Berkshires.

"Towards night," he writes, "took up an essence vendor for a short distance. He was returning home, after having been out on a tour two or three weeks, and nearly exhausted his stock. He was not exclusively an essence-pedlar, having a large tin box, which had been filled with dry goods, combs, jewelry, etc., now mostly sold out. His essences were of aniseed, cloves, red-cedar, wormwood, together with opodeldoc, and an oil for the hair. These matters are concocted at Ashfield, and the pedlars are sent about with vast quantities. Cologne-water is among the essences manufactured, though the bottles have foreign labels on them. . . . This man was a pedlar in quite a small way, making but a narrow circuit, and carrying no more than an open basket full of essences; but some go out with wagonloads. He himself contemplated a trip westward, in which case he would send on quantities of his wares ahead to different stations."

An old bill made out by G. C. Goodwin of Boston to Cook and Ranney of Ashfield shows that the drug business flourished to such an extent that it could not be wholly supplied from local sources, and that importations were necessary. This document mentions, among other things, *Mitchell Bitters, Indian Vegetable Sassafras Bitters,* and *Wild Cherry and Sarsarparilla Bitters.* The last was recommended in a note from the wholesaler as "a new article in great style for Peddlers." Since its wholesale price was three dollars and a quarter a dozen, while it retailed for one dollar a bottle, it must have well merited the description.

Thus, in the year 1848, when pottery was added to the list of merchandise sent out from the little Berkshire town, we see Ashfield as a well-established manufacturing and trading post. It is more than coincidence that the making of stoneware was almost wholly abandoned in Whately in that same year, or the year before. The Ashfield pottery was an attempt to continue the craft in a location considered more favorable on account of opportunities for distributing the product. The pottery firm did, in fact, carry on its own retail business.

Although there are no less than five firm names to be found on Ashfield stoneware, only three successive organizations actually operated the pottery. The other two marks were used for selling purposes. With this in mind, a clearly defined history of the business may be traced.

Orcutt, Guilford & Co.

The Ashfield pottery building was erected by Walter Orcutt, of the neighboring town of Conway, on land owned by the Guilford family. John Luther Guilford, son of John Guilford of Ashfield, although he appears not to have been himself a potter, retained a one-third interest in the business throughout its duration. Walter Orcutt was his uncle, as was also Eleazer Orcutt, a potter, who may, or may not, have been a member of the firm. Pitkin says some of the ware is marked *W. & E. Orcutt & Co.*, but I have found no firm of this name in the town records; neither have I seen a piece of pottery so marked. Orcutt, Guilford & Co. is first taxed in 1848 for "1 ½ acre & the Potery," valued at six hundred dollars. In the following year the names are given in full as "Walter Orcutt & John Guilford & Co." Their unpretentious little building was placed on the east side of the road from Ashfield, a short distance above the South Ashfield four corners and just south of the Mill Pond Brook, which crossed the road at that point and again wound southward back of the pottery land. Today the spot may be found diagonally across from the South Ashfield post office and a little north of a deserted blacksmith's shop with some tumbledown sheds in the meadow behind it.

Walter and Eleazer Orcutt were sons of the Stephen Orcutt

who, in 1777, was Whately's first potter. Their mother was Miriam Frary. Eleazer, born at Whately December 7, 1796, married Jane Giles of Troy, New York. The *History of Whately* (James M. Crafts, *1899*.
On Whately pottery see ANTIQUES for August 1925, *p. 77*) records that he was "a potter by trade" and a resident of Troy, New York. His connection with the Ashfield concern must have been an interlude between his days at Whately and at Troy. According to Pitkin, Eleazer Orcutt attended to the firing of the kiln. Walter was born at Whately May 7, 1799, and is recorded as a resident of Whately, Troy, and Conway. During his ownership of the pottery he lived in Conway, where he died March 1, 1854. His wife was Ann Eliza Blatchford. Little is known concerning the other workmen who were associated with the Orcutt family, except for David Belding, another Whately man, who became their successor. A brother of Guilford, William Frank, sold the pottery goods from a peddler's cart, traveling the country over. That the ware was distributed both by peddling and by local sales is indicated by the marks *Orcutt, Belding & Co.* and *Walter Orcutt & Co.*, which appear on sundry examples. Neither of these firm marks signifies a change in organization. In 1849 Orcutt, Belding & Co. was taxed for three horses and stock in trade, worth three hundred and seventy-five dollars. This was obviously a peddling outfit, distinct from the pottery concern, but allied with it. In 1850 Walter Orcutt & Co. was assessed for a house, barn, store, half an acre of land, and stock in trade. Orcutt was running the general store and post office of South Ashfield at that time. Pottery marks indicating the name of the distributor rather than that of the maker are not uncommon, but they do add to the confusion of the collector. In this case they explain the next step in the destinies of the Ashfield enterprise.

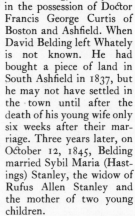

Fig. 2 — SALT-GLAZED STONEWARE
a. Churn, marked *Hastings & Belding/Ashfield, Mass. b.* Lipped crock, marked *Orcutt, Guilford & Co./Ashfield, Mass. c.* Covered jar, marked *Walter Orcutt & Co./Ashfield, Mass.*
From the collection of Austin G. Packard

Hastings & Belding

In 1850 Walter Orcutt sold his share of the "stone-ware factory" to Wellington Hastings and David Belding, while John Luther Guilford still retained his one-third interest. Belding, as we have seen, was already connected with the pottery and was probably the prime mover in taking over its management. The son of Elisha Belding, he was born in Whately, Massachusetts, March 7, 1813. His daughter, still living in Deerfield, and other members of the family have always spelled the name *Belden*. Local history shows that the two spellings are interchangeable, one being a corruption of the other; but the original Whately family was *Belding*, and the Ashfield potter so stamped his name on his jugs. Hence I use the latter spelling here. David was brought up among potters in the days when Whately had twenty-one native master workmen, besides journeymen potters, at work. He probably received his training in the art from Thomas

Fig. 3 — TWO-GALLON SLIP-GLAZED CIDER PITCHER
Marked *Orcutt, Guilford & Co./Ashfield, Mass.*
From the collection of Dr. Francis George Curtis

Crafts, whose daughter Triphena he married, November 10, 1842. A mute record of his Whately days survives in the form of a small gray stoneware churn marked *D. Belding/Whately*, now in the possession of Doctor Francis George Curtis of Boston and Ashfield. When David Belding left Whately is not known. He had bought a piece of land in South Ashfield in 1837, but he may not have settled in the town until after the death of his young wife only six weeks after their marriage. Three years later, on October 12, 1845, Belding married Sybil Maria (Hastings) Stanley, the widow of Rufus Allen Stanley and the mother of two young children.

Wellington Hastings was the brother of Belding's second wife. He and his brother Chauncey came to Ashfield from Wilmington, Vermont. The family, descended from the Earl of Huntington, had settled originally in Salem, Massachusetts, and had subsequently moved to Vermont by way of Hardwick. Wellington, the son of Gardner and Hannah Axtell Hastings, was born in Wilmington November 6, 1812.

Belding had gone into insolvency in 1847. What was his business at that time, the court records do not show. Three years later he had recovered sufficiently to join with his brother-in-law in the potting venture. The Hastings and Belding partnership lasted four years, and the majority of the jugs, crocks, and churns found around Ashfield bear their mark. We are permitted to know rather more about the pottery in this period than in its beginnings or its ending. In 1908 Albert H. Pitkin went to Ashfield, where he gleaned some valuable bits of information from the step-daughter of David Belding. These I have since confirmed with the aid of the family. At the time, this step-daughter was living in South Ashfield, the wife of John Luther Guilford of the pottery. She was thus doubly connected with the firm.

From the Guilfords, Pitkin learned that the pottery employed only seven men, of whom three worked at the wheel, and that it had only one kiln. One of the turners was named Wight. He was exceedingly skilful in making offhand pieces and was considered the best workman. Another was Staats D. Van Loon, who first appears in the Ashfield tax list in 1851, and who remained to become a member of the third firm. Ashfield tradition says that some of the potters came from Pennsylvania. It seems likely that Van Loon, at least, had migrated from the Pennsylvania region, or from New York.

Van Loon & Boyden

In 1854, the Hastings and Belding firm went into receivership. Thereupon the business was taken over by Van Loon and George Washington Boyden, with Guilford still holding his one-third share. The pair struggled on for two years more without great success, and in 1856 abandoned the undertaking. I have been able to learn almost nothing about these closing years. Jugs bearing the Van Loon & Boyden mark are exceedingly scarce, so that little tangible evidence of the period remains. Family history discloses no information of value. The Boyden *Genealogy* states that George Boyden was born in 1830, and died April 16, 1858. He married Minerva D. Graves of Conway, who died in Ashfield three days after the birth of a son, Frank Dickinson. In 1856 George Boyden owned a house, grist mill, and other property in Ashfield, but that was after the pottery had closed. It is probable that his connection with the business was purely financial, Van Loon attending to the potting. After the industry failed, Van Loon disappeared from Ashfield, perhaps to drift to Bennington or to some other of the Vermont potteries.

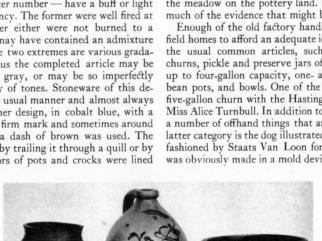

Fig. 4 — Slip-Glazed Pieces
Quart measure marked *Vinegar*.
a and *b*, *from the collection of Mrs. Harold Flower; c, from the collection of Mrs. Arthur J. Chapin*

The Wares

The wares made by Orcutt, Guilford & Co., Hastings & Belding, and Van Loon & Boyden are not distinguished one from another by any points of difference. They are all stoneware of rather ordinary quality made of clay brought from Perth Amboy, New Jersey. Some pieces have a dense gray body; others — and they represent by far the greater number — have a buff or light brown body of porous consistency. The former were well fired at a high temperature; the latter either were not burned to a proper degree of hardness, or may have contained an admixture of native red clay. Between the two extremes are various gradations of color and quality. Thus the completed article may be light brown, buff, or a bluish gray, or may be so imperfectly burned as to exhibit a variety of tones. Stoneware of this description was salt-glazed in the usual manner and almost always decorated with a spray, or other design, in cobalt blue, with a blue swash over the impressed firm mark and sometimes around the handles. Less frequently a dash of brown was used. The colored slip was applied either by trailing it through a quill or by means of a brush. The interiors of pots and crocks were lined with slip glaze, black, dark reddish brown, or light brown in color.

In addition to their blue-decorated gray stoneware, the Ashfield potters produced a good deal of ware covered with a dark slip glaze inside and out. The pitcher in Figure 3, marked *Orcutt, Guilford & Co.*, is an example of this type. The bowl with ear handles and the jelly mold in Figure 4 belonged to Mrs. John Luther Guilford, and may also have been made during the first period.

All Ashfield stoneware chips easily, especially when it has been allowed to stand

Fig. 5 — Salt-Glazed Stoneware
a. Marked *Orcutt, Belding & Co./Ashfield, Mass. b* and *c.* Marked *Hastings & Belding/Ashfield, Mass.*
a and *b*, *from the collection of Dr. Francis George Curtis; c, from the collection of Austin G. Packard*

in a damp place. This is a serious defect, and, in itself, affords sufficient explanation for the failure of the works and the inability of its output to compete with the hard, durable products of Bennington.

In September 1933 I discovered, near the bank of the brook, the site of the pottery's waste pile. On the surface of the ground, where they had been thrown eighty-five years ago, lay fragments of all types, including a piece with the Orcutt, Guilford & Co. mark. Shards buried in the moist soil had partly disintegrated. Among the pieces was half a crock cover, warped in the making and discarded. Its upper face was embossed by molding into a conventional leaf pattern. These recovered fragments, although their number was limited, proved of great assistance in studying the pottery. Most of the pottery débris was buried by a minor catastrophe years ago. In 1878 the Mill Pond dam at Ashfield Plains, during a freshet after heavy snows and a sudden thaw, burst, flooding the valley below and the village of South Ashfield. The old pottery building, then in use as a blacksmith's shop, was swept away, only part of a shed remaining at some distance from its original location, while tons of sand and débris were washed into the meadow on the pottery land. This flood effectively removed much of the evidence that might be so instructive today.

Enough of the old factory handiwork has been saved in Ashfield homes to afford an adequate idea of its character. There are the usual common articles, such as egg and butter crocks, churns, pickle and preserve jars of different sizes, molasses jugs up to four-gallon capacity, one- and two-gallon cider pitchers, bean pots, and bowls. One of the largest utilitarian pieces is a five-gallon churn with the Hastings & Belding mark, owned by Miss Alice Turnbull. In addition to these useful pots I have seen a number of offhand things that are far more interesting. In the latter category is the dog illustrated in Figure 8. This animal was fashioned by Staats Van Loon for one of Belding's children. It was obviously made in a mold devised from one of those bisected iron dogs that were used to embellish the side rails of parlor stoves, or were mounted on marble plinths to serve as door stops. Photographs of an original iron dog of the type and of its duplicate in glass appeared in the October 1929 issue of Antiques. Van Loon's pottery canine is entirely covered on the outer surface with a rich cobalt blue.

The potter Wight made, as a gift for Belding's stepdaughter, a toy bank with the inscription running twice across it, *Harriet Sophia Stanley, 1850. Aug. 17th*. This was presented on the child's tenth birthday.

A miniature churn, made by Wight for the same little girl, was bought by Pitkin and may now be seen in his collection in the Wadsworth Atheneum, Hartford, Connecticut. A perfect copy of the larger churns, even to the mark — *Hastings & Belding/Ashfield, Mass.* — it is inscribed with the date *August, 1852*, in cobalt blue. A moustache cup and a sand shaker from the Ashfield pottery are other offhand pieces recalled by descendants of the Belding family. The shaker is now owned by John Tomlinson, Jr.

More important from a ceramic point of view than any of these trifling objects is the water cooler illustrated opposite page 237 of Spargo's *Early American Pottery and China*. Not only is this a good piece of potting of graceful shape and fine proportions, but it is also elaborated with ornamental handles and a figure of Diana in relief. That it is an Ashfield product there can be no doubt, for it bears the Hastings & Belding mark, although its sophisticated style points to craftsmanship of the English school. Even without the initials FW, which may be faintly discerned on the band under the figure, it would be safely ascribed to the same Wight who delighted in making presentation pieces. Examination of the Ashfield town records reveals the fact that in 1852 and 1853 a poll tax was paid by one Franklin Wight. Here then, we may assume, is the full name of the man whose work must give him an important place among New England potters. As John Ramsay has pointed out in his excellent article *Early American Pottery* in ANTIQUES (October 1931), the Ashfield water cooler is one of the few examples of native stoneware that have departed from "unimaginative plainness." It is now preserved in the Wadsworth Atheneum collection.

Whether the idea for this monumental cooler originated in the fancy of Franklin Wight is a question that will be raised by comparing the picture of the Ashfield piece with another serving as the frontispiece of Mr. Spargo's book. The latter is a cooler, slightly different in proportion, but in decoration the same, marked *L. W. Fenton/St. Johnsbury, Vt.* The potter's personal initials are, however, missing. Did Wight make this jar, too? Did he copy Fenton's work? Or are both coolers adaptations from some English original? The date of Fenton's works — 1808 to 1859 — would admit of Wight's having been employed at St. Johnsbury either before or after his stay at Ashfield. Further investigation into the history of the Fenton pottery may illumine this point. [The St. Johnsbury potters were Richard Webber Fenton and his son, Leander W. Fenton. Richard was the brother of Jonathan, the Dorset potter.]

Fig. 6 (left) — TWO-GALLON CIDER PITCHER
Marked *Ashfield, Mass.*
From the collection of Mrs. Arthur J. Chapin
Fig. 7 (right) — STONEWARE JAR
Marked *Van Loon & Boyden/Ashfield, Mass.* The word *Hope!* indicates that this is one of the first pieces made by this firm.
From the collection of John Tomlinson, Jr.

Failure of the Pottery

More than one factor contributed to the failure of the struggling enterprise in Ashfield, as well as to that of many other small potteries scattered through the New England states. The year 1857 was a time of financial panic. The closing of the Ohio Life and Trust Company in August undermined the stability of the country's entire banking system. In New England conditions were much the same as in our recent crisis, and a period of inactivity and unemployment ensued. Van Loon & Boyden must have succumbed in the general business collapse.

Inability to compete with the larger and better established works at Bennington and to produce an equally durable ware were also important elements of weakness. A third reason, too, probably doomed the pottery to failure from the outset: the westward movement had begun to be felt in Ashfield. It was found that peppermint oil and other essences could be manufactured more cheaply and on a larger scale in Michigan than in Massachusetts, and ambitious young men were leaving town. Between 1840 and 1850 Ashfield's population dropped from 1,610 to 1,394 — the greatest decrease in any ten-year period of the town's history.

Ashfield Marks

The regular custom in marking Ashfield pottery was to impress the firm name over *Ashfield, Mass.*, but this rule was not invariably followed. Much of the stoneware is stamped *Ashfield, Mass.* without the maker's name. Occasionally the firm name was used alone, as on a brown stoneware Hastings & Belding molasses jug owned by Austin G. Packard; but the omission of the town mark was probably an oversight. It is interesting to note that the firm signature and the Ashfield mark were applied separately by hand; for the Orcutt, Guilford & Co. fragment that I picked up has the first line of lettering upside down. It is impossible to estimate how large a proportion of Ashfield pottery was unmarked. We do know that the slip-glazed ware was unsigned, and some of the stoneware may also have been left without marking.

The marks in chronological order are as follows:

Orcutt, Guilford & Co.	1848 to 1850
Orcutt, Belding & Co.	
Walter Orcutt & Co.	Distributors
Hastings & Belding	1850 to 1854
Van Loon & Boyden	1854 to 1856

(*The author acknowledges with grateful appreciation the kind assistance of Mrs. Harold Flower and Austin G. Packard in assembling information for these notes.*)

Fig. 8 — MOLDED DOG
Rich underglaze blue.
From the author's collection

Ohio Pottery Jars and Jugs

FIGURE 2 (FIGURE 1 *centre*)   *By* RHEA MANSFIELD KNITTLE   FIGURE 3

OHIO is noted for its clay products, which range from brick and drain tile to excellent ornamental wares. Toward the close of the eighteenth century, pioneers migrating from the eastern states into the "Western Country" were quick to avail themselves of the variety of clays in which the region abounds. The first potter in Ohio of whom I have record came to the territory from Kentucky in 1795. Somewhat later, artisans from the great pottery districts of Europe were attracted to Ohio, and, during the middle of the nineteenth century, when large industries were being established, East Liverpool became for a time a world centre of potterymaking. Nearly every Ohio county boasted at least one pioneer potter, and the Ohio and Muskingum River Valleys teemed with early little kilns.

Ohio soon produced virtually all the pottery styles and techniques attempted in the coastal states, in many cases improving upon the latter in quality of clay and glaze. For stoneware it developed an ornamentation peculiarly its own. The early glazed earthenware bowls, pitchers, plates, and jars followed, in part, the

Pennsylvania German and Swiss traditions and, in part, the Connecticut. *Sgrafitto* decoration on earthenware was seldom employed. Many of the old-world forms and motives likewise found their counterparts in Ohio. The later glazed ware in the Rockingham manner, manufactured at the larger potteries in eastern Ohio between 1850 and 1870, was patterned after the English product, as were the similar wares of Bennington, Baltimore, and Trenton.

Fortunately for us, it was not unusual for an early potter to inscribe his work with his name and occasionally with that of the town where he worked, together with the name of his particular patron. This inscription was customarily incised; infrequently it was applied in brown or blue slip; sometimes it was both incised and applied. Dated pieces are also found. The oldest dated jar of which I have record is marked *1804*.

The accompanying illustrations afford a fairly representative view of Ohio pottery jars and jugs. All the pieces pictured are in perfect condition and each is, in its way, a significant specimen. All but one were found by Earl J. Knittle of Ohio.

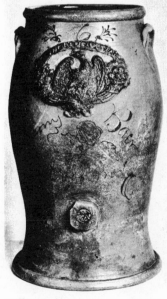

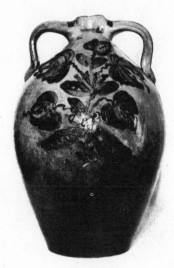

FIGURE 4   FIGURE 5   FIGURE 6

FIGURE 7

FIGURE 8

FIGURE 9

Fig. 1—UNGLAZED POTTERY WATER JAR OR WINE COOLER
Very early piece, notable for soft, natural coloring, ample proportions, and effective simplicity of decoration. Clay of blended tones of buff and a warm gray. Neck and shoulders incised with narrow reeding. Bunghole has no surrounding ornamentation, an unusual feature in Ohio water or wine jars. Sole decorative motive consists of incised and applied sheaves of wheat upon a raised circular medallion on upper part of body. *Origin:* Northeastern Ohio.

Figs. 2 and 3—REMARKABLE GRAY STONEWARE WINE COOLER, HEAVILY SALT-GLAZED (*1856*) (*obverse and reverse*)
Elaborate handles, splotched with blue slip and decorated with crimpings and applied buttonlike bits of clay, terminate in five large rosettes, which were applied to the body by squeezing wet clay through a funnel-like device made of heavy linen. Applied strapwork, circles, and impressed starlike forms encircle base and collar of jar. *Obverse:* Ornamented with applied flowers and foliage, hearts, clasped hands, rosettes, some of which are decorated with blue slip. Bung is in centre of a large applied heart, upon and above which are incised tiny houses. *Reverse:* High on shoulder the numeral *5* (signifying five gallons) is formed of applied circular motives. Side of jar is almost covered with large block letters incised and painted with blue slip: MADE BY E. HALL/OF NEWTON TOWN SHIP/MUSKINGUM CO: OHIO./AT W. P. HARRISES FAC/TORY. A HOLESALE AND/RETAIL DEALER IN STONE/WARE. BUCK AND BRECK/TO JOSHUA CITES. The date of the marriage of Joshua Cites, *January 13, 1856*, is scratched on side of jar. The larger letters OHIO cut above base border are likewise ornamented with blue slip. *Origin:* Newton Township, Muskingum County, Ohio.

Fig. 4—GRAY STONEWARE WATER OR WINE COOLER WITH HIGH-DOMED COVER
A decorative piece, heavily salt-glazed, its major ornament washed with blue slip; inner surface is brown-glazed. Square bunghole, at base, is decorated with starlike applications. Name of purchaser, *A. A. Morgan*, blue-slipped on front and back of piece. *Capacity:* 3 gallons. *Origin:* Formerly stood in an early tavern in McConnellsville, Ohio.

Fig. 5—VERY LARGE WATER JAR OR WINE COOLER
Mottled buff and warm gray; outer surface salt-glazed; inner surface glazed with Albany slip. Octagonal bunghole protrudes from surface immediately above actual bottom of jar, which is some inches above hollow base. Bunghole ornamented with four imitation screws incised in the clay. Decoration of two kinds: flat blue slip — sprays, and inscription *Anthony Baer / Cleveland / Ohio*; superimposed clay — emblematic ornament composed of upright eagle in oval formed of two horns of plenty and ribbon bearing the

words *Ne Plus Ultra*. This device is painted strong cobalt blue. *Height:* 20 ½ inches; *capacity:* 6 gallons. *Origin:* Attributed to one of the Western Reserve potters, a little south of Cleveland; made for Anthony Baer, tavern keeper, of Cleveland.

Fig. 6—GRAY STONEWARE TWO-HANDLED CIDER JUG, HEAVILY SALT-GLAZED
Obverse: Flowers and foliage painted in rich, cobalt slip in a large, free manner. *Reverse:* Undecorated except for the incised inscription, painted with blue slip, directly below the mouth: *J. C. Smith / Mogadore Ohio. Capacity:* 4 gallons. *Origin:* Mogadore Potteries, Ohio. Butter crocks with similar decoration, from Lancaster County, Pennsylvania, suggest the likelihood of a Pennsylvania-German prototype.

Fig. 7—BARREL-SHAPED WATER COOLER OF GRAY STONEWARE
Covered with a fine quality of salt glaze. Four hoops in applied clay encircle the barrel. Top and bottom of piece are solid, with an opening in top for filling, and a bunghole just above base. Incised sun and fish are decorated with blue slip. *Capacity:* 1 gallon. *Origin:* Cincinnati, Ohio.

Fig. 8—GLAZED, SLIP-DECORATED EARTHENWARE JUG
Rough, pitted, brown earthenware body, unevenly washed with a greenish-brown glaze. Opaque white, brilliant green, and black slip applied to each side, down the front, and on the jug's handle. The date of potting, *1831*, appears in glaze on one side. Rare. *Capacity:* 1 gallon. *Origin:* This buttermilk jug was made in new Philadelphia, by potters who migrated from Switzerland to Ohio.

Fig. 9—COVERED COOKIE JAR
An outstanding piece, well-proportioned and unusually large. Yellow clay body with rich all-over glaze of mottled brown and yellow slip in the Rockingham (England) manner. Well-executed decoration in high relief, depicting a mythological group on either side of jar. Drooping handles overhang gracefully extenuated acanthus motives. A ring of smaller acanthus leaves encircles sloping rim of jar. *Capacity:* 4 gallons. *Origin:* East Liverpool, Ohio.

Fig. 10—HARVESTER'S CIDER JUG
An exceptionally fine piece. Of chocolate-colored clay, glazed with the same color. The generous handle is ornamented with a heavy twisted vine that at one end merges into finely modeled grape leaves. Decoration in relief: below the spout, a mythological figure, probably a bacchante; below the filler, another female figure; on each side, a large medallion of grape leaves, boldly modeled. *Capacity:* 2 gallons. *Origin:* Attributed to Tuscarawas County, Ohio.

Fig. 11—BUTTER OR SUGAR CROCK WITH DOMED COVER
Yellow clay body with rich brownish glaze. Overhanging lid topped by a finial composed of six petals. Handles in similar petal-like form attached above petal motives on the body. *Capacity:* about 10 pounds. *Origin:* Zanesville, Ohio. A typical example of everyday potting, pictured to show the excellence of both form and ornamentation exhibited by the commercial output.

FIGURE 10

FIGURE 11

Early Rhode Island Pottery

By Charles D. Cook

Illustrations from the author's collection

THE first New England potters were Indians, but, because of the dampness of the coastal climate and the comparative scarcity of suitable clay, they did not make so much pottery as did the Indians west of the Hudson River. In fact, our local aborigines constructed most of their cooking utensils from the accessible and easily worked soapstone, which could withstand much heat without cracking. Still, many bits of Indian pottery and fragments of clay pipes may even yet be found scattered about Rhode Island, and are readily recognizable as a native product from their admixture of clay and pounded shell — a compound favored by the red Rhode Island potters.

Some of the early settlers of Rhode Island and their eighteenth-century followers were doubtless potters by trade and possibly made earthenware; but, broadly speaking, the pottery industry on a commercial scale was not maintained in Rhode Island or, indeed, to any great extent in New England before the latter half of the eighteenth century.

Walter A. Dyer states that no pottery of consequence was made in America until after 1750. He adds that before the Revolution earthenware or porcelain was not common in the average American home, except in the more prosperous towns. My own investigations carried on quite independently have led me to the same conclusion.

One of the earliest potteries established in Rhode Island was that operated at East Greenwich by the Upton brothers. Doctor D. H. Greene in his *History of East Greenwich*, written in 1877, gives the following account of this establishment:

"At the commencement of the Revolutionary War, a man by the name of Upton came from Nantucket to East Greenwich, and manufactured earthern ware for a number of years. The pottery where the articles were made, and the kiln where they were baked, stood on the lot now occupied by the dwelling house of John Weeden, on the corner of King and Marlboro streets. The articles made there consisted of pans, bowls, plates, cups

and saucers. As there were no porcelain manufactories in America at that time, and the war prevented the importation of such articles from Europe, many of the people here were obliged to use these coarse clumsy plates, cups and saucers for want of better. They were made of the coarse red earthen ware, which we see at the present day in the form of milk-pans, jars and jugs. A table set out with such rough looking specimens of crockery would look very strange at this day, but we presume that many a good dish of tea was drunk out of those thick, heavy cups and saucers, and many excellent dinners were eaten off of those red earthen plates. The clay for making those articles was brought from Quidnesett at a place called Gould's Mount, on the farm now belonging to Henry Waterman, and where great quantities of the same kind of clay still remains. Shortly after the termination of the Revolutionary War Mr. Upton returned to Nantucket, and no earthen ware has been made here since."

In an endeavor to verify Mr. Greene's account, which has been followed unquestioningly by such subsequent writers as Alice Morse Earle, I found that the printed historical material relating to Nantucket failed to disclose any reference to a potter named Upton. The East Greenwich *Town Records*, to which I next turned my attention, proved more fruitful. Here I found that, on December 9, 1771, Thomas Aldrich sold to Isaac Upton and Samuel Upton a lot of land in East Greenwich bound southerly by King Street and westerly by Marlborough Street. Several years later, that is in 1783, Isaac Upton, at this time a resident of Berkley, Massachusetts, deeded to Samuel Upton of East Greenwich, for two hundred and fifty Spanish milled dollars, all of his share in the dwelling house and potter's shop in East Greenwich, the same land that had been deeded to the two men in 1771. Both Isaac and Samuel were called "potters" in this deed. The East Greenwich Council records show that they were both living in East Greenwich in 1777.

Having thus determined the given names of these potting

Fig. 1 — COVERED JUGS AND TWO TEACUPS (*Rhode Island, eighteenth century*)
Surfaced with a characteristic jade green glaze that, in conjunction with the nature of the clay employed, seems to identify the product of the Upton brothers' pottery at East Greenwich

Uptons, I turned to the Upton genealogy, and found they were brothers, Isaac having been born about 1745 and Samuel about 1747, at Bedford, Massachusetts. Their father was Edward Upton, a glazier by trade, who came from Danvers, Massachusetts, where for many years the family had been settled. This Danvers connection gives us

Fig. 2 — RUM OR VINEGAR JUGS AND PITCHER (*Rhode Island, eighteenth century*)
In body and glaze so similar to the items illustrated in Figure 1 as to be attributable to the Uptons

an interesting clue. Probably it was because of their friends and relatives at Danvers that the Upton boys took up the trade of potters, which they undoubtedly learned from the famous Danvers potters. They both married Yarmouth girls, and perhaps lived for a time on Cape Cod. Tradition may have confused Cape Cod and Nantucket. This I believe to be the case; for I have also been told that pottery was made on the island. Samuel is said to have followed the sea when not engaged in pottery work.

No marked specimens of the Upton product have been found, and it is indeed very probable that the brothers never used a potter's mark. It is, however, possible to identify with considerable assurance a number of examples of their work. Four pieces made of the peculiar red clay characteristic of Gould's Mount, and known to have been used by the Uptons, were discovered years ago, tucked away in East Greenwich attics or cupboards. All four are pictured in Figure 1. Two of them are tall, wide-mouthed jugs with covers. The other two are teacups, made without handles after the time-honored fashion of the Chinese. Jugs and cups alike are glazed with a very beautiful and unusual jade green that has a character so individual as to indicate the same authorship for all the earthenware on which it occurs. The two smaller jugs of Figure 2 are from farmhouses in Exeter and northern South Kingston, within the natural selling field of an East Greenwich pottery. The pitcher was secured in Providence, where many objects of East Greenwich manufacture naturally found their way. It will be noted that the specimens shown are similarly somewhat crude in workmanship and design, a circumstance that, taken together with the characteristic red clay and the peculiar glaze, fairly establishes their identity of origin.

The curious, old, wide-mouthed jug with cover (*Fig. 3*) is evidently not an East Greenwich product. It is a particularly rare piece and differs materially in texture, workmanship,

Fig. 3 — COVERED JUG OR JAR (*Rhode Island, eighteenth century*)
Olive green glaze with large orange-colored mottlings. Ascribed to Joseph Wilson, who was potting in Providence as early as 1767

and glaze from the previously discussed specimens. It is of about the same time, but probably a little earlier — of the Colonial rather than of the Revolutionary period. It is of odd shape, with a decidedly high neck, and is covered with a rich, olive green glaze through which irregularly round orange spots or blotches are visible. Many years ago, in the old Sherman house at Pawtucket, this jug was found, covered with a layer of thick paint. From time out of memory it had been in use as a doorstop. Rescued from such ignoble service and relieved of its heavy coat of paint, the piece in all its pristine beauty again literally came to light and to recognition as a noteworthy *chef d'œuvre* in a collection of about a thousand specimens.

Historically it gains special importance from the fact that it is unquestionably the work of Joseph Wilson, one of the earliest, if indeed not the earliest, Rhode Island potter to manufacture on a commercial scale. Wilson was potting in Providence as early as 1767; and, since his advertisement appeared in the *Newport Mercury*, it seems safe to conclude that he marketed his wares not only throughout the entire Plantation but also in parts of Massachusetts and Connecticut. The advertisement referred to appeared in the *Mercury* for June 22, 1767, and read as follows:

"Joseph Wilson — potter

"At the North End of Providence Informs the Public, that he can Supply them with Earthen Ware at a cheap Rate, made in the best Manner and glazed in the Same Way as Practised in Philadelphia — All persons in this Town may be regularly supplied by Means of the Boats which constantly pass between this Place and Providence."

Wilson, it would seem, learned his trade from the Swiss and German potters of Pennsylvania, while the Uptons followed the traditions of the Danvers industry. It is interesting to note that, within the space of five years, workmen from two great but widely separated early American centres of pottery-making should have set up their workshops in Rhode Island.

It is hoped that collectors will not pass by this early American earthenware, even though its jugs and pitchers may be crude, for the collection and preservation of the few specimens of it that still exist will enable connoisseurs to piece together much of interest regarding our early potters and the products of their handiwork.

The potters of Poughkeepsie

BY JOHN P. REMENSNYDER

I KNOW OF ONLY TWO published articles on the potters of Poughkeepsie, New York: "Poughkeepsie Was Also a Jugtown," by Thomas H. Ormsbee, which appeared in the *American Collector* for February 1936; and "The Caire Pottery at Poughkeepsie," by Dr. J. Wilson Poucher, originally published in the *Hudson River Magazine* for November 1939 and reprinted in the 1941 *Year Book* of the Dutchess County Historical Society. Both mention a pottery which appears on a 1780 map of the village of Poughkeepsie, and both begin the story of the Pough-keepsie potters with the appearance of John B. Caire in 1840. Mr. Ormsbee (Dr. Poucher concurring) says that although a pottery had apparently existed continuously on the original site, "just what sort of jugs and crocks were made remains a matter of conjecture down to the time when the Caire family came to Poughkeepsie to live and work."

I have not been able to locate that 1780 map. However, a pottery is clearly shown on a map in the office of the county clerk of Dutchess County inscribed *Corporation of the Village of Poughkeepsie Surveyed May 10th 1799 by Henry Livingston.* (Most of the documentary material mentioned here also came from the county clerk's office.) The pottery is located on Union Store Road about 660 feet from the edge of "Hudson's River," or on what is today Union Street extension about halfway between Water Street and the river bank.

I believe that a pottery was established here early in the eighteenth century. So far I have been unable to determine who the first potters were or what they made, though their products were almost certainly bricks and redware. I base my belief in the early existence of the pottery in part on the names which occur on documents relating to the land (later designated as Lots 9 and 10) where the pottery shown in Colonel Livingston's map was located. These include a John De Graff who sold the land in 1766 and who may well have been related to Jan a. De Graff, listed as a potter in Albany as early as 1657 (see Robert G. Wheeler's check list of Albany potters published in *New York History,* October 1944). James Winans and his wife were the purchasers, and the tract remained in the hands of their descendants until by 1804 or shortly thereafter both lots were owned by Elizabeth Winans and her husband, James Reynolds. At this time we do know definitely, from the Livingston map, that there was a pottery here; and I strongly suspect that a stoneware jug in my collection (Fig. 1) incised *Isaac Adriance* and dated *1813* was made there. Adriance is very much a local name (as witness the Adriance Memorial Library), but I have been unable to document my suspicion beyond the listing of an Isaac Adriance in the Poughkeepsie records at this period.

In May 1823 James and Elizabeth Reynolds sold Lot 10 and the northern part of Lot 9 to William Nichols. The sturdy water cooler shown in Figure 4 indicates clearly that Nichols operated the pottery; it is the earliest piece

1

2

3

4

5

6

Fig. 1. Stoneware jug incised in script ISAAC/ADRIANCE/1813 on the front, and ADRIANCE [in printed capitals] /1813 on the back. Simple manganese decoration; height 15⅝ inches. *Except as noted, all illustrations are from the author's collection.*

Fig. 2. Stoneware jug of early shape marked W. CARROLL/POUGHKEEPSIE. Decoration in cobalt; height 11¼ inches. The collection includes a small jar with the same mark. Since no documents have been found to connect Carroll with a pottery, he may or may not have made these.

Fig. 3. Stoneware jar marked J G BALL & Co./POUGHKEEPSIE. Decorated in manganese and cobalt; height 8¾ inches. According to Smith's *History of Dutchess County* (1882), a pottery was established at Poughkeepsie by John Ball about 1820. The collection contains a jug with this same mark.

Fig. 4. Stoneware water cooler marked W. NICHOLS./ PO,KEEPSIE. Decorated in cobalt; height 15⅞ inches. In 1823 William Nichols owned the Poughkeepsie pottery site shown in a 1799 map of the area.

Fig. 5. Two-gallon stoneware jar marked T. G. BOONE & C. / PO'KEEPSIE N Y. Decorated with cobalt; height 11 inches. Boone was in Poughkeepsie from an undetermined date until 1839. In 1840 he appears in the Brooklyn, New York, directory as "Stoneware Manufacturer."

Fig. 6. Stoneware gallon jar marked PO'-KE'PSIE/ W. REYNOLDS/1. Decorated in cobalt; height 8½ inches. After Nichols' death in 1824 William Reynolds acquired the pottery from his estate, and apparently held it (but without necessarily operating the pottery for the entire period) until 1837.

I have been able to attribute to it. The *History of Dutchess County* (1882) says that John Ball established a Poughkeepsie pottery about 1820, and the jar shown in Figure 3 and a jug in my collection with the same mark are proof that there was such a pottery, though I have not found any other evidence of its existence. Somewhere in here, too, a local pottery was being run by Thomas G. Boone (Fig. 5). According to an article by Preston R. Bassett which appeared in the *Long Island Courant* (publication of the Society for the Preservation of Long Island Antiquities) for March 1965, Boone, who listed himself as "Stoneware Manufacturer," came to Brooklyn from Poughkeepsie in 1839 and operated a pottery there with his sons for a number of years. Stoneware has been found marked with the firm name T.G. BOONE AND SONS and SANDS ST. or NAVY ST., BROOKLYN (the pottery was located at the corner of these two streets). However, there is no indication as to how long Boone had been operating in Poughkeepsie before he moved to Brooklyn, or where his Poughkeepsie pottery was located.

By contrast, the line of descent of the pottery on Lots 9 and 10 is fairly clear. William Nichols' sister Julia was the wife of Nathan Clark, the outstanding early-nineteenth-century potter of the Hudson Valley, whose pottery had been established in Athens (across the river from the town of Hudson) in 1806. Upon William's death in 1824 Clark was appointed guardian of his children, and in that capacity conveyed the pottery and land to William Reynolds (possibly a son of the James Reynolds who had owned them until 1823). One of William Reynolds' well-designed jars is shown in Figure 6.

I do not know how long Reynolds operated the pottery. The 1831 Poughkeepsie assessments list includes the firm of Orcutt and Thompson, whose Rockingham pitcher appears in Figure 7 but no address or occupation is given and there is no way of knowing where their pottery was located; and C.W. Thompson & Co. are listed in the *New York Annual Register* for 1835 as proprietors of a stoneware factory in Poughkeepsie, but the same is true of this firm. In 1837 Reynolds and his wife conveyed Lots 9 and 10 to Solomon V. Frost, who had established a local foundry in 1831 and probably never engaged in the pottery business. In 1839 he sold the property, which was then leased by Mabbett & Anthone (Fig. 8) to William Colson and William Sanderson of Athens and Ed Selby of Poughkeepsie, they to take possession upon the expiration of the Mabbett & Anthone (Antoine?) lease in 1840. The 1839 Poughkeepsie town assessments show Selby, Colson, and Sanderson as operators of a "Pottery Bakery corner Union & Laurel" with a valuation of $1500. The gallon jug shown in Figure 9 carries the firm name of Selby & Sanderson. I know of a jug marked SELBY & COLSON POUGHKEEPSIE, and I have a two-gallon jar marked WATSON & SANDERSON/POUGHKEEPSIE. These firms cannot have been very successful: by 1841 the property was back in Frost's hands, and he sold it to Ed Selby and Levi Emigh for $3,750. I have in my collection an Albany-slip-coated jug marked SELBY & EMIGH.

By 1843 the Poughkeepsie directory listed three members of the Caire family as potters on Main Street: John, George, and "Jacob Caire & Co." Levi Emigh and Ed Libby were "potter bakers" on Union Street—the old site—and Henry Stockwell and Abraham Conover were also in the business, on Main Street. There is some confusion here. In 1842 Lilley & Sanders, of whom I have found no

other record, had sold their pottery at 141 Main Street to John B. Caire, who had come with his family from Bavaria in 1839. John later conveyed this property to his son Jacob, who conducted the pottery as Jacob Caire & Co. until 1857. However, the stoneware jar in Figure 10 bears the mark of JACOB CAIRE, UNION STREET, so he must have done business at the old stand at least for a while. After this all mention of the Union Street pottery disappears; it may have been abandoned, or the railroad may have bought the site.

Examples of Caire pottery are fairly common. I show three marked pieces (Figs. 10, 11, 12) and it is very possible that the daisy-pattern pitchers in Figure 13, and the scroddle pitcher in Figure 14, are Caire products. Incidentally, Caires were working as potters in other sections as well as Poughkeepsie. Bassett, in the article cited above, says that the Boone firm in Brooklyn employed a Jacob Kair who was "without doubt, another of the Poughkeepsie family who came to Long Island to carry on his trade." He also notes that Frederick J. Caire "of the Caire family, famous potters of Poughkeepsie . . . was induced by his father-in-law to come down to Long Island and operate the [Huntington] pottery as manager."

Early in 1857 Jacob Caire was succeeded at the Main Street pottery by Thomas Lehman and Philip Reidinger (Fig. 15), and for a few months the Caires were not connected with it. However, later that same year Lehman retired and Adam Caire, one of Jacob's brothers, returned to Poughkeepsie (like Jacob and Frederick, he had been plying his trade outside of the village) and joined Reidinger. As Reidinger & Caire they ran the pottery together for twenty years, until Reidinger's death in 1878. After that, until his own death in 1896, Adam Caire was sole proprietor.

Both Ormsbee and Poucher tell a good deal about the products of the pottery under Adam Caire's management. Of particular interest to both were some mugs made off-hand for commemorative purposes. Ormsbee mentions one inscribed with the signatures of fifteen members of the Vassar Class of '95; *Eleanor Gedney, 349 Mill St., Po'keepsie* is incised on the bottom of this one. Poucher mentions these mugs, but says regretfully that he has not been able to locate one. He also reports the indignant denial of a member of the Class of '95 that they were used, during class festivities, for drinking beer to the tune of "If it wasn't for beer we wouldn't be here"—a reference, of course, to the source of the fortune with which Matthew Vassar founded the college. The editor of the *Year Book* did find one of the mugs in the Adriance Memorial Library in Poughkeepsie, and appended to Dr. Poucher's article a note to the effect that one of the ladies listed on it identified the group as members of "Professor Salmon's seminar in history." Another member of the class told the editor that these mugs were not official class souvenirs, but were "acquired by girls associated with each other in small intimate groups." I am happy to be able to show here (Fig. 17) the Vassar mug owned by the Adriance Library, as well as another commemorative example. These are far from being the most important products of the Poughkeepsie potters, but they have their own appeal.

ANTIQUES

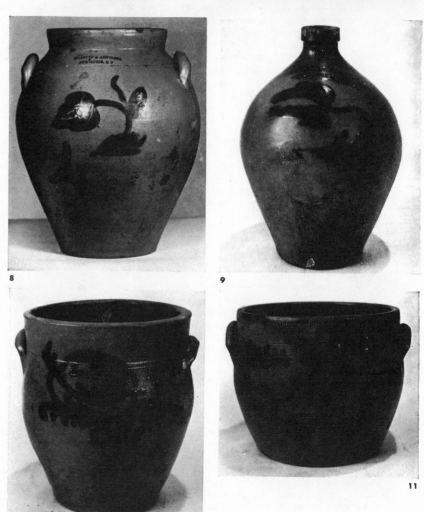

Fig. 7. Pitcher marked *American/ Manufacture* on one side, and Or-cutt & Thompson/ Pokeepsie on the other. Earthenware with Rock-ingham glaze, molded decoration; height 11 inches (the collection in-cludes an identical pitcher in red-ware with a dark glaze). In 1835 Orcutt & Thompson apparently had leased the pottery from Rey-nolds, and were making these nicely molded pitchers in various sizes.

Fig. 8. Four-gallon stoneware jar marked Mabbett & Anthone/ Po'keepsie, N Y. Decorated in co-balt; height 14⅝ inches. Mabbett and Anthone (Antoine?) leased the pottery in the later 1830's.

Fig. 9. Stoneware gallon jug marked Selby & Sanderson/Po,-keepsie N Y. Cobalt decoration; height 11⅜ inches. This firm appar-ently operated the pottery between 1839 and 1841.

Fig. 10. Stoneware jar marked Jacob Caire, / Union Street, Poughkeepsie. Decorated with co-balt; height 11½ inches. Several Caires, including Jacob, are listed as on *Main* Street in the first Poughkeepsie directory, issued in 1843.

Fig. 11. Two-gallon stoneware jar marked Jacob Caire & Co. / Po'-keepsie. Decorated in cobalt blue; height 11 inches. The brushed-on 2 indicates the capacity of the jar, as do similar numerals on other vessels shown here.

12

13

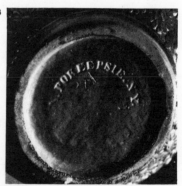

14

Fig. 12. Outsize hound-handled pitcher marked on base J B CAIRE & Co/ POKEEPSIE/ N Y. Stoneware with Rockingham glaze, undoubtedly made in a mold designed by the well-known Daniel Greatbach; height 11¾ inches.

Fig. 13. Pitchers molded in an allover daisy pattern, marked on base POKEEPSIE. N Y. and probably produced by the Caires. *Left*: earthenware; *center and right*: stoneware; all with brown slip, height of tallest, 6⅝ inches.

Fig. 14. Pitcher with gadrooned body; neck molded in daisy pattern. Unmarked, but probably from the Caire pottery. An extremely rare example of scroddled ware; height 7⅝ inches.

Fig. 15. Two-gallon stoneware jug marked LEHMAN AND REIDI .../ POUGHKEEPSIE N Y. Thomas Lehman and Philip Reidinger took over the Caire pottery in 1857 and operated it until Lehman retired in the same year. Cobalt decoration; height 13½ inches.

Fig. 16. Pint container for Post's root beer, a Poughkeepsie product of the late nineteenth century. Unmarked, but known to have been made in quantity by the Caire pottery. Inscribed *Post's* in cobalt blue; height 10⅜ inches.

Fig. 17. Stoneware mugs, unmarked but traditionally made at the Caire pottery. *Left*: inscribed *July 20th/ G.[?] H. Ransom/ Apokeeping* [an earlier Indian name for Poughkeepsie] / *Boat Club*. *Right*: inscribed with the names of nine members of the Vassar Class of 1895—Alice F. Learned, Ida H. Poppenheim, Frances Albee Smith, Christie Hamilton Poppenheim, Julia Swift Arvis, Julia Emery Turner, Mabel I. Jones, Bess Updegraff, Gertrude Witschief—a crude shield containing the year, 95, and an equally crude cipher of *V* over *C. Adriance Memorial Library, Poughkeepsie*.

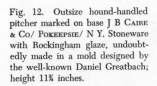
15

16

17

Fig. 1 — North Carolina Pottery
Left to right: Plate with cream ground, decorated in pumpkin brown and black; shaving dish with pumpkin-brown ground decorated in cream and black; plate dated *1812*, chocolate ground decorated in pumpkin brown, cream, and green; canteen bottle showing a bird that may be either a stork or an ostrich; plate with red-brown ground decorated in cream and green. *Diameter of plates*, approximately 13 inches. *From the author's collection*

A Note on Early North Carolina Pottery

By Joe Kindig, Jr.

Note. The following brief discussion pretends to be no more than a note in passing. Nevertheless, it deserves more than fleeting consideration; for it directs attention to one of the most delightful, albeit least known, types of early American pottery — that made by German settlers in North Carolina. It will be noted that in his observations Mr. Kindig is extremely careful to avoid dogmatic generalization. He reports only what he has seen, while at the same time presenting a sufficient number of illustrations to justify his opinion as to the fine quality of the North Carolina wares and their superiority, in certain respects, to the corresponding pottery of Pennsylvania.

That the North Carolina product betrays local characteristics clearly differentiating it from Pennsylvania analogues seems evident. The reason for this phenomenon is, however, far from obvious. A valuable article, *The Beginnings of the Pennsylvania-German Element in Rowan and Cabarrus Counties, North Carolina,* by William H. Gehrke, published in the *Pennsylvania Magazine of History and Biography* for October 1934, tells us that, as early as 1737, "and certainly in 1747," Germans were living in the piedmont section of North Carolina. Apparently with few exceptions they had drifted in from the north. "While a few immigrants, besides pastors and teachers, left Europe with the intention of settling in North Carolina . . . the dominating majority spent a few years in Pennsylvania." Among them were Swiss, as well as the usual quota of Germans stemming from various parts of the Fatherland.

Such individuality as we discover in the pottery turned out among these folk in their new environment must, it would seem, be ascribed primarily to chance. That is to say, the influencing tradition is not primarily of Pennsylvania, but of the European district from which the potters who migrated to North Carolina happened to come. Diluted and diverted as it must have been by local vicissitude, that tradition would probably defy tracing to its primal source or sources. Nevertheless, given a sufficient number of examples to serve as a starting point, some fruitful comparisons might be made between the decorated pottery of North Carolina and its foreign prototypes. In advance of any attempt in that direction it would be essential to classify the American product. A wide gulf separates the superb plate of Figure 4 from the splotchy items beside it, and a similar disparity exists between the obviously early jug of Figure 3 and its attendant sugar jars. Are these evident variations in artistic quality explicable on the grounds of time, of place, or of craftsmanly skill? Just now no one can tell.

What we know historically concerning the early North Carolina potters we learn chiefly from the archives of the Moravian congregation at Bethabara and Winston-Salem as they are quoted in Rice's *Shenandoah Pottery* (*pp. 271 et seq.*) from Elizabeth L. Myers' compilation of passages in church diaries and other manuscripts translated by Adelaide Fries. According to this account the Moravian brethren at Bethabara began building a pottery in 1756. In August "Brother Aust glazed pottery for the first time." By 1757 the quantity produced was sufficient to permit sales outside the community. On June 15, 1761, people came from a radius of fifty and sixty miles, and so great was the demand that the supply was exhausted before noon. During succeeding years, pottery products were shipped by wagonload to Salisbury and other outlying points. The record as quoted by Rice ends with the demolition of the old Bethabara pottery in 1777.

Meanwhile, the Moravian pottery at Salem had been in operation for eleven years. Brother Aust had moved thither from Bethabara, in July of 1768, with the promise of having "his own housekeeping, and . . . a certain sum annually." Here, again, the demand of the countryside exceeded the local supply. In 1773 a potter named Ellis was imported from Charleston. This man claimed to know the secrets of stoneware and of burning and glazing "queensware." Apparently Ellis' performance belied his promises. The newcomer dallied from December to May over the production of queensware and then departed without ceremony from amid the Salem brethren.

Quotations from this account terminate with the year 1779. In May of the preceding year Brother Aust had been told to discontinue sales to outsiders "on account of the crowd it draws." This decision on the

Fig. 2 — North Carolina Plates
Left to right: Pumpkin brown decorated with two diamond-back terrapin and a fish in cream slip. Brown ground with bird in cream and light red. *Diameters,* 13 and 15 inches. *This and succeeding illustrations from the Titus C. Geesey collection*

part of the church authorities becomes comprehensible when we learn that many purchasers came with only butter to exchange for earthenware and that the over-supply of the dairy product caused some embarrassment. On one occasion, however, Brother Aust succeeded in gathering other media of barter such as "cotton, flax, and two guns."

Concerning the later history of the North Carolina potteries further information will, no doubt, be forthcoming. At present, almost no material is available to permit ascribing dates to surviving examples of the ware. A dish or plate in Figure 1 is inscribed for the year 1812. It would be reasonable to assign the more elaborate dish of Figure 4 and the extraordinary example at the left in Figure 2 to a somewhat earlier period. The exceptionally handsome pitcher of Figure 3 seems certainly to be of the eighteenth century. As to the age of the other articles illustrated, judgment may well be reserved pending the discovery of more comprehensive data.

— *The Editor.*

I HAVE never seen any *sgraffito* ware from North Carolina. All the decoration known to me is in slip. Nor have I seen any North Carolina plates bearing inscriptions, such as we frequently find in Pennsylvania. Such negative evidence, of course, does not afford proof that *sgraffito* and inscribed items were never made in North Carolina; but it is safe to say that they were, at least, very rarely produced. Furthermore, I have seen only one dated piece. It is marked *1812* in slip. A few pieces occur with initials scratched on the back, evidently before firing. The clay used apparently was very similar to that employed by the Pennsylvania makers of slipwares — light red in color, though perhaps a little lighter in tint than Pennsylvania clay. I have examined a few pieces whose body was almost white. Like that of Pennsylvania, North Carolina pottery is glazed on one side only.

The range of North Carolina glaze colors is wide, wider than will be met in corresponding Pennsylvania products. Backgrounds are usually of a light red as in Pennsylvania slipware; or a creamy white, very similar to the prevailing color of Pennsylvania *sgraffito* ware. Yet a third background varies from a dark reddish brown, through chocolate, to an almost black tone. Against such foundations the decoration is applied in slip of sundry hues. The light shades run from a creamy white to a rather dark yellow. Shades of green, red, brown, and black also occur.

The utensils made in North Carolina were, in general, similar to those produced in Pennsylvania. The majority of surviving items are plates and dishes ranging from about six inches in diameter to a rare maximum of fifteen and one half inches. In cross-section, a North Carolina plate almost invariably exhibits a wide rim and a fairly deep bouge. I have no recollection of finding any

Fig. 3 — NORTH CAROLINA JUG AND SUGAR JARS
Left to right: Cream ground with red, black, and green slip decoration. *Height,* 11 inches. Red ground with cream, green, and black slip decoration. Pumpkin ground with black and cream slip decoration. Note horizontal placement of handles on jars

Fig. 4 — NORTH CAROLINA LAMP, PLATE, AND MUG
Left to right: Yellow-brown ground decorated in black, green, and cream slip. *Height,* 6½ inches. Black ground with cream, red, and green slip decoration. *Diameter,* 12 inches. Pumpkin ground mottled with black and cream slip

of the type, frequent in Pennsylvania, which approximate the form of a rimless deep dish. Of course, in Pennsylvania we find both types; but in North Carolina apparently we find only rimmed dishes (*Fig. 2*).

Next to plates, the most usual North Carolina pottery items are sugar jars. So, at least, these vessels are locally known, and I have found several that still contained some sugar. Collectors may term the large examples cookie jars and the small ones sugar bowls; but North Carolinians assure me that both were dedicated to the same sweet end. The lidded jars of Pennsylvania are of a different shape, with straighter sides, larger mouth, and proportionately more expansive lid. The handles of Pennsylvania jars are usually set vertically. North Carolina jar handles, on the contrary, are invariably horizontal and often extremely small. Pennsylvania lidded jars pass by various names, but I have never heard one referred to as a sugar jar. All the North Carolina jars that I have observed have been decorated with conventional ornament. Birds, flowers, animals, and the like have been notably absent.

Though plates and sugar bowls are the commonest articles of North Carolina decorated pottery, I have seen a few pitchers or jugs. The one illustrated in Figure 3 is an unusually pleasing example. I have also found a few Betty lamps like that in Figure 4. Flat, lidded shaving dishes partitioned into two divisions — one for soap, the other for water — were also made. Pottery flasks and small kegs, apparently for conveying liquid refreshment to workers in the fields, occasionally turn up. Other articles doubtless were made; but I have yet to meet surviving examples of them.

North Carolina potters were fond of conventional borders. In fact, I believe that they often surpassed their Pennsylvania contemporaries in the use of abstract forms. On the other hand, their use of floral motives, of which they were fond, is less convincing than that of their Pennsylvania cousins. Occasionally they introduced birds in the centre of plates, and, in one instance at least, a fish and two diamond-back terrapin. North Carolina potters did not approach the Pennsylvania craftsmen in variety of designs. It is solely in conventional decoration that they seem to have excelled. For such superiority the Brother Aust mentioned in the early records may have been chiefly responsible. The man was evidently a skilled potter and a trustworthy supervisor. It is unfortunate that nothing is known of his antecedents.

FIG. 1 — HEART-SHAPED SAUCER LAMP. Attributed to David Spinner, who plied his trade at Melford in Bucks County from 1800 to 1811. This lamp is a mere three inches long, with a single wick channel. Its heart shape suggests that it may have been a wedding present

FIG. 2 — SPOUT LAMPS. Of the same red-brown tone as Figure 1. From Berks County. *Left*, quite apparently copied from a mug; three inches tall; spout of the same length. *Right*, probably modeled after a teapot or jug; stiff, straight spout. Height, 4 5/16 inches; spout 3 1/2 inches long

EARLY POTTERY LIGHTING DEVICES OF PENNSYLVANIA

By WILLIAM J. TRUAX

FIG. 3 — CANDLESTICK. An amusing example in lighthouse form, whose wide saucer might support a betty lamp. Incisions in the sides form the letters *ISI* so that this combination candlestick and lamp stand might be classed as a signed piece. So many potters claim these initials, however, that they are not an exact identification. This piece was made in Lebanon County. The glaze is very dense, with green and dark-brown spots running through it, and slip of yellowish brown. Height, 7 1/8 inches; top diameter, 4 15/16 inches

PENNSYLVANIA pottery occupies an unquestioned place in the domain of antiques. Indeed, since much of it has been unmistakably earmarked by time, we may be sometimes inclined to look upon the whole colorful category as a survival from the distant past. Yet Jacob Medinger, the last of the old-school Pennsylvania potters who were responsible for much of the ware that collectors prize today, died but a decade ago. The craft of making redware pottery in the early manner survived in Pennsylvania because of the rather astonishing fact that the people, though in constant communication with other parts of the changing continent, clung tenaciously for over two centuries to many early methods, customs, and superstitions. Yet, while they perpetuated the customs of their forefathers that seemed to them sound and good and appropriate, they shrewdly adopted new designs that came to the pottery kiln, and sometimes the happy combination of old and new lifted the products of their craft into the realm of art. One writer has observed that almost any antique found in any one of the original states has its counterpart in the Dutch country of Pennsylvania, but that the counterpart always reveals the characteristic local touch.

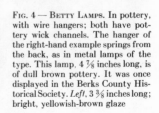

FIG. 4 — BETTY LAMPS. In pottery, with wire hangers; both have pottery wick channels. The hanger of the right-hand example springs from the back, as in metal lamps of the type. This lamp, 4 7/8 inches long, is of dull brown pottery. It was once displayed in the Berks County Historical Society. *Left*, 3 3/8 inches long; bright, yellowish-brown glaze

Though the Pennsylvania potter spent the greater part of his days in making more or less standard commercial products such as pie plates and crocks, he expressed his individuality in the fashioning of numerous odd objects that are to us utterly delightful. Whistles in the form of birds — a whistle could hardly be caged more appropriately; small houses to be used as children's banks; flowerpots with fine pie-crimped edges, designs on their sleek sides, and often an inscribed date; and tremendous dishes for the bride-to-be, abundantly and happily adorned with a medley of tulips and love birds and inscriptions, all in rich, bright colors — such varied objects we find today, a persistent monument to the play spirit of the industrious potter of yesterday.

Lighting devices seem to have offered a special invitation to the personal touch. That the Pennsylvania potters produced lamps of almost every conceivable design is evident from the great variation in extant specimens. The majority of these are of redware glazed in plain colors. Their lack of elaborate decorations may be due to the small surface of the pieces. Occasionally fine specimens turn up with variegated or speckled glaze or with ornamentation in slip. Others, though lacking distinctive coloring, are unusual in form, and sometimes excellently proportioned. No two are alike, and the forms were frequently copied from unrelated objects that caught and pleased the potter's eye. Most of

them embody the simplest principles of illumination, providing a receptacle for grease and a channel for holding the wick in place. Still, as some of the illustrated examples testify, more complex devices are to be found.

To the collector of old lighting fixtures the matter of date is important. Yet, in the case of these pottery devices, unless a piece is dated or bears the individual and unmistakable mark of a certain potter, it is difficult indeed to say when it was made. And such identifying marks are rarely found. According to John Ramsay's *American Potters and Pottery*, the eastern Pennsylvania counties of Chester, Montgomery, and Bucks became a pottery-making center before the middle of the eighteenth century; the first recorded pottery in the district was built in 1740. It is generally accepted that the earliest potteries were in Chester County, and several collectors and dealers with whom I have discussed the subject feel that pottery was being made there soon after 1700, if not before that date. So far as I know, however, there is not one existing example of Pennsylvania pottery earlier than a platter inscribed *1733*.

While some of the lighting devices here pictured are of a type used in this early period, I am not credulous enough to believe that any of them can boast an age of two centuries and more. The persistence of old patterns, and the primitive character of many late pieces that were turned out simultaneously with superior work, make the task of dating with any accuracy almost impossible. It is safe to say, however, that the lamps here illustrated represent the century of potterymaking between the years 1770 and 1870. The forms are characteristic of what the collector may expect to find, though the condition of the members of this group is above the average.

Pottery lamps are being copied today, but the discriminating collector will soon learn to differentiate between old ones and new. The latter have a lighter, more porous body, and lack the patina that comes only with age. The fact that old lighting devices in Pennsylvania pottery are not half so numerous as specimens in metal or glass only adds zest to the collector's chase.

FIG. 5 — GREASE LAMP. The molding of the standard resembles linen-fold paneling; three small knobs decorate the handle. Height, 7 ¼ inches; base diameter, 4 ⅞ inches. The color is light brown. This lamp has the characteristics of Berks County production

FIG. 6 — GREASE LAMP. Short, open-top, saucer-base example covered with a glaze almost black in color. Though discovered in western Pennsylvania, it may be an Ohio piece. Height, 4 ⅛ inches; diameter of base, 5 ¼ inches

FIG. 7 — CANDLESTICK. While not particularly appealing in design, this piece has the distinction of an inscription, incised in the base: *W.A. and A.D. No. 22, 1866*. The known list of potters fails to throw light on this bold marking. This stubby specimen was found in Montgomery County. Height, 2 ½ inches. The scalloped saucer base is 5 ¼ inches in diameter. The glaze is speckled brown and green

FIG. 8 — THREE-WICK LAMP. Shape possibly inspired by a quill holder and ink pot, which it resembles. The wick tubes, and the known fact that the well once contained oil, not ink, prove that it is a lamp. The other lighters here illustrated could have been outfitted with wicks made from a piece of oil-soaked rag, but this piece calls for the solid round wick used in camphene lamps. Discovered in Berks County. Height, 2 inches; diameter of bowl, 4 ⅞ inches

American pottery lamps

BY LURA WOODSIDE WATKINS

Fig. 1. Lamp of unglazed red earthenware made at Morgantown, West Virginia, by John W. Thompson, probably before 1840. Height, 5 inches. *The Smithsonian Institution, United States National Museum.*

EVERY LARGE COLLECTION of American lighting devices includes one or more pottery grease lamps. These are primitive affairs, usually with a simple open reservoir on a standard, a saucer base, and a handle or handles. The greater number have a slight beak in the bowl-like reservoir where the wick may rest, others have spouts, while a very few have wick supports.

Such fat lamps are now comparatively rare, but in their day they were probably rather common. They were fashioned by local potters who made a business of supplying household utensils of whatever clay was available. Red-burning clay was the material most often used, but lamps were also made of stoneware. Most surviving specimens date from the first half of the nineteenth century.

Almost all the lamps of this type have been found in areas of German settlement, principally in Pennsylvania and Ohio, among the Moravians in North Carolina, and to some extent at a late period in Tennessee. It is more than probable that all American pottery lamps, even when made by potters of British descent, originated among the German settlers. This theory is bolstered by the fact that no pottery lamps of any kind were made by the hundreds of clayworkers of English descent in New England. Neither do they appear to have been produced by any of the numerous English and Irish potters whose histories have been recounted by Arthur E. James in *The Potters and Potteries of Chester County, Pennsylvania.*

Judging by the probabilities alone, the German settlers would have made the style of lamp familiar to them in their homeland. That they actually did just this we know for the reason that similar lamps were in use among the peasants of northwestern Europe, in Hungary, and in Sweden. Continental lamps differ in the respect that they usually have a pouring lip in the saucer base, but they show the ancestry of our American examples.

The lamp shown in Figure 1 is referred to by Walter Hough in his *Collection of Heating and Lighting Utensils in the United States National Museum* as having "English ancestry." By this he probably means that it was descended from an English lamp type known as a "Cornish chill," examples of which are to be found in the Penzance and Truro museums in Cornwall. One of these

Cornish specimens has the lip in the base found on Hungarian and Swedish lamps. There is evidently a relationship between the Cornish and Continental types, but the latter, brought to us by German immigrants, are more likely to be the originals of our own clay lamps.

Hough obtained the lamp shown in Figure 1 in Morgantown, West Virginia, from a daughter of John W. Thompson, the potter who made it. Thompson's father had taken his family over the mountains from Bel Air, Maryland, in 1785, and John became an apprentice in the first pottery west of the Alleghenies, founded by one Foulk at the very beginning of the settlement. This pottery supplied the demand for household wares then so expensive to obtain from Baltimore or other seacoast sources of supply. Thompson succeeded to Foulk's business and continued to make redware until about 1840, when the manufacture of stoneware was begun. The lamp illustrated must have been made between 1800 and 1840. Hough surmises that it may have been a potter's lamp. Although it was perhaps designed for the potter's own use, we now know that it is a type often repeated in the middle Atlantic states. It is most primitive in construction, being simply a lipped saucer on a stand with saucer base and a handle.

A similar example, made in Tennessee of stoneware clay, was illustrated by H. C. Mercer in *Light and Fire Making.* He says of it: "From the boat-shaped earthen lamps of ancient Rome, from the green majolica ones of candlestick shape used by the Moors of today, to this miniature boat-shaped one of stoneware set upon a stemmed dish, in which opossum or 'coon' fat might have burnt for the Tennessee moonshiner, where I found it two years ago in the hill country of White County, Tennessee, there is no change of character or make." He further adds: "There J. T. Goodwin baked it for me of blue clay in 1895."

Such instances of a lamp by a known maker are rare. A lamp that was sold at the auction of the Alfred B. MacClay collection in 1939 was marked on the base, *J. L. Blaney, Cookstown, Pa.* This lamp must have been made between 1825 and 1854, since Cookstown had different names before and after those dates. Needless to say, such a marked lamp is a priceless rarity.

Fig. 2. Stoneware lamp glazed with Albany slip, found in Ohio. Height, 5½ inches. *Author's collection.*

Fig. 3. Lamp with globular reservoir, glazed red earthenware, attributed to Pennsylvania. Height, about 5 inches. *The Smithsonian Institution, United States National Museum.*

Fig. 4. Lamp with two handles and spouts, dark brown glaze. Height, 6⅝ inches. *Henry Ford Museum.*

Fig. 5. Lamp with a true spout, dark brown glaze. Height, 5¾ inches. *Henry Ford Museum.*

Fig. 6. Lamp with fully developed spout, glazed red earthenware. Height, 2¼ inches, length, 4¾ inches. *Author's collection.*

At the pottery centers of Bethabara and Winston-Salem, North Carolina, Moravian potters were working as early as 1756 and as late as 1830. Lamps from this area have a light red earthenware body and are decorated with a combination of brown, black, cream, and green slips on a yellow-brown ground.

The large stoneware lamp in Figure 2, with a lipped open reservoir and an Albany slip glaze, was found in Ohio. John Ramsay illustrates an almost identical example in his *American Pottery* (page 158). Albany slip glazing on stoneware was a nineteenth-century technique, and these lamps may have been made about 1840. A pair of lamps of a similar shape were made and used in a rural community in Tennessee as late as 1905.

A number of grease lamps have reservoirs of globular form. The one shown in Figure 3 has a slight lip for a wick rest. It is attributed to Pennsylvania and is distinguished by a rudimentary decoration of tooled straight and wavy lines. Some globular reservoirs are slightly closed in at the top, and have chunky projecting spouts to serve as wick channels. An example with two handles and two spouts is in the Ford collection at Dearborn, Michigan (Fig. 4). The spouts, of triangular shape, are simply contrived. A similar lamp, owned by Mrs. Rhea Mansfield Knittle, is shown in John Spargo's *Early American Pottery and China* (plate 31).

Lamps with true spouts are great rarities, probably because they were difficult to make. Since the reservoirs of all these lamps were turned on the potter's wheel, they are fundamentally cups or bowls adapted to the purposes of illumination by the addition of lips or spouts. A lamp with a true, albeit rudimentary, spout is shown in Figure 5. This displays the novel feature of a reservoir partly closed to prevent the spilling over of oil or grease. A more fully developed spout may be seen on the lamp in Figure 6, which has the wick opening on the upper surface of the beak. Here, as rarely, no stand was provided, and the result is a lamp as primitive as those of ancient Greece or the Near East and not much different from some of them. A lamp of this type, provided with a carrying handle, was illustrated in an article by William J. Truax in ANTIQUES for May 1940. Mr. Truax also showed an example with a deeper reservoir, which might possibly have been intended for a lamp filler.

Another class of pottery lamps is equipped with tubular or gutter-shaped wick supports, which allowed any surplus grease to drip back from the wick into the reservoir itself rather than onto the outside of the lamp. A notable example of this type is that shown in Figure 7. Its wick tube is a perfect cylinder at the outer end, but is opened and spread apart towards the center of the bowl. The lamp with rudimentary spout in Figure 8 has a ceramic trough or channel (the more usual form) inside.

At least four examples of pottery Betty lamps with interior wick supports are known, all from Pennsylvania. One, illustrated in the article by Mr. Truax, has a handle and was not designed for suspension. The lamp in Figure 9 has a punched opening in the tab at the back for the accommodation of a wire or string. Two others of unique form appear in the group shown by Mr. Truax. One is complete with the regular type of twisted iron handle and hook so familiar on iron Bettys; the other has been pierced at the sides in a wholly original manner for an iron suspending wire and hook.

The Bettys are the aristocrats of American pottery lamps and must have a strong appeal for those who like to reflect upon old customs and ways. They represent the successful attempt of their makers to provide a wanted necessity when the usual materials were not at hand. All these lamps, in fact, must give us added respect for the ingenuity of those masters of the wheel.

Fig. 8. Lamp with pottery wick trough in bowl leading to spout, red earthenware with rough reddish-brown glaze. Height, 5½ inches. *Henry Ford Museum.*

Fig. 9. Betty lamp with pottery wick trough, glazed red earthenware. Diameter, 4½ inches. *Author's collection.*

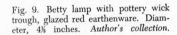

Fig. 7. Lamp equipped with pottery wick tube in bowl, the standard partly hollow, red earthenware with dark brown glaze. Height, 7 7/10 inches. *Landis Valley Museum.*

BY MARGARET MATTISON COFFIN

Decorated tinware

Photographs by Charles Coffin

Fig. 1. Document box with typical Connecticut design, probably from the Filley shops. *John J. Vrooman.*

THE FIRST AMERICAN TINSMITHS, Edward and William Pattison, settled in Berlin, Connecticut, in 1738. Until this time, the few pieces of tinware used in the Colonies were expensive imports. In 1749 the English parliament passed a law prohibiting rolling and plating mills in the Colonies. There was no production of tinplate here until after 1829, when Amherst's Professor Hitchock discovered tin near Goshen, Connecticut. (Tinplate is sheet iron rolled very thin and coated with layers of molten tin.)

The Pattison brothers imported sheets of tinplate from Wales, then the sole producer of tinplate for export. They worked up an assortment of household utensils in their home, and sold it door-to-door. The demand soon grew so great that the Pattisons had to hire peddlers.

In 1750, roads in rural areas were non-existent, and the tinmen walked, carrying baskets. Later they traveled on horseback, with packs hanging on either side. By 1800, peddlers started using brightly painted carts, usually red, but sometimes yellow or green. Doors of the carts swung down, revealing compartments filled with tinware.

Routes of peddlers were extended as turnpikes were built. When Shubael Pattison inherited his father's tinware business in 1787, his peddlers had routes in Canada. He himself did some peddling there and traded for furs, which he hired girls to make into muffs. When he died in 1828, he was wealthy, and was said to have had the largest funeral ever held in town.

In Maine, peddlers started out from Stevens Plains, where Zachariah Stevens opened one of the first tin shops in 1789, and "Old Briscoe" first peddled tinware. An old-time peddler, writing for the Portland *Argus* reported that most peddlers were "green young men from the farm who wanted to see the world and earn enough money to buy some land."

The South was a profitable field for peddlers. Northern roads were passable only from May through the middle of November. In autumn, peddlers loaded their carts and started southward. When supplies were sold, they headed north again, sometimes selling horses and carts to return by boat.

Distances covered by the tin peddlers are amazing. Timothy Dwight wrote, "I have seen them in 1797 on Cape Cod and in the neighborhood of Lake Erie—distant from each other more than 600 miles. They make their way to Detroit 400 miles further—to Canada and to Kentucky, and if I mistake not, to New Orleans and St. Louis."

New York State had many tinmen. Augustus Filley, manager of the tin shop in Lansingburg, New York,

Fig. 2. One typical kind of Pennsylvania pattern, with orange acorns, the paint smudged when wet into the "saucer" of the acorn. *Author's collection.*

Fig. 3. Document box which looks like the work of Ann Butler. *Ruby M. Rounds.*

Fig. 4. Large domed-top box, with one kind of decoration found in New York State. *Mr. and Mrs. A. P. Robertson.*

Fig. 5. Typical pattern found on canisters and boxes along the Vermont-New York border. *Mr. and Mrs. George Pierce.*

wrote to his cousin Oliver in Connecticut on July 17, 1815: "The Canady peddlers wanted more tin than I could let them have . . . Albany City tinmen was here Thursday & wanted $200 jap. tin." "Honest" Wilson peddled tin along the eastern state line, coming down from Barre, Vermont. Hiram Lahue, a cripple, lived near Granville, in Washington County, and always carried striped stick candy and spruce gum to encourage youngsters to care for his horse. Erma Shepherd Griffith of Binghamton, New York, reports that Paul Phelps, born in Mansfield, Connecticut, in 1786, settled in Palmyra, New York, and drove a tin peddler's cart throughout that section for years. Peddlers were so much a part of rural New York life that Danforth Brayton and his wife added an extra room to their house at East Lake George just for peddlers.

The tin peddlers served their countrymen well. They offered a means of delivering goods, and took the place of present-day radios and telephones. By about 1900 the era of the tin peddler had passed. Tin kitchen utensils became impractical, as hundreds of new industrial uses for tin were found. The romance of the tin peddler passed away, and now only the few remaining pieces of the tinware they sold remind us of the peddler's cart clattering up a country lane, as dogs barked, children shouted with excitement, and mother set another place for dinner.

The tinware carried by the first peddlers was plain, but very soon japanned and decorated wares became popular. These first American-decorated pieces were done with brushes and oil paints, not stencils. Backgrounds were most often "japanned"—painted with asphaltum, a transparent substance with a tar base, which required heat to dry. The names Mygatt, Hubbard, Francis, and North were prominent among the early Connecticut decorators, who were also in demand in the Filley branch shops in other states. Their designs were stylized, and they favored a white band surmounted with a design over a japanned surface (Fig. 1). Variations of brush strokes and swags were used as borders. Almost transparent green leaves showed fine black veins, stems, and tendrils. Some of the yellow used was ochre, brownish and transparent. Pastel shades were occasionally used. Striping was plentiful.

The Stevens Plains decorators—Zachariah Stevens, the Francis girls, Oliver and Mary Ann Buckley—produced more realistic designs. Background colors used in Maine were often bright, and of solid colors, without banding. Much of "Uncle Zach's" work which has been preserved was done on a cream-colored or a mustard-yellow background. Sally Francis was a prolific rose painter, and her roses have been found on trays and caddies, coffeepots and table tops. Leaves in the Stevens Plains decoration are often chubby, with straight veins, sometimes resembling the leaves of the strawberry plant. Zachariah Stevens produced some scenic decorations, but flowers and fruit were preferred—peaches, strawberries, clusters of cherries, whitish flowers with gay accents. Designs of yellow and vermilion alone are found. Stevens Plains borders are unusual—a distinguishing characteristic; one looks like a string of pearls and another combines berries and leaves with symmetric artistry.

Pennsylvania tinware designs resemble peasant decorations from the central countries of Europe (Fig. 2). They are often symbolic, and at times appear to be an impression rather than an accurate representation. Pennsylvania craftsmen sometimes used asphaltum and sometimes

112

bright background paints which did not adhere properly. Red was a favorite background, while blue, yellow, and brown were used in designs. (Brown was rarely used elsewhere.) An orange-vermilion appears sometimes in stems, and many designs are placed on white circles. The popular tulips, pomegranates, and star-shaped flowers are often outlined in black. Some Pennsylvania decorators used their fingertips to blend wet paint of different colors, at times leaving distinct fingerprints.

In New York State, unique decorating was done by Ann and Minerva Butler, daughters of Aaron Butler of Greene County, who ran a peddling and decorating business from 1824 to 1859 (Fig. 3). Their flowers and leaves are formed by brush strokes neatly laid together. Many patterns include delicate cross-hatching in flower centers. White bands, dotted lines, and "zig-zags" are characteristic. Stems are hair-like, of green, yellow, or vermilion, and tiny dots form forget-me-nots. Some greens are olive, others emerald; the vermilions are bright but not orange and the yellows and blues bright and clear. Backgrounds are either of dark asphaltum or black

paint. Borders vary, but the "rickrack" and "rope" types were the most favored.

Another type of decoration found in New York State is characterized by large vermilion flowers, with alizarin crimson and white over-strokes (Fig. 4). Dark green leaves with yellow veins resemble either elongated elm leaves or willow leaves. Yellow brush-stroke tassels abound.

A group of pieces found in western Vermont and eastern New York State has simple designs on an asphaltum base (Fig. 5). A spray of dark green stems runs diagonally from the lower left-hand corner to the upper right, and flowers are formed of elongated brush strokes of vermilion, with accents of dark blue, sometimes blended into white.

The various decorating formulas which may thus be distinguished teach us a little more about a truly American folk art. The best of these designs reveal expert craftsmanship. The Stevens, Butlers, Filleys, and others have left us an artistic heritage of which we may be proud.

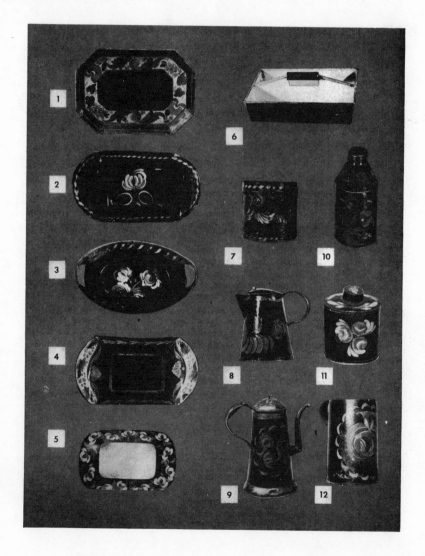

Fig. 6. Chart of tinware shapes. (1) Octagonal tray, Pennsylvania. *Metropolitan Museum of Art.* (2) Bread tray, Butler. *Mr. James C. Stevens.* (3) Oval bun tray, Butler. *Author's collection.* (4) Bread tray, Connecticut. *Mrs. Robert Wilbur.* (5) Rectangular bun tray, Maine. *Mrs. Clyde Holmes.* (6) Knife and fork tray with marbleized finish, found in New York State. *Author's collection.* (7) Round, flat-topped canister, New York. *Author's collection.* (8) Syrup pitcher. *Mrs. Robert Wilbur.* (9) Crooked-spout coffeepot, Pennsylvania. *Metropolitan Museum of Art.* (10) Tea caddy, found near Vermont-New York border. *Farmers' Museum, Cooperstown, New York.* (11) Squat, oval caddy. *Miss Florence Wright.* (12) Measure, Pennsylvania. *Miss Florence Wright.*

Decorated tinware east and west
In New Mexico

BY E. BOYD

WHAT IS POPULARLY KNOWN as "old Spanish tin" did not exist in our Southwest. The first tin articles came, ready made, over the Santa Fe Trail during the second quarter of the nineteenth century. These, from records, seem to have been tin candle molds and tin-framed looking glasses. As in other Spanish countries, candles had been made by dipping; but the molds must have found buyers—we find copies of them, country-made from tin scraps pieced together. The looking glasses are mentioned in several contemporary accounts; they hung in churches as well as in private homes. In 1846, Lieutenant Colonel W. H. Emory spoke of "Yankee looking glasses without number"—all hanging so high that they could not be looked into!

After the military occupation of New Mexico by the United States in 1846 and the steady influx of emigrants from our eastern states, various staples in tin containers were freighted over the plains. When the tins were empty, they were salvaged for reworking by ingenious native artisans. To understand how desirable tin, as a material, was in the eyes of New Mexicans at that time, we must remember their perennial lack of metals. For more than two hundred years small tools, hardware, nails, and bolts were brought by caravan from Central Mexico by a long and dangerous route, and there were never enough to supply even the rudimentary needs of the northern frontier province. As a result, every scrap of worn-out metal was made to serve again and again. Local folk artists supplied secular and religious decorative pieces, ingeniously contrived from local materials, but they had nothing to satisfy the human fondness for sparkle and brilliance. Tin had this property, it was easily worked with blacksmithing tools, and it could be had for the taking from gringo trash heaps.

Early New Mexico tin pieces have several distinguishing characteristics: very heavy tinning of soft pewter color, the presence of brand names and other commercial marks on the reverse, and the fact that each object was pieced together from assorted snips of tin cut without relation to the structure—the result of their having been made from cut-down containers instead of from new sheet tin.

Candle sconce made of 13 scraps of tin joined with pine rosin. *Except as noted, illustrations are from the Museum of New Mexico.*

Glazed tin *nicho* with panels of painted paper, predominantly blue, and candle sockets at lower right and left. Note piecing of both tin and glass.

With the exception of candleholders and molds, tin was used in New Mexico purely as an ornament. The lack of commonplace implements made of tin is the more surprising when we learn that iron or copper vessels were itemized as valuable properties in last wills and testaments, while dippers, mugs, bowls, and other kitchen trifles were made at home, whittled from wood, cow horns, or gourds. The profound religious devotion of the province offers an explanation: the silvery tin was reserved for the little pantheons of saints and holy persons then seen in every home as well as in the churches. A tin frame, or a *nicho* (small glazed tin shrine), was made for an old family image, which might be a locally-made *santo* or an engraving brought by a pilgrim from some Mexican shrine. In record time for those days, the enterprising N. Currier sent out a series of colored lithographs of religious subjects for the new Spanish Catholic market. Later on European clergymen who came after Archbishop Lamy to the diocese of Santa Fe, created in 1851, distributed inferior prints from France, Germany, and Benziger Brothers' Cincinnati press.

Candleholders, the functional form in which tin was used in New Mexico, were obviously a vast improvement over wooden ones. Shapes ranged from a single sconce of a tin scrap bent at a right angle and fitted to a socket, to ceiling chandeliers with a central lantern form and perhaps twelve candle sockets on curved straps. Like most of the tin pieces, these were not only much pieced but made from several different tins, as the original stamping and factory grooving of different parts of the same piece show. Later in the nineteenth century cut-out fins, floral and bird forms were soldered among the tiers of candelabra.

Among other useful and attractive innovations brought by the Anglos to New Mexico, such as fashions in dress and the distilling of spirits, were two items taken for granted by most of the population east of the Mississippi—window glass and wall paper. It is a matter of record that in 1846 the only building in the Territory with glazed windows was the Palace of the Governors. Yankee families who came to stay sent to St. Louis for

window panes and rolls of wallpaper, to recreate in strange adobes the mid-Victorian parlors they had left behind. The earliest tin pieces contain heavy plate glass with air bubbles in it like the surviving original panes in the old Palace itself. The oldest wallpapers, which have been preserved in tin pieces but not on walls, are in William Morris neo-classic patterns. After these we find a sequence familiar to anyone who has seen old sample books, or our grandmothers' homes. Since tin was so often combined with glass and wallpaper by New Mexicans, we must give due consideration to all three materials in dating any example, as well as to the image which forms the central motif.

In recent years it has become a custom to paint gay designs on windows in New Mexico style interiors and to call the result "Spanish colonial painted glass," but if there was almost no glass before 1846 how can painting on glass be a "Spanish colonial" craft? In the course of twenty-five years of keeping notes on indigenous Spanish artifacts, I have noted only three examples of small wooden panels in which irregularly cut ovals of hand-blown glass were painstakingly inlaid, with a small tempera painting on paper of a religious image, more or less in the manner of the folk artists who made *santos*, under the glass. It is the glass in these three pieces which is remarkable, and the labor which went into its inlay indicates its rarity at that time. When scraps of window or picture glass did become available to tinsmiths, they adapted the process described above to tin pieces. A pattern of wavy lines and floral scrolls was painted on common paper, laid under a small clear glass panel, backed with tin or makeshift cardboard, and the whole

Multiple-windowed frame of the type used for family portraits in the East, with N. Currier print dated 1848 of Our Lady of Guadalupe of Mexico. Each section was separately made, the whole soldered together and braced by ornamental bosses.

Tin chandelier, circa 1850, made in vicinity of Santa Fe and used in church at Cañoncito, New Mexico. *Wash drawing by the author, Index of American Design, National Gallery of Art.*

Frames in "Federal" style, with motifs copied from cabinetwork brought west by emigrants. Surface decoration was done with the point of a nail or small dies already in use for stamping leather.

Cross of mid-nineteenth-century wallpaper, in terra cotta, black, and yellow, mounted in tin.

was soldered together with a narrow tin rim. (Since tinsmithing as a profession did not exist prior to Yankee influence, solder did not arrive in New Mexico as quickly as tin containers, so some of the first locally re-fashioned tin pieces were put together with pine rosin which is still visible.) Multiple panels, each carefully sealed, were joined to make larger pieces. The painted inlays, which are usually more attractive to today's collectors, were not used as frequently as wallpaper.

One of the first designs for frames, which seems to have been copied from furniture in the Federal style, was a vertical rectangle with corner bosses and a pediment of the spread eagle or other motif. Later versions had small rosettes of tin, or curlicues, soldered around the rim. The repetition of simple geometric figures gave added sparkle to the tin, and was used with pleasing restraint. After the Civil War an amusing adaptation of the family portrait gallery frames, common in the East in the form of a heavy oval or polygonal wooden molding with multiple openings to show small photographs of many members of the family, was made of the same tin, glass, and wallpaper scraps, with a religious subject at the center.

After the railroad reached the Rio Grande in 1880, there were more commercial items and more variety in materials. Storekeepers offered oil paints for woodwork and wagons, and tin pieces were pointed up with gaudy colors rather thickly daubed on. Objects grew larger, and flying superstructures in flamboyant shapes were attached. Neither functional nor well made, these gaudy pieces have seldom survived intact. The earlier reserva-

tion of tin to the greater honor of religious images seems to have been forgotten, and an increasing supply of colored prints, magazine and catalogue covers, advertising and greeting cards, found its way into tin frames. When cheap copies of gilded plaster or dark wooden frames reached local stores, tin itself became démodé, except in distant villages where the old crafts persisted well into the present century.

The many artists who moved to New Mexico in the past two generations encouraged native artisans to revive tincraft as a means of livelihood, and the WPA Federal Art Project gave further impetus. Now, under the direction of various regional craft shops using traditional and recent designs, it has gone into a more mass-produced phase to supply the new demand for this type of ornament so appropriate to southwestern adobe homes.

Tin and glass trinket box with commercial colored cards inset. Reverse shows cards for Peter's Cornstarch and Ayer's Cherry Pectoral—"For the Cure of Coughs, Colds, Asthma, Croup, Bronchitis, Whooping Cough and Consumption." 1885-1890.

Quart-size cottage cheese colanders in conventional shapes, round, diamond, and—by far the most popular—heart. Solidified cheese retained the shape and pierced design of the mold.

Decorated tinware east and west

In Pennsylvania   *BY EARL F. ROBACKER*

THE FONDNESS OF THE Pennsylvania Germans for ornamenting even the simplest of their handicrafts is proverbial, and the piercing or punching of the sheet tin used for household objects as a means of enhancing their beauty seems to have been particularly popular. True, pierced tin performed both a utilitarian and a decorative function in the familiar "Paul Revere" lantern, and in the more or less ubiquitous footwarmers, both of which are of eastern seaboard rather than purely local provenance; but it remained for the Pennsylvania German craftsman to turn a merely convenient practice into something of an art.

Tinware, pierced or punched, seems to be almost entirely a nineteenth-century product. Such few dates as are found range from the 1830's to the 1860's, with more falling in the 1840's than at any other time. In a few instances the piercing of tin for ornamental purposes seems to have continued up to contemporary times.

"Piercing" and "punching" are, of course, two different things. As the name implies, piercing denotes a complete perforation—a chisel making a slit, a nail a round hole. The rough surface created by the process is always on the outside of the object decorated. Punching, done with a hammer and nail or a hammer and a fine die, dents the surface of the tin but does not cut it. Punched objects were usually intended to hold liquids.

At once the most important and the most distinctive pierced tin object is the pie cupboard, or pie safe, the primary function of which was to provide storage space after the weekly or semi-weekly orgy of baking. It is curious to note that museums seem to have neglected this most characteristic—in function, design, and meticulous execution—of Pennsylvania German products. The cupboard is a simple, sturdy framework of pine, either pegged or nailed, with a hinged door or pair of doors constituting the entire front. Over this framework are tacked the perforated sheets of tin which provided circulation of air while the pies cooled, at the same time protecting them from insects or mice. The decoration may be an over-all one, as in the hanging cupboards, or may be executed in small identical panels in the stationary type. The rare eagle motif is particularly sought by collectors; also desirable are the six-pointed geometric design sometimes erroneously referred to as a "hex" sign, and the five-pointed star. The free design of scrolls or arabesques is more usual. Large six-pointed figures were evidently laid out with a compass; smaller designs were probably done by following a pattern superimposed on the tin.

Similar to the tin panels of the pie cupboard in details of fashioning are the colanders for shaping cottage cheese, into which was poured the scalded milk for draining and eventual solidifying. Heart-shaped strainers of

Perforations on the door of this foot-warmer—which held a hot brick wrapped in flannel—show representative heart motif.

Three hearts at center back form the sole embellishment of this simple punchwork candle sconce.

Important pierced tin pie cupboard with unusual rooster and four-pointed star motifs. Typical projecting corner posts at top are bored so cupboard can be strung with rope and suspended from the ceiling. Taller cupboards, with two vertical doors, were stationary.

All illustrations from author's collection; photographs by Alden Haswell.

Already a rare item because of its limited vogue in the early days of the parlor store, the "ash protector" was placed on the iron hearth before the grate to check draft and keep hearth neat.

The punched tin coffeepot on the left is a prize specimen complete with maker's name, initials of recipient, and date: *J. Ketterer, H.G., 1843;* central decoration, an urn filled with tulips and other flowers, is this maker's favorite. Heart motif on pot at right occurs infrequently in coffeepots. An interesting variant is the miniature, dated 1860, with its single elaborate tulip.

this type—some of them obviously of recent manufacture —are still in use in the Pennsylvania German country. Some strainers have lids, others do not. Early examples are likely to be footed; both early and late ones may have convenient tabs or wire handles for ease in manipulation and for hanging.

As is the case with pie cupboards, the actual perforation is done before the pieces are assembled and soldered. Designs are usually elementary, with stars and rayed concentric circles predominating. Nail punching makes a neater, more compact, and more attractive design here than chisel perforation because of the limited area for decoration.

Other objects decorated by the Pennsylvania Germans in pierced tin were nutmeg graters, foot warmers, and "ash protectors"—the last in use for only a very brief time, since space heaters improved and changed so rapidly.

Compartmented bureau box with six-pointed punchwork geometric figure.

It is in punched tinware that the student will find the most finely detailed work, with coffeepots the best specimens. The punching was done with great care—a single too-vigorous indentation would have ruined the entire undertaking. At the same time, it is doubtful that these capacious and attractive pots ever saw active duty; they belonged then, as they do now, to the category of things kept "just for fancy."

Modest craftsmen that they usually were, the Pennsylvania Germans refrained from putting their mark on any but pieces that were obviously a matter of pride; it is significant, therefore, that of all punched tin objects, coffeepots alone are commonly identifiable by maker. Three names occur: J. Ketterer, M. Uebele, and W. Shade; but even these artisans did not, apparently, mark all their pieces. When the name does occur, it is die-stamped on the handle.

Exterior evidence indicates that punched tin coffeepots, like the best sgraffito or slipware pottery, were made as special presentation pieces, possibly for brides. Frequently the initials of the recipient—or of the owner—appear, one on either side of the central motif. When the date is added, the *18* appears at one side on the reverse and the two remaining numerals on the other. Designs frequently use the profile tulip of fractur, of dower chests, and of ironware. The heart occurs infrequently, as do comet-shaped figures (the Chinese *yin* and *yang* symbols), conventionalized floral patterns, and stars —usually four-pointed.

Other than in coffeepots, punchwork occurs only incidentally. One instance is the candle sconce shown. Occasional cooky cutters have elementary punchwork designs, presumably for identification, and one specimen has an elaborately outlined *F* for the same purpose.

THE CASE FOR
PENNSYLVANIA GERMAN PAINTED TIN

By EARL F. ROBACKER

THE PAINTED TINWARE of German Pennsylvania, or what the late Esther Stevens Brazer was wont to call "country tin," has long been something of a puzzle to collectors. Possessing, as it does, characteristics which set it apart from the painted tinware of New England, it seems also to evade a satisfactory classification among bona fide Pennsylvania German antiques. The important questions as to where, when, and by whom it was made have thus far found no satisfactory answer, a circumstance not at all unusual in the matter of establishing provenance in a number of antiques felt to be Pennsylvania German. Records of all kinds are so elusive in the Dutchland that it is, as one writer says, "like sailing over an uncharted sea" to attempt to fix even a few points of exactness. This lack of records, while it has not operated to any marked degree against a satisfactory classification of such obviously Pennsylvania German items as dower chests or *handtücher*, for instance, has caused more than a few students to look upon the tinware fraternity as suspect, or at best as interesting but lacking in the authentic touch.

Before dismissing the subject — and more than a few important surveys in the last few years have veered sharply away from it — one would do well to bear certain circumstances in mind. "Pennsylvania German," or "Pennsylvania Dutch," for all its seeming definiteness, is not an entirely clear-cut term, but is broader than is commonly supposed and covers several progressional steps in development. So loosely is the expression used nowadays that unless one stops to take thought he is prone to tuck away a purely empirical concept of what is Pennsylvania German in a special compartment in the larger field of antiques where, by comparison with such well defined categories as Connecticut, Philadelphia, or Virginia, it loses its finer — and now and then its more important — nuances of significance.

The developmental aspect of Pennsylvania German artistry needs emphasis. Only a few years ago it came as a surprise to many, to discover that a rather highly developed Pennsylvania German literature, flourishing side by side with the main branch of

American letters, had grown up in the Dutch country. Where the written word exists, it needs only the piecing together by the research worker to demonstrate how growth and development have taken place. When, instead of the written word, the evidence is in the form of unsigned and undocumented bits of household wares and decorative objects, it may take longer to show a comparable periodization, but the analogy is significant.

The layman is likely to think of Pennsylvania German motifs largely in terms of hearts and tulips, which take us back to the very beginnings of things Pennsylvania German. In Pennsylvania these motifs are to be found in the very earliest ironwork, dower chests, *fraktur schriften*, and pottery, some of it dated and signed, more of it not. In those early days the individual craftsman, when he had completed a bit of work in which he took pride, had time to affix his name or his initials and the date if he were not content to be lost in anonymity. The late 1700's and the early 1800's in particular are date-bearing years, with more actual dates and signatures then than in any other period in *fraktur*, dower chests, and pottery. Historically this corresponds to the time when German Pennsylvania was richest in individual craftsmanship. It was before westward expansion had taken its toll of the farming country, and homes and farmsteads were more the product of the thought and work of a single family than they were ever to be again.

The artistry of this time was, of course, largely untutored, and as such was often cumbersome and labored; yet it possessed a degree of individuality not attained by any other section of the New World. It is to this period that contemporary collectors and writers commonly refer when commenting on what is and what is not Pennsylvania Dutch, and if they are speaking purely in terms of "folk art" artistry they are correct. At the same time they are ignoring a later period which is equally interesting, and yet remote enough from the present to be possessed of characteristics untouched by the machine age.

This second period, the time in which the outside world began to thrust itself upon the Pennsylvania German, marks at once the decline of individual craftsmanship and the beginning of the time in which manufacturing and decorating were done by those whose skill or facility took the form of a regular business enterprise. It was the day of the itinerant country peddler, soon to be followed by the day of the country store. No matter how beautiful the early dower chest may seem to us, it was heavy and cumbersome, took a long time to make, and eventually had to give place to the lighter and more serviceable chest of drawers. No matter how carefully detailed the pottery, it was both fragile and heavy, and finally had to yield to lighter and more convenient vessels. No such austere respect attached then as now to articles made entirely by hand; for all that a sound craftsman put his best effort into his creation, whether it were a chest or a pottery mug or a baptismal certificate, when it became possible to secure something not the fruit of his own hard labor, and something which he actually

(*Front row*) MINIATURE "blicky," or tin pail, child's cup, miniature "book," another blicky, and a tall cup. (*Back row*) Tall canister, handled measuring cup, sugar bowl. Sugar bowl, child's cup, and book are in yellow, hardest to find in tinware colors. (Note similarity to "tree of life" motif on sugar bowl.) Canister and second blicky are in red, a color hard to find and, unfortunately, one lacking in durability, since the paint has a tendency to flake off.

(*Front row*) CANISTER, teapot, herb pot (sometimes called a cream pitcher). (*Back row*) Coffee pots. With the exception of the side pourer, all these articles are japanned rather than painted, for durability, and in each case the background is the translucent dark brown common to japanned ware. Note the consistent and expert use of petal strokes in leaves and fruit, and the use of cross-hatching for highlights. "Fancy" coffee pots were generally considered too attractive for use.

almost no tin available, either at home or from abroad. England was shipping very little tin at that time, and, even if she had been exporting much, the Pennsylvania Germans were not then buying imports. Not in the years of mass production, either, because it bears too many marks of individual craftsmanship. Punched, unpainted Pennsylvania German coffeepots frequently contain such identifying data as initials, name of maker, and dates, but they are unique among identifiable tin pieces. Painted ones — or japanned, for there is a distinction to be made — have not thus been identified, nor is there any distinguishing clue in workmanship or decoration, any more than there is in tea pots, caddies, canisters, measuring cups, trays, and other pieces.

We know that such fine decorated toleware pieces as tall urns, bureau boxes, chestnut roasters, tilting teapots, and galleried trays were imported from Europe; we know, too, that some of the more mundane painted tin of New England was imported. There are records to support that fact. It would hardly be fair, therefore, in the absence of documentary evidence, to deny the possibility that some or all of the Pennsylvania ware was imported. On the other hand, the tinsmiths or whitesmiths of New England made many of their boxes, cans, containers, and trays, and New England artists decorated them. There is at hand ample evidence to indicate that Pennsylvania German tinsmiths were equally accomplished (*cf.* the punched tin coffeepots of Ketterer and Uebele); it is possible that all Pennsylvania German tinware may have been made, decorated, and sold locally. It would seem that, if such were the case, it must have been done in some fairly large town or city such as Philadelphia or Lancaster, or possibly Reading or York, for it was done in greater quantity and with more competence than would seem likely in a small community. In a small village or town, too, local pride would probably have retained some landmark or recollection of a once thriving industry that has now apparently vanished, leaving no trace behind, whereas in the city such a disappearance would be commonplace,

liked better, the new convenience was secured and the homemade article was laid aside.

Thus it was that, very early in the new century, a second category of what have by now become Pennsylvania German antiques appeared in the Dutch country, at first side by side with the earlier handmade wares, and then as replacements for them. Spatterware, with its bright new patterns, took the place of dishes of wood and pewter and pottery, and for very special occasions the even more colorful gaudy Dutch was employed. Though not made in Pennsylvania, they so appealed to the Pennsylvania German taste in color and design that they were almost immediately adopted. To the purist they are not really Pennsylvania German, but it would be a hardy collector who, fully cognizant of the Staffordshire origin of this colorful ware, would turn down a fine schoolhouse plate or a peafowl cup and saucer on the ground that it is not Pennsylvania German. By association, by tradition, such items have become Pennsylvania German, in the same sense that in an earlier day Swiss bride's boxes, so inalienably associated with the life of the people, were considered Pennsylvania German.

In this period, the transitional years between the era of handmade things and the era of mass production, in the decades between 1800 and 1840, Pennsylvania German handcrafts are at their most colorful. Gay chalkware ornaments appeared on mantels; gorgeous patchwork quilts blossomed under the easy availability of commercially bought fabrics; painted and stenciled chairs, settees, and rockers replaced earlier, more massive furniture; gay and gleaming chinaware came into its own. Bear in mind, however, that the human touch was still there. Chairs may have been made by sets and offered for sale, but they were still hand made and hand decorated. Chinaware may have been shipped in by the boatload, but it was still decorated by hand — more competently and with more professional skill and flourish than might have been expected, but essentially an individual product.

Now where, in this scheme of things, does painted tinware belong? Not in the earliest days of heart and tulip, because there was

GROUP of octagonal trays. While the tulip pattern of the tray at lower left is often seen, and the leaf design of the one at the right is not uncommon, the shell motif is seldom encountered. The use of tendrils, attached or unattached, is characteristic, and is also to be found on Pennsylvania German painted furniture. The effect of crystals obtained by washes such as aqua fortis and sal ammoniac before the varnish was applied in japanning lends a sparkling touch to trays like the one at lower right. Small trays of this sort are said to have served as teapot bases.

A GROUP of utilitarian objects, all showing signs of much handling. (*Front*) Jointed nutmeg grater, knitting needle case with needles, shaker, sander. (*Back*) Unusual deep apple tray with favorite tulip design, infant's milk warmer, hanging case. The ingenious milk warmer, with its kerosene burning vessel in the base, bears a stenciled design sometimes found on furniture of the "Painted Period." The hanging case, too small for comb or brush, may have been intended for matches.

particularly when the occupation may have been in the nature of a sideline to some larger business.

In spite of the possibility that Pennsylvania German painted tin may have been imported, the writer inclines to the belief that it was made in America. One reason is that its shapes and designs do not overlap with those of New England as closely as would be the case if it were simply a product made up abroad for export to a common colonial market. There is a homogeneity in the Pennsylvania product that sets it apart, in the mass, from the bulk of the New England ware. This homogeneity consists in its fundamental simplicity, its design, its repetition of local motifs, and its bold, unrestrained use of color — color with fewer delicate tints and shades, fewer pinks and mauves and puces than in early New England ware or later typical Victorian ware. Also, some Pennsylvania pieces have no New England counterparts.

A still stronger argument for home manufacture, however, is the degree of kinship that exists between the artistry of Pennsylvania German craftsmen as applied to the painted furniture mentioned above, and the artistry employed in decorating tinware. This kinship is a matter of common devices, of sameness in technique, allowing of course for the different media, and an awareness of spatial proportion that did not exist earlier. A similar correspondence is not to be met with in New England, which did not enjoy a "painted period" like the one which held sway for fifty years or more in Pennsylvania.

Eventually, perhaps, we may discover the missing facts which will put an end to speculation, and settle for good and all the present controversy, but for the present the case appears to rest

about as follows: Painted tinware has for many years been found in long established Pennsylvania German homes. It is not a product of the earliest days of the colony, but probably became popular not long after 1800, and continued so for a matter of fifty years or more. While it has points of correspondence with the tinware of New England, as can be seen from the accompanying illustrations, it has a strong enough degree of individuality to mark it as of local provenance, and this individuality is of a piece with other painted objects known to have been made in German Pennsylvania. If it was not actually made and decorated by the Pennsylvania Germans, at least it met with their hearty approval, filled a specific want or need, satisfied their characteristic and definite tastes, and became theirs by adoption.

A GROUP of document boxes, among which the oval one, with its red background and tulip motif, is unusual. The box at lower left, with its petals on the lid arranged as in the good luck symbol, is also in red. Pennsylvania German tradition has it that receptacles of this sort served as cash boxes on trips made by Conestoga wagons. Oblong boxes are commonly found outside of Pennsylvania, frequently in the German territory about Saugerties, New York.

WHILE there is enough similarity in design and execution to mark trays of this sort as the work of one individual or group of individuals, no two are exactly alike. Central designs, like those on almost all Pennsylvania German tinware, are brush work, but the borders are stenciled in gilt with occasional touches of color. "Chippendale" edges, as well as edges in many of the better made oblong trays, are reinforced with heavy iron wire. The floral motifs are almost exactly repeated on locally made furniture.

PENNSYLVANIA COOKY CUTTERS

By EARL F. ROBACKER

Illustrations from the author's collection

WHILE collectors have for years been on the trail of the tulip, the peacock, and the pomegranate in Pennsylvania *fraktur* and on spatterware, it is only recently that a byroad in the same general direction has led explorers in search of the lowly tin cooky cutter. Without doubt, tin cooky cutters have been used in every part of the country, and probably from earliest times. New England has yielded a few, and many more might have been rescued from ashheap and oblivion had anyone taken them seriously. Some turn up in Maryland and Virginia and farther south. But it is not surprising that the finest examples come to light in the Pennsylvania-German country, where delight in color, love of ornamentation, and appreciation of good food have been manifest in a variety of household gear.

Just who the first cooky-cutter makers were will never be known, and does not really matter. It is not improbable that each early family could boast some member who could turn out a recognizable, if not anatomically accurate, tin pattern for horse, mule, star, heart, or tobacco pipe. By the beginning of the 1800's, however, itinerant craftsmen, including tinsmiths, were making their way over the countryside, and from then on if the "Dutchman" himself still made the cooky cutters for his wife before she began her Christmas baking, it was by choice and not from necessity.

The tinsmith was a welcome visitor in many a rural home, where he might spend a day or a week according to the number of odd jobs he could persuade his host were desirable. Somewhere along the line of his endeavors, after the cake tins, dippers, funnels, pans, and pails had been fashioned, came the cooky cutters. These were constructed for the most part from left-over scraps of tin, and even from the flattened remains of tin canisters or cooking utensils. A stately deer, for instance, bears an unmistakable baking-powder-can ridge across his back, and a dog proudly displays the letters —FRAM. So far as is known, not a single early craftsman thought highly enough of his cutters to mark them with his name.

It has commonly been assumed that early cooky cutters were made by fitting a strip of tin (the cutting edge) around a wooden mold of the desired shape, then soldering it to a strong backing. After removal of the mold, the backing would be trimmed down, roughly following the outlines of the design, and sharp edges cut off or bent under slightly. While some credence may be given to this theory, so few molds exist which might conceivably have been used for the purpose that there

FIG. 1 — HEARTS AND TULIPS, WITH VARIATIONS
Both motives were popular in Pennsylvania

FIG. 2 — HUMAN FIGURES AND FACES
Showing more or less stylization

may be more than reasonable doubt about this method. A few comparatively heavy steel-plate patterns have been found that may possibly have served in such a capacity; but, again, little more than speculation may be offered in their behalf. A more telling indication that the mold method was not generally used is the almost complete lack of duplication among surviving cooky cutters. Had a tinsmith taken the time and trouble to fashion a pattern, he would hardly have used it only once; yet it is virtually impossible to find one cutter that appears to be a replica of another. A large elephant cutter in my collection seems to have been constructed by first placing the cutting edge about a flat pattern, and then soldering the whole to its backing. It is equally possible, however, that the "pattern" was merely a reënforcement, since the cutter is a very large one.

The probability is that from the earliest specimens, which are perhaps too crude to have been made by a self-styled tinsmith who must look to his reputation, to those whose design indicates a date well after the Civil War, cooky cutters were constructed "freehand," by the use of such simple tools as would form the necessary curves and angles.

The pattern, crude though it may be, is one of the best indications of the cutter's age. A Continental soldier on horseback, closely resembling figures seen on Pennsylvania sgraffito plates, may reasonably be ascribed to the period between the Revolution and the end of the century. Many cutter patterns are clearly related to the hearts on Ephrata fraktur, cut-paper work, and furniture; to the conventional designs on painted chests and bride's boxes; to the bird figures on enameled glass; and to the peacocks on samplers and door towels, many of which are dated. The artisan in tin may usually have complied with the artistic demands of his patrons; but it is probable that, more widely traveled and familiar with the "outlands" than they, he may likewise have contributed patterns of his own suggestion, such as the eagle, the Forty-Niner, the preacher, the plain-clothes sectarian, the broad-hatted "Dutchman," and the lady in a puffed-sleeve gown. In search of new ideas after executing the universally popular tulip, star, heart, and peacock, the tin worker frequently drew his inspiration from whatever domestic objects happened to be visible. This would account for the rough approximations of

bottle, clothespin, broom, basket, gun, hatchet, shoe and boot, pitcher, and coffeepot. Flowers, curiously enough, are rare, except for the tulip and the thistle- or carnation-like blossoms. Patterns that recur so often as to indicate a perennial popularity are variations of the tulip and the characteristically shaped Pennsylvania-German heart — more squat than the modern valentine heart — as well as birds whose close counterparts appear on fraktur dating from the late 1700's to 1840 or even later.

Pattern is of course not the only criterion of age. Equally important considerations are the character and condition of the material, and the method of soldering. Early cutters are as a rule very heavy, made of a strong, thin steel plate generously coated with tin. In many instances, the plating has worn away or rusted heavily. The method of soldering is an indication not only of the age of the cutter, but also of the degree of the artisan's skill. Containing a large quantity of lead, probably about fifty per cent, and with a flux that was undoubtedly rosin, the heavy

FIG. 3 — CHRISTMAS PATTERNS
Reindeer, Kris Kringle, Christmas trees, bell, camel, sheep, stars

FIG. 4 — ANIMALS AND FISH
Rabbits, dogs, cat, pigs, calf, donkey, goat, squirrel, skunk, bear, fish

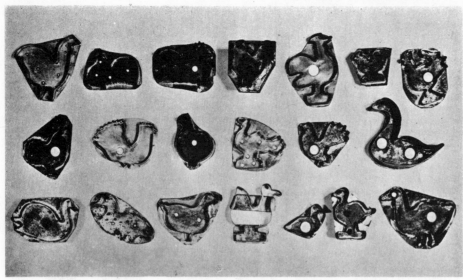

FIG. 5 — DOMESTIC FOWL
Hen, setting hens, roosters, turkey, peacock, guinea hen, bantam, fan-tail pigeon, swans, ducks, ducklings, goose

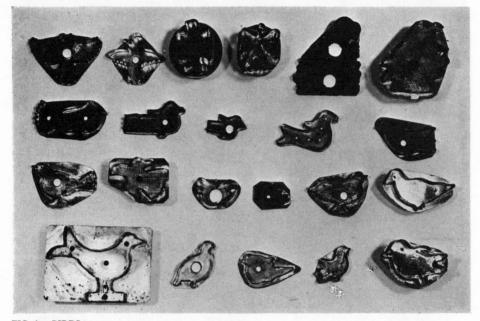

FIG. 6 — BIRDS
Note resemblance of certain forms to birds depicted in *fractur*

soldering usually goes a much lighter, cheaper quality of tin, and, toward the end of the 1800's, a less elaborate design — a concession to the busy housewife who, in her cookymaking, had little time to bother with hard-to-handle beaks, legs, or wings.

In early examples, made for hard service, the backing was seldom a geometrically cut piece of tin, but was sheared close to the outline of the pattern. A circular, oval, or octagonal backing may safely be considered indicative of late origin, and customarily displays, by way of corroborative evidence, an over-shininess, a thin solder, a design lacking in detail, and few signs of wear. As far as wear is concerned, however, only the most popular of the real Pennsylvania-German cutters are greatly worn, for they were seldom used except at Christmas; and similarly, those which show signs of hardest wear are generally found to be the oldest. Plain circular forms and those with fluted edges served for ordinary occasions, and the "fancy" designs were kept carefully packed away.

Cherished figures must sometimes have been claimed by certain children of the family for their own, for once in a while a scrawled name appears, scratched in an unformed hand. Occasional words in more mature writing indicate, perhaps, a means of identification for other purposes. Still other tokens of ownership are a lightly punched initial, tin-lantern style, an asterisk, or a comparable symbol.

amalgamating ingredient was originally applied by hand, according to what is still known as the soft-solder method. In earlier forms the cutting edge was laid on its backing and the solder was applied in several places along the outer edge. Enough was used to make sure that it would last for time and eternity: a whole cutter will often rust away before a single piece of solder lets go, even though the soldering iron had been used in only a few spots. Later a shinier solder, indicating a higher percentage of tin, was employed, and a smoother, more even coat applied, revealing fewer tool marks. If the entire cutting edge has been secured by a thin, almost invisible line, the chances are that the article is not much more than forty years old. Along with more modern

Variety is likewise to be found in the handles applied to the backing, though they offer relatively little help either in identifying or in authenticating patterns. For the most part, handles were formed by flat strips of tin, the edges more or less neatly turned under for reënforcement, and the whole then curved and fitted to the backing. Some of the earliest examples never had handles. Often handles have been bent out of shape by hard use, and a great many of the oldest ones are missing, though the solder still remains.

An evidence of quality in workmanship is the hole occasionally punched or stamped in the backing. Its purpose was to allow the air to escape when the cutter was applied to the dough.

The perforations range from about an eighth to three quarters of an inch in diameter, and were strategically placed where they would be most useful. Some cutters are carefully supplied with as many as six, while others have only one. Sometimes a supplementary nail hole has been punched by the house-wife to facilitate her work. This helps to explain why certain older cutters are found in good condition. Hard-to-handle patterns, such as horses with their four slender legs, ears, long neck, and tail, often exhibit but one perforation, usually in the middle of the back. Obviously making cookies with such cutters took a good deal of time and patience, and punching nail holes was dangerous since the neces-sary pounding might weaken the solder or bend the cut-ting edge. Resoldered cut-ters are probably evidence of an attempt to right this sad condition. The owner's simplest solution to the difficulty, of course, was to use the complicated cut-ter seldom or never.

Cutting edges range in depth from less than a quarter of an inch to as much as an inch and three quarters. With a few notable exceptions, one finds that the older the cutter, the deeper the cutting edge. Three quarters of an inch seems to have been a satis-factory working dimension. However, the oldest heart form known has a cutting edge less than a quarter of an inch deep, and that of a strange, horselike creature measures just under two inches. In very late forms the cutting depth decreases to three eighths of an inch.

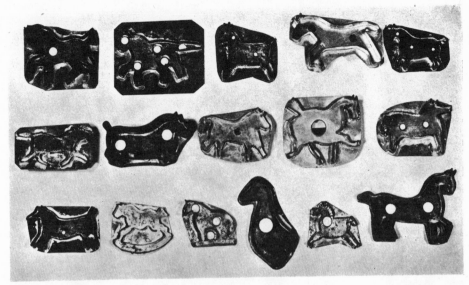

FIG. 7 — HORSES
Galloping, standing still — and rocking

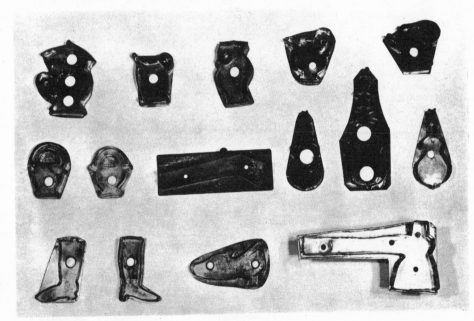

FIG. 8 — DOMESTIC IMPEDIMENTA
Pitchers, coffeepot, baskets, gun, fiddles, boots, shoe, hatchet

Subsidiary cutting edges, set within the pattern outline, were occasionally used. In some cutters the exterior cutting edge and the inset were of exactly the same depth, so that holes could be made through the dough. In others, a shallower inset simply im-pressed a design upon the cooky's surface. Cut-out and impressed line were sometimes combined, with effective results.

Overall measurements of cooky cutters vary. Some miniatures could be covered by a quarter-dollar; on the other hand, an astounding gingerbread man in the Bucks County Museum stands more than fifteen inches tall, and is, moreover, outfitted with hat, coat, buttons, shoes, pipe, and all the other trimmings. Apparently the smaller sizes were popular, since they show greater signs of wear. Tiny figures seem not to have been used a great deal, perhaps because the housewife could not make rapid progress with them in her baking, perhaps also because nobody wanted to see too small an allotment of cooky fall to his share. The delicate problem of just how many little ducklings equaled a large horse may help to explain why cooky cutters of extreme sizes are in such flourishing condition today.

Naïve in design, humble in origin, inextricably associated with memories of bygone Christmases, a few tin cooky cutters are even today passed about among the great-great-grandchildren of their original owners. Others, retired from active service, are taking their place among informal but appealing collectibles.

Zachariah Brackett Stevens

Founder of the Japanned-Tinware Industry in Maine

By ESTHER STEVENS FRASER

FOR many years, the name of my great-great-grandfather, Zachariah Brackett Stevens, has been listed on my genealogical chart very simply as "tinsmith," the first in four generations to abandon the paternal craft of blacksmithing. But in surmising that my ancestor made only kitchen tinware on a small scale for use in his own community, I have done him a great injustice. In reality he founded an amazingly active industry employing many workers, whose products were marketed by peddlers throughout Maine and New Hampshire, as far north as the Canadian border. Many of these wares were gaily decorated tin boxes, bread trays, teapots, and tea caddies, the character of whose ornament becomes our best means of identification. Besides the "tin-plate knockers," craftsmen who fashioned pewter, britannia ware, horn combs, and hairbrushes acquired land of Zachariah's father, until a busy craft centre was established on Stevens Plains near Portland, Maine.

Since there is no printed history of Stevens Plains, let us turn back to the year 1765, when the locality belonged to Zachariah Brackett (grandfather of Zachariah Stevens the tinsmith), who lived in the shipbuilding backcove region of Portland, or Falmouth, as it was then called. Isaac Sawyer Stevens, a man small in stature but mighty in muscle, due to his blacksmithing trade, assisted Brackett in clearing the land of pitch pines. In 1767 he married Brackett's daughter Sarah, and with his bride set up housekeeping in the big, two-story square frame house that he had built for the purpose. This spacious dwelling, the first on the Plains, was destined to become the centre around which the life of the entire community revolved. Here Isaac and his wife were living quietly with their two children, Sarah and Isaac junior, when the rumblings of war were heard so ominously that the husband and father felt that his greatest duty was to leave home and assist in defending American liberty. Thereupon Mrs. Stevens, resourceful in emergency as Maine housewives have always had to be, opened her

Fig. 1 — ZACHARIAH STEVENS: TINSMITH OF STEVENS PLAINS
From a daguerreotype taken late in life. An extraordinary portrayal of a remarkable New England character. Stevens was born in 1778; died, 1856. *From the author's collection*

home as a tavern and met with such success that "Stevens's" is listed in early handbooks for travelers as the chief ordinary for Portland. Situated, as it was, on the main road from Boston to Augusta and other points in Maine where settlements were rapidly extending, the Stevens home was a convenient way station. Portland, on a promontory to the eastward, was less accessible for through travelers to more distant places.

In the family tavern-dwelling house, Zachariah Brackett Stevens the tinsmith, fourth child of Sarah and Isaac, was born in 1778. Here he spent his early and uneventful childhood. Where he passed his apprenticeship in tin working is a puzzling question. Certainly there was no one at Stevens Plains to teach him so intricate a craft. Family legend maintains that he lived for a time in Cambridge. This I might easily believe, since his tinware shows a familiarity with craftsmanship of *urban*, not rural quality. Numerous small pointers lead me to surmise — though they do not *prove* — that the shop where Zachariah learned his trade may have furnished the "Japanned tea trays in sets" (see Paul Revere's advertisement for the year 1785) or other tinware sold by Paul Revere, at his place in the North End of Boston. At any rate, there was a very definite relationship between the Revere family and the folk of Stevens Plains.

Jumping over the possibility, even the probability, that during his service in the Revolution Isaac Sawyer Stevens met Paul Revere, we know definitely that Revere's nephew, Phillip Rose, stopped at Stevens Plains in 1791 or shortly thereafter. The family still possesses two ornamental drawings made for them by Rose: one commemorating the marriage "together" of Isaac S. Stevens and Sarah Brackett; the other, a genealogical listing of their nine offspring. As a decorative device, Phillip Rose was wont to fill a border strip with a tortuous line which kept doubling back upon itself — a method that I have often observed on painted trays, and nowhere else. Perhaps Rose had been apprenticed or employed

Fig. 2 — PINCUSHION BOX
Made by Zachariah Stevens for his daughter Emmeline, born 1811, who married Rufus Dunham, pewterer, and died young.
From the collection of Mrs. O. H. Perry

Fig. 3 — FLOWER HOLDERS
Made for Zachariah's wife, Miriam Stevens.
Light asphaltum finish, decorated in black.
From the collection of Mrs. O. H. Perry

Fig. 4 — THE STEVENS FAMILY CAKE BOX
From the collection of Mrs. O. H. Perry

Fig. 5 — MINIATURE FRUIT BASKET
From the collection of Mrs. O. H. Perry

Fig. 6 — BOX FROM THE STEVENS HOME
From the author's collection

in a tray-decorating shop. Also, in 1803, came Thomas Brisco, the first tinsmith "from foreign parts" to take active part in the tin industry. Brisco had married Revere's niece, Sarah Rose, sister of Phillip, the decorator.

After Brisco came other tinsmiths. Each bought land for his dwelling and tinshop from Isaac Sawyer Stevens, who had become proprietor of the Plains by purchase from his widowed mother-in-law, Judith Brackett. Since no less than eleven Plains tinsmiths may be identified in addition to Zachariah Stevens and Thomas Brisco, I have had to pick my way very carefully through the tinware which seems indigenous to this locality. By tracking down pieces still owned by Zachariah Stevens' descendants, I have found an early group which I believe to have been made by him. The other and later ware I am forced to segregate as "Stevens Plains tinware."

Zachariah's home, built in 1800, is still standing across the street from the site of his general store and adjoining tin shop. For Zachariah was quick to observe the need for a general trading post, where merchandise taken in barter for tinware might be disposed of. As the community developed, he doubtless withdrew gradually from tinsmithing to devote himself to local affairs. Still he was so fond of color that one cannot imagine him completely abandoning the painting of tin boxes. In 1823 he became coroner; later, selectman, deputy sheriff, and, in 1833, postmaster for Stevens Plains, *Westbrook* as the town was now called. Zachariah is also spoken of as auctioneer, an office that, with his quick wit and keen sense of humor, he must have performed admirably.

As a man, he is said to have been deeply religious and positive in his convictions. "With him it was either a friend or an enemy, but far more friends than enemies." The Sabbath he wished to see strictly observed, often chiding neighbors who cut hay on Saturday afternoon, and felt forced to bring it in on Sunday. In 1814, it is said, he repudiated the idea of future punishment, and thereafter doubtless enjoyed a more cheerful mind.

Strict though he was, he had his human and humorous side, eloquently revealed in the daguerreotype taken in his old age

(*Fig. 1*). His crooked smile seems to tell us that a huge joke has just occurred to him, and will be sprung the moment this photographic ordeal is over. To the townspeople, he was universally known as Uncle Zach. Yet, despite this endearing appellation, he was hardly indulgent in his own household. His young daughter Cordelia — she who was to be teacher of drawing and painting at Westbrook Seminary — yearned long and in vain for a box of colors. Not until she resorted to wild berry juices to supply her tints did Zachariah finally relent. To his credit, be it said, he bought her a fine box of paints and thereafter proudly displayed the girl's handiwork.

In an attempt to learn just what manner of tinware Zachariah Stevens made and decorated, I have visited his home and analyzed the pieces still remaining there. While some of these appear to be of poorer quality and later date than others (perhaps the work of the sons, Samuel and Alfred Stevens, after Zachariah had passed his business to them in 1830), a number of early pieces may safely be accepted as Zachariah's own. There is, for instance, a small pincushion box, octagonal in form, upon which a padded velvet top has been sewn through tiny holes in the cover rim. Within a delicate decorative frame the name *E. Stevens* is painted, unquestionably for Emmeline, Stevens' daughter, who was born in 1811. The background coloring on this box is a rich ivory white, against which the pattern in vermilion, red, green, and black stands out most effectively. The rose is painted by a method used on lace-edge trays whereby a vermilion circle is the basic foundation, and the rose form is superimposed in filmy, semitransparent tones (*Fig. 2*).

For his wife Miriam, Zachariah undoubtedly made the pair of double-cone-shaped objects shown in Figure 3. They stand about six inches high, the lower section filled with lead as if to fortify them against unstable equilibrium. About one inch down from the top is soldered a circular disc of tin through which the only aperture is a central hole about the size of a small steel knitting needle. My guess is that these pieces were fashioned as flower pots for sprays of artificial flowers. The supposition is reënforced by my aunt's remembrance of her grandmother's

Fig. 7 — TRINKET BOX *(front and top view)*
From the collection of Mrs. Mary Mountford

Fig. 8 — BOX WITH SLIDING DRAWER
An early item dating 1795–1800. Perhaps made when Zachariah was an apprentice as a gift for his future wife, Miriam Berry, whom he married in 1798.
From the author's collection

making a similarly shaped cardboard flower pot back in the 1870's. This grandmother was a daughter-in-law of Zachariah, the wife of his oldest son, Samuel Butler Stevens. At any rate, these tin standards are finished in a pale golden asphaltum, and decorated with a typical tin-painter's brushstroke design, enclosing the initials *M.S.* These two, and the pincushion box, are the only *initialed* pieces possessed by the family. It is significant that they still repose in Zachariah Stevens' home.

Here we may also see the generously proportioned family cake box betraying evidence of hard and prolonged use. It was once painted cream white as to background, and decorated in green, blue, yellow, and vermilion. The lid once bore conventional flowers, but the front portrayed an elaborate rural scene with green-trimmed house and ell, flanked by various stately trees (*Fig. 4*).

For one of his little daughters, Uncle Zach made a toy bread or apple basket, measuring about three inches over all. Its four semicircular lobes bend outward and downward, the better to display their decoration of miniature rosebuds and forget-me-nots. The rectangular body of this little piece tapers sharply to the point where it joins a saucerlike base. To fashion this tapering shank, Zachariah cut the tin into narrow ribbons, removed every other strip, and interwove the remainder into a basket pattern. Nothing could better illustrate Zachariah's extraordinary fluency in so handling tin as to produce articles of marked individuality (*Fig. 5*).

Then there is the little yellow box which was found at Zachariah's home by the late Charles L. Woodside, who graciously

presented it to me. If religion developed certain stern inhibitions in Uncle Zach, it in no wise constrained his use of color. All compunction was thrown to the winds when he painted this little box a sulphur yellow and decorated it with his blue, green, red, and vermilion (*Fig. 6*).

Last of all, among the tinware at Zachariah's home, we see two black boxes which are more hurriedly painted than usual, and may be typical of later work done "for the trade" (*Figs. 12, 13*). Quite probably he lavished more time and ingenuity upon presentation pieces for members of his family, inasmuch as the Stevens descendants possess articles more exquisitely decorated than any to be found in present-day antique shops. Under stress of rapid production, the competent tin decorator would have achieved his effects with few but very accurate strokes. It is such expertness of brush handling that must be appraised in tracing Zachariah's work.

Again to be ascribed to Zachariah is Alfred Stevens' large document box (probably used when he was surveyor and tax collector) fitted at one end with small transverse compartments in which official papers were kept. The front and ends are ornamented with festoons of colored flowers, reminiscent of the pendulous pattern on my sulphur-yellow box, while around the cover runs a conventional brushstroke border in yellow (*Fig. 14*).

At the same house we find a charming trinket box possibly made as a wedding present in 1826 when Nancy Buckley became Zachariah's daughter-in-law. The piece is most individual in construction, with molded lid, slanting sides, and an applied rolled molding at cover and base line. Only an ivory-white background could adequately reveal the infinite and lovely detail of its adornment of varicolored flowers; only a patient and skilled hand could execute such an elaborate yet fragile design. This box is one of those examples which lead me to believe that Zachariah wrought more painstakingly for members of his family than for the general public that was served from the carts of the tin peddlers (*Fig. 7*).

Direct descendants of Samuel Butler Stevens, Zachariah's oldest son, apparently possess no decorated tinware that may be attributed to Zachariah. But in the house of neighboring Goodrich cousins have been found three boxes which are probably examples of my great-great-grandfather's work. One, in the characteristic cream-white paint used by Zachariah, displays on its cover the same weeping willow tree that confronts us on the family cake box of Figure 4. Here, too, we encounter the novel feature of a tiny drawer (the only *tin* box drawer that I have ever met), quite the kind of individual touch that would occur to Zachariah. We might easily leap to the conclusion that space within the box around the drawer is wasted. Looking within, however, we find soldered over the drawer a tin platform shaped like an inverted V. In the centre back of this platform appears a small hole accommodating a plug which, when inserted, locks the drawer. At the left is a depression or well, large enough to store beads or other small trinkets; at the right is a similar till with hinged cover (*Fig. 8*).

To me this white box is more or less of a mystery. It may have been made during Zachariah's apprentice days.

Fig. 9 — PAIR OF BOXES
Perhaps painted as a gift for Maria Francis at the time of her marriage to Walter B. Goodrich, tinsmith of Stevens Plains, in 1829 or perhaps painted in 1826, when Goodrich first came to the Plains.
From the author's collection

Fig. 10 — TRINKET BOX   *From the author's collection*

Fig. 11 — SMALL SPICE, TRINKET, OR MONEY BOXES   *From the collection of Mrs. Arthur Oldham*

In the decoration we find an intricate spray of roses and star flowers executed in silver leaf on which detail lines in pale green are superimposed. The edge of the tiny drawer, as well as the box lid, is bordered with a quarter-inch band of gold leaf. It is far from customary to find gold and silver leaf on country tinware, and this is the one time that it appears at Stevens Plains. Only the craftsman who has seen the laying of a pattern in gold size attempts to handle gold and silver leaf. If, then, Zachariah made this box during his apprenticeship in a Boston or Cambridge tinshop, where precious-metal leaf was in use, we could understand why he undertook such a unique form

of ornamentation. Supporting this hypothesis is the fact that the rest of the decorative design is amateurish, wrought not with bold, effective strokes, but with tiny hesitating dabs that consumed too much time and lack essential brilliance.

The same family of Goodrich cousins formerly owned a pair of black boxes that also seem to be Zachariah's work. They may have been painted about 1826 when Walter B. Goodrich, tinsmith from Connecticut, first came to the Plains. I am aware of the danger of attributing these boxes to the wrong maker; possibly they were *constructed* by Goodrich, but the decoration seems undeniably to reveal Uncle Zach's own hand. Certain

Figs. 12 and 13 (left and right) — COMMERCIAL BOXES BY STEVENS
From the collection of Mrs. O. H. Perry

Fig. 14 (below) — DEED BOX
From the collection of Mrs. Mary Mountford

Fig. 15 — BREAD TRAY AND BOX

The box with its light ground and the delightful frontal decoration, which is extended to stray over the ends of the box, may have been a presentation piece. It will be noted that most, if not all, of the Stevens tinware thought to have been devised for gift purposes is creamy in color, a circumstance that recalls Simon Willard's tendency to dress his bride's clocks in white and gold.
From the author's collection

motives here used repeat themselves upon other family-owned Zachariah tinware, thus forging a strong chain of evidence. Both these boxes, I am happy to say, were given to me for my Stevens Plains collection (*Fig. 9*).

In the home of Miss Annie Stevens, who descends from William, brother of Zachariah, we find a tiny book-shaped box whose decoration matches that of the Emmeline Stevens pincushion box. Beside the same rose and rosebud pattern painted upon the same cream-white background, we here meet with a new border motive, alternating green leaves and red berries growing on a central stem.

So much for the family-owned pieces of Zachariah Stevens tinware. Suppose we turn now to those which have drifted into other homes and into local antique shops. The examples illustrated are, in my estimation, true Zachariah pieces. Those with a black background are most difficult to identify, for tinsmiths, the country over, were turning out similar items, decorated in corresponding colors on a dark ground. So far as I have observed, no Zachariah piece exhibits a wide cream-white band behind a decorative border, commonly found in Connecticut and Pennsylvania.

We must figure the conclusion of Zachariah Stevens' tinsmithing at the year 1830, when his son Samuel Butler Stevens signed a six months' note for six boxes of tin 13 by 19¾ inches at $58.50. This undoubtedly represented the entire stock of tin plate of which Zachariah was at the time possessed. The ultimate fate of Stevens-made tinware was doubtless settled April 11, 1842, when "Fire broke out this morning about two o'clock at Stevens Plains, in the blacksmith shop of

Z. B. Stevens, and soon communicated to the tin-ware shop of his son Samuel B. Stevens. Both shops were consumed. Mr. S. B. Stevens lost his books, ware, tin plate, etc. amounting to $1500.00, insured $300.00. The fire extended to the shop of Rufus Dunham, block tin manufacture, which was also destroyed with contents. Loss $1000.00 to $1200.00. The citizens turned out with great spirit, and disputed the ground with the fire adversary so successfully that the buildings nearby contiguous to those destroyed were saved, including a large amount of property." (The Portland *Argus*, April 11, 1842.)

Pewter enthusiasts may notice that Rufus Dunham was known in the heyday of his craft as "block tin manufacturer." Indeed, so little was the difference between the trades of pewtermaking and tinsmithing that, when Dunham went West for a year or two, he left his business in the hands of one of our Stevens Plains tinsmiths, Walter B. Goodrich. We also notice that a higher valuation was placed upon Samuel Stevens' tin shop than upon the Dunham place of business.

Thus ends the story of Zachariah Stevens tin; but the tale of those other busy tinsmiths who worked at Stevens Plains is yet to be told. How Uncle Zach contributed to the growth of a lively, hustling town, and how the downfall of the tin industry caused the community to shrink, will be considered in a subsequent article. Without Zachariah Stevens as a pioneer in an important industry, Stevens Plains might never have occupied its significant place in the history of Portland.

(For valuable assistance with the history of Stevens Plains, I am gratefully indebted to Miss Stella Davis.)

OLD-TIME FOOT STOVES

By LURA WOODSIDE WATKINS and EVAN W. LONG

Note. The following article is an amalgamation of two articles on the same subject, independently submitted by the authors. — *The Editor.*

FROM ancient times various types of portable heater have been dedicated to warming the extremities of humankind. Some of these contrivances harbored burning substances such as charcoal or oil; others merely conserved and distributed the heat of bricks, stones, boiling water, or lumps of iron, whose temperature had been raised by contact with fire before they were placed in their appropriate containers.

The Japanese favored a pocket stove curved to fit the person and utilizing a slow-burning charcoal composition. In China devices for heating feet and hands were made of pottery covered with basketwork and filled with hot coals. These efficient braziers afforded twenty-four hours of relative comfort. In the latter part of the sixteenth century metal spheres with screw caps were filled with hot water to serve as hand warmers. The Ashmolean Museum, in Oxford, England, owns an object which an old booklet describes as "a brazen ball to warm ye nunnes hands."

In England from the fifteenth century to the nineteenth the warming pan, a lidded metal basin to be filled with hot coals and wielded by means of a long handle of wood or iron, occupied a place of honor by the kitchen fireplace. It was the housewife's pride to keep the lid of this pan — ordinarily of brass or copper — so brightly polished that its luster rivaled that of the near-by flame. And as she polished she could pause and refresh her virtue by reading the pious exhortations often engraved around the rim of the lid. In his diary for 1669 Pepys mentions a "noble silver warming pan" that had just been presented to him. A warming pan of pewter, the work of William Will, is pictured in Kerfoot's *American Pewter* (Figs. 25 and 80). From England the warming pan came to this country with the early settlers who used the instrument chiefly to mitigate the midwinter anguish of diving into a cold and clammy bed. The pierced or engraved copper or brass lid gave coppersmith and brazier opportunity to display their artistic skill. Among household furnishings bed warmers were important enough to warrant their frequent mention in wills. In the probate records for the Massachusetts county of Essex from 1635 to 1681, warming pans appear almost as frequently as any other item.

The foot stove probably had its origin as a lamp, or as a pan of embers or burning charcoal, placed beneath a footstool. From this beginning the once separate parts were combined, apparently in Shakespeare's time, into a single portable unit. Howard G. Hubbard reports that in 1594 Hugh Platte, at Lincoln's Inn, London, wrote:

> Warming pinnes, or froes, are put into thin cases, and those cases wrapped in linnen baggs, to serve to heat bedds, and to cast one into a kindly sweat. The like device is used in conveying such iron pinns into hollow boxes of wood, first lined inwardly with metal, either to laye under their feete when they write, or studie, in cold weather, or in their coches to keep their feete warm.

Although as already noted warming pans are frequently mentioned in early inventories, we find no references to the use of foot stoves among the first American colonists. The lack of these conveniences must be attributed to pioneer conditions, since foot warmers were commonly used in the 1600's by the people of the Low Countries, and the settlers must have been familiar with them. The Dutch *genre* painters, who portrayed so many household accessories in their compositions, have left

FIG. 1 — BRASS WARMING PAN
Made by William C. Hunneman of Boston (*1769–1856*), an important manufacturer of metal wares large and small. The lid of this pan is slightly pierced and elaborately engraved. Handle broken. A pewter warmer by William Will of Philadelphia is illustrated in Kerfoot's *American Pewter*, Figures 25 and 80

FIG. 2 — BRASS WARMING PAN
Lid pierced with only 12 holes as against 21 in the preceding example. Engraving more formal and correspondingly less interesting. The turned handles of these pans are often very handsome

FIG. 3 — EARLY FOOT STOVE FROM CONNECTICUT (*c. 1800*)
Constructed of wood, with ventilating holes arranged in a decorative pattern. The front panel may be lifted to permit ingress of a tray of hot coals. A form of stove too likely to catch fire. *From the collection of Lura Woodside Watkins*

ample evidence that the *stoof* was a recognized necessity. In at least three of his pictures Jan Steen, who died in 1679, introduced the familiar wooden box with tin lining and iron "pinn" (*Twelfth Night, The Sick Girl*, and *The Doctor's Visit*). This type of stove was introduced into America by the Dutch colonists, and handsome examples decorated with carving and piercing may occasionally be found.

The New English Dictionary quotes a writer in *Harper's* for 1883 who speaks of "charcoal to put in the little foot warmers used by all womankind in Dutch churches." This may be not quite correct. Charcoal and red embers from the fireplace are not the same thing, and burning charcoal liberates dangerous fumes unsafe in close or crowded churches and homes.

A simpler variety of stove, also betraying Dutch influence, was made in Connecticut (*Fig. 3*). This wood-enclosed stove resembles the pierced tin form, except that its door slides up instead of swinging on hinges. It has no lining of metal or other protection against the heat of the coal pan.

The Dutch also made foot stoves of elaborately ornamented brass. One specimen, dated *1733*, combines repoussé and openwork ornament, employing the familiar tulip for motive. It is round instead of rectangular.

Such contrivances were common in England and America by the early eighteenth century. In 1716 the playwright Gay wrote, "The Belgian stove beneath her Footstool glows." History records that, in 1744, the First Church in Roxbury lost its third edifice as a result of fire caused by foot stoves. Thereafter their use in the building was prohibited. One shudders to think of that chill New England meetinghouse in zero weather, when even the comfort of warm feet was denied the suffering congregation! In 1748, David Blasdell, the Amesbury clockmaker, made two stoves for the tithing men, receiving one pound four shillings for his labor. He was typical of the handy artisan of his time, for he not only worked on clocks, but also made and repaired augers, andirons, steelyards, and gunlocks, repaired tin and brassware, made nails, shod horses, molded spoons, forged ironwork for vessels, made tow combs, sold groceries, dry goods, meat, and wood, and operated a

FIG. 4 — CARVED WOOD FOOT STOVE (*eighteenth century*)

Either a Holland example or of Dutch inspiration

cider mill. No doubt the majority of handwrought foot warmers were made by local tinkers possessed of similar universal capabilities. The demand for foot stoves was large, and since their making involved no serious difficulties almost every smith must have tried his hand at the job. Not improbably such stoves were piled on the wagons of countless Yankee peddlers, as a regular item of merchandise to be distributed among habitations in the wilderness.

In the eighteenth century, the early form of the word — *stow* — was often heard. We find that Agnes Lobdell of Boston, reporting her losses by the fire of 1760, lists "1 Tin Stow" worth two pounds and five shillings. Easter Tinkom mentions "1 Stow & frame"; Rachel La Mottee, "Stove & pan," at three pounds ten shillings; and Jonathan Mason, "1 Tin Stove & Case."

Evidently the tin stove had come into its own in New England by this time, and its popularity continued for another century. The usual type of the early 1800's is a wooden frame with turned corner posts, enclosing a pierced tin container for the iron or tin fire pan. Glowing embers from the fireplace provided the heat, which radiated through the small openings, bathing in a genial warmth the pedal extremities that rested on the barred frame above. The punched decoration is, of course, the interesting feature of this type of stove. Hearts, circles, and geometric designs predominate. The four pictured examples in Figure 5 are representative. They are for individual use. The stove at the right was carried to service in Bradford, Massachusetts, about 1830. On many a Sunday its owner filled it with hot coals at the old house on the corner of Salem Street, the first home of Bradford Academy, where members of the congregation were supplied with fresh fuel before church began.

Figure 6 illustrates two somewhat larger stoves that may conceivably have been enjoyed by two persons at once. The unusual round example has a wooden top with large openings for radiation, tin sides, and a round coal pan. A family-size affair, similar to the square one shown in Figure 6, is owned by Miss Eleanor Hudson. It is fully four times as large as an individual foot stove

FIG. 5 (*below*) — METAL STOVES IN WOOD FRAMES (*first half of nineteenth century*)

A safer form than that of Figures 3 and 4. The woodwork merely constitutes a frame for a tin box within which a pan of coals may be placed. The example at the left is from Ohio and displays more elaborate piercing than most New England stoves of the period. The ap-

proximate date of stoves of this type may be judged by the character of the turned corner posts. In none of the stoves here illustrated do the turnings display any such refinement of proportions and elaboration of members as would indicate eighteenth- or even very early nineteenth-century craftsmanship. The example at the right is known to have been used in the 1830's. The one at the left was taken to the Western Reserve by settlers from New England.

Left, from the Ohio State Archeological and Historical Society; others from the collections of Eleanor Hudson and Lura Woodside Watkins

and was probably placed in the center of the pew, where father, mother, and the children could share its genial outgiving of warmth. This Gargantuan heater is illustrated in Figure 15.

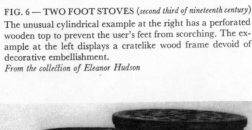

FIG. 6 — TWO FOOT STOVES (*second third of nineteenth century*) The unusual cylindrical example at the right has a perforated wooden top to prevent the user's feet from scorching. The example at the left displays a cratelike wood frame devoid of decorative embellishment.
From the collection of Eleanor Hudson

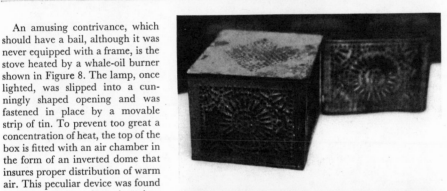

An amusing contrivance, which should have a bail, although it was never equipped with a frame, is the stove heated by a whale-oil burner shown in Figure 8. The lamp, once lighted, was slipped into a cunningly shaped opening and was fastened in place by a movable strip of tin. To prevent too great a concentration of heat, the top of the box is fitted with an air chamber in the form of an inverted dome that insures proper distribution of warm air. This peculiar device was found in Connecticut, where ingenious Yankees often turned their wits to inventing and patenting such contraptions, in spite of their questionable practicability.

A combined lantern and foot stove, manufactured by Francis Arnold, of Middle Haddam, Connecticut, was exhibited at the New York Exposition of 1853. It might well have been the affair shown in Figure 9. It will be seen that a whale-oil burner provides both light and heat. Windows on the front and sides and a substantial handle for carrying make the box a veritable lantern. When the upper section is tipped back on its hinges, a sloping surface, nicely carpeted, with a ledge for resting the heel of the shoe, is revealed.

In fact, at various times foot stoves intended to serve a multitude of collateral purposes came on the market. In England, in 1781, a patent was issued for a heater with an earthenware case for the purpose of warming beds, dishes, plates, and feet in carriages or in churches. An 1846 patent covers a combination foot and bed warmer and a potato roaster.

At the Philadelphia Centennial in 1876 an English firm exhibited a pottery device to be filled with hot water and placed in boots for the purpose of drying and heating these intractable articles of footwear. That any of these all too ingenious inventions were actually manufactured and marketed may be doubted.

While the warming pan was the chief instrument for preheating the old-time bed, the more compact foot stove was requisitioned for long winter drives and for counteracting the Sabbath chill of unheated churches, where the rule of four-hour services was not relaxed in deference to Boreas. Prior to 1825 the adequate heating of churches or other places of public assembly was hardly thought of. Even in 1840 only the larger houses of worship were equipped with sizable coal or wood stoves. In an attempt to afford the congregation at least some foot comfort, dogs were frequently permitted to enter the church and to lie across their master's feet, while in some churches a fur robe tacked to the seat might be wrapped around the nether

FIG. 7 — ALL-METAL FOOT STOVE (*first half of nineteenth century*) Made in Pennsylvania and exhibiting characteristically elaborate piercings. The absence of a wood frame fails to constitute proof that the stove was not originally equipped with such a safeguard

FIG. 8 — OIL-BURNING FOOT STOVES (*1830–1850*)
Left, of wood lined with tin and equipped with a lamp.
From the Bucks County Historical Society, Doylestown, Pennsylvania.
Below, pierced tin stove, heated with a whale-oil lamp. A device within the stove evenly distributes the heat. Found in Connecticut.

From the collection of Lura Woodside Watkins

ANTIQUES

limbs of the shivering worshipers. In some localities, during the noontime intermission in the preaching the congregation would repair to a near-by house for luncheon. Such a refuge was often erected specially for the purpose and was known as the "Sabba-day house." It appears to have been little more than a shed with horse stalls at one end and a large fireplace at the other. From the latter shrine the assembled folk would select fresh embers for their foot stoves before repairing to the sanctuary and enduring the second installment of the sermon. The hardier, and perhaps more devout, souls viewed foot stoves as crass material substitutes for the celestial fires which should have been kindled solely by the hortatory friction of the sermon. But certain it is that most of the women and even some of the men, whatever their spiritual reliance upon the parson, preferred to plant their feet firmly on a diminutive but cozy heater. Watson, in his *Annals (1842)*, says that the more prudent and feeble women carried foot stoves to church with them. Howells, writing in *Longman's Magazine* in 1882, mentions "the foot stove which one of his congregation carried to meeting and warmed his poor feet with."

Even the small comfort yielded by the foot stove was declared unhealthful by an English writer of 1818, who in a discourse on the art of preserving the feet observes, "Our English travellers should always be on their guard against the use of feet stoves." Even in those days, apparently, America was a materialistic land of creature comforts.

Various other means of warming the feet, either at home or abroad, were resorted to in olden days. One of the commonest was a large slab of soapstone that could be heated in the fireplace and then placed, well wrapped, in bed or carriage. Iron handles for lifting it were inserted in holes bored in the soft stone (*Fig. 11*). A smaller version was dedicated to warming and drying cowhide boots (*Fig. 12*). Hot-water bottles proved comfortable on long journeys, and to that end they were shaped to fit the feet pressed against them (*Fig. 14*). They are a product of the mid-nineteenth century and were made in mottled Rockingham ware both at the Bennington works and at some of the smaller potteries in New England. The same kind of bottle was turned out at Portland, Maine, in stoneware washed with dark-brown slip. Some specimens marked *J. T. Winslow, Portland, Me.* will be found. The elongated stoneware bottle of Figure 14 represents a type of foot warmer used until quite recently. Earlier containers of the same shape were made in gray stoneware and in glazed redware.

Home-contrived substitutes for special hot-water containers were many. Often the family cider jug was requisitioned. A hot

FIG. 9 — COMBINATION LANTERN AND STOVE (*c. 1850*)
A double-service device, equipped with whale-oil lamp. Closed, it serves well as a portable lantern spreading its beams in three directions. Open, it affords a carpeted rest for chilled feet.
From the collection of Eleanor Hudson

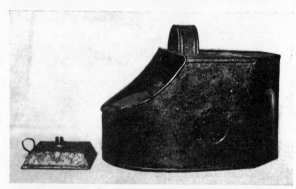

FIG. 10 — COMBINATION FOOT WARMER AND CARRIAGE LANTERN (*c. 1830–1850*)
Another double-service device, capable of heating and lighting simultaneously if placed under the front seat of a vehicle. Made of tin, with wire ventilator at side; equipped with whale-oil burner.
From the collection of Mrs. Bertram K. Little

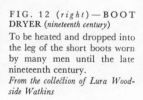

FIG. 11 (*left*) — SOAPSTONE FOOT WARMER (*nineteenth century*)
Heated in the fireplace or oven and wrapped in wool cloths, these soapstones remained at least tepid for several hours.
From the collection of Eleanor Hudson

FIG. 12 (*right*) — BOOT DRYER (*nineteenth century*)
To be heated and dropped into the leg of the short boots worn by many men until the late nineteenth century.
From the collection of Lura Woodside Watkins

brick wrapped in cloth was a frequent companion of slumber or of a sleigh ride. A crude but efficient means of heating a bed was to employ a log of green wood about eighteen inches long and nine inches in diameter. This log was heated either in front of the fireplace or in the kitchen oven, then wrapped in cloth. A family in eastern Pennsylvania reports that a log, christened "Uncle John," served thus faithfully for twenty-five years prior to the advent of the rubber hot-water bag and electric pad.

Men and women may come and go, but, if legend may be trusted, cold extremities have been the lot of humankind at least since Noah's day. No doubt they will continue forever to be a plague exorcisable only by close personal contact with an appropriate talisman. But though there is greater potency in today's electric pad than in all the metal and earthen heaters employed by our ancestors, the old-time devices possess certain mystical powers that no mechanical ingenuity can duplicate. Even when stone cold, they can still warm the heart — a capability denied to their modern rivals even when their temperature has been raised to the boiling point.

FIG. 13 — CARRIAGE OR SLEIGH FOOT WARMER (*mid-1800's*)
Earthenware with warm chocolate-brown glaze. Metal screw cap and brass-mounted thermometer. Probably made at Zanesville, Ohio.
From the Krantz collection

FIG. 14 (*below*) — HOT-WATER FOOT RESTS AND A STONEWARE BED WARMER (*c. 1850*)
From the collections of Mrs. John O. De Wolf, Eleanor Hudson and Lura Woodside Watkins

FIG. 15 — FAMILY-SIZE FOOT STOVE
This tin-and-wood heater was carried to church or meetinghouse, where the whole shivering family could enjoy its comforting warmth on a winter's day. It is four times the size of the largest of the individual foot stoves. A number of these distributed through the church would compensate for the absence of central heating. Some communities maintained "Sabba-day houses" where during the noon intermission the congregation could eat lunch and replenish the fuel in their foot stoves, before the afternoon session.
From the collection of Eleanor Hudson

A VICTORIAN FOOTSTOOL

THE above article by Mrs. Watkins and Mr. Long provides a comprehensive discussion of the varied devices to remedy cold feet which were used up to the mid-nineteenth century. Perhaps later articles designed for the same worthy purpose do not need or deserve consideration. Yet ANTIQUES cannot resist illustrating a combination footstool and foot warmer which must once have relieved the chill formality of a Victorian parlor of the 1850's or 1860's (*Fig. 16*). Its frame is of pine, veneered in mahogany and ornamented with a band of inlay. Its top is upholstered in red plush. To the casual observer, the stool is a stool and nothing more. Release the catch at one side, however, lift the top, and discover within a neatly fitting brass container for hot water. A seal impressed in the metal carries the inscription *Chevalier / à Paris /*

Brevete. A brass and wood handle is provided for loosening the flat screw cap, and sliding grips at either end of the can facilitate removal of the container from the stool. When the can is filled with hot water and replaced in the stool, a gentle heat penetrates the unlined fabric cover and unobtrusively protects decorous toes from drafty floors. How early Chevalier of Paris secured the *brevet*, or patent, on his invention we do not know. It may have been later than the 1850's, though his product suggests that decade. At all events, the footstool is as neat a gadget as one could wish for although hot water would not provide warmth for nearly as long as did embers in the earlier devices. From the collection of Miss Helen S. Stone and Bromley S. Stone, it is here pictured through the courtesy of the Cooper Union Museum.

FIG. 16 — COMBINATION FOOTSTOOL AND FOOT WARMER (*c. 1850*)
From the collection of Helen S. Stone and Bromley S. Stone. Photograph by courtesy of the Cooper Union Museum

NOTES ON THE NEW ENGLAND BLACKSMITH

By MALCOLM WATKINS

HOES, SCYTHES, HAMMERS, NAILS, andirons, toasters, door hardware, plow shares, and a host of other tools and implements lay close to the basis of colonial economy. Until the industrial era all these were of hand-forged iron, handiworks of the black-smith's art. "We can scarcely fix upon a single utensil, vehicle, or instrument which does not owe its origin, either directly or indirectly to the blacksmith." (Edward Hazen, *The Panorama of Professions and Trades*, Philadelphia, 1836)

In England, smithing was subdivided into specialized skills. The blacksmith made rougher sorts of implements; and if he made only horseshoes at his forge and was a veterinarian as well, he was then known as a farrier. Whitesmiths, on the other hand, "polish their work to a considerable degree of nicety; some include in their business bell-hanging . . . others are chiefly employed in the manufacture of locks and keys."

A new set of conditions prevailed in New England, however. Immediately upon the founding of the Colonies the demand for skilled labor outran the supply, and any sort of smith necessarily had to turn his hand to whatever he was able. This situation appears to have existed until the industrial period.

George Francis Dow (*Arts and Crafts in New England*) lists only one white-smith who advertised himself as such, and he had newly arrived from London to manufacture "Smoak Jacks" in 1757.

On the other hand, a blacksmith, Robert Hendry, in 1751 advertised "Horse Shoeer, Spinning Wheel Irons, . . . all sorts of Locks are made and mended." He later called attention to "fine White-Smith's Work; also Spades, and the best sort of Steel Shovels." Similar advertisements indicate that the blacksmith was a jack of all trades within, and sometimes outside, the limits of hand forging, even in such a large center as colonial Boston.

In 1638 John Josselyn (*Two Voyages to New England*) listed the equipment essential for a family settling in New England, and the different kinds of wrought-iron ware appearing on this list approximate those itemized in household inventories for the next two centuries. Among the iron things he recommended were "howes," saws, hammers, file, augers, broad axes, chisels, gimlets, hatchets, frows, nails, spikes, locks, chain, pitch fork, plow shares, a ten-pound coulter, iron pot, kettles, frying pans, spit, grid iron, and skillets.

EIGHTEENTH-CENTURY NEW ENGLAND LATCHES. The two large examples are typical early eighteenth-century exterior door latch handles, whose approximate counterparts are seen in Eastern Massachusetts and other parts of New England. The three small latches are frequently found on interior doors of colonial and post-Revolutionary houses. The center example, known as a "bean-head" latch, was a common English type that was imported into New England.

TWO LARGE NORFOLK LATCHES. (The term "Norfolk" distinguishes latches with continuous back plates from the more common "Suffolk" latches.) The scrolled example at left suggests other than New England design. The latch at right is from Moodus, Connecticut.

TWO LATCH HANDLES from house in East Haddam (*built c. 1788*). The more ornate "sword-fish" example is probably the work of the smith who worked in Haddam-Hampton-Moodus area.

For the first few years, certainly, such articles were imported by the colonists themselves as they came over, then by the merchants and businessmen who soon established themselves in the trade. Dow (*Everyday Life in the Massachusetts Bay Colony*) mentions the shop of George Corwin of Salem who, as early as 1651, was selling a general variety of imported goods, including iron locks and hardware.

Martin S. Briggs, speaking of the early colonists in *The Houses of the Pilgrim Fathers in England and America (1620-85)*, says, "The simplest ironwork required for their doors and windows may be taken as typical of much other craftsmanship. In the first fierce years of the settlement, all hinges and handles and locks had to be brought from home, as appears from early writers . . ."

The advertisements of Andrew and Jonathan Belcher in Boston in 1711 list imports from England which included nails, brads, "Hammers of sundry sorts & sizes, Spring & Stock Locks, Chest ditto, & Padlocks of several sorts . . . Hinges of several sorts", Steel Spades, Scythes, "and many other sorts of Iron Ware."

Deeds and inventories show the extent to which iron tools and utensils were used. They are seldom far from the minimum recommended by Josselyn, yet their diversity in spite of this indicates how important they were. The explicitness with which they are listed suggests, too, the value which was placed upon them. John Kitchin of Salem, whose inventory was made in 1676 (*Essex County Probate Records*) owned a "Jack, Andirons, Fire Shovels, Tongs, 2 spitts & a pr. of Stilliards, 2 smoothing Irons, hakes, Fenders & chafing dish with some other small Iron Things . . . . 3 payles whereof Two with Iron hoopes & bayles." Another listed "slice, a paire of tramells, a spit, fire shovell, pot hooks, tongs, frying pan, one iron foot, 2 chaynes and a span shackle."

Elsewhere are Broiling Iron, Flesh hooks, Toasting Iron, Cob irons, Dog Irons, Dripping pans, Fender, Fire dogs, Fire forks, Fire slice, Flesh forks, Grates, Hearth irons, Heaters (for irons), Apple roaster, Cheese tongs, Kettles, which were usually of cast iron; and various tools were uniformly mentioned.

The tremendous influx of newcomers that followed the first wave of set-

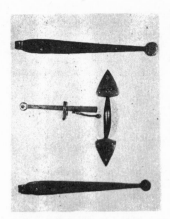

(*Left*) PAIR OF STRAP HINGES AND LATCH from house in South Glastonbury, Connecticut. The latch, which was used on the front door, is dated May 3, 1757. Other similar hinges and smaller arrow-head latches from the interior of the house are not shown here.

(*Right*) MISCELLANEOUS HARDWARE. The two strap hinges are of a type found on grain chest lids, trap doors, and the like. The butt on the left-hand example is perhaps unique, while that seen on the other is made from a salvaged ox shoe, a trick sometimes used in the country, where iron and the blacksmith's time were both scarce. The H and HL hinges may have been made in New England, although many were imported from the mother country. The S-shaped device at top is a shutter fastener.

tlers in the seventeenth century increased the demand for these basic implements in direct proportion to their own numbers. With even only a few blacksmiths and founders among the new arrivals, it was natural that a native iron industry should spring into being, particularly when New England hills were veined with ore and pond bottoms were coated with sesqui-oxide of iron.

The story of this industry and the rapid expansion of foundries and bloomeries and rolling mills and slitting mills by enterprising Yankees belongs elsewhere. But allusion to it should be made, because blacksmithing, reliant at first upon expensive imports of Russian and Swedish bar iron, necessarily owed its growth in every town and hamlet to the native foundries where bog iron was transformed into pig iron, and to the triphammers and forges where the pig iron was beaten into bars fit for the blacksmith to use.

Described often in other accounts was the exclusive privilege granted by the Massachusetts General Court in 1644 to the "Company of Undertakers for the Iron-Works," giving them the right to make iron for twenty-one years, provided they made after two years sufficient iron for the country's use. The initial foundry at Saugus was the first successful one in America. Although this enterprise was faced with difficulties which delayed its success, nevertheless it must surely have stimulated the local manufacture of iron utensils by blacksmiths, since the charter provided that the company should furnish all sorts of bar iron. The facts that they advertised the "richness of the ore and the goodness of the Iron" and that in subsequent years American bar iron was held in high esteem by British ironmongers lead further to this conclusion. At any rate, within the next hundred years there were foundries and forges scattered through the New England countryside, providing bar iron for the blacksmith to finish into tools

and into other hardware.

Most fine tools continued to be imported throughout the colonial period, although tools of a sort were made by blacksmiths. H and HL hinges were principally an English product, as were many of the smaller "bean-head" latches that are still found in early houses.

But there was an increasing output of hand-forged iron, made locally in each town, usually as a part of the barter system on which village economy was founded. The products themselves, based at first on traditional designs, soon began to assume a character distinct from English or other foreign prototypes. Most probably to save iron, though perhaps because of an inherent chasteness in creating design, New England blacksmiths made utensils which are light, delicate, and restrained. A fork will have a slender, flat handle, ending in a feathery rat-tailed loop. A pair of gooseneck andirons may have a lightness that belies their strength. Skewers and skewer holders often have the nicety of silver. Now and then, especially in the latter part of the eighteenth century, when there was more occasion for developing esthetic skill, some blacksmith would emerge here or there whose eyes and hands were those of an artist, and produce latches like those below. Such a worker was the blacksmith who, in the 1780's and '90's, made the elaborate latches still to be seen in the vicinity of Haddam, Connecticut.

Yet throughout the seventeenth and eighteenth centuries, and into the early nineteenth, there is evidence of a shortage of iron utensils, especially in the interior towns, as though there were never enough blacksmiths, or else enough iron. The inventory of Stephen Fitch of Windham, Connecticut, whose house is now an exhibit at Old Sturbridge Village, shows only the following articles of iron in 1806: 2 Wedges, 1 Iron bar, 1 pr. Hand Irons, 1 Draft Chain, 1 pr. Broken Tongs, 1 pr. Tobacco Tongs, 1 Fire Peal, and less cast- and

(*Left*) WROUGHT-IRON HARDWARE FROM GREAT BRITAIN. *Left*, Scottish Norfolk latch. The loose ring, called a "tirling pin," which the visitor drew up and down over the ridges of the twisted handle to announce his presence, is a unique Scottish feature. *Upper center*, cockshead hinge. Such hinges were imported from England and used in seventeenth-century houses in New England. *Lower center*, H hinge with ornamented ends. Also a characteristic English hinge type of the seventeenth and early eighteenth centuries, found in early houses here. *Right*, hinged hasp from seventeenth-century Scottish chest lid. The plain strap hinge has its origin in such designs.

(*Right*) GROUP OF THREE CONNECTICUT LATCHES. The small handle at left is a late eighteenth-century piece. The two large examples, probably made for churches, allegedly came from the vicinity of Litchfield. The upper point of the center latch is missing. The example at right, much heavier and solider, is probably considerably earlier than the other two. The flat thumb press with its straight lift bar (shown at extreme right), commonly an early feature, supports this view. The braced catch is shown, but the latch bar is missing.

sheet-iron objects than Josselyn felt were necessary in 1638. When Stephen Fitch Junior's inventory was taken in 1815, only a few tools, steelyards, and a trammel appeared in addition to the former list.

Scarely more elaborate is the 1771 inventory of iron belonging to Solomon Richardson of Podunk, Massachusetts, whose dwelling has also been moved to Old Sturbridge Village. It is interesting that none of these lists is essentially different from those of a century and more earlier. (It may also be noted here that the groaning weight of iron and other utensils that crowd the kitchen hearths of many of our restored colonial houses has no support from these contemporary records).

Probably few communities had sufficient blacksmiths. The Beards (*The Rise of American Civilization*) point out that in the colonial period special privileges and bounties were offered to entice skilled English workers to come to America, but with little success. Those who did come were prone to move westward with the settling of new communities, rather than to stay in one place.

The restrictions which stifled the expansion of the iron industry as a whole after 1750 probably had little direct effect upon the blacksmith, since pig-iron manufacture was encouraged. Nor did the relaxing of these restrictions after the Revolution and the consequent stimulus upon the iron industry have any perceptible effect on the rural blacksmith until mass-produced cast iron began to change the country's economy radically after 1840.

Perhaps a typical country blacksmith was William Skinner, Jr. of Woodstock, Connecticut, who carried on at his forge immediately after the Revolution. His account book, carefully balancing a record of his work against one of payment in goods or in

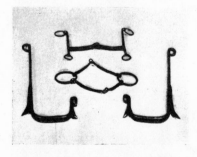

TWO WROUGHT-IRON BRIDLE BITS, and a pair of stirrups.

WROUGHT-IRON TOASTER. "Toasting Irons" appear in early inventories.

WROUGHT-IRON BROILER of simple design.

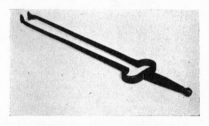

PAIR OF FIRE TONGS. Although its shape is characteristic of seventeenth-century tongs, this pair is dated 1826.

labor by his debtors, is preserved in Old Sturbridge Village. It illustrates beyond doubt how thoroughly the community depended upon the blacksmith.

The following entries, selected at random, are characteristic: "mending tongs; for loom irons; for an inch auger, partly your iron; a day upon tainterhooks; Riming Sieve; Beaming plow; to seting shoe on the lame creature; 2 hundred of Board Nails (Hazen in 1836 pointed out, "Workmen by practice . . . in making wrought nails . . . acquire surprising dispatch in this business; and this circumstance has prevented the general introduction of the machines which have been invented for making nails of this description."); for making Crane &

Eyes; fixing 2 pair of hinges; 5 pair of Hinges, 4/0 per pair; 2 small pair of Hinges; for a chissel to trim appletrees; for 2 Hoes; for newlaying an Ax and mending head; to a new worm & putting on gripe; 12 links for log chane; for making 24 spikes for Hetchel & Bailing Tea Kittle; to mending Hook of a Chane."

Quite similar to this is another blacksmith's account book kept in Southbridge, Massachusetts, in 1827: "Making a clapper for Bell; Repairing Stage; splicing chain for pot rack; cutting and welding a tyre; one pair of gallopers (*sic*); making irons for Jail chain and spikes; one large pair of hinges, 20 lb. of iron; repairing Gun lock; one grid iron; making a door latch; making 16 paire of hinges."

Conspicuously missing here, however, are references to nails. Cut nails were being made by machine to some extent, and Hazen stated in 1836 that nine tenths of all wrought nails were said to be imported because of the difference in labor costs here and abroad. The great change was thus by this time showing itself. Volume production by machine was to drive down the costs of finished products and raise the price of skilled labor. Cast iron latches, machine-made plows, mechanically-cut nails, standardized parts, and factory-made tools were to reduce the blacksmith to a horseshoer, and that merely as a survival of a bygone era.

The "undertakers" of Saugus marked the direction of this industrial change, which might have blossomed many years earlier except for the restraint placed by Parliamentary acts upon expansion, and thus indirectly upon invention.

Meanwhile, the blacksmith — resourceful, mechanical, and frequently an artist — was one of the mainstays of colonial New England, as indeed he was in all the Colonies.

All illustrations are from Old Sturbridge Village, Sturbridge, Massachusetts.

GROUP OF KITCHEN HARDWARE. The fork, ladle, and spatula are typically New England in their design. The two trivets with handles are smoothing-iron rests, while the swastika-shaped example is for resting a small kettle over the coals.

Notes on Early Ohio Lighting Devices

By RHEA MANSFIELD KNITTLE

FIGURE *1.* Combination rush and candle floor light fashioned during the frontier period of Ohio's settlement. The wrought-iron standard is supported by a rough, hand-hewn base, made from the burl of an ash tree. The adjustable fixture is dexterously forged into a combination of candle cup and clip rushlight holder. This fine specimen was used in Trumbull County, and it is in original condition.

During the opening of the trans-Allegheny country suitable tallow for candles and material for wicking were very difficult to obtain. Fortunately, however, rushes abounded in swamp and swale. The pithy parts of the rush stems were pressed together and soaked in bear grease (or that of some other wild animal). The rushlight was, of necessity, employed in this section of the country a century or more after its use was discontinued along the Atlantic seaboard. As late as the 1840's the inhabitants of wild and sparsely settled sections of Ohio carried pitch-pine flares at night.

Figure 2. An unusual wrought-iron rushlight floor device that does not conform to any type of early fixture with which I am familiar. The slender perpendicular rod terminates abruptly at the top, and at the base is supported on a low tripod with expanded, circular feet.

The bracket is an oblong platform from which rise two iron tubes hollow from top to bottom, with openings only sufficiently large for a rush. No candle sockets of any sort have been attached to these tubes, which are original. The inner section of one side of the adjustable frame is missing.

Note. All of the objects here illustrated were found in Ohio. It seems probable that the majority, if not all, were, as tradition insists, made in that state, which almost from the beginning of its settlement boasted a surprising number of competent craftsmen among its inhabitants.   — *The Editor.*

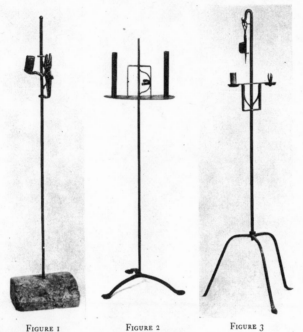

| FIGURE 1 | FIGURE 2 | FIGURE 3 |

| FIGURE 4 | FIGURE 5 | FIGURE 6 |

The piece came from the descendants of the original owner and was forged about 1800–1810 in the Muskingum Valley, where malleable bog iron was found prior to 1805. This valley became a mecca for proficient pioneer craftsmen, among whom were many ironworkers well versed in "the art and mistery" of blacksmithing.

Figure 3. An excellent example of a Pennsylvania-Dutch blacksmith's ingenuity as practiced in Lancaster, Ohio, in the early days of Ohio's statehood. Candles were so scarce that this device was contrived as a partial remedy for the situation. The platform holds both a deep candle socket and a three-pronged pricket, upon which the stub of the candle could be stuck and completely consumed after it had burned to the socket level. The tripod base is extremely wide and high, and the shaft, terminating in a crook at the top, is set through the base and strengthened at the joining by an iron ring. This specimen of early wrought iron was in Lancaster County until 1931, at which time moldy tallow was still adhering to it.

Figure 4. Ratchet-type of wood candlestand. Apparently both jackknife and plane were used in its construction. The parts are pinned together by both wooden pegs and early, short wrought-iron nails. Socket holes for candles extend through the platform. The latch that regulates and holds the ratchets is attached to both sides of one upright bar. This piece came from the environs of Tiffin.

Figure 5. A Mid-western frontier oak floor candlestand. Notice the octagon form of the lower portion of the shaft; the finely cut screw, which still operates perfectly; and the construction and balance of the arm with its metal sconce — made to hold a very slender candle — projecting through the base. Two of the three splayed legs, doweled into the oaken ball, are original. Standing where it was exposed to the elements, this sturdy little light survived the neglect. It came from Carroll County.

Figure 6. Uncommonly tall and somewhat light standard made of wood and tin. Its height was necessitated by the use to which it was put. The first communist settlement in the United States was established in Tuscarawas County in 1817 by the Separatists Society of Zoar, who migrated in the spring of that year from Germany. Among the community undertakings was weaving, and there was a weaving room, where material for clothing, blankets, and coverlets was produced on hand looms. This light was used by the side of a loom.

The shaft resembles an elongated broomstick. In it oaken pegs are inserted at regular intervals, for supporting the adjustable wooden arm, into which the little standard slides and is firmly held in position. The cup of this standard is badly charred. It still holds a small tin receptacle for grease or fluid of some sort. The burner or wick tube is missing; so also is the handle which was attached to the side of the vessel. A unique specimen, of interest both as an antique and as an historical item.

Figure 7. Wrought-iron open grease lamp of the frontier era, a type known variously as "slot," "slut," and "open betty." In this particular example, which came from Tuscarawas County and was probably fashioned from local bog ore, the sides are deeper, the handle is longer, the bowl is more circular, and the spout is more adequate than one sees on most lamps of the type. Bear or other animal fat was used in these little lights, a twisted rag wick emerging over the spout. It was better than no light at all, and was easily carried.

Figure 8. Iron betty lamp embodying every good feature that a lighting device of this kind should have. Each part is perfectly

FIGURE 7

FIGURE 8

wrought — hanging staple, handle, chain, and wick-pick (used for removing the constantly recurring carbon or soot from the end of the wick), sliding cover with thumbpiece, the vessel itself, the trough, the spout, and the wick tube. The oak stand or pedestal was at some time stained a dull red. Betties were made in Ohio from various metals — iron, tin, brass, and copper. This example was made in a section of Ashland County when it was still a part of Knox County. The stand came from the Amish district in the adjacent county of Holmes.

Figure 9. Primitive pottery grease lamp, built up by hand from coarse local clay and glazed with chocolate-colored slip of inferior character. The well for grease, oil, or some kind of animal fat has a central circular aperture through which it was filled and two spoutlike openings for the wicks. The base is sufficiently capacious to hold the drippings. This crude device is as sturdy and strong as the backwoodsmen who probably modeled and used it. It came from the vicinity of Winesburg, and is very early. It may have been fashioned by two Swiss potters who erected a pothouse in the near-by wilderness prior to 1818.

Figure 10. Another earthenware fat lamp, potted at least a quarter of a century later than Figure 9. This device and similar contemporary forms are attributed to the Routsons of Doylestown and Wooster, Wayne County, potters from Pennsylvania. The clay has been pugged and built up more carefully than that of the preceding example. The glaze resembles Albany slip, which it may be, for this slip was brought into Ohio in the 1840–1850 decade and was used to glaze the interior of Dutch or apple-butter crocks. The bulbous bowl has two wick spouts, and a generous handle is attached to the standard.

Figure 11. This lamp is similar in body, texture, and glaze to Figure 10. The shape is more sophisticated, and the handle is unique in so far as Ohio pottery lamps are concerned. The bowl is very wide and shallow, and only one spout occurs. The saucer is greater in diameter than that of any similar light that I have observed. This

FIGURE 9 (*above*)
FIGURE 10 (*left*)
FIGURE 11 (*right*)

FIGURE 12

FIGURE 13

FIGURE 14

example is attributed to the hand of an experienced and efficient potter, Curtis Houghton, who migrated from the Vermont pottery district in the 1840's and settled in a rich clay centre now known as Dalton. *Pottery lamps similar to Figures 10 and 11 are now being reproduced; also iron floor stands somewhat resembling Figure 3.*

Figure 12. Tin oil lamp of a type frequently found in Ohio. The cylindrical chamber is capped by a double wick burner and is set into a larger lipped standard. The panlike base and the handle are soldered to the standard.

Figure 13. Three metals enter into the composition of this choice lighting device: The open top reservoir is of copper, and swings on two side pivots. The supporting arms branch out from a slender stem, of iron, sunk into a tin pedestal, which in turn is attached to a tin saucerlike base. A delicate chain containing more than the usual number of little links is attached to one of the arms, and a slender pick is fastened to the other end of the chain. This light came from Portage County.

Figure 14. Tin oil lamp with small detachable triple burner and prominent tubular opening through which to pour the fluid. The chamber is covered with a slightly convex stationary top. Footless, very thin tin snuffers hang by a little hook. The blade end of these snuffers is curled in an unusual manner. Even the box is scalloped around its edge. The ensemble will interest our lighting-device collectors, some of whom may know who patented it. It was found in Coshocton County, where it had been in use.

Figure 15. Pewter swinging lamp made by Homan and

FIGURE 15

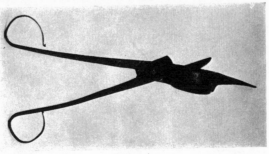

FIGURE 17

Company of Cincinnati between the years 1857 and 1872, for use in the home and on Ohio River boats. The original wholesale price was twelve dollars per dozen.

This type of lamp is a development of the New England whaler's lighting device. Although such devices were manufactured as late as 1872, a perfect specimen is now difficult to find.

Figure 16. Tin lard-oil lamp made for a broad, flat wick. The wick holder has three narrow parallel openings in one side whereby the wick could be conveniently "picked up." A slide in the top of the lamp covers a good-size circular aperture for filling. The handle is not in evidence in this picture.

An interesting circumstance in connection with this lamp is that, with five identical brothers, it was found, in 1932, in the attic over an abandoned tin shop in central Ohio. Neatly wrapped in a cobwebby box were the separate parts, cut and marked, ready for shipment — to be assembled at a destination which they never reached. So they were soldered together in 1932, and, as the photograph shows, the tin is almost as shiny as when it was first rolled and cut.

Figure 17. Wrought-iron combination snuffers and wick-pick. This piece has never had feet, or rests, and the handles taper to a delicate thinness seldom found in iron work. The blacksmiths of Ohio's pioneer period wrought not only for utility and durability but also for grace.

The devices pictured, while somewhat crude and homely, are, nevertheless, proof of definite skill and of a desire to combine good workmanship with utility.

FIGURE 16

STAGECOACH LUGGAGE

By I. T. FRARY

IT'S a long shot from the slowly bouncing, swaying stagecoach of a century or two ago to the cloud-piercing airplane of today. It is quite as far from the gay, paper-covered bandbox which the crinoline-upholstered maiden carried with her into the coach, to the streamlined luggage with which the smart miss of today soars aloft.

The baggage of traveling ladies has run the gamut from neat little hair-covered trunks to mammoth Saratogas whose capacious interiors engulfed unbelievable quantities of silken goods, stitched by misguided seamstresses into garments planned to obliterate all hint of the feminine form that lurked somewhere within billows of frills and flounces. Then came the efficient wardrobe trunk (still with us), cursed by sweating baggagemen, with its immense poundage of ingeniously built-in cupboards, drawers, and cubbyholes. From this, by easy stages, we come to airplane luggage with its achievement of infinite lightness.

The evolution is easily traced to changing means of transportation; to the necessity for economy of space and weight in the stagecoach; to increasing disregard for such restrictions, as baggage cars became more capacious, and back again because of sharp limitations enforced today by a conveyance that is dragged up into space by magnified pinwheels.

And now the gay bandboxes of our grandmothers and great-grandmothers are being retrieved from shadowy attics, and installed among the rarities of collectors' loot.

Bandboxes derived the name from their employment as receptacles for the protection of linen neckbands in the seventeenth century, when fashion dictated their use in place of the lace ruffs that had irritated the necks and chins of earlier generations. These bands, in turn, were superseded during the early nineteenth century by collars, from which mankind has not as yet been emancipated. Although the bandbox ministered to the pride of man in its early existence, it was ultimately preëmpted by woman as a repository for hats and bonnets, to say nothing of such other items of wearing apparel as could safely be stuffed into it.

Doctor Samuel Johnson refers to the bandbox, in his celebrated dictionary, as "a slight box used for bands and other things of light weight." He proceeds to illuminate the subject by quoting Addison, who wrote, "My friends are surprised to find two bandboxes among my books, till I tell them that they are lined with deep erudition."

The Oxford Dictionary defines the bandbox as "a slight box of cardboard or very thin chip covered with paper for collars, caps, hats and millinery, originally made for the bands or collars of the 17th c." The Universal English Dictionary allies the bandbox with the ministry by asserting that it was "originally a case in which a clergyman kept his linen bands; now a light case of cardboard for holding light articles, esp. hats." Here, too, we find reference to our good old phrase, "He looks as though he had just stepped out of a bandbox."

The makers of bandboxes produced them in various sizes and shapes. Some were of wood, cut to veneer thinness; some were of heavy cardboard; some had thin boards forming top and bottom; some were round and others oval; but all were covered with block-printed paper enriched with fanciful designs of widely varying character.

One can scarcely credit their age, in view of the excellent preservation in which many are found today; but this may be due to the excellent care that was bestowed on these fragile objects. Often they were shrouded in cases of chintz, or other inexpensive material, when "on the road." Moreover, they belonged to a less prodigal age than ours, an age when possessions were usually come by through sacrifice and hard work, and could not be casually replaced by telephoning to the nearest department store. Necessity and poverty of resources gave value to all that one possessed.

The paper with which most of the earlier boxes were covered was printed especially for the purpose. Later, wall paper was cut from rolls and applied. Many of the patterns are valued today quite as much as records of contemporary events and places as for their decorative charm. Inasmuch as the boxes were to be used mostly in traveling, it was natural that the designers of the paper coverings should turn their minds to subjects that the traveler might encounter. So we find picturesque representations of current means of transportation — horse, stagecoach, canal boat, railroad, and sailing ship. Even the balloon was used as a motive, recalling the interest in aviation that was even then agitating the minds of inventors, and occasioning heated

FIG. 1 (*above*) — THE CITY HALL, NEW YORK. Blue background

FIG. 2 — THE UNITED STATES CAPITOL. Blue background

FIG. 3 — BUILDINGS OF YALE COLLEGE. Green background

FIG. 4 — WINDMILL AND RAILROAD. Yellow background

debates as to whether or not God ever intended man to fly.

The wonderful sights vouchsafed those fortunate enough to go on long journeys were also seized upon by designers as suitable subject matter for bandboxes. We find the Capitol at Washington, the City Hall at New York, and various hospitals, schools, and public buildings, depicted with varying degrees of bad draftsmanship to which we grant absolution on the grounds of "quaintness."

A statement that will bear investigation appeared in an article on bandboxes, published several years ago in a magazine that was not named ANTIQUES. One of the architectural designs was referred to quite innocently as a *View of the Deaf and Dumb Asylum,* later *Columbia University.* We refrain from comment.

Sentiments of patriotism were aroused, we suspect, by these inspiring views of buildings that recalled important episodes in our nation's history, and by dashing military gentlemen mounted on cavorting steeds, no less than by striking representations of the grand American eagle. More tender sentiments were suggested by deer dashing through well-groomed wildernesses, and very well-fed squirrels snuggling lovingly together beneath diminutive trees, the apotheosis of domestic bliss.

The backgrounds of these designs were usually in soft tones of blue, green, and yellow. Blue was most common. The design was printed in gray and white, with accenting touches of contrasting colors. The same design was sometimes produced in colors.

An important collection of old bandboxes has been assembled by Mrs. Harry G. Sloan of Cleveland Heights, Ohio, who by persevering search has garnered a rich harvest of these colorful luggage carriers. Some have been preserved intact; others have been flattened out and framed under glass. By this method they can be shown to excellent advantage, are preserved from damage, and — well, just imagine trying to house even a few dozen bandboxes in an ordinary home!

While Mrs. Sloan includes in her collection most of the known designs, her preference is given to the historical scenes. Among these she has views of numerous famous buildings, such as New York's City Hall, the United States Capitol, the buildings of Yale College, and old Castle Garden. This last design as it appears on a bandbox still complete and unframed is reproduced on the Cover of this issue of ANTIQUES.

Then there are depictions related to events of current interest. These include a balloon in ascension, and a magnificent horse-drawn train of the Baltimore and Ohio Railroad. Another shows the Grand Canal (presumably DeWitt Clinton's Erie Canal) with a boat being hauled in state through a lock by a horse and rider of not overly prepossessing appearance; another boat is being made ready for the breathtaking ascent in the lock. And finally, there are the various designs involving beasts of the field and birds of the sky, together with the inevitable floral effects.

The designers and printers of the bandbox papers, and the makers of bandboxes, have been lost sight of to a large extent. We could hardly expect serious-minded historians to concern themselves with such lowly folk, to record them with portrait painters, silversmiths, or even furniture builders. Theirs was a very humble craft, and a peaceful one. Historians want drama.

Fig. 5 (*top*) — THE GRAND CANAL. Blue background

Fig. 6 (*above, left*) — THE BALTIMORE AND OHIO RAILROAD. Blue background

Fig. 7 (*above, right*) — WESLEYAN UNIVERSITY. Blue background

Fig. 8 (*below, left*) — VIEW OF THE DEAF AND DUMB ASYLUM

Fig. 9 (*below, center*) — CLAYTON'S BALLOON ASCENT

Fig. 10 (*right*) — SURRENDER OF CORNWALLIS. Blue background

Fig. 11 (*below, right*) — THE BRITISH QUEEN. Green background

Now and then, however, the name of one of these workers with veneers, paper, and glue, comes to light. We can point with assurance to the following as bona fide practitioners in boxmaking:

H. Barnes, Bandbox Manufactory, Jones Alley, Philadelphia

Thomas Day, Jr., Bandbox Manufactory, 396 Pearl Street (presumably New York)

Putnam and Hoff, Paper Hanging, Bandbox Manufactory, Hartford, Connecticut (*early 1830's*)

Barnard Andrews, Bond Street, New York

Hannah Davis, Jaffrey, New Hampshire (*1784–1863*)

The father of Hannah Davis was a manufacturer of cheeseboxes. Hence it is not surprising to learn that Hannah, brought up among cheeseboxes, made her own bandboxes, and made them from the same thin, pliable wood that her father incorporated in his own commercial product.

The collector of bandboxes can hardly make practical use of his treasures, as may the owner of old glass, china, or furniture. Though examples are to be found which are still perfectly serviceable, every-day use might soon prove too much for them. But their ornamental value is high. Their soft colors and fascinating patterns make them striking and attractive elements in any decorative scheme. Thus they are the delight and despair of the collector.

Paintings on
Velvet

By Louise Karr

*Illustrations, except as noted,
from the collection of
Mrs. Isabel Carleton Wilde*

~✇⊚✇~

Fig. 1 — Theorem Painting on Velvet
(c. 1812)
By the talented Lydia Hosmer of
Concord, Massachusetts. This picture
represents theorem painting at its best.
Size: 20 by 24 inches.
*From the collection of the Concord
Antiquarian Society*

WHEN we speak of paintings on velvet, we usually mean a type of art work that, a century ago, was considered the flower of all things desirable in the education of young ladyhood. Paintings of the kind are familiar enough among heirloom relics and the treasure-trove of the antique shops. Usually they represent arrangements of flowers, or fruit, or a combination of the two overflowing from a wicker basket. Occasionally they offer more ambitious themes, such as landscapes and figure subjects.

Their advent appears to mark the temporary decline of embroidery as an elegant accomplishment, and the concurrent rise of painting and drawing as essentials in the curriculum of schools for highly genteel females. The cynic may perhaps regard them as evidence of a disciplinary breakdown in the educational world. For half a century before the vogue of painting, embroidery had grown steadily less meticulous. Before the 1800's, stitchery and painting mingled freely in the same designs. Now painting reigned almost alone. Some of it was executed on Bristol board, some on velvet. It was known variously as mezzotint, Oriental tinting or Chinese painting, velvet painting, and theorem painting. But whatever the name, the process remained virtually constant and essentially mechanical. It consisted primarily of tracing a design on transparent paper, cutting out the pattern, and using the result as a stencil.

True, the velvet paintings were sometimes drawn directly on the material by placing the latter over an engraving held against a well-lighted window and tracing the outline thus revealed through the fabric. Color was subsequently applied as genius prompted. The great majority of these pictures were, however, composed according to what was called the "theorem method." Hence they were known as "theorem paintings."

According to the dictionary, a theorem is a rule or formula. But the inventors of novelties in the way of art exercises for young ladies — or older ones, for that matter — were not particular about the accuracy of the terms that they applied to their various methods. Thus Oriental painting was the somewhat

grandiloquent designation used for floral and bird patterns painted in transparent colors on glass, surrounded with a field of lamp black, and given the adventitious glitter of a tin-foil backing. The result is described in Tilton and Company's *Art Recreations* (Boston, 1860) as a "gorgeous array of brilliant colors, with sparkling aids."

The process of coating engravings with turpentine and varnish until their substance was rendered sufficiently transparent to transmit colors applied to the back of the sheet was dignified with the name of Grecian painting, because of its "sombre and antique appearance." Hence we need not be surprised to learn that a "theorem," in the art-teacher parlance of the early nineteenth century, was one of the many stencils employed in theorem painting. The method was also known as "Poonah painting" — in tribute to its assumed origin in Poona, Bombay — and also as Oriental painting, tinsel work to the contrary notwithstanding. The style, we are informed by *Art Recreations*, "is better adapted to fruits, birds, and butterflies than to landscapes and heads. It will enable you to paint on paper, silk, velvet, crape, and light-colored wood."

The employment of theorems on all these varied materials forms a subject too complicated to pursue. Furthermore, its most interesting manifestations are the pictures on velvet, though our authority cites "ball dresses painted, with belts and neck ribbon to match; also white crape dresses, with vines of gold and silver." For such pictures "firm, white cotton velvet was selected and stretched." That was the easiest part of the performance. Preliminaries might occupy a period ranging from two days to a week.

First, according to one authority, it was necessary to find a subject — usually an engraving — suitable for copying. Where such things were procured is beyond my knowledge; for I have never yet encountered a theorem painting that bore a striking resemblance to any original work of art of my acquaintance. Nevertheless, some of them recall late eighteenth and early nineteenth-century European engravings, while still others seem directly or indirectly related to the fruit and flower compositions of Currier and Ives. Perhaps special patterns were issued to serve the purposes of theorem devotees. Perhaps, and more than probably, few people ever took the trouble to follow the laborious and obscure directions in the books; but procured their theorems ready-cut from the art teachers. Even then, sufficient trouble lay in wait for them.

Assuming, however, that a satisfactory engraving was found, it was now necessary to prepare the theorems, or stencils. "Horn paper" was a first essential. To make this substance drawing

Fig. 2 — Theorem Painting on Velvet (c. 1820)
The watermelon cut to expose its pink flesh punctuated with dark seeds was a favorite motive for fruit arrangements
From the collection of Brooks Reed

paper was coated on both sides with linseed oil, allowed to dry, recoated with spirits of turpentine or fir balsam and again subjected to a drying process. Some writers allow two days for this undertaking; others insist upon more than a week. Meanwhile our engraving is impatiently waiting to be copied. If it is not to be damaged in the course of transfer we may as well begin, while our horn paper is drying, by tracing the outline of our print on white paper, with a soft lead pencil.

This done, "mark those parts [of the design] which do not touch each other, with a figure 1." Let us hope that the horn paper is now dry — many sheets of it, since we shall need them all. Now "lay [a sheet of] horn paper over the sketch, and trace [cut out] with a sharp-pointed penknife, or large pin, all the objects marked 1. Mark another piece of horn paper for theorem 2, and cut again;" and so on until the whole pattern has been reduced to a set of stencils.

The reason for confining each cutting to non-contiguous parts is clear. If wet colors were applied too closely side by side they might easily run into each other, with disastrous results. One after another the theorems were placed on the velvet, and held

firmly in place by weights or tacks, while the surface of the material revealed through their apertures was carefully painted. "Commence with a leaf; take plenty of paint, a very little moist, on your brush, and paint in the cut leaf of the theorem; hold the brush upright, and manipulate quickly with a circular motion. It is best to begin a little distance from, and work toward, the edge." Shading was accomplished by cutting a templet of horn paper with one edge following the contour of a major vein. This templet was laid on the already painted leaf, while more color was worked in from the edge of the templet toward the border of the leaf. Thus was produced a somewhat mystifying effect of modulated tone. Stiff brushes were used to apply the color, though "stalks, fibers, dots, etc." were a postscript addition, executed with camel's-hair pencils.

Such, in essence, is the method of theorem painting as described in *Art Recreations*. However, at the time when that engaging volume was prepared, the process was nearly or quite dead. At any rate, it had passed from popularity, a fact attested by the relatively few pages devoted to it in our reference work compared with the space given over to minute rules for spoiling engravings to render them Greek, or for rivaling the splendors of Oriental art with the aid of tinsel pasted on the back of glass.

No doubt the author, or authors, of *Art Recreations* borrowed a good deal of material from earlier publications, revising some of it, and accepting the rest as they found it. I am not sure that their description of the making of the theorems is entirely correct. They seem either to be discussing a later and more summary method than that employed by earlier workers, or else to have misunderstood the rules as laid down by previous writers.

A reading of *Art Recreations* would lead one to believe that each stencil included a number of

Fig. 3 — Painting on Velvet (probably c. 1812)
If, as seems likely, the building portrayed is the old Capitol at Washington, this curious picture may well have been painted before 1814. It shows no signs of the use of theorems or stencils. *Size: 20 by 24 inches*

noncontiguous units in the original design. Direct examination of the paintings themselves leads to the belief that each element, or motive, in the pattern was cut as an individual stencil, and that these stencils were assembled, more or less independently, to suit the whim or convenience of the artist. One leaf stencil might serve for several leaves of the same type. Each rose petal, on the other hand, might require its own specific theorem. Despite its mechanical aspects, the method called for extreme care and considerable deftness of hand. Likewise it allowed some latitude for expressing individual preferences in the arrangement of parts, a fact that accounts for the slight variations of a similar theme to be discovered among any considerable group of theorem paintings.

Precisely the same technique was employed in stenciling the Hitchcock chairs of the 1820–1830 decade. Such Hitchcock decorations were theorem paintings pure and simple. Later, however, the procedure was changed, and what I may call fixed stencils, with the entire design cut in one piece, were substituted for the previous smaller units. The substitution speeded the work of the decorator, but it resulted in a more rigid arrangement of parts, and a flatter and far less

Fig. 5 — THEOREM PAINTING ON VELVET
The separation of the various landscape elements leaves no doubt as to the use of stencils for most of this painting. But the fuzzy foliage can have been achieved only with the free hand. *Size: 12 by 18 inches*

Fig. 4 — THEOREM PAINTING ON VELVET (*1828*)
A mourning piece in whose making theorems were used, at least to some extent. The marble tomb retains the color of the velvet, delicately shaded. *Size: 12 ½ by 16 ½ inches.*
From the collection of the Concord Antiquarian Society

interesting surface effect. If theorem painting continued as late as the 1860's, which I doubt, it may by that period have been reduced to little more than pushing colors through the apertures of fixed stencils.

As to the exact nature of these colors, at any period of theorem work, I still harbor doubts. I find them described at some length in J. W. Alston's *Hints to Young Practitioners in the Study of Landscape Painting, to which are added Instructions in the Art of Painting on Velvet*, published in Edinburgh, 1804; in Maria Turner's *Young Ladies' Assistant in Drawing and Painting*, an American publication that saw the light in Cincinnati, in 1833; and in sundry other books and short articles. In general, I believe them to have been colored powders mixed with gum tragacanth and water until they attained the consistency of starch. I have found, however, one or two suggestions that oil colors mixed with turpentine proved a satisfactory medium.

I can see no good reason for here repeating the dreary receipts for extracting the needed hues by boiling French berries, saffron flowers, powdered indigo, and so on, in "separate earthen pipkins," or the equally dreary and still more complicated prescriptions for mixing the dyes to obtain intermediate tints. I am inclined to suspect that quite as few persons paid attention to these printed directions for preparing colors as attempted to make horn paper and cut stencils. Matters of that kind were better left to the teacher. My suspicion is deepened by the perusal of some parts of Mr. England's verbose treatise on certain dyes of his own invention for use in painting groups of flowers and fruit on velvet, "by means of the Ispahan formula."

For my acquaintance with the pompous Mr. England, I am indebted to the Department of Textiles of the Victoria and Albert Museum in London. His treatise, written apparently in the 1840's, gives us two valuable clues. He himself does not use the word theorem; but he speaks of *models*, which appear to have been colored sketches "properly shaded, done on paper at a price even less than many groups could be hired for." This somewhat obscure statement certainly implies that Mr. England himself devised the compositions that his pupils were to follow. Likewise it fairly disposes of the idea that engravings were actually traced by aspiring neophytes. Whether it also means that the advertiser supplied stencils with his models, I am unable to judge. But when he speaks of the price which many "*groups* could be hired for," he must refer to some practice of renting ready-cut stencils.

In short, I think it reasonable to believe that most of the theorem paintings on velvet are copies of professionally made "models" and that they were executed with professionally cut stencils, by pupils working directly under the watchful eye of a teacher like the redoubtable Mr. England. This would be true particularly in the case of fruit and flower pictures whose similarities can be accounted for by no other hypothesis.

With the far less common landscape and figure subjects on velvet the case may have been materially different. Indeed, I am inclined to question whether all of them were really executed by the theorem method. Some indicate the use of stencils in parts.

Fig. 6 — THEOREM PAINTING ON VELVET
Evidently based on an old needlepoint picture, and very neatly wrought with stencils and a little free-hand painting. *Size: 12 by 18 inches*

almost certainly, between 1800 and 1840. No art manual of the eighteenth century so much as mentions them. I find their technique described in a work of 1804. In *The Female Student*, published in 1836 by Almira Phelps, former vice president of the Troy Female Seminary, they are spoken of disparagingly, and their production is belittled as lacking any "tendency to refine and elevate the taste like most other departments of the art" of painting.

Among actual examples, the earliest that I have heard of is reported to me by Mrs. Foster Clarke of Boston, who once owned a mourning piece, painted on velvet and dated *1808*. Lydia Hosmer's decoration reproduced in Figure 1 is believed by Mrs. Cummin, curator of the Antiquarian Society at Concord, to have been done about 1812, the same year in which the industrious Lydia won a prize for an embroidered picture that she exhibited at the Agricultural Fair. The mourning piece of Figure 4 bears the date *1828*. Two very fine flower pieces by Mrs. Boutwell, wife of President Grant's War Secretary, I had the privilege of examining at Groton, Massachusetts. They were probably painted in the 1830's.

Cora Helen Coolidge reports a similar painting given her

Others look as if they had been traced on the material and then colored by rubbing in slightly moistened pigments. Where considerable masses of a single shade were required, as in the foliage of the weeping willow of Figure 4, it seems not unlikely that the tinted gum-water was considerably diluted and washed into the fabric from behind, so as not to mat the pile unduly. Matting the pile was always a danger, for the avoidance of which various means are described in the treatises, together with remedies in case of unpreventable disaster.

Despite my personal doubts as to the extensive use of theorems in landscape and architectural paintings, their employment in such connections is elaborately related in the books, with much insistence upon finding the true horizon line, and placing trees, houses, fields, and figures in proper relation thereto. Skies and clouds, which were no subjects for theorems, were done free hand. After such features as these were safely and smoothly in place, other elements could be

Fig. 7 — PAINTING ON VELVET
Theorems were evidently employed to some extent in painting this romantic scene, but the straight-edge is responsible for much of it. *Size: 24 by 30 inches*

added at will, provided they showed sufficient deference to the all-important horizon line. I imagine that many an anxious moment was experienced as the unity of a theorem landscape hung in the balance. In fact, some pictures are so mysteriously off the perpendicular as to suggest the untimely absence of the teacher or the complete collapse of the pupil's nervous system.

In preparing architectural specimens such as castles, churches, bridges, and dwellings, frequent recourse to rulers, compasses, and other drawing instruments was necessary. Every detail had to be very exact. One old lady tells me that an aunt of hers, long since dead, was accustomed to execute the fine, sharp outlines of her velvet architecture with the aid of a hot steel point. In no other way could she have secured the keenness of long lines essential to the unyielding severity of her geometric structures.

When were these paintings on velvet made? Most of them,

mother in 1858 by an old lady who had treasured it from her girlhood days in Vermont. Harriet Lewis Jones of Olean, New York, tells of four paintings on velvet, the work of her grandmother (*1809–1840*), who was educated in a convent school where she was taught both fine sewing and painting. One of the four is a fruit and flower piece, the others are "historical scenes." They probably date from the 1820's. From Hollywood, California, Mrs. William Wirt Stevens writes to tell of a velvet picture, emphasizing a watermelon, painted by her grandmother about 1830–1840. In Athens, Georgia, Miss M. A. Frierson owns three fruit and flower designs painted by Sarah Hancock about 1822.

I may be generous in assuming that the popularity of theorem paintings or any other kind of paintings on velvet outlasted the 1830's. At any rate, the needle found revenge on the briefly popular brush in the advent of the craze for Berlin wool work.

BY GEORGE H. ECKHARDT

The Henry S. Borneman collection of

Pennsylvania-German fracturs

THE ACQUISITION of the Pennsylvania-German *Fraktur Schriften* collection of the late Henry S. Borneman by the Free Library of Philadelphia opens the door to a wider knowledge and appreciation of an American folk art that is unique. These illuminated manuscripts took the form of house-blessings, birth and baptismal certificates, and moral texts. They were displayed in the homes of which they were a part, and therefore were far more than pages of books buried in libraries for the pleasure of the few. They were expressions of the inner thoughts of a people.

The Prodigal Son; 16 by approximately 13 inches.
All illustrations are from the Henry S. Borneman collection
at the Free Library of Philadelphia.

During his long and active life Mr. Borneman collected more than six hundred examples of this art, no two exactly alike. Since he had an intimate understanding of the Pennsylvania German, and an appreciation of art in a broader sense, he was well qualified to create this outstanding collection. Although he published two handsomely illustrated books based upon it (*Pennsylvania German Illuminated Manuscripts*, Pennsylvania German Society, 1937, and *Pennsylvania German Bookplates,* Pennsylvania German Society, 1953), and parts of it were exhibited from time to time, the collection was never before really accessible for study.

Fraktur is a German word and refers to a certain design in Gothic lettering; a type face known as Fraktur, founded upon the old hand-lettering, is still used in printing. *Schriften* means "writings" — hence *Fraktur Schriften* means "writings in a certain design of Gothic lettering." The term is often shortened to simply *Fraktur* —or, in American usage, fractur.

These fracturs of the Pennsylvania Germans are often spoken of as illuminated manuscripts. Now if one wishes to be precise—and technical—an illuminated manuscript is a work written by hand and "illumined" with gold or silver; but today the term may apply to a work in which the text is embellished by ornamentation of the initial letter with bright colors. The decorations may extend to the margin of the paper and take the form of miniatures. Incidentally, "miniature" as used here does not necessarily refer to a painting in small scale. The word comes from the Latin *minium*—a red paint often used in decorating manuscripts.

In the fracturs of Pennsylvania we see an art which flourished in the medieval monasteries of Europe and then suffered an almost total eclipse, emerging as a folk art among a people in a strange land some two centuries later. To understand this we must try to understand the Pennsylvania German, and we must also go back to the early days of the art itself. The question of how an art might remain dormant in a people for two centuries or more and then spring up among them in a new environment may be answered in the words of Sean O'Faolain—"the folk mind is the repository of its own riches." Thoughts and art may be stored and preserved there as well as in libraries and galleries.

The first Germans came to Pennsylvania in 1693, only one year after Penn himself. The migration steadily increased until it reached its height between 1730 and 1750, although it continued until after the Revolution. While the art of illuminating manuscripts in Pennsyl-

Vorschrift (example of writing);
approximately 8 by 13 inches.

Vorschrift;
8 x 13 inches.

vania goes back to 1750 or earlier, it became really widespread in the first third of the nineteenth century.

What manner of people were these Rhine Valley Germans who availed themselves of Penn's invitation to dwell in a land of peace? Basically they sought religious freedom and they found it. They were not all of one sect—there were Mennonites, Amish, Schwenkfelders, and others, each group with its own interpretation of the Scriptures.

The Pennsylvania German was a farmer, passionately fond of the soil. He did not linger in Philadelphia but settled in the rich and fertile regions of Lancaster and adjacent counties. He kept very much to himself and seldom married outside his own sect. He developed a language of his own and made little effort to spread his religious beliefs beyond his own circle. He was peace-loving, industrious, thrifty—and an individualist to the point of sheer stubbornness. His religion taught asceticism and he lived according to strict rules, but his life was robust and lusty. He and his family dined well—so well that his cooking became proverbial. He built solid barns and raised fat cattle. Though his personal garb was drab, he loved color—especially reds and blues. He was a

realist, though there was something of the mystic about him too (and far too much emphasis has been placed upon this side of his character).

The illuminated manuscript was an almost perfect form of art expression for such a people. The religious or moral substance of the text furnished the note of asceticism, and freedom was permitted in the decoration.

The fracturs were done by the people themselves. The colors were often homemade, and the quill pens were cut from the feathers of the barnyard geese; in many instances only the paper was bought.

It is doubtful whether anyone ever received formal training in painting fracturs. Naturally some became more proficient than others, and a "master" who had established a local reputation might paint fracturs for his neighbors for small fees. There is a tradition that one man paid off a mortgage on his farm by illuminating manuscripts; but this would be unusual. More commonly the craft was practiced by schoolmasters and ministers, or some member of the family became proficient and painted fracturs for the others as a labor of love.

The educational value of the fracturs must not be overlooked. They were, in addition to all else, exercises

Baptismal certificate dated 1816;
8 by 10 inches.

Baptismal certificate dated 1823;
8 by 13½ inches.

in calligraphy, yet they represented more than a desire to achieve a skill in handwriting: they were part of the discipline of education itself. Many fracturs are embellished with ornate alphabets reminiscent of the sampler, and in the Borneman collection there are school-books in which the triangles and circles of the geometry lessons are beautifully and ingeniously colored.

The decorative designs used commonly fell into two general classes: birds and flowers, and geometric. Both were often used in the same fractur. The birds and flowers permitted a wide freedom. Much has been said about the symbolism involved, but it was an obvious symbolism: for instance, it takes no stretch of the imagination to understand that the dove represents peace. The tulip is probably the flower most seen. This has been attributed to Oriental influence, but such an attribution is rather far-fetched. The tulip was well known to the Pennsylvania German, the flower is easy to draw, and it makes a pleasant design. The late Henry S. Borneman went very thoroughly into this matter of possible Oriental influence in the fracturs, and dismissed the theory. He was most competent to make such a study because he was familiar with the illuminated manuscripts of the East, and in addition to his fractur collection he had a very fine collection of Korans.

While birds and flowers were freely represented, geometric designs were subject to the rigid discipline of compass and ruler. The folk artist might display unlimited ingenuity in design, but this design was always kept within the mathematical bounds of the geometric rules.

As time went on certain printers in the Pennsylvania-German regions issued printed fracturs in black and white, often with blank spaces for names and dates; these were then hand-colored by individuals. In the collection will be found several examples of the same basic fractur colored by different people.

Aside from their artistic interest, the fracturs at the Free Library of Philadelphia will add greatly to the genealogical record of early Pennsylvania. Under Miss Ellen Schaffer, rare-book librarian, all names, places, and dates mentioned in the collection are being catalogued and cross indexed—a work which will be most valuable. For further study one must go to the Schwenkfelder Library at Pennsburg, Pennsylvania, where the second largest collection will be found.

SHAKER INSPIRATIONAL DRAWINGS

By EDWARD D. ANDREWS

EVER SINCE that time in Manchester, England, about 1772, when the Lord Jesus appeared to the imprisoned Ann Lee, the mill girl and prophetess who became the first leader of the Shaker sect, the "Shaking Quakers," or Believers in Christ's Second Appearing, have been visionists and mystics. The reality of spiritual presences was re-demonstrated when, after Ann's release, a mysterious power protected her and her followers from the clubs and stones of their Lancashire persecutors, and again when she was enabled to confound her accusers by speaking in unknown tongues. Shortly before the little band, seeking freedom of worship, embarked for America in 1774, James Whittaker, Ann's chief disciple, had a vision of the new country, and "saw a large tree, and every leaf thereof shone with such brightness, as made it appear like a burning torch, representing the Church of Christ, which will yet be established in this land" (*Fig. 3*). On the ship Mariah, during a severe storm, two angels were seen standing by the mast assuring the passengers of a safe arrival in the new world; and the first religious dances were learned from visions of angels dancing around the throne of God.

As the Shaker movement spread through New York and

HUNDREDS of the Shaker drawings here discussed — no one knows how many — once existed in the eighteen main branches of the United Society of Believers. Most of those here illustrated, with others, chiefly from New Lebanon, New York, and Hancock, Massachusetts, are in the author's collection. About eighty-five have been documented. The present article is based on an unpublished monograph.

New England, and after the turn of the century into Kentucky, Ohio, and Indiana, the tenets of the faith — celibacy and purity of mind, separation from worldliness and the world, confession of sin, community of goods or "joint interest"—continued to find support and validity through supernatural agency. Leaders were chosen, and their authority sanctioned, by divine revelation. The statutes governing the organization and administration of church order were inspired laws. Visions abounded. In the rapture of sensing the imminence of the holy spirit, diverse "gifts" were received by young and old, and songs and rituals found their strange origin.

Some fifty years after the establishment of the United Society a great revival — known as "Mother Ann's Work," or "Ann's Second Appearing" — broke out among the Shakers, during which such gifts flowered in many remarkable forms. In the spring of 1838, about eight months after the first "manifestations" at the Niskeyuna (New York) colony, messages from the spirit of the prophetess were received at New Lebanon, in the same state, through the medium of chosen "instruments." Speaking in the name of their heavenly parent, these inspired visionists called upon the Believers, in meeting, to return to the true order of the church, to purge out disorders and superfluities, to confess their sins, to mortify the flesh by bowing, reeling, shaking, and kissing one another's feet. It was not long before similar ceremonies were observed in the other seventeen societies. Blessings were bestowed on young and old. Spiritual wine was dispensed "which carried a great evidence of its reality, by the paroxysms of intoxication which it produced, causing those who drank it to stagger and reel, like drunken people." A particular phenomenon was the distribution of spiritual presents, symbolic of the virtues of the Shaker life but bearing the names of material things: gold leaf, books, musical instruments, fruits and flowers, diamonds, numerous articles of ornament, boxes and baskets, implements of hand labor, weapons of war, and sacks full of all kinds of rich treasures. From the instruments, as well as from others subject to the mysterious influences of the revival, proceeded a stream of messages — prophecies, warnings and exhortations — many new dance forms, and hundreds of "gift" or "vision" tunes and songs.

Action was pantomimic, gestures may sometimes have been grotesque, but the emotions which accompanied the bestowal and acceptance of gifts were genuine. When presents or communications were received by the Believers from their "heavenly parents" (Christ and Mother Ann), their "spiritual parents" (Father Joseph Meacham, the American-born organizer of the order; Mother Lucy Wright, his successor as head of the church; Father William Lee, Ann's brother; Father James Whittaker; and other early leaders or biblical prophets), and finally, from their "eternal parents," Almighty God and Holy Mother Wisdom,

FIG. 1 (*above*) — SACRED SHEET. Sent from Holy Mother Wisdom, by her Holy Angel of many signs, for Sister Adah Zillah Potter. Received March 5, 1843. Written March 22, 1843. In the first Order on the Holy Mount (New Lebanon). Instruments, Semantha Fairbanks and Mary Wicks. Design in black ink on white paper, 8 by 13 inches.

FIG. 2 (*right*) — HEART GIFT OR REWARD. The Word of the Holy Heavenly Father. To a child of his Delight, James Goodwin. Inscriptions on both sides, and symbols on one side of white paper. Pen and ink. New Lebanon, 1844.

338

— the illusion in the Shaker mind was absolute and highly dramatic.

For several years the manifestations were ritualistic, behavioristic, spontaneous. In 1840 scribes were chosen to record, in beautifully written hymnals and journals, the songs, testimonies, and messages, but no attempt was made to picture the mystic experiences of the revival until about 1845, when the afflatus itself was beginning to subside. True, Mary Hazzard, an eldress at the church family in New Lebanon, had "pricked"· one of her lovely songs around the border of a leaf design in a hymnal dated 1839. Cryptic "sacred sheets" symbolizing the orderly beauty of heaven (*Fig. 1*) appeared in 1843. The leaf "rewards" — delicately inscribed green paper cutouts representing leaves from the tree of life — were first exchanged in the period 1843-1844, and the pink, yellow or white paper hearts (*Fig. 2*) — where decorative devices such as angels, crowns, swords, doves, and the like make their initial appearance — in 1844. But these tokens of love and merit, in a sense, were tentative forerunners of those designs in which the artist's imagination, hitherto suppressed by prohibitions on all display and ornament, was fully released. The major drawings, covering the years from 1845 to 1859, seem indeed the expression of "emotions recollected in tranquillity," the "remembrance of things past," recalling Proust's contention that there is nothing significant in any occurrence until it is remembered.

These later inspirationals fall into two general groups, not too distinct: those depicting

FIG. 5 (*below*) — A TYPE OF MOTHER HANNAH'S POCKET HANDKERCHIEF. Drawn by Father James for Jane Blanchard. New Lebanon, 1851. Design in colors, 14 by 17 inches. Reference is to Mother Hannah Goodrich, the first leader, "on the female side," at Canterbury and Enfield, New Hampshire, or to Mother Hannah Kendall, who occupied a similar position at the Harvard and Shirley, Massachusetts, communities.

simple floral and arboreal designs and emblems, variously interpreted, usually done in color, with the Tree of Life as a favorite device; and those in which the symbolism is more elaborate and abstract. Floral motifs and plant forms persist in the latter, but do not dominate a carefully planned and often detailed pattern rich with allegorical meanings; some are in color, while others are delicately rendered with a pen in blue, or blue and red inks. There are also two main, though sometimes merging, sources of inspiration: the beauty of nature, as represented in fruits and flowers, arbors, leaves, trees, plants, gardens, fountains, rivers, precious stones, the sun, moon, and stars; and the Scriptures, especially the books of Genesis, Esdras, and Revelation. As to the first, the mystic communion of the Believers with God involved a sensitive kinship with nature, a love of color and form subtly revealed in many ways and now openly expressed. They had built their communities in beautiful places, had "redeemed" the soil with affection, had cultivated plants and flowers for the health of body and spirit. Perhaps, before they had become Shakers, they were familiar with the floral patterns on appliqué or embroidered quilts, hooked rugs, samplers, wall papers, needlepoint, or stencils. Perhaps they adapted their designs from biblical allusions. Whatever the source, the limners turned to the beauty surrounding them for the fittest expression of a perfect immortal world. That the Scriptures furnished an equally rich field of images is apparent from the emblems and legends in many, especially the more complex drawings: the well of Samaria, the ark, "the cup from which the Saviour drank at the well," Abram's altar, the Red Sea, "Sarah of old," Jephtha, the woman of Samaria, shew-bread, and so on. The wine press and vineyard, angels, doves, trumpets, harps, and fountains (a symbol, with the ancient Hebrews, of life-giving power and celestial happiness) were favorite subjects. The sickle, the lamps and candlesticks, the seals, the golden chariots, the pillar of light, "the moon turned to blood," the chart of the heavenly Jerusalem, the cross, the all-seeing eye, the lamb and dove, the bread plant, the fig and weeping willow trees, the Cedar of Paradise, the bower of mulberry trees, may all be traced to the same origin.

However, the meanings ascribed to such emblems were seldom stereotyped. A tree may be

The Tree of Life, all pure and clean
Of God the Fathers planting;
On Zions hill, it firm doth stand,
And well establish'd, by God's hand.
Not like the house, upon the sand,
But firm by heaven's granting.

But it also may represent a celestial plum tree, a cedar of paradise, the "cherry tree brought from spiritual England," a tree bearing manna or "strange fruits," "the gospel union, fruit bearing tree," or a tree of light, comfort, order, virtue, or protection. Similarly, a rose may signify love or chastity, though sometimes it may typify patience, perseverance, or faith. As in the spiritual "gifts" exchanged in meeting, there were balls of light, love, and union; diamonds of peace and comfort; chains of strength and union; boxes or baskets of treasures.

Objects precious and rare in a worldly sense — golden chains, crowns, ornaments, and exotic flowers and foods — served more literally to suggest the wonders and joys of a supernatural world. And when clocks or watches, angels with protective wings outspread, or "a ship of safety," are used the intent is obvious. Yet there was, on the whole, considerable freedom and individuality of expression. Not only in the ascription of emblems, but in the decorative borders of some of the

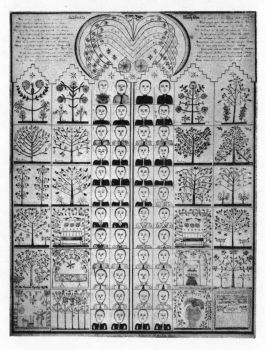

drawings, the free use of color, and the explanatory legends and inscriptions, there is evidence of original and versatile talent. The period in which the drawings were composed was too brief, indeed, to produce a "school."

Most if not all of the inspirationals were done by sisters of the order, though some were dedicated to, and perhaps actually presented to beloved brethren and sisters, to elders and eldresses, and especially to the Ministry or "lead." Apparently the heart, leaf, fan and seal tokens were freely exchanged, but the larger designs, if employed as gifts, were — in accord with the code against ornament and individual privilege — never displayed.

In fact, we cannot be sure whether there was a clear purpose behind their creation. The only allusion in Shaker literature is the following passage in Isaac Young's manuscript history (1857): "There have been many notices to individuals this year past [1843] . . . with many drawings, signs, and figures of objects in the spirit world, with mysterious writings, etc. which will, it is said, at some future time be revealed and explained."

There is a Shaker tradition that the writings and drawings were sometimes automatically controlled or "dictated by a spirit," and in at least one example, a tree design by Hannah Cohoon of Hancock (*Fig. 7*) — notable because the signature appears on the work — the artist testifies that its identity was revealed to her

FIG. 6 (*left*) — FLORAL WREATH. From Father James, Father Joseph, Mother Lucy and Mother Dana for the Ministry at the City of Peace (Hancock), December 4, 1853. Design in colors. 12 inches square.

FIG. 7 (*center*) — TREE OF LIFE. Design in colors. City of Peace (Hancock), July 3, 1854. Seen and painted by Hannah Cohoon. Size of drawing, 18 by 23 inches.

FIG. 8 (*left*) — AN EMBLEM OF THE HEAVENLY SPHERE. A Gift from Mother Ann, Given January, 1854. Dictated by the Prophetess Deborah. (Judg. iv) Hancock community. Design in colors, 19 by 24 inches. Forty-eight "saints in order" are represented, beginning with Mother Ann, Father William, and the Savior, and including biblical figures and Christopher Columbus.

by Mother Ann's moving the hand of a medium "to write twice over, Your Tree is the Tree of Life." The inspirationals were the product of a profoundly moving experience and it may be argued that the forces of spiritualism unlocked the doors of the subconscious Shaker mind, sanctioning an open expression of human desires and the vicarious enjoyment of the same. Unused to games or recreation, the Believers tossed to one another glistening "spheres of love." Opposed to instrumental music, they listened with rapture to spiritual harps, to shining trumpets, to the "holy musical instrument of God" with its "fifteen connecting instruments." Intolerant of jewelry, they imagined themselves adorned with chains of pure gold, with diamonds, pearls, amethysts, and sapphires, with golden finger rings and costly gems. Living in plain dwellings, they envisaged the ornamental structures of heaven. Used to the simplest food, they relished the "sweet scented manna" and the exotic fruits of the tree of life. Long accustomed to utensils of pewter, wood, and stoneware, they found satisfaction, during their symbolic sacraments, in drinking from silver cups and eating from golden bowls. Denying the state and refusing to bear arms, they thrilled to the waving of flags, and buckled upon themselves swords, breastplates, and spiritual armor. On sheets of gold and on rolls in radiant colors were the heavenly messages delivered. Humbly laboring without wage or material reward, the Believers welcomed the mantles, crowns, and wreaths spiritually bestowed, the golden sacks of comfort, the golden chariots ready to take them to their eternal home. Was it not as a compensation for their own plain apparel that the Shakers, before marching to their hill-top festivals, joyfully clothed themselves in the garments of the blessed?

Though an element of compensation may have entered into the content, the control of form and precision of execution (involving in some instances the aid of a compass, ruled lines, and preliminary sketches) are evidence of deliberate creation, far removed from the crude scrawls and indeterminate pictures accepted as automatic. The "vision" of the instrument was not immediately committed to paper,

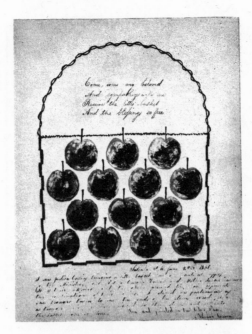

FIG. 9 — FRUIT DESIGN. "Seen and painted in the City of Peace [Hancock] by Hannah Cohoon." Inscription: "I saw Judith Collins bringing a little basket full of beautiful apples for the Ministry, from Brother Calvin Harlow and Mother Sarah Harrison. It is their blessing and the chain around the bail represents the combination of their blessing. I noticed in particular as she brought them to me the ends of the stems looked fresh as though they were just picked by the stems and set into the basket one by one." (Brother Calvin and Mother Sarah were the first "lead" at Hancock.) In colors. Date, 1856.

FIG. 10 (below) — TREE OF COMFORT. "A Gift from Mother Ann, August, 1859, to Eldress Eunice [Hastings], with the Heavenly Fr. and holy Mother's blessing." Design in colors. Hancock.

nor always drawn by the one who had the vision or idea. Though the Shakers themselves have been noncommittal, and in some cases have repudiated the testimonies of the period and disposed of the drawings, there is evidence that those members of the order with a natural talent for drawing and penmanship were encouraged to render in graphic form, as a means of promoting the afflatus, the experiences which were common to the whole membership. Like the songs and dances, the messages from the instruments and other gifts, they thus served an educative purpose. This view receives confirmation in an account of a mountain meeting in which the Savior, speaking through an instrument, declares: "I would instruct those that do not clearly understand the work of God, by means and ways that ye may understand, comparing heavenly and divine things to the similitudes of earth." And again, in one of the remarkable books published at the time, the author, Philemon Stewart, writes: "All the presents . . . have been sent forth in this degree or nearness and semblance of material things that do exist on earth, that you might be better able to appreciate in lively colors, and thrilling sensations, the real adornings and beauties of the spiritual world, or the abodes of the righteous, in the paradise of God."

However, if such were the purpose of the drawings, probably not all of them were thus employed. With the possible exception of the small gifts, they received little publicity; few Believers at the time, or since, knew of their existence. That they were sanctioned by the ruling order, the ministry, is obvious; but in retrospect they seem neither automatic nor didactic expressions, but rather purely creative compositions produced by selected individuals as a reaction to an experience which was personal, but which at the same time reflected the spiritual outlook of the whole community. As such the drawings should properly be considered a religious and a true folk art.

In the preface to a book which contains an account of the manifestations at Canterbury, New Hampshire, the Shaker author found it fitting to quote the following lines from Lamartine:

Beauty's the form of things unseen,
Save to the soul's desire.

COUNTERATTACK

archenemy

PAUL HOBLIN

MINNEAPOLIS

Darby Creek
A division of Lerner Publishing Group, Inc.
241 First Avenue North
Minneapolis, MN 55401 U.S.A.

Website address: www.lernerbooks.com

The images in this book are used with the permission of:
Front cover: © Erik Isakson/Blend Images/CORBIS.
iStockphoto.com/Ermin Gutenberger, (stadium lights).

Main body text set in Janson Text 12/17.5.
Typeface provided by Adobe Systems.

Library of Congress Cataloging-in-Publications Data

Hoblin, Paul.
        Arch enemy / by Paul Hoblin.
            p.   cm. — (Counterattack)
        ISBN 978–1–4677–0306–2 (lib. bdg. : alk. paper)
        [1. Soccer—Fiction. 2. Toleration—Fiction.
    3. Lesbians—Fiction.] I. Title.
    PZ7.H653Ar 2013
    [Fic]—dc23   2012022445

Manufactured in the United States of America
1 – BP – 12/31/12

▦ ▦ ▦

FOR MY FRIENDS. AND, IT GOES
WITHOUT SAYING, FOR MKTK.

"a winner is that person who gets up one more time than she is knocked down."

■ ■ ■

MIA HAMM

chapter 1

I f you ask me, the hardest part about playing high school soccer is *not* playing high school soccer.

Honestly, if I had a choice, I'd never leave the soccer field. I'd roll out a sleeping bag and snooze right on the grass. If it rained, I'd move the bag under the bleachers.

But that's the thing: I *don't* have a choice. Everyone else chooses for me. The state athletic association. My teachers. Coach Berg.

Even my awesome parents and supersweet teammates. Ever since last year, when Mr. Lenders caught me juggling a ball while I was supposed to be in class so many times that he suspended me for a whole school week, everyone has kept a really close eye on me.

"You been going to all your classes, Williams?" Coach Berg will say. (That's me— Williams. Addie Williams.)

"Need help studying for your Algebra II test, Addie?" a teammate will ask.

"Remember, Addie," my parents like to remind me, "you're a student first, an athlete second."

They're all worried that I'm going to get suspended a second time—but they shouldn't be. Because of the suspension, I missed two games last year, and there's no way I'm ever letting that happen again.

Still, it's not easy sitting in a desk when I could be galloping across the soccer field— especially on days like today.

Game days.

Today is Fraser High's fourth game of the season, which means I've spent the entire school day waiting for the final bell to ring. When it does, I practically leap out from my desk and bolt for the hallway. As I weave through the crowd, I imagine it's filled with my opponents. I pretend there's a ball at my feet as I sidestep a sophomore and juke out a junior. The kids moving in the same direction as me are my teammates, and I guide the invisible ball toward one of them as I open the door to the locker room. Soon I'll be in my uniform and headed for the field.

Except when I open my locker, I find a note on top of my uniform shorts:

Dear Addie,
You suck at soccer and life. Do us all a favor and quit.
Sincerely,
Coach Berg

chapter 2

would feel more freaked about the letter if it were actually from Coach Berg.

But it obviously isn't.

For one thing, it's written in pink ink. The letters are loopy. There's no way Coach Berg's handwriting looks like this.

Besides, I already know who wrote the letter. It's the same girl who wrote me dozens of letters last spring—the same girl who used to call me her best friend.

Eva Riley.

Clearly, she *wants* me to know she sent the letter. If she didn't, she would have disguised her handwriting or used a different pen.

She may have signed *Coach Berg*, but she knew I'd figure it out. Because over the last few weeks, it's become clear that she's no longer wants to be my best friend.

She wants to be my archenemy.

chapter 3

he first note I ever got from Eva was during the last day of my suspension. It just so happened to be the last game of the season. That's right—I got suspended during the *playoffs*. I'd been cutting class all spring. But Mr. Lenders, hall monitor extraordinaire, didn't do anything about it until I was preparing to play the most important games of my career.

While my team was losing on a neutral

field, I was standing on our home field, passing the ball back and forth with Belle.

Belle, by the way, is my dog. She's a Brittany spaniel, and she's way better than your average dog. Remember Air Bud, the sports star-slash-retriever? Belle's like a real-life version of him. Whenever I kick the ball to her, she kicks it right back to me.

Okay, *kicks* might be a stretch. More like *nudges*. She pushes the ball forward, inch by inch, with her nose. Pretty impressive, I think, for a dog.

Still, it takes forever for Belle to return my pass, and my mind tends to wander. As I watched her nudging the ball that day, I thought about the game I was missing and couldn't help feeling sorry for myself. I looked at the empty bleachers and imagined all the fans who were probably cheering Fraser High at that very moment. I looked across the empty field and imagined all my Copperheads teammates racing from one end to the other.

My gaze returned to Belle. She stood perfectly still, one paw raised. Her head was turned up and away from me. A growl came from deep in her throat.

I turned my own head just in time to see another dog—a beagle—charging toward us. It looked like it was coming straight for me with its tongue flopping out of its mouth. But when it was only a few feet away, Belle started yelping at it, and it changed course. As the beagle veered toward Belle, a piece of paper flew out of its collar and fluttered to the ground.

Belle yelped in alarm, then flipped around and pounced on the beagle. They continued growling and yelping as they rolled around with their teeth bared. I closed the gap and started yelling, "No! Get away! Bad dog! Get away!"

By then, I was in front of Belle. I lifted my right leg and got ready to stomp on the beagle. Did I mention I was wearing my cleats? My entire uniform, in fact. If I couldn't play on the team, at least I could dress like my teammates. One good stomp, I thought, would send this maniac dog running.

"Skittles, come!"

I didn't recognize the voice, but the beagle seemed to. She stepped away from Belle and trotted past me. A girl stood in the corner of the field and called for her dog again, "Come on, Skittles! That's a good girl!"

She crouched down, and the dog jumped into her arms. Standing up, she headed my way, her beagle squirming and wiggling but unable to get free. The girl wore a spring dress and strappy heels. With each step, one heel or the other sunk into the ground. When the girl was a few feet from me, she crouched again. I thought she was going to set the dog down, but she didn't. Instead, she picked up the piece of notebook paper on the ground.

"Sorry about that," she said to me. "Skittles was supposed to deliver this note,"— she unfolded the paper for me to read—"but I guess she found her own friend to play with instead."

In big, pink, bubbly letters, the note said, "Wanna play soccer?"

"Not sure I'd call what your dog was doing

playing," I said.

"She's totally harmless, I swear."

I must have made a face like I didn't believe her because the girl said, "Besides, your dog totally liked it."

I looked at her skeptically. "My dog's always been more of a cuddler than a fighter."

"All dogs are fighters," the girl said. "Look."

Sure enough, Belle was sitting below the girl's arms, growling and standing up on her hind legs to paw at Skittles. The girl lowered Skittles to the ground and Belle pounced. Within a few seconds, the dogs were rolling around again and growling. Now that I wasn't so freaked, I could tell that it was happy growling.

"I'm Eva," the girl said. "Just arrived in town, like a second ago." She was short, with dark hair and plenty of makeup. "My parents are setting up the house. They wanted me to get Skittles out of their hair." We were standing close enough that I could see some freckles behind the concealer she'd caked on her face. She interrupted my thoughts, "Miss the bus to your game or something?"

"Something like that," I said. I didn't feel like talking about my suspension.

"I know—the bus left as you were strapping on those calves. Is that it?" She gestured toward my legs.

That's another thing I don't think I mentioned: I have huge calf muscles. Seriously. I got them from my dad, who was an Olympic-hopeful ski jumper. For most of my life, I thought my calves were really freakish. But when I realized I could jump higher than everybody else on the soccer field and hit headers to my teammates, I changed my mind about my calves. I think they're awesome now—like a superpower. Eva seemed to agree.

"I mean, those things are amazing," she said.

"I do what I can," I said.

We looked at each other for a second, both of us laughing. "I'm glad you missed the bus," she said.

"Yeah?" I asked.

"Now you can play soccer with me instead."

"In those?" I pointed to her heels.

"I've got my soccer bag." She gestured to the lumpy, black duffel bag lying in the grass a few feet away. "Mom and Dad want to check out the church down the block soon, but I'm sure they can wait a little while for me. After all," she said, showing me her best pouty face, "they don't want their daughter to be the new kid with no friends, do they?" She was already walking over to her soccer bag, her heels sinking. Then she stopped and turned around. "Besides, there's Skittles's social life to consider too."

chapter 4

I t's weird to think that Eva and I might have never become best friends if she hadn't stopped by the field that day. We might have never spent all summer together, playing soccer and hanging at each other's houses.

We might have never become archenemies.

Really, the more I think about it, the more I wish Eva's parents had brought her to church like they wanted to. We might have never become best friends, but at least we'd be on speaking terms.

As it is, we played the first three games of this new season without saying a word to each other—which is pretty incredible, considering we play across from each other on defense. And considering we used to talk nonstop.

During summer league, we even came up with a code. We told each other all the usual stuff, of course: *Get back!* and *Go left!* and *Line!* and *Man on!* But we also had two phrases of our own.

Hey-o! was one of them and meant, "I'm not open, so you shouldn't even bother looking my way."

Whoop! was the other and meant the opposite: "I'm wide open on the other side of the field if you need any help."

We heard an old lady using these phrases on the Fourth of July. She was sitting next to us on a hillside. Every time a new firework exploded across the sky, she'd yell, "Hey-o!" or "Whoop!" at the top of her lungs. She was being completely serious, so it would have been really mean to laugh at her—but that we couldn't laugh out loud just made it funnier. She yelled other stuff too, such as, "Awesome blossom!" and every time she yelled, she leaned her chair back like she was trying to get a better view of the sky. During the grand finale, she leaned back too far and fell flat on her back. We helped her up and made sure she was okay, then laughed all the way back to Eva's house. We decided then and there that we were going to find a way to use all the lady's sayings on the soccer field.

Unfortunately, we still had a bunch of sayings left to use by the middle of fall when we stopped talking to each other completely.

chapter 5

I t's spring now. We're playing the fourth game of the season, and Eva and I still haven't said a single thing to each other. We're playing Cardinal Creek, who luckily aren't very good, because Eva and I have been really careless on defense all game. Twice we've let a Cardinal Creek player get behind us with only a bad pass bailing us out.

Coach Berg is having a fit on the sidelines. "Communicate!" he keeps yelling. "Are you trying to cost us a goal?"

"*Ask Eva!*" I want to shout. After all, she's the one who stopped talking to me first. But I don't. I don't see what good it would do. Coach Berg views the defense as one unit— one player's mistake is everyone's mistake. If I blamed Eva, Coach would just tell me to take responsibility for myself.

Besides, if I don't blame her, maybe she'll finally forgive me.

"Addie!" shouts Alyssa Duncan, our goalie. "Take the ball!"

At least *she's* still talking to me.

I take two aggressive steps forward and block a Cardinal Creek player's pass with my body. I push the ball past the oncoming opponent and keep pushing it toward midfield. It's an aggressive move, and as I enter the crowd of other players, I wonder if it's too aggressive. The Cardinal Creek players are closing in fast. If I'm going to get rid of the ball, I need to do it quickly.

"Whoop!"

I can't believe it. Just when I thought Eva

and I might never talk again, there she is, on the other side of the field, ready to save the day.

"Whoop!" she says again.

If you need any help, she's telling me, *I'm wide open.*

She and I performed this maneuver so many times over the summer that I don't even need to look: I know exactly where she'll be. I send a big, field-switching pass and watch the ball soar over the Cardinal Creek players' heads toward the empty space on the other side of the field. Of course, the space won't be empty for long. By the time the ball hits the grass, Eva's foot will be there to stop it. Then it will be her turn to jump-start an attack.

Except she never shows up. The space stays empty. The ball lands and bounces out of play.

"Williams!" Coach yells. "Get your head in the game!"

chapter 6

"**P**ut that one front and center," Eva told me.

This was late last spring, in her bedroom. I was helping her finish moving in. Specifically, I was helping her tape tons of crinkly magazine pictures to her walls and ceiling. Most of the pictures were of male soccer players or models posing shirtless in soccer shorts and cleats.

Eva called them her soccer studs.

Her room was on the top floor of an old house, which meant the ceiling was also the roof. It slanted from maybe twelve feet high almost to the floor. The bottom half had already been covered with six packs, but Eva wasn't tall enough to reach any higher.

That's where I came in. It was my job to stand on her bed and put up the rest of the soccer studs.

"Right here?" I asked.

"Let me see," she said. She flopped down on her bed, and I almost lost my balance. Then she tilted her head to the side and squinted, mulling over the placement of the picture. "Perfect," she finally said. "Too bad I can't sleep with my eyes open, huh?"

I looked at the picture. Up close, the crinkles looked like wrinkles. "Ummm, yeah. I guess so." Suddenly I wanted to change the subject, so I hopped off her bed and cracked open a window. It was almost summer and getting hotter every day, but there was still a nice breeze. It felt good inhaling the fresh air. Like Eva, who had changed without showering into a spaghetti-strapped shirt and flowered skirt after going for a run with me, the room smelled of perspiration and perfume.

As I took another deep breath, I heard a series of growls and yelps. "Hope Belle and Skittles are still getting along," I said.

"Are you kidding?" Eva said. "They're BFF. Just listen to them down there."

No matter how many times Eva insisted that they were only play fighting, the dogs' roughhousing made me nervous—even though I knew she was right. Despite all the biting, neither had ever broken the other's skin.

"Maybe we should bring them up here," I said.

"No way," Eva said. "You'll never get out of here alive."

"What?"

"Skittles hates when people leave her. When someone tries to leave a room that she's in, she doesn't let them."

I still didn't get it.

"She goes right for the person's ankles and won't let go," Eva said.

"Yikes."

"It's kind of endearing, if you think about it. You know that she loves people that much."

I can't say I drew the same conclusion. "So you can never bring her in the house?"

"Only when strangers are here. For some reason, she doesn't bite family members. Maybe she trusts that we're coming back." Eva bit her lip and looked away, thinking about what she just said. "Of course, you're not exactly a stranger, so maybe we could bring her inside and see what happens."

I imagined Skittles gnawing away at my leg. "Maybe some other time," I said. "When she gets to know me a little better."

Eva nodded and then went back to the task at hand. She stuck pieces of tape on the back of the picture she was holding and pointed to another bare patch of ceiling. I took the picture from her and stepped on the bed.

"Here?" I asked.

"Yes, please," she said, licking her lips.

"Eva—time to go!"

It was her dad's voice.

Eva rolled over, grabbed the phone on her side table, and checked the time. "Yikes." She turned her head and yelled, "Coming!"

"Where are you going?" I asked.

"Church," Eva sighed.

"You go to church on Thursday?"

Addie nodded. "And Friday and Saturday and Sunday and Monday and Tuesday and Wednesday."

It had never occurred to me that the church was even open on weekdays. For the last couple years, my family hadn't even gone on Sundays.

"Wanna come?" Eva asked.

"Think I'd rather pass the soccer ball with Belle," I said.

Eva bent her knees and got up like she was doing a sit-up. "No fair," she said. "You'll be playing soccer while I'm yawning in a pew." She picked up the stack of studs. "Will you at least do me a favor?" she asked.

"What?"

"Before you leave, will you finish putting these pictures up? Otherwise, I'll have to ask my dad to help, which would be totally weird."

"As weird as me being here alone in your house?"

"Why is that weird? Mi casa es su casa." She held out the pile of pictures.

"How am I supposed to lock up when I leave?"

"Don't worry about it," she said. "We leave our house unlocked all the time. Mom and Dad say a community is a neighborhood that keeps its doors open."

I didn't know what to say to that, so I stopped arguing and took the pictures.

"Eva!"

This time it was her mother's voice.

"I said I'm coming!" Eva hollered. She brushed past me, and I got another whiff of her. When she got to the door, she turned back toward me. "Thanks, Addie," she said and closed the door behind her. A few seconds later, the door opened again. "Feel free to take a picture home with you. Any soccer stud your heart desires."

She waved her hand across the room, said,

"See ya," and closed the door again.

I scanned the wall and the stack of pictures in my hands—but I didn't take a soccer stud. I took a soccer babe. It was an action shot. The model was just about to kick the ball. She had on a sports bra but no jersey. I didn't find the picture on the walls or in the stack. I hadn't even noticed it until the breeze from the open window sent the picture fluttering through the air. Where had it come from? The top of a dresser? Under her bed?

In any case, I figured she wouldn't miss it much, so I folded it neatly and stuffed it into my soccer bag.

chapter 7

Our fifth game of the season comes three days after my whiffed pass to Eva against Cardinal Creek. I spend each day in between trying to convince myself she didn't intentionally sabotage me.

Yes, she's been mean to me ever since last fall.

Yes, she wants me off the team.

Yes, she said, "Whoop!" when she wasn't actually open.

Until now, she's never tried to sabotage me *during a game*. Because doing that is as bad for her as it is for me. Worse, it's bad for the team.

So maybe, I think, she just got the code wrong. Maybe she mixed up "Whoop!" and "Hey-o!"

Right.

At least, she finally spoke to me during a game.

And she kept talking to me during the next couple practices too. Then again, Coach made her. He kept shouting things like, "I can't hear you, Riley!" and "Speak up, Williams!" I think the only reason he isn't going to bench us is because Fraser still managed to beat Cardinal Creek.

Whatever his reasons, I know Eva well enough to know she'll do just about anything to stay on the field. So will I.

░░ ░░ ░░

In any case, the only thing worse than Eva not talking to me might be Eva talking *too much*.

We're playing Ironwood today. Over the roar of their fans, I can hear Eva yelling at me again for no reason. She's spent the whole game barking orders and reminders at me. She tells me to watch the ball and to pay attention even though I'm already doing both of those things. A couple times, as I'm about to clear the ball by booting it up the field, she shouts, "I'm *not* open, Addie," as if I need to be reminded not to pass the ball to a guarded player. Another time, she simply tells me to "Pass it!" just as I'm doing exactly that. Toward the end of the game, an Ironwood player tries to lob the ball into the penalty area. I camp under the pass, ready to spring into the air with my superhero calves and head the ball safely away from our end of the field. Just as I'm about to launch, Eva says, "Get it, Addie!"

Her comments might seem harmless, but they're super annoying. Especially the way she says them—like I need to be reminded how to play soccer. Like soccer isn't my life and isn't as natural to me as breathing or blinking.

They're the kind of comments neither of us would have dreamed of making during the summer.

Back then, we talked in code. Back then, we trusted each other completely.

chapter 3

Trust must have had something to do with why I found myself in front of New Hope Church on a Wednesday night in July. Eva and I had been juggling the ball in her yard when she said she knew a place with more room. It turned out she was talking about the church lawn.

We tied Belle and Skittles by their leashes to a tree and practiced yelling, "Whoop!" and passing to each other. After a few minutes, people in nice clothes began shuffling up the sidewalk. Two of those people were her parents. "There you are, Eva," her mom said. "I hope you brought a change of clothes."

"Yes, mother," Eva said, clearly annoyed.

"Well," her dad said, "you better go use the restroom to change. The service starts in a few minutes."

Once again, I'd forgotten all about church on weekdays.

"*Okay*, dad," Eva said.

I watched her parents pass the tall pillars at the front of the church. When I turned back to Eva, I saw her pulling a summer dress out of her soccer bag.

"You knew church was about to start, didn't you?" I asked.

She grinned guiltily and then pulled the dress over her head. "Thought it might be less boring if I went with a friend."

"I'm not really a churchgoer," I said.

"Oh, c'mon." She was still wearing her shirt and shorts under her dress. "It'll be fun. Trust me."

There was that word again. Trust.

Of course, I didn't trust her—not about this. I hadn't been to New Hope in years, but the last time I was there, it definitely wasn't fun.

And yet, there I was anyway—sitting with Eva in the balcony of the church, my legs sticking to the pew, and hoping no one would recognize me. It wasn't just sweat that made me uncomfortable or that I was still wearing athletic clothes. It was the memory of my mother storming out of this church and dragging me with her. It was the sound of Pastor Meyer's voice, then and now.

That's when I heard a sound I wasn't expecting.

Giggling.

Eva's giggling.

She had her makeup compact open. I looked back at the pastor and saw him squinting. That's when I realized what she was doing. The last sunlight of the day was shining through the stained glass windows, and Eva was using the mirror in her compact to redirect it toward the altar.

Into Pastor Meyer's face.

The pastor squinted and blocked the light with a forearm as the congregation turned their heads and followed the beam of light to the back of the church. Eva's parents were sitting several rows up. They were the first ones to locate the light's source. Maybe Eva had pulled this stunt before. They swiped their hands across their throats, the universal sign for *Cut it out*!

By the time Eva closed the compact, the whole congregation was glaring at her—and I didn't blame them. But that doesn't mean I joined them. I giggled with Eva.

Eva had been right. Church really *could* be fun.

Except it was weird. Afterward, Eva was no longer in a laughing mood. Maybe her parents had scolded her. Or maybe it was because of something I said.

"You went to church so much," I said to her over the phone. "I was worried you were like super religious."

There was a pause.

"I *am* super religious," Eva said. "Why would you say I'm not?"

"I just thought—you know, because of the prank you pulled—"

"Just because the pastor is boring doesn't mean I don't believe what he says."

Like I said—it was weird. At church, she'd been laughing. But she had turned deadly serious.

I changed the subject. "We still playing soccer tomorrow?"

"Whoop!" Eva said.

chapter 9

A couple hours after the Ironwood game, I'm in my bedroom, juggling my soccer ball. I should be happy. We won the game, and this time I didn't have any major screwups.

Eva may have been annoying, but annoying is better than nasty. I'll take what I can get.

Yeah—happy. That's what I should be. So why aren't I?

As I'm thinking all this, I try to keep the

ball in the air with my feet and thighs. My eyes are fixed on the ball as it drops onto the laces of my left cleat. Belle is on my bed, her eyes moving up and down with the ball too.

Mom took me out to eat after the game and asked why I don't hang out with Eva anymore. I lied and told her that I'd been too busy studying to worry about my social life. She was impressed. Somehow or other, she blames last year's suspension on my grades. No matter how many times I remind her that I was suspended for cutting class, not failing it, she still blames my classroom performance. It's weird because I'm not that bad of a student. I mean, I'm not pulling As out of my pockets, but I get a lot of Bs and Cs.

I felt bad lying to my mom about why I don't hang out with Eva anymore, but I didn't have a choice. If I had listed all the things Eva's been doing to me, Mom would've made a huge deal about it. So would my teammates, come to think of it. If Mom did know the whole situation, she'd try to convince me to tell Coach and anyone else who could help.

She'd have told me to take a stand against injustice. Mom's a social activist. So for her, there's no issue that isn't worth fighting for.

That's what she was doing three years ago when she left the church: fighting on my behalf. The pastor at New Hope said that two girls liking each other *that way* was a sin—the word he used was *abomination*. Mom dragged me out of the church pew and never brought me back. For a while, we experimented with a few other churches in neighboring towns. Some were more welcoming, but eventually, we just stopped going altogether.

The stuff with church didn't end there, either. Mom wrote a letter to the editor of *Fraser Daily*, our local newspaper. It said the Pastor Meyer should either quit being hateful or quit his job. She suggested she might be able to sue him—which was a bluff, she told me later—and things just got uglier from there.

I'm really grateful for what she did for a couple of reasons. It was her way of telling me I had no reason to feel ashamed. And it ended up being a chance for lots of other people to tell me the same thing—including my dad, although I already knew he was proud of me. My teammates too, who called a team meeting to tell me that they would always have my back.

Still, the whole thing was *really* public— too public. I'm not like my mom. I don't need to fix things all the time. The only place where I *do* like to take a stand is on the soccer field. And the only issue I like to stand against is the other team scoring on the Copperheads. By the time Eva arrived last spring, the controversy had pretty much vanished, and my life was finally just about soccer again. Which is how I want to keep it.

"How you doing, Addie?" my dad asks from the doorway. His voice is so calm and quiet that I'm hardly startled at all. If Mom had said my name, my soccer ball probably would have went flying into a lampshade or out my window and into the street. Instead, I bump it into the air one more time with my knee and catch it.

"Hey, Dad."

He's standing in the doorframe, sipping from a mug of hot chocolate. This is as far as he's going to come, I know, unless I invite him into my room. He's really good about not invading my privacy. Belle hops off the bed, crosses my room, and presses her body against Dad's leg. She loves the guy.

"I saw you at the game tonight . . ." he says. I can tell he's really concerned. Not because of the tone of his voice but because of his calves. I can see them bulging underneath his wind pants as he rocks from toe to heel. This is a sure sign he's tense. We laugh about his "tell" all the time. He says it's a good thing cards are played at a table. Otherwise, he'd never get away with bluffing. He must not want me to know he's concerned, though, because he stops rocking and crouches down to pet Belle. "Anything you want to talk about?"

Unlike my mom, who usually works really long hours, my dad's a manager at Sportsville, a local equipment shop, and his hours are pretty flexible. When I look up to the bleachers during my games, I can usually spot him sitting somewhere near the middle, watching closely. He's not a soccer expert, but he *is* a great athlete, so I know he can tell whenever something isn't right on the field. I also know he'll never push me into talking about anything if I don't want to.

He takes another sip of hot chocolate, which is his favorite drink, even though it's almost always really hot in North Carolina and hot chocolate seems like just about the worst beverage choice in the world. I asked him about it once, and he said it reminded him of sitting in the lodge after ski jumping—which strikes me now as really sad.

"Why'd you give up ski jumping?" I ask.

The question might seem out of the blue, but it's not. I've been asking him this exact question for years, and each time he gives me the same answer: "Because I fell in love with your mother. There's nothing wrong with having two loves, Addie—but sometimes you have to choose one over the other."

Usually that answer is enough for me, but

today I want to know more. "So Mom made you move to North Carolina?"

"She didn't make me, but I knew that's what she wanted."

Fraser is my mom's hometown, but it's never made much sense to me that she wanted to return after college. It's not like she has tons of friends or even family here. When she's fighting against yet another injustice, it can even feel like everybody here is her enemy.

"Why'd she want to come back here?"

"You'll have to ask your mother that," Dad says. "But it's always suited me just fine."

Unlike my mother, who has dark brown skin, Dad's skin is pasty, freckled, and burns in a matter of minutes. Still, somehow he seems to fit in better than she does.

"Don't you ever regret giving up something you loved so much?" I ask.

"Sure. But not for very long. I may have loved ski jumping, but I love your mom more. You're not too bad either," he says, smiling.

I smile too. "Gee, thanks, Dad."

"If you need to talk about anything, just let

me know, okay?"

"Okay."

Dad pats Belle on the top of the head and steps back into the hall.

A few moments later, a crumpled object flies through the open window and lands at my feet. I pick it up and unfold it. It's a magazine picture—the same picture I took from Eva's room last summer. In pink ink, Eva has drawn a speech bubble next to the soccer babe's mouth.

"Quit staring at me, perv!" the soccer babe says to me.

chapter 10

I returned the picture of the soccer babe to Eva around the end of July.

Actually, I wasn't the one who returned it. Skittles did.

She and Belle were in Eva's room with the two of us—a situation that was still pretty recent. A couple weeks earlier, Eva had brought her dog into the house for the first time while I was there too, just when I was about to leave. It was a test, Eva explained.

If Skittles didn't try to bite me, then she no longer considered me a stranger. Eva assured me she had a good grip on her dog's collar, but I still hustled for the door. I liked my ankles how they were—without any dog teeth attached to them. Luckily, Skittles didn't lunge for me or act distressed in any way. "You come here so often," Eva said, "she probably thinks you're family. Either that or she's intimidated by your calf muscles."

Anyway, the four of us—two people, two canines—were in Eva's room when Skittles stuck her nose into the unzipped side pocket of my soccer bag.

"Skittles!" Eva yelled.

The beagle took her snout from my bag and backed away, opening and closing her jaw.

Eva grabbed her tail, reeled her in, and pried open Skittles's jaw. She pulled out a ball of crinkly paper. "What's this?" she asked, unfolding the picture.

I took a look at the picture and remembered. "It's just—earlier this summer you told me to take a picture, and—"

Eva interrupted me. "Where did you find this?"

"In here. It was—"

"You shouldn't have taken it," she interrupted. She sounded really mad.

"Sorry. I just—"

"You were supposed to take one of *those*," she said, pointing to her ceiling of studs.

"I . . . I didn't want to."

Eva's mouth was open, but she didn't say anything for what felt like a long time.

"Look, Eva," I continued, "maybe I should have told you earlier—it's really not a big deal—but I'm not into what's in those pictures. Because—because I like what's in *this* picture . . . you know?" I nodded my head at the soccer babe.

When she didn't reply, I thought maybe I shouldn't have said anything. I thought about Pastor Meyer and how Eva said she agreed with the stuff he said. I thought that maybe we weren't close friends after all, not really, even if Eva kept saying we were. If we were truly friends, I'd be able to tell her this, wouldn't I?

All the sudden it was my turn to be mad. I wondered if this was how Mom felt when fighting for one of her social causes.

I focused my fury on Eva, ready to plead my case. That's when I realized her cheeks were no longer red. Instead, she was crying. And smiling.

I didn't know what to think.

"Me too," she finally said. She wiped away a tear and smudged her eyeliner.

"Yeah?"

She nodded her head and rubbed her eyes some more. "I just wasn't sure if anyone else around here would get it," she said.

We smiled at each other for a while, and then she went to her bedside table and pulled open the drawer. When she spun back around, she had four pieces of tape dangling from her fingers. "Hold this," she said and handed me the picture.

She put the tape on the back corners of the picture and then pointed me to one of the few remaining bare spots on the ceiling.

chapter 11

When the balled-up soccer babe landed in my room, I went to the window in time to see Eva sprinting away in a sundress and thought maybe enough was enough. Maybe it was finally time to talk to Coach or my parents to turn her in. Maybe I had no choice. She'd been harassing me for months, and I wasn't sure I could take it any longer.

But for some reason, I couldn't—not when I thought about her running away in that dress. There was something so pathetic about it, so desperate. It reminded me of late August, which was the last time I saw her running away. She was trying to hurt me that evening, I knew, because I had hurt her back then.

▦　▦　▦

Our sixth game of the season is away at Woodvine. We play them twice a year, and they're a way better team at home. Some teams are like that—as if you're getting two different teams depending on where you play them.

Woodvine's stadium is actually really cool. It's set into a hillside and feels like you're playing inside a bowl. It also feels like Woodvine's fans are sitting way closer than fans at our stadium. All their chants are way louder. Way meaner too.

Woodvine's athletic director must have lost the memo about student conduct because the fans are ruthless today. Boos rain down on us during the entire game. So do insults—

many of them pretty creative. When Dayton Frey fails to control a pass and turns it over to Woodvine, the fans chant, "club foot!" and keep chanting it anytime Dayton touches the ball. When Coach subs out Elise Heisel, one of our weaker players, the fans chant, "Forced retirement!"

I feel sorry for Elise, but the truth is that this is really fun. Nothing fires me up more than opposing fans. Besides, it's hard to dwell on Eva's constant comments when I can hardly hear them—and when the Woodvine fans' comments are way more brutal.

With only a few minutes left against Woodvine, I'm pretty sure that not turning Eva in was the right decision. I can handle her antics as long as I get to play in games like this.

Especially when she plays this well. We're winning 1–0, and we have Eva to thank for the lead. She's been racing around all over the place.

We're in the closing minutes when Woodvine invades our side of the field for the last time. The ball is to my right and glued to a Woodvine forward's foot.

"Mark her, Faith!" yells Alyssa, our goalie, and Faith Patel moves in to do just that. Except before she gets there, she stumbles, and all of a sudden, there's no one between the Woodvine forward and the goal box. She pushes the ball ahead of her, and Alyssa has to make a decision to back up or come out of the goal in a hurry. As always, Alyssa's decisive— she bursts out of the goal and pounces on the forward. She's too late though. The forward has just enough time to chip the ball over her outstretched hands.

I watch the shot floating toward the goal, and there's nothing I can do about it. I'm too far away. In less than a second, Woodvine will be celebrating a game-winning goal.

But then, out of nowhere, Eva swoops in and heads the ball out of harm's way.

It's a great play—but Woodvine has a corner kick coming up.

So, it's my time to make a great play of my own. I take my station in the corner of the goalie box and think, *C'mon, Woodvine. Kick the ball nice and high.*

Which is exactly what happens.

I watch the ball arc through the air as I get ready to launch off my feet. That's when I feel someone's hand tugging at my jersey. This is nothing new—opponents try to keep me grounded by grabbing my jersey all the time. Without taking my eyes off the airborne ball, I make my hand into a fist and hack away at the player's arm. Usually, doing this is enough to get free of someone's grasp.

But not this time.

The hand still has my jersey in its clutches, and I don't have any more time to free myself. The ball has arrived, and I jump up as high as possible with somebody trying to pull me down.

Luckily, it's high enough. I get my forehead on the ball and redirect it away from the goal. Madison Wong, who has dropped back to help out, gets to the ball and clears it across midfield.

We've dodged a bullet. I breathe a sigh

of relief as I turn to see the opponent who grabbed me.

But the player behind me isn't an opponent.

It's Eva.

chapter 12

his isn't the first time Eva's hand has been a problem.

By the end of last summer, it was an area of huge concern. Not because it was grabbing my shirt, but because it was grabbing *my* hand.

For a while, after the soccer babe picture found its way out of my bag, things seemed really cool. It was nice to have the issue out in the open. If anything, we seemed more comfortable around each other than ever. But then all of a sudden, Eva started holding my hand whenever we were alone together. And I let her—more out of surprise than anything else. I didn't know what else to do.

The hand-holding wasn't the only thing that was new. She also got in the habit of writing me lots of notes that she stuck on Skittles's collar. Each note was written on lined paper she'd torn from some notebook. Sure, she'd done the same thing on the first day we met—but these notes were different. I started to wish she'd just text me like everyone else—or stop sending the messages altogether.

Sometimes, the notes were jokey. While we sat on the edge of her bed reading *Sports Illustrated*, Eva would giggle and plop Skittles on my lap. "I think she has a note for you," she'd say.

I'd take the note out of her collar and read things like *U R Awesome Blossom!* These notes were always signed *Love, Skittles*, so I'd give the dog a thank-you pat on its head and get back to my *Sports Illustrated*.

But then, one day in late August, I got a

note that wasn't from Skittles. My parents had taken me on a weekend trip to tour some colleges in the area. As I unpacked from the trip, a balled-up piece of paper flew through my window.

In her usual pink ink and loopy letters, Eva asked herself a question: *Did you miss Addie Williams?*

Below the question, she'd written her answer: *Whoop!*

It all would have seemed harmless enough if I could have thanked Skittles and maybe complimented the beagle's throwing arm. But I couldn't do that because underneath the answer, it said, *Love, Eva.*

I poked my head out the window, and there Eva was, a huge smile across her face.

"Hey!" she said. "Long time no see."

It hadn't been *that* long.

"Hey, Eva."

"Well," she said, "are you coming?"

"Coming where?"

She arched an eyebrow. "It's a surprise. C'mon!"

I didn't want to go with her. She was wearing a dress and heels, for one thing, and there weren't any places I wanted to be that required this sort of attire.

"I'm just wearing a T-shirt and shorts," I told her.

"You look perfect," she said.

So much for that excuse. "I'll go get Belle," I said.

"Let's leave the dogs out of it, just this once, okay?"

Suddenly I really didn't want to go—not after the way she said that, with her eyes locked on mine. But I did go because I couldn't think of an excuse not to.

And it turned out I really was dressed appropriately because our destination was the Fraser High soccer field. At midfield, Eva had laid out a blanket and a picnic basket. She guided me to the blanket, her heels sinking into the turf with each step.

That's when it occurred to me that she was wearing the same shoes as the first time we met. The same dress too.

She sat down on the blanket with her legs folded under her and waited for me to do the same.

I didn't.

"Did you bring a ball?" I asked, looking over my shoulder at the parking lot. She'd driven us here in her parents' minivan.

"No," she said. "Sorry."

"Are you sure? It's a big car. Maybe there's one in the trunk or between the seats."

"I didn't bring you here to play soccer," Eva said. She grabbed my hand. "Sit down, okay? I have something I want to tell you."

I almost did sit down. Her hand and her words were so gentle, it would have been easy to give into them.

But I couldn't.

Now, looking back, I realize how much courage it took Eva to do all of this. The letter, the picnic, the words she was about to say—all of it was a risk. She'd cluttered her room with soccer studs so she could hide a soccer babe without anyone noticing. But here she was, sitting on a picnic blanket with no studs in sight. There was only me. She wanted to talk to me—and we both knew about what.

Eva had even chosen to say what she wanted to say *in public*. The more I think about it, the more amazing that is to me. Okay, no one was around, but they could have been. This wasn't her bedroom. It was a place where a couple dozen people usually performed for crowds of onlookers.

Which was, as much as anything, the reason I couldn't—I *wouldn't*—sit down.

Because if I did, it felt like the Fraser High soccer field, my favorite place in the world, would be forever changed. It could never again be just a soccer field. And I wasn't ready to give that up. I wanted Eva to keep being my friend, but more than that, I wanted her to be my teammate. Being anything more than that was too big a risk. It had taken a couple years for the New Hope Church controversy to go away, and I didn't want to have to deal with any other non-soccer-related issues. This wasn't about shame or fear. It was about priorities.

Eva signed her name under the word *Love*. I thought I might even feel the same way. But like my dad always said, "Sometimes you have to choose one love over another." And that's what I did. Dad chose a person over athletics, and I'm glad for my sake that was his choice. But I chose soccer over a person, and at the time, it felt like a no-brainer.

It still does.

So instead of sitting next to Eva and letting her say what she'd come here to say, I pulled my hand out of hers.

"I'm sorry," I said. "I don't feel the way you do. I just want to be teammates. And friends. But . . . not anything more."

Eva didn't say anything for a long time. In fact, she didn't do anything at all. She'd been stunned so badly that her body was frozen stiff. When she did move, she collapsed. Her chin fell to her chest. Her shoulders sunk. Her hands dropped into her lap. She started bawling.

It was terrible to watch. After I don't know how much time, I finally sat down next to her on the blanket.

"I'm sorry," I said. "I'm really, *really* sorry." I reached for her heaving shoulders and tried to hold her steady. But she flinched, lashing out at me with her elbow.

"I don't know what you think I was going to say," she said, her voice weirdly loud. "But you must have misunderstood."

"Okay," I said. Both of us knew I hadn't misunderstood.

"You don't need to apologize," she said. "Just a misunderstanding, that's all."

"Are you okay?" I asked.

"Of course, I'm okay. Why wouldn't I be okay?" She stood up. "I'm not a . . . I'd *never. . .*" Then, standing over me, she said, "I don't know how anyone could be like that. I don't know how *you* could be like that."

"You can't control it!" I said.

"Yes, I can. Maybe *you* can't. But I can."

She turned around and walked away. Or she tried to. Her heels kept sinking into the turf until she reached down and yanked her shoes off. I sat on the blanket and watched her run across the field and away from everything that had just happened.

chapter 13

"What's this?" Mom asks. She sounds alarmed.

I've just gotten back from the Woodvine game and I'm still in my uniform, plopped down on my bed.

"What?" I ask, sitting up.

Unlike my dad, Mom has no problem striding right into my room. "*This*, Addie." She holds up the crumpled picture of the soccer babe.

"Where'd you get that?" I ask.

"From the pocket of your pants. I was doing laundry. Where did *you* get it?"

She's standing with her feet spread out and her knees slightly bent. It's what Coach Berg would call an athletic position. Her feet are planted, but not so much that she couldn't pounce on me if I tried to escape. Neither one of us is going anywhere until I answer her question.

So I do. I tell her everything. What happened at the end of the summer; what's been happening ever since. I'm surprised that I start to tear up—I'm not usually the crying type. I'm even more surprised that *she* starts tearing up. Mom's a sort of professional activist. She works for the state and deals with people getting harassed (or worse) all the time.

"You've got to report this, Addie," she says.

All along, I knew she'd say that, of course. That's why I waited so long to tell her. *How could I possibly tattle on someone*, I wondered, *who only a few months ago was my best friend?*

"I'll help you if you want, but you—"

"It's okay," I interrupt. "I'll do it."

Because after what Eva pulled at the Woodvine game, tattling suddenly seems a whole lot easier.

chapter 14

Eva didn't start harassing me right away.

For a while, it seemed like she never wanted to be near me again. She didn't call or come over. She definitely didn't speak to me. We had only a couple more summer soccer games, and she skipped both of them. After all the on-field yelling and bantering we'd done, those last games were depressingly quiet. Often, when I looked around the field, I was surprised that Eva wasn't there. It was like my brain couldn't believe that she was gone. I'd only known her for one summer, but soccer didn't make as much sense without her.

When school started up, the only time we saw each other was in the hallways. Eva would duck her head and pretend she didn't notice me.

At the time, it was really sad. In one afternoon, I'd lost my best friend, apparently forever. But now, I'd do just about anything to go back to the way things were in the fall. Loneliness was bad, but I could handle it. If Eva had spent the rest of her life avoiding me, I could have spent the rest of mine as I had before we met.

But then one day she stopped avoiding me and started getting in my way. She would brush against me in the hallway and then hiss, "Get away from me!" She would tell me that seats were saved at the lunch table when I tried to sit by my teammates. When the other girls gave me a seat, Eva stormed off and found a new table.

Then she got a boyfriend.

His name was Joe Anderson, but I didn't

know much about him beyond that. I don't think Eva did either. Maybe she picked him out of the yearbook. His last name *did* start with an A.

The only thing they seemed to have in common was a willingness to stick their tongues down each other's throats. *A lot*. Right in front of me.

Everywhere I turned, there they were—slobbering all over each other. I'd close my locker door and see them leaning on the next locker, her hands shoving his face into hers or shoving his hands into her back pockets.

When I tried to maneuver around them, Eva would say things like, "Got a good look?"

I don't know who dumped who, but Joe didn't last long. So Eva got another boyfriend. And then another.

I knew what she was trying to do, of course. She was trying to prove something to me—and probably to herself too.

But knowing why someone does something doesn't stop them from doing it. Ignoring them doesn't always work either.

chapter 15

The only way to make Eva Riley stop is to report her to people who can make her stop.

Except I can't report her. I know I told my mom I would, and I know I'm probably being naive. But I can't turn her in.

Not yet. Not until I try to talk to her. She deserves that.

Okay—maybe she doesn't *deserve* it. Maybe what she deserves is to be expelled or worse.

But I can't stop thinking about the summer—about how we spent almost every day together and about how it all ended—and I can't stop thinking about her running away from the picnic she'd made for us.

Which is why, when I see Eva hanging outside my fifth-period English classroom necking with Tim DeLoy, I walk right up to her.

I don't bother clearing my throat or waiting for her to notice me. "We need to talk," I tell her.

Eva gives Tim's earlobe a tug with her teeth and turns to me. "I have nothing to say to you."

"I have something to say to you," I say as kindly as I can. "It's important. Please."

Eva can tell I'm serious. Her sarcastic smile goes away. Her hand, which was scratching the small of Tim's back, falls to her hip. She nods. "Meet me at the field in five minutes."

"We have class then."

"I thought you said it was important."

"It is," I tell her. "It's just—"

"You can't be a few minutes late to class?"

"You know what happened last year . . ."

"You got suspended for skipping class, not being a few minutes late."

I sigh and shrug my shoulders. "Why the field?"

"Can you think of a better place?"

I can't. It seems right to have our conversation there. That's the place where it all started.

"I'll be there," I tell her.

.

chapter 16

arrive at the field first.

As I stand at midfield and wait for Eva to show up, I think about just how stupid it is for me to be here. Honestly, I'm not sure why I agreed to step out in the middle of the school day. Eva's reasoning actually seemed logical at the time. But the more I think about, the more illogical it becomes.

Being a little late to class might not be the same thing as cutting class, but what about being *a lot* late? It's not as if what we have to talk about will take only a couple minutes. Issues need hashing out.

When Eva gets to the field, I'm going to tell her that I'm sorry, but I can't talk right now. After school, absolutely. But not right now.

I check the time on my cell phone. Eva should be here. I decide to wait two more minutes. Then I have to get back inside.

If I hurry, I'll only be a little late. Three or four minutes, tops. I'll rush into the classroom and tell Ms. Banks I'm really, really sorry. Worst-case scenario, she'll mark me tardy.

Right?

You can't suspend someone for being tardy, can you? Even if they have a prior record of cutting class? No—no one would do that. Still, I have to get back inside.

I check my cell phone clock again. Sorry, Eva, time's up.

Except as I speed walk out of the stadium, I almost smash right into Mr. Lenders.

"Ms. Williams," he says. He has a giant belly and wheezes when he breathes. "I am truly disappointed to find you here." More wheezing. "I thought the suspension last year had taken care of your aversion to class."

"It's not what it looks like," I say. "I was only out here because . . . " Because...what? Because I was meeting someone? Because I really had to talk to her? What can I say?

"Save it, Ms. Williams," he says. "One of these days, you're going to have to start taking responsibility for your actions."

"I know—I do—it's just—"

Mr. Lenders raises his hand to silence me. "Last year, you said it was my fault for waiting until the playoffs to suspend you," he says. He has caught his breath, and his voice is steady. "I wonder, when are the results of your actions going to be *your* fault?"

That's when it hits me how he found me. Eva. She must have told him. Why else would he walk all the way out to the track? "I'm not saying it's not my fault, Mr. Lenders. I'm just saying—"

He raises his hand again. "In any case, I won't make the same mistake twice. We'll let Principal Collins figure out a suitable punishment here and now. I doubt he'll be in favor of keeping you on the soccer team given your prior record. I hope you'll use this time to think about *your* actions and not the actions of those around you."

chapter 17

Everything seems to be happening exactly as it did last year.

Like last year, Mr. Lenders escorts me through the halls of the school.

Like last year, he's taking me to Principal Collins's office.

Like last year, Mr. Lenders's route to the principal's office takes us through the athletic department hallway. Coach Berg's office is at the end of the hallway. I wonder if—like last year—he'll be sitting at his desk as I walk by. Is he going to take the news as badly as he did last year when he heard about my suspension?

No, I tell myself. *It'll be better this time.*

It has to be.

After all, unlike last year, I won't be missing playoff games. And, really, maybe I won't be missing any games at all. Last year, my suspension was entirely my fault. Even though I was angry about the timing, I knew deep down that I was getting what I deserved. This year is different. I'm not saying I should have cut class, but I have reasons for doing it this year that I can explain. Reasons that adults will be able to understand. Maybe, once Principal Collins and my parents and Coach Berg hear my side of the story, they'll drop the suspension completely.

Or maybe not.

Because as I pass Coach Berg's office, I see that he's not alone. Eva is in there with him.

▦ ▦ ▦

I can see Eva's whole plot clearly now. Eva told me to meet her outside, ratted on me to Mr. Lender, and then headed to Coach Berg's office. She wants me to get suspended again. And just in case getting caught leaving the school isn't enough to do it, Eva's going to seal the deal with lies about me. It's so obvious that I wonder why I didn't see through her plot earlier.

Okay, maybe it's not obvious. Maybe Eva's not really evil enough to do all of this to me— but right now, after all she's done to me, it seems totally possible.

As I sit outside the principal's office, I think about all the nasty lies Eva might have told Coach Berg. I imagine her telling Coach . . . what? That she's uncomfortable with me on the field? That she wants to play with someone she can trust? I'm not entirely sure, but I know it's not good.

The more I think about it, the more of a hurry I'm in to talk with Coach. After all, the longer Eva's version of what happened between us sits alone in Coach Berg's head, the more likely he'll think it's the truth. Mom talks all the time about how this happens in her job. When the media reports only one side of a case, the public immediately assumes it's the only side—even if the facts tell a different story later. The trick, Mom says, is to get the truth to the public as quickly as possible. If people have a chance to compare what *really* happened to what supposedly happened, they're more likely to be able to tell the difference. But you have to reach them before they've made up their minds.

That's why I need to talk with Coach Berg ASAP.

Except I can't. Not as long as I'm stuck in the lobby of Principal Collins's office, waiting for my parents to arrive. I've been staring at the door for what feels like forever, silently pleading for my parents to walk in.

Open, door, I tell it. *C'mon. Please. Open.*

When the door doesn't open, I'm actually mad at it for not cooperating. In fact, I'm mad at lots of inanimate objects right now. The chair I'm sitting on for being so hard and uncomfortable. The brown carpet for being exactly the same color as scum and dirt— intentionally. All the carpet in this school is this color because adults are worried kids will get actual dirt on it. Kids can wear muddy shoes or spill whatever they like, and it will blend right into the natural color of the carpet. Adults think they've solved the problem, when they haven't solved anything. They've guaranteed that their carpets will always look dirty, even when they're clean. Adults can be really illogical if there's no one there to point out the flaws in their thinking.

Hurry up, Mom and Dad! I need to point out the flaws in whatever's in Coach Berg's head!

Almost on cue, the door opens and my dad steps in. He's wearing wind pants, a T-shirt, and sneakers—his usual attire.

"Where's Mom?" I ask.

"On her way," he says. "What's this all about, Addie?"

I know he's concerned because he's rocking back and forth from toe to heel. I can see his calves bulging through his wind pants.

"Nothing—I mean, not nothing. I'm definitely in a lot of trouble, and I definitely can explain what happened. But not right now, okay? Right now, I have to explain it all to Coach Berg because I need him to understand what happened between me and Eva—not some other version of it. I'll tell you everything—I promise—but not until I tell my coach first. Trust me."

I stop talking and take a deep breath.

Dad does some more rocking.

"Of course I trust you," he says.

He opens the door for me and tells me good luck.

chapter 18

oach is still in his office when I get there, but there's no sign of Eva. I'm a bit surprised. I'd gotten so used to the idea of her spinning her lies that I assumed she'd be right where I last saw her, talking crap about me.

I'm so relieved she's not there that I actually reconsider my theory. Maybe she didn't stop in to bad-mouth me. Maybe Coach called *her* into his office. Maybe she'd been on her way to meet me at the soccer field, just like she said she would, when Coach saw her rushing by and pulled her aside to talk strategy.

Maybe—but not likely.

"Hey, Coach," I tell him as I step inside and take a seat. "I don't know what you've heard, but I just got caught cutting class and—"

"I heard plenty, Williams," he interrupts.

Uh-oh.

He rubs his buzzed head, something he does whenever he's feeling stressed. Or angry.

"Well, I wanted to warn you that I might be suspended and have to miss a few games. I'm really sorry, Coach, but—"

"You're not going to miss a few games."

"I'm not?"

"Nope."

More head rubbing. Maybe it's not anger after all—maybe he's here to support me. "Thanks, Coach. But I really want to explain why—"

"You're through, Addie. You're off the team for good."

The words hit me like a soccer ball to the stomach from close range.

"Eva told me everything. You've been erratic on the field, and I've done my best to tolerate it. But I won't tolerate this. The situations you put her through off the field . . ."

"Coach?" The words barely make it out of my mouth. I'm not even sure he heard me.

"Who you're attracted to is none of my business. But the way you treat my players is. You have no right to harass Eva, no matter how you feel about her. As far as I'm concerned, you're done."

⸱⸱⸱ ⸱⸱⸱ ⸱⸱⸱

I walk out of Coach Berg's office in a daze. I tried and tried to explain what happened, to give him the truth, but he wouldn't listen.

You're through, Addie. You're off the team for good.

Nothing makes sense. How did this happen?

You have no right to harass Eva.

Me? Harass her?

I go over the conversation again and again. "She's lying, Coach," I tried to tell him. "That's not what happened," I tried to say.

But he wouldn't listen. He wouldn't even let me get the words out.

Save it.

It doesn't make sense. This can't be happening. But I know it is. It already did happen. I'm off the team. Case closed.

That's when I realize I'm no longer in the school hallways. I'm not in the principal's office either. I'm in the parking lot.

Actually, this *does* make sense. If I'm not going to be a soccer player, then there's no reason for me to be a student.

I spot my mom's car toward the back of the lot. She must be inside right now with my dad, waiting for me to return from Coach Berg's office. But I'm not going back to the principal's office. I'm getting out of here.

When I reach Mom's car, I dig in my pockets for the spare key she gave me. I click the unlock button. I put the key in the ignition and turn it.

I don't know where I'm going. I just know it's as far away from this school as possible.

chapter 19

I don't decide where I'm headed until I'm well out of town. After unlatching the glove box, I take out my mom's GPS and plug it in.

Dad and I gave Mom the GPS this year for Christmas. Dad paid for it, and I entered the addresses to all the schools in Fraser High's conference. Mom works late hours and often can't attend my games. But just in case she got out of work early enough to catch the second half, Dad and I wanted to make finding the field as easy as possible for her.

My first stop is Ironwood, about twenty minutes away, but I only stay long enough to see that the players have started practice. I get back in the car and look up the way to Yeopin Valley. The players there are in their practice gear too. My next destination is Greenridge High, then it's Cardinal Creek, and then Willow Woods Upper School. I'm surprised by how quickly I arrive at each school. Pregame jitters always made the bus rides seem longer.

I'm not sure exactly why I'm doing this. Nostalgia? Is this a way for me to say good-bye? Whatever the reason, it feels good. Sad but good.

By the time I get to my last stop, Woodvine, the stadium is empty. I sit in the bleachers and look down at the field. I imagine I'm down there at the bottom of the valley, clearing a soccer ball out of Fraser High territory as a Woodvine player closes in on me. I imagine the crowd groaning as another potential goal is kicked away by Addie Williams.

Then I realize it's me groaning, not the crowd. I'm groaning because I'll never get to deny Woodvine or any other team from scoring again.

And yet there I still am, on the field, as Woodvine charges once more at Fraser's goal. The imaginary crowd around me gets more and more excited as a Woodvine forward crosses the ball to the middle. Of course, they shouldn't be excited. They shouldn't stand or cheer or hold their collective breath. Because I'm down there with my superhero calves, waiting to launch into the air and head the cross away.

Except I can't jump. I can't even move. Eva Riley has her hands wrapped around me and is holding me down. She's driving with her legs. She's tackling me.

The real me stands up from the bleacher bench just as the imaginary me falls to the ground.

All this time, I've been in a daze—driving

from one field to another, trying to get used to the idea of never playing soccer again.

But I'm not dazed anymore. I'm mad.

I'm not the one who's going to give up her spot on the soccer field. At least, I'm not the *only* one. If I'm going, Eva's going with me.

chapter 20

It's getting dark by the time I pull into Eva's driveway.

The driveway's empty, as I knew it would be. Her family is at church like they are every night.

The front door is unlocked as usual.

I take out my phone and look at the time. 7:51 P.M. They usually go to the seven o'clock service on weekdays, but I'm not exactly sure how long it takes. An hour, maybe? So I'd better hurry.

"You first, girl," I say.

I'm talking to Belle, who I brought with me. I was worried my parents would catch me when I stopped at home to get her, but they weren't there. They're probably out looking for me, I know, but I can't worry about that now.

I have blackmail material to find.

I follow Belle into the house and let her go racing through the house to find her friend. They haven't seen each other in months, and Belle is frantic with excitement. She's got a great nose, so to her the whole house must reek of beagle.

I listen to her dash around the downstairs as I head up to Eva's room.

Truthfully, I'm not exactly sure what I hope to find in here. Something incriminating, I guess. Something that will prove Eva's the one who's been harassing me and not the other way around. A diary, maybe. I don't know for sure that Eva keeps a diary, but I think there's a pretty good chance. After all the letters she's written to me, maybe she writes to herself too.

Still, even if she does have a diary, it's not like I can just show it to the world—not unless I want people to know I trespassed in her house. But maybe I can blackmail her with it. *Unless you tell the truth*, I could tell her, *I'm going to make your FEELINGS public knowledge.*

Yikes. Who knew I was capable of being this nasty?

A part of me thinks I'm not—that even if I find a diary, I'll never use it to blackmail Eva, no matter what she's done. But another part of me—the angry part—kind of likes this plan.

As I search the room, I can't help noticing how messy it is. Clothes are everywhere, which is strange. Eva's not a neat freak, but she's no slob either. What's even stranger is all the dresser drawers. The bottom drawers are open and look rummaged through. Pant legs and sweatshirt arms spill over the drawers' edges. The top drawers have been pulled completely out and toppled over. Balled-up socks and bunched-up underwear clutter the floor.

I spot an empty jewelry case just as the dogs start barking loudly.

"Woof!" Belle barks.

"Arf!" Skittles howls.

"Ow!" another voice yells from downstairs. I freeze.

This voice belongs to a human. And it doesn't stop: "Owwww!"

It doesn't sound like Eva or her mom or dad. Whoever it is, he's swearing now, something Eva's parents would never do. Without thinking about it, I bend down and pick up a soccer cleat that's lying on the floor.

I should stay up here. Even in my adrenaline-crazed state, I know I should. But I don't. Maybe it's because of the adrenaline or because the screaming voice sounds more pained than fierce—but rather than lock Eva's door I open it. I sprint down the stairs.

I race through the kitchen with the soccer cleat raised above my head like a tomahawk.

As I round the corner and enter the living room, I see that the shoe won't be necessary. The dogs have the situation under control.

Each has her incisors deep into an ankle of the burglar, who is sitting on the floor and still yelping in pain. He's swatting vainly at the pooches, who are too busy chewing on his jeans to notice.

As for the burglar, he's nowhere near as scary as the ones on TV. In fact, he's just a pimply faced kid with his pockets full of jewelry and a couple laptops stacked next to him. My guess is the kid is thirteen years old. Fourteen, tops.

"Who are you?" I demand.

"He says his name is Tony," a voice says from behind me. I turn and see Eva standing in the entryway, looking straight at us.

chapter 21

va's parents walk in a few moments later. They ask what's going on, and Eva says, "Ask him." That's when Tony tries to escape but quickly changes his mind. For one thing, his ankles are well chewed and don't offer much stability. For another, Skittles and Belle lurch at him so aggressively that all he can think to do is get into the prone position.

Eva's dad says, "I guess we'll have to call the cops." He looks at us. "Girls, why don't you help him wash out those cuts?" Leave it to Eva's parents to say something like this. They leave their door unlocked because they believe so much in community, so why wouldn't they treat a burglar like a guest?

"What?" Eva says. "Why would we help this creep?"

"Because everyone deserves to be helped out, Eva."

"But—"

"Please, girls," Eva's mom says. "I think the dogs really did a number on the poor kid."

⸭ ⸭ ⸭

"Owwww!" Tony says.

"Quit your whining," Eva says, giving his ankle another splash of hydrogen peroxide.

We're in the bathroom, cleaning out the bite marks on Tony's leg. I can hear Eva's dad talking to the police on the phone. Eva's mom hung out in the bathroom for a few minutes but then decided no adult supervision was necessary. Tony's a little too pathetic to do anything worse than yelp in pain. In fact, he hasn't stopped shaking for a second since the dogs attacked.

"Owww!" he says again.

Really, the bites don't look too bad. More like scratches than cuts. When we first lifted Tony's pant legs, I thought we were going to find really nasty wounds, but his jeans protected him pretty well.

"Just wait until the cops get done with you," Eva says. She has Tony's foot propped on the toilet seat so all the peroxide and blood drip into the bowl. "They'll cuff your wrists so tight you'll get permanent scars."

What is she so mad about? I wonder, remembering how angry I am with Eva. After all she's done to me, what right does she have to threaten anyone? I'm mad at her for being mad at him. He's just a dumb kid.

"You might as well sic the cops on me while you're at it," I say. My voice gets louder as I talk. "I snuck into your house too."

This gets everyone's attention. Eva stops roughly wiping Tony's ankle. Tony stops yelping in pain. They both stare at me silently.

Which is good, because I'm not done talking. Not even close. I tell Eva about the whole plan. When I'm finished with that, I go back further. I go over everything she's done to me this year and all the horrible ways she's treated me. I tell her how I got kicked off the team, and just like that, I'm bawling my eyes out. Next thing I know, I'm so angry I'm shaking. "How could you? After all that happened this summer, how could you do this to me? Huh?" I glare at her through bleary eyes. "How does someone do these things to another person?"

But Eva doesn't answer me. First, she glares at me and I think she's about to yell and then her eyes fog up with tears. I think her hand is trembling because she spills some peroxide and Tony gives another yelp.

▦   ▦   ▦

Despite Eva's threats, the cops don't handcuff Tony. Eva's family doesn't even press any charges. Her parents agree that he's learned his lesson. "There's no lesson like forgiveness," her dad says, patting Tony on his shoulder. I wonder if he'd say the same thing if he found out Eva liked soccer babes more than soccer studs. Based on her behavior this past year, I doubt it.

Eva and I watch Tony limp out the front door, and Eva says, "I'm sorry, Addie."

We've both been holding onto our dogs' collars for several minutes, but now that the cops and Tony are gone, we finally let go. I can hear Eva's parents doing one more sweep of the upstairs, making sure everything is where it's supposed to be.

"I know that's not even close to good enough, but I really am sorry. Tomorrow I'll go to Coach and tell him what really happened, okay?"

I almost say thanks but stop myself. Why should I say thanks when she's just doing the right thing?

"I don't know how to explain all the stuff I've done to you this year," she says. "I'm not even sure I can explain it to myself. At first, I thought I could just stay away from you—but that just made it worse. It was like you weren't even the same person to me. You were just this person I hated. The fact that I could do terrible things to you proved that you had to be a terrible person, if that makes any sense."

It doesn't—not really. But I'm glad she's trying to explain it, even if there's no way she totally could.

Because I've already said everything I have to say and there's really nothing else either of us can say, I change the subject. "Did you see Belle back there? Chomping on that kid's ankle? She's never done anything like that before."

"She must've learned it from Skittles." We watch the dogs start to wrestle each other again. "We do lots of strange things because of the ones we care about," Eva says.

chapter 22

I t's late in the season, and we're playing Ironwood again. We've won most of our games, and were looking ready for the postseason until our goalie, Alyssa, got a concussion. During practice, it seemed like her replacement, Becca, was going to be solid, but now I'm not so sure. Coach has spent the whole game screaming his lungs out at her.

I feel really bad for Alyssa because I know how hard it is not to be able to play. I feel bad for Becca too. I also know how brutal Coach can be. But honestly, it's nice to have something to focus on besides what happened with Eva.

She fessed up to everything she did to me, just like she said she would, and wound up suspended from school for a week. She was also kicked off the team. Mom said I should consider suing, and I did—but in the end, I couldn't go through with it.

For one thing, I couldn't bear to do that to our dogs. Eva and I don't see each other much, but when we do, it's to reunite our canine companions.

Besides, Eva has apologized more than once, but she has never asked me to forgive her, and there's something I admire about that.

She stayed away from our games for a while. But eventually, she started coming as a fan. That is where she is now: in the bleachers, cheering us on.

A few moments later, a ball comes bounding my way, and I advance it to midfield. Things are congested in front of me, and I have a decision to make. Where should I go with the ball next?

"Whoop!"

It's Eva's voice, from the stands, and I have to decide whether to trust it.

She said during our last doggy play date that she was thinking about trying to return to the team next year. She wanted to know if I'd be okay with that. I told her I'd have to think about it.

But I don't have any time to think right now. I have to act—and I do just that. I send the ball sailing over the Ironwood players' heads. As I watch the ball fly through the air, I can see Eva nodding from the stands.

Just as the ball lands on the other side of the field, Faith swoops into view. She takes the pass and runs with it, charging forward with no opponents in sight.

about the author

PAUL HOBLIN HAS AN MFA IN
CREATIVE WRITING FROM THE
UNIVERSITY OF MINNESOTA.
HE LIVES IN SAINT PAUL,
MINNESOTA.

archenemy

As a defender for Fraser High, Addie used to be ready for anything. But now the biggest threat on the field is her former best friend.

the beast

When a concussion takes Alyssa out of the lineup, her rising-star teammate Becca takes over in goal. Will Alyssa heal in time for playoffs? And how far will she go to reclaim the goalie jersey?

blow out

Lacy spent the winter recovering from a knee injury that still gives her nightmares. Now Raven is going after her starting spot. Can Lacy get past her fears and play the way she used to?

offside

It might be crazy, but Faith has a crush on her coach. Can she keep her head in the game? And when Faith's frenemy Caitlyn decides that Faith's getting special treatment, will Faith become an outcast?

out of sync

Since childhood, Madison and Dayton have had soccer sync. But lately, Dayton is more interested in partying than playing soccer. Can Maddie get through to her best friend?

under pressure

Taking "performance supplements" makes Elise feel great, and lately she's been playing like a powerhouse. But will it last? How long can she keep the pills a secret?